To
you who had [illegible]
[illegible]
from
[illegible signature]

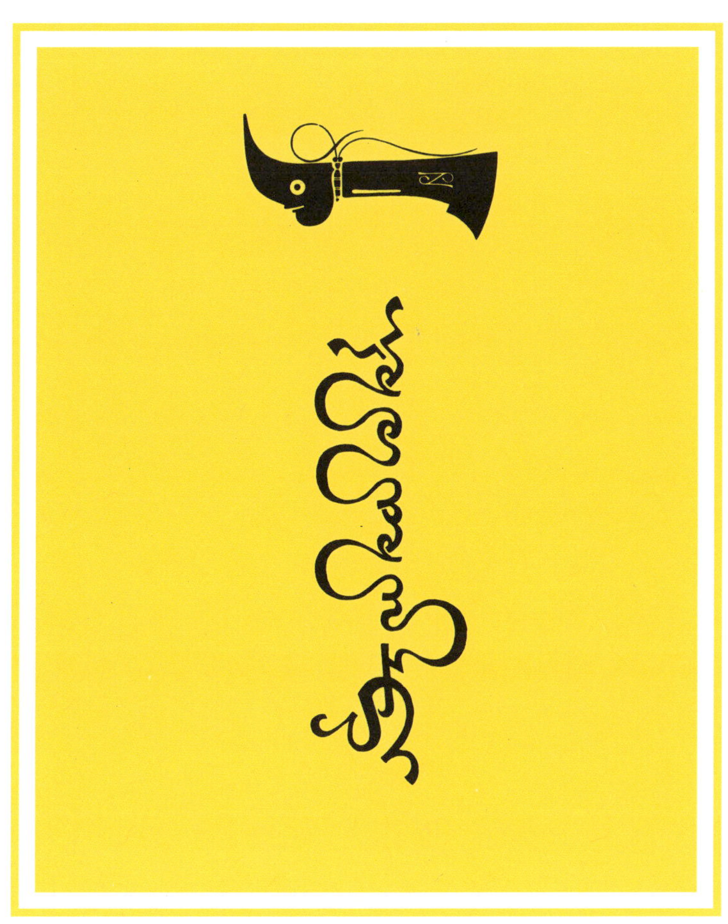

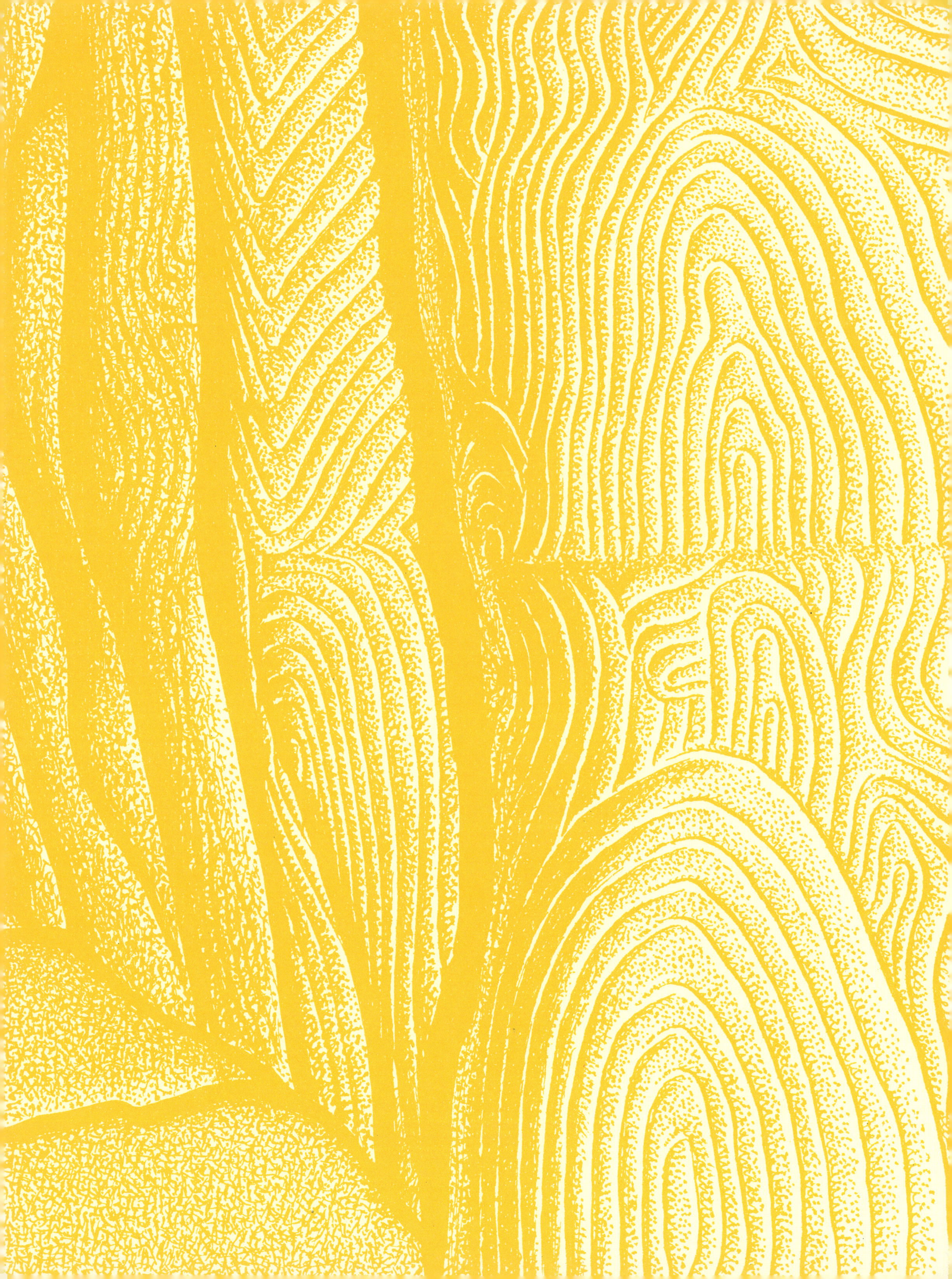

STANISLAV SZUKALSKI

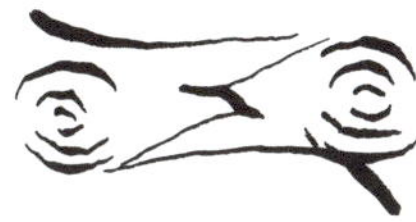

BEHOLD!!! THE PROTONG

■

Extracts from the 39 volumes of my science "Zermatism," based on new interpretations of petroglyphic communications, in which will be revealed the most precedent-shattering and up-turning of all notions on our origins. Including samplings from *Anthropolitical Motivations*, *The Deluged Gods*, and *Listen to These Stones*

■

FOURTH EDITION

Introduction by **ROBT. WILLIAMS** | Obituary by **RAY ZONE**

Edited by **GLENN BRAY** and **LENA ZWALVE**

LAST GASP

SAN FRANCISCO

2019

Edited by Glenn Bray and Lena Zwalve
Book Design by Piet Schreuders, Amsterdam
Original artwork scanned by Glenn Bray
"Katyn" photos by Nick Springett
Special thanks to Suzanne Williams

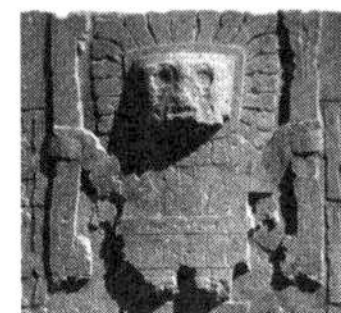

COVER IMAGE
Detail of the "Dawn Gate" in Teotihuacán (Bolivia),
representing the God Wirakocha (see image #117)

Published by
Last Gasp of San Francisco
777 Florida Street, San Francisco, CA 94110
www.lastgasp.com
ISBN 978 0 86719 876 8

Third printing
Printed in Canada

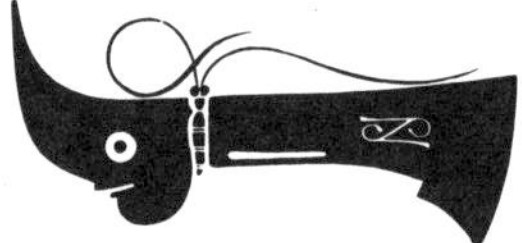

Official online source of all things Szukalski:
Archives Szukalski, *www.szukalski.com*

Respectfully dedicated to

**JOAN AND STAS
TOGETHER FOREVER**

Easter Island, July 30, 1988

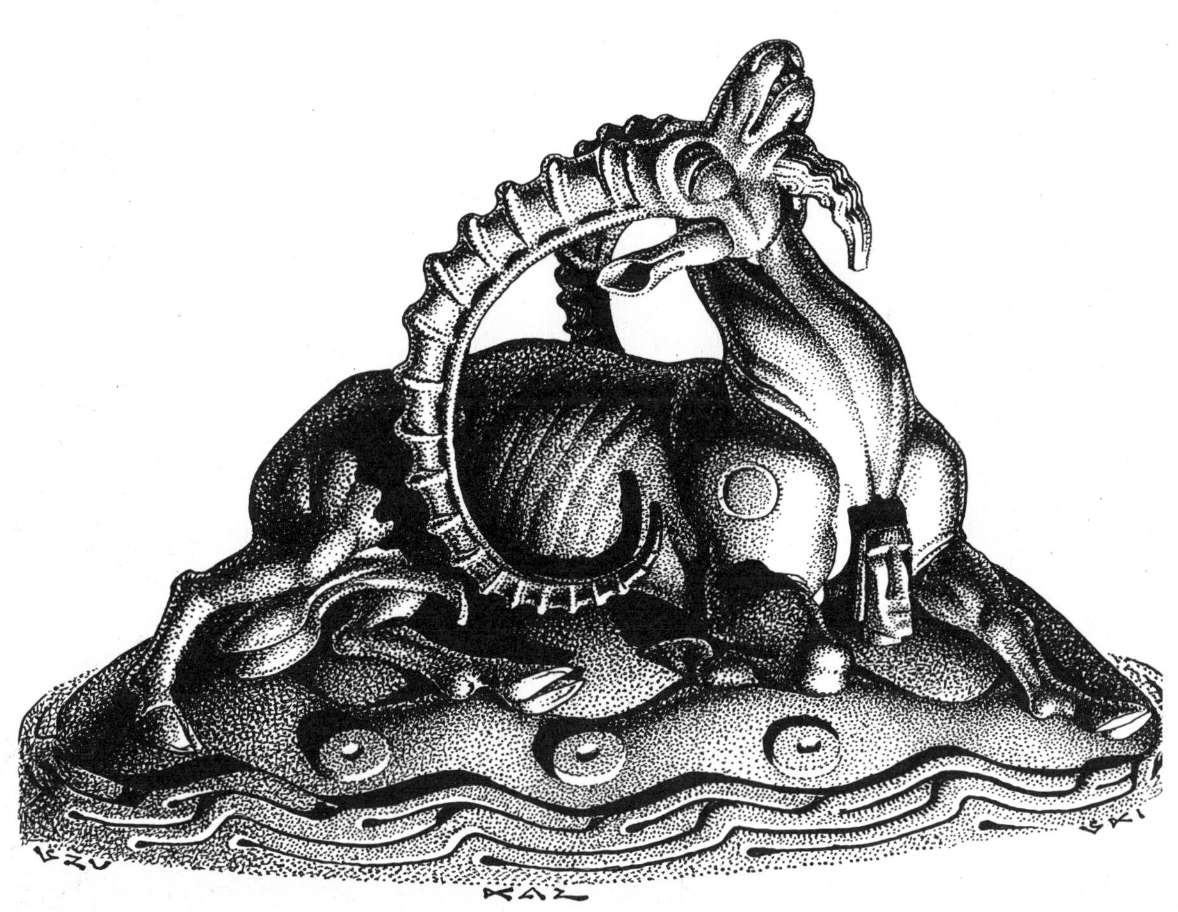

SZUKALSKI'S COAT OF ARMS

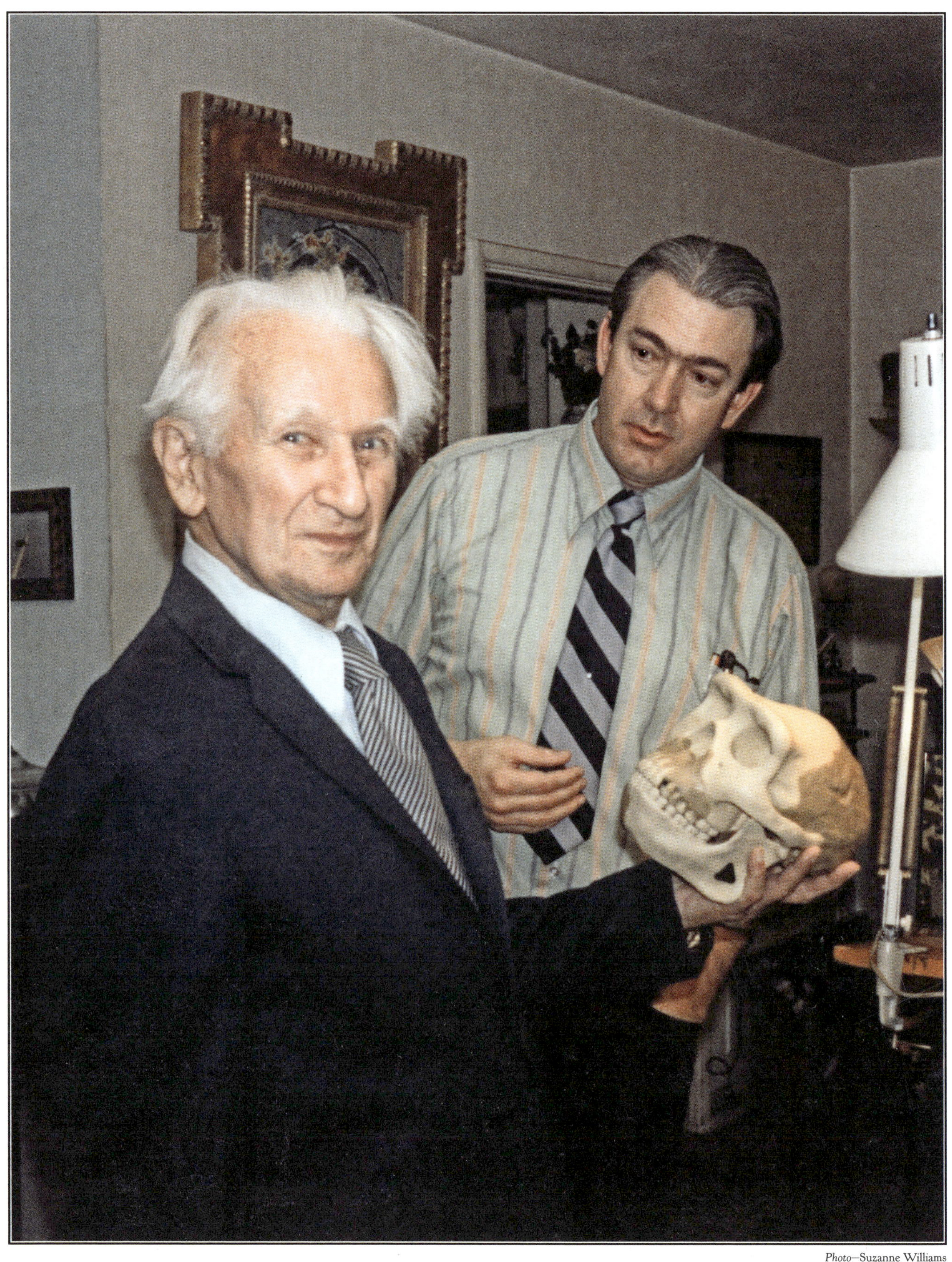

Photo—Suzanne Williams

STANISLAV SZUKALSKI WITH ROBERT WILLIAMS
December 13, 1984

Introduction

A N artist's work, life and philosophy are almost always linked in some way. With the Polish sculptor Stanisłav Szukalski, all facets of his existence were tightly locked together in a well-orchestrated logic, free of outside philosophies. He called his idiosyncratic superview Zermatism.

Szukalski was a friend of mine and my wife, Suzanne. I met him through Glenn Bray in 1973. By then he was but an energetic shadow of what was once a great man.

Born in 1893, as the son of a Polish blacksmith, Szukalski at an early age showed a proclivity for artistic expression—particularly sculpture. In 1909 the Kraków Academy of Fine Arts accepted his request for enrollment. He was fifteen years old. From that point on he was a force unto himself.

The art modes at this time, still the world of imperial salons, were trying to come to grips with Impressionism and Expressionism. The very theoretic nature of modem art allowed Szukalski to exercise his most creative predilection, unencumbered philosophical forays. It was in this fertile territory that he slowly started to mentally ferment Zermatism.

In Szukalski's opinion, the accepted knowledge of our time, while innocent and honest, lacked accuracy, and because of his acute artistic intuition he could more lucidly ferret out the basic truths—particularly regarding matters like man, man and his anthropological place, past world, and related cosmology.

Szukalski espoused serious notions that the planets were slag that had been ejected off the sun. He interpreted the 26,000-year period of the earth's rotating procession as periods of calm with intervals causing continents to rise and fall (hence the disappearance of Atlantis) and the waxing and waning of the ice ages.

Szukalski envisioned great floods brought about by these global changes and saw mankind ravaged by these deluges. From these ancient survivors he surmised the first language spoken to be a proto tongue, or as he called it, Protong.

One of his primary sociological concepts proposes the premise that among the human races of the world was the blood link of troglodytal near-men that walked among us. Some were almost identical to us, while others who failed to breed with our ancestors were still in the basic form visiting us today as Yetis, Bigfoot, and the Abominable Snowman.

Szukalski should not be thought of as just an eccentric. The man was energetically poetic and saw humanity as lost children he could help—but he did not compile volume upon volume of hand-written codices about Zermatism for fools.

Stanisłav Szukalski fits the definition of genius; his observations, though in question, were brilliant. Whether his theories are worthy of a large conscientious following, you must be the judge.

Robt. Williams
2000

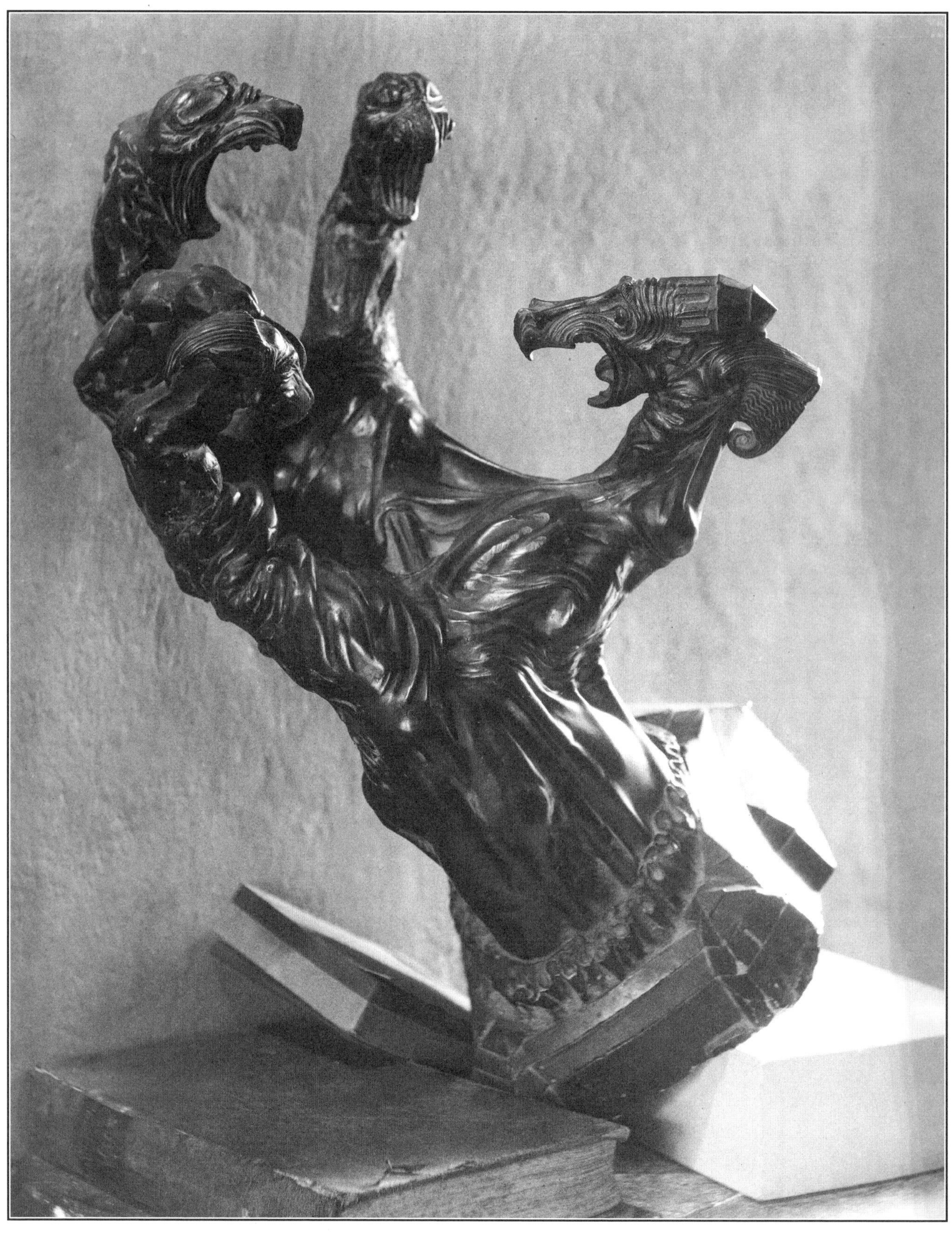

Photo—Szukalski circa 1917

STRUGGLE

1917

Obituary

IN his classic study of mythology, *The Hero With a Thousand Faces,* Joseph Campbell writes, "It is not society that is to guide and save the creative hero, but precisely the reverse. It is the hero or artist who is the true avatar of civilization; the individual, not the group, preserves and advances culture."

Stanisłav Szukalski was one such avatar, an unsung creative hero who toiled away in Burbank, California, without the recognition he was due. At 93 years of age, Szukalski is dead. Just prior to his death, Szukalski was still maintaining a one-man assembly line of symbolic sculptures, drawings, and writings. Despite this, and despite a reputation as a celebrated artist that spanned two continents in the '20s and '30s, Szukalski was virtually unknown in Los Angeles. In the '30s he was considered Poland's greatest artist; he is all but unknown to the art community here. In the face of monumental indifference, Szukalski maintained a prodigious creative output.

Who was Szukalski and what is his art?

Szukalski was a son of Poland, born in 1893 in the town of Warta, who established himself as an artist at a very early age. At the age of fourteen he had his first exhibition at the Kraków Art Academy. Soon after, he immigrated to America with his blacksmith father and settled in Chicago.

As a young artist living in Chicago, Szukalski met luminaries such as Ben Hecht, Carl Sandberg, Sherwood Anderson, Harriet Munroe (the editor of *Poetry* magazine), and Clarence Darrow. Because he liked working on sculpture while discussing a variety of different subjects, he proposed they form a "Vagabond Club," which met fortnightly in his loft on Wabash Avenue. The motto of the Vagabond Club expressed a progressive vision Szukalski says he has never abandoned: "All those who eagerly perceive the as-yet-unnamed are Vagabonds."

In 1923, Covici-McGee published their first book on Szukalski's art, *The Work of Szukalski.* Typical of the works of this period is the piece titled *Struggle,* and it is a key to Szukalski's imaginary world and his individual philosophy. It depicts the human hand, a few times larger than life-size, with the thumb in fierce opposition to the fingers.

"The thumb," Szukalski explained, "is Quality and the fingers are Quantity. They turn against him. They dig a hole so that they can try to get away from him. Civilization is not created by the brain, it's created by the thumbs. Without thumbs, we couldn't make tools, we couldn't make civilization. Out of a dozen people, one person will be creative, the one who provokes and proposes ideas. This individual is sent by Nature. He is the means by which a people can historically survive against adversity."

In 1936, Szukalski was summoned by the Polish Minister of Art and Culture to return and create sculpture on commission. He returned to Poland with a tremendous cargo of sculptures and drawings to find himself hailed as Poland's "greatest living artist." He was given a large studio in Warsaw by the government, and it was proclaimed the Szukalski National Museum. Commissions to erect sculptural emblems of Polish glory in the country's major cities showered down upon him. World War II put an end to all that. Nazi bombs obliterated the Szukalski Museum.

Months later, Szukalski returned to Los Angeles. Researching the origins of language in an intensive study of pictography led to his discovery of what Szukalski called "Protong," short for "Proto-tongue," or "First Language." In the book of *Genesis*, it is stated that "There was once one language and one speech in the world." Szukalski claimed that this speech was Protong, an archetypal language expressed in pictography and common to all cultures.

There was only one Szukalski and we will never see his likes again. He was a monumentalist in an age of the miniature, a realist in an era of the abstract. There's no doubt that he was a creative font, a protean cultural thumb.

Ray Zone
1987

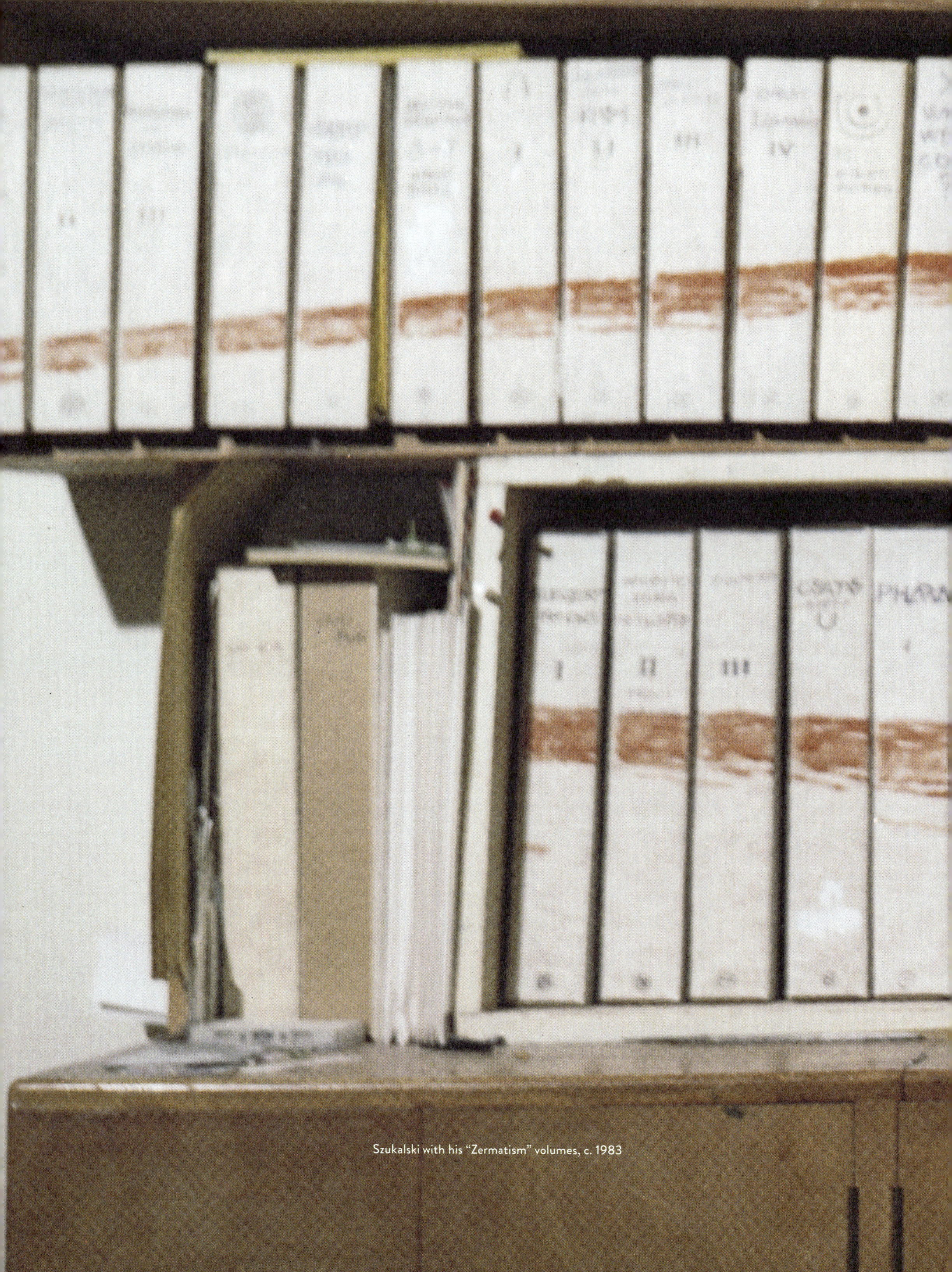

Szukalski with his "Zermatism" volumes, c. 1983

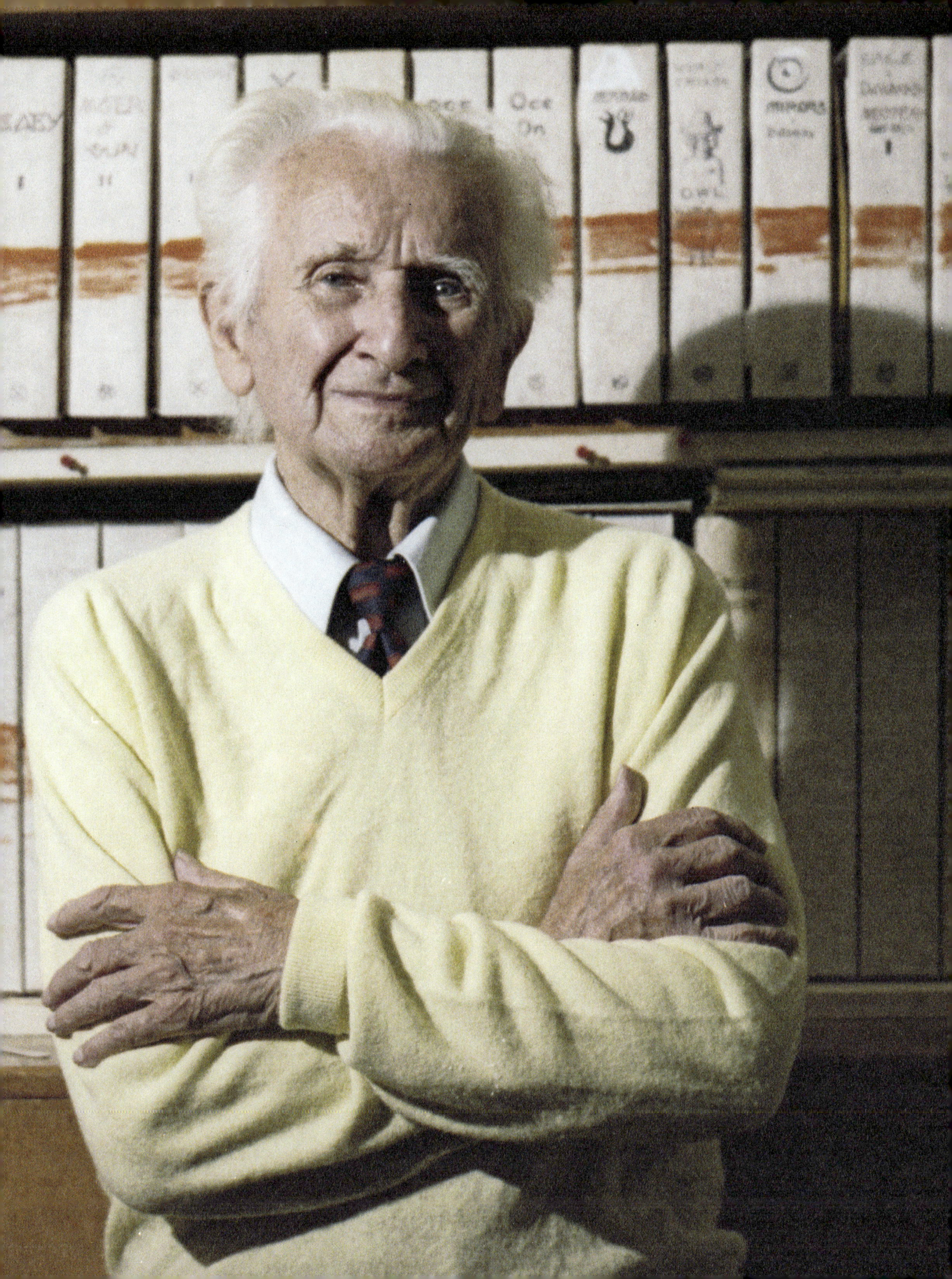

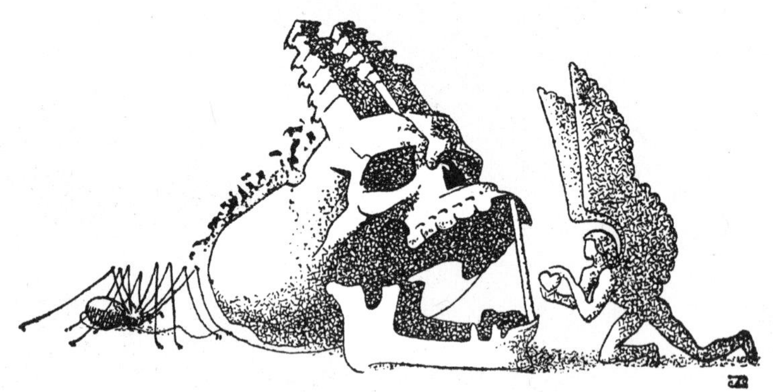

VIGNETTE BY SZUKALSKI
from *KRAK* #1, December 1937

Art and Justice

IN all things, preconditions have to be right before there can be success. If you are a midget, do not attempt to be a baseball player. If your bowel-laboratory converts load after load of food and you cannot gain weight, do not aim at being a Sumo wrestler. If your chromosomes made you an honest person, do not study law, as to ready yourself to be an American politician. If…

However, in becoming an artist, there is no need for preconditions. Whether you are a savage or a sophisticated aristocrat with a dazzling erudition in the history of Culture and its Arts, you are on the par with each other as to the opportunity to become the genius of the age. Whatever your background and circumstances, you can be the finest painter or sculptor in the world; be you a student of all the academies or as unworldly as an Eskimo or country bumpkin, you are instantly ready to become a celebrated artist or… you never will make it, regardless which of the Modernist parishoners you claim to be.

Democracy cannot stomach the individualist though it simply adores Picasso, Henry Moore and Miró. You have never heard of them? How lucky for you. Apparently, you do not care if you are included among the "Intellectual Elite" who make the preponderance of the intrinsically uncultured. Actually, the presumptive Snobs make the vast bulk of that self-anointed elite. They are the Nouveau-Cultured, whose make-up shows its rough edges at every second word. But after all, Culture does begin to function among the obnoxious Snobs.

Their origin lays in England. When the landed Esquiry accumulated newer wealth from the produce off their estates, one of them took it upon him to become the initiator of the democratic treatment of youth, the sons of his stable managers, giving them the same good education as his own sons, so that, by becoming more wordly, they would know how to find wider markets for his yearlings and how to deal with prospective buyers. Their higher education allowed them to sign various agreements with their own names, provided they would add beneath, "Without Nobility." The new class of "superiors" agreed to the condition, but insisted that it was more "learned" to write this in Latin, *Sine Nobilitas.* Actually, their insistence was intent on deceiving the ignorant masses, who did not understand that the two Latin words did not mean "Equal with the Best of Aristocrats," but "Without Nobility Whatsoever."

The sudden elevation of servelings into a superior class began to bear down on all who came in close contact with the chosen "clerks" who soon abbreviated the Latin phrase to "*S. Nob.*," this becoming associated with the most obnoxious people. Thus, all phony pretenders showing ill-acted superiority towards all human beings when there is no reason for conceit, have become regarded as snobs.

Who are the Snobs today? Those who simply have orgasmic ecstasies when they see something done by the— due to a press that does not know any better than to blemish its pages with pretended enthusiasm over their excrements— over-advertised charlatans of Art. But then, in the pond that has no fish, to a pathetically frustrated angler even the frog becomes a fish. It was the presumptive, sterile "critics," the abominable pests that infected the world with the plague of "Modernism."

This is the epoch of the total eclipse of Art. Our nations are suffering from physical and moral Decadence, from Karl Marx and Picasso to Roosevelt's Yalta Conventicle and Henry Moore's Sabertooth-Tiger-left-behind-dumplings with warm perforations. If these are acclaimed as our Art, the materialization of our innermost Aspirations, then which of the snob-specialists on Culture is wiser than the next psychotic fool, posturing heroically and no better than the other 1200 Napoleons in the insane asylum? The more books, treatises and doctorates they write, the more ridiculous and pompous their pseudo-learned discourses sound. No writer on Art deserves to be

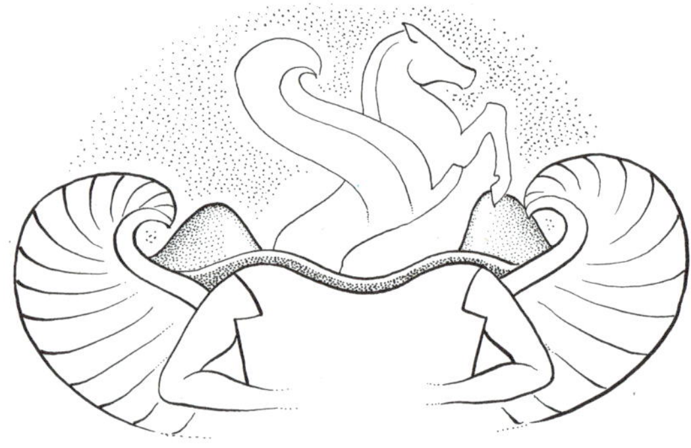

After Perseus decapitated Gorgon, the blood gushed upwards from her body, and from that fountain the **White Horse Pegasus** was born. Note the undulating watery horizon joining the Twin Perished Continents. (Ancient Grecian "crater" painting)

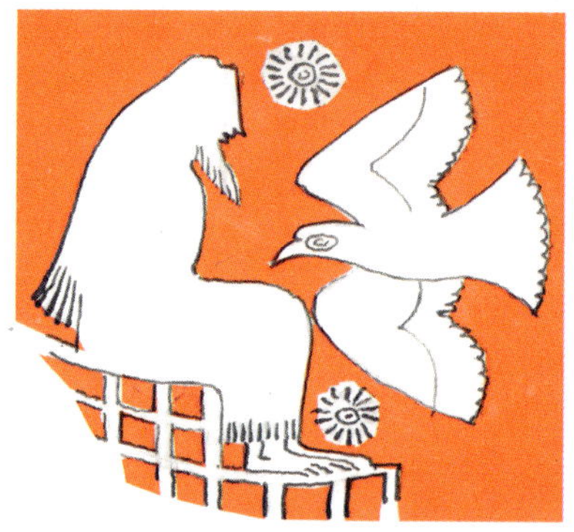

God **Zeus** on his throne, commanding his White Eagle to do an errand. (Greek vase painting)

listened to, since all their theorizing comes out of the drags of an empty bottom. There was no epoch in the history of the world as impoverished, as totally sterile, as suicidally thrashing as a fish out of water, as ours. We are the victims of "Modernism" that was encrusted on this pooped-out, ancient volcano by total absence of Talents, the chief carriers of this plague being the "critics of Art." They destroy our Culture, what remains of it.

We have founded thousands of Art Schools, which suck in millions of psychotic misfits of every nation. The incubators of mass-produced "artists" enter just anybody, as long as they can pay for their tuition, adding more zeros to the democratic numbers for which stands no arithmetical digit. It is rare that a youth who has made drawings from early childhood on, drawing the attention from everybody in the neighborhood, enters these factories. Most of the candidates for genius come from the class of black sheep, who NEVER had an inkling of a notion of what they would like to be, tailors, mailmen or Art critics. On seeing that a creature so depraved as Picasso—a talentless failure who, instead of committing suicide, becomes a "Modernist"—can get a few million dollars for a toilet paper segment with his post-nasal drip dried and varnished, these sterile nonentities finally turn to Art as their haven instead of to mental institutions.

Hermitage and Metropolitan Museums are the proud possessors of the worst examples of our cultural decline and decadence. To the contemporary Snob, whether a *kulturyi* Russian, American or Japanese, any doodle you cannot recognize and does not in any way resemble the Ancient Arts, is "Modern Art." Not knowing which end is up, you, the Modern Public, listen to and read the opinions of the Art critic, the Pied Piper of Hamlin, as if these were Holy Scriptures.

We have not yet lost all our senses, for we still hold back democratic notions in the Olympic Games, where only the ultimate athletes can compete and real, physical talent dares come to the fore.

I am an American, despite my Polish name, having been granted full citizenship, but… not the right to exist in this country as a creative man. Though I had to pledge allegiance to you, you have not been obliged to be loyal to a "foreigner." I was world-renowned, even in my early twenties, yet despite my dwelling in the Los Angeles vicinities for the last forty years, I apparently was nobody, for the press would not report anything about my worth, not even if I broke two blocks worth of windowpanes on Wilshire Boulevard.

But it was not always this way in the United States. When I was known in this country, two large monographies came to the public attention, *The Work of Szuakalski* (1923) and *Projects in Design* (1929). They were published in Chicago, the first by Covici McGee, the second by Chicago University Press. Initially being sold for $20, they are $220 on the rare book market now. But World War II came and Franklin Delano Roosevelt altered everything.

The United States helped to destroy the Nazi Nightmare that killed 42 million people on both sides of the conflict, freed the conquered nations, and turned around to leave with its traitorous co-conspirators after signing away eleven nations to Communist Russia at the Yalta Conventicle, without a single shot being fired, which crime against humanity was RATIFIED by the Anglomerican Senate and Congress.

While prior to Roosevelt, Americans were friendly and partial to Poland and Polonism, this land became, after his Yalta Conventicle, an unproclaimed enemy country to the Poles, born here or naturalized. They could not get a job at any learned institute, in radio or TV, unless they had real English

The **White Eagle** still under
the horizontal water bars
(therefore, turned left) in
the Atlantic region. On
the other side of the globe,
the upside-down Pacific
Ocean bottom empties
the three Landmasses
of the Motherland. The
shape of the Serpent here
represents the earth's
Horizon Jars.
(N. W. Australia)

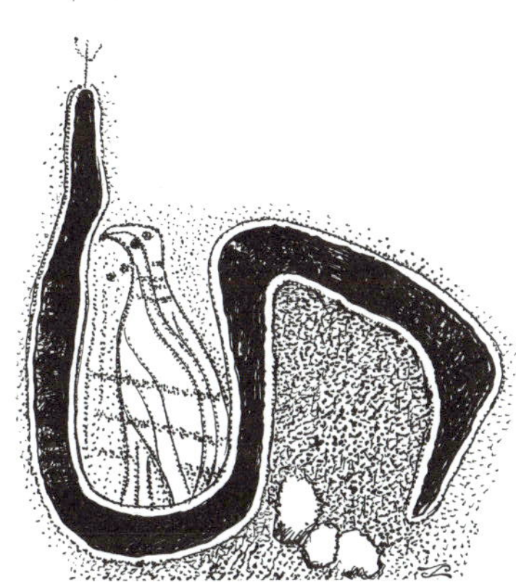

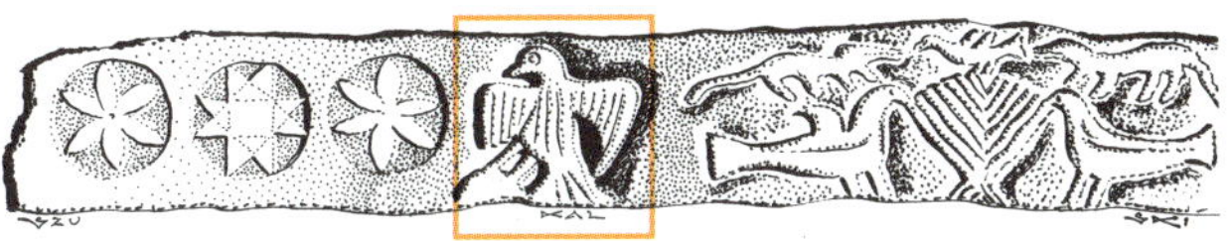

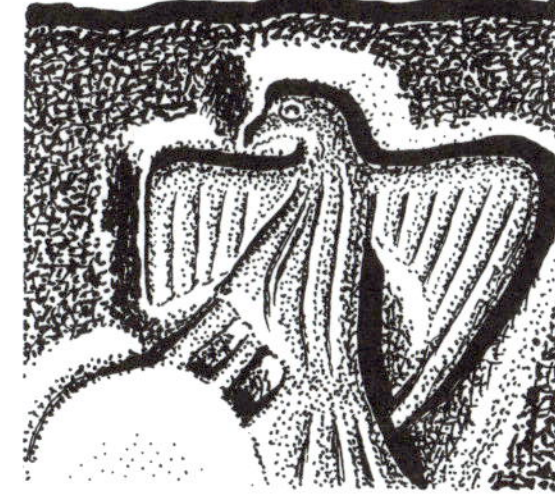

The **White Eagle** attempting to raise Easter Island with the water of
the Pacific streaking down his body. At right, the same Eagle at Sunrise
(turned left) and Sunset (turned right), attempting to raise the rebusal
tree (meaning " Where Water"), assisted by the Twin Lion Cubs.
(From Brando, Corsica, 5th Century. A.D.)

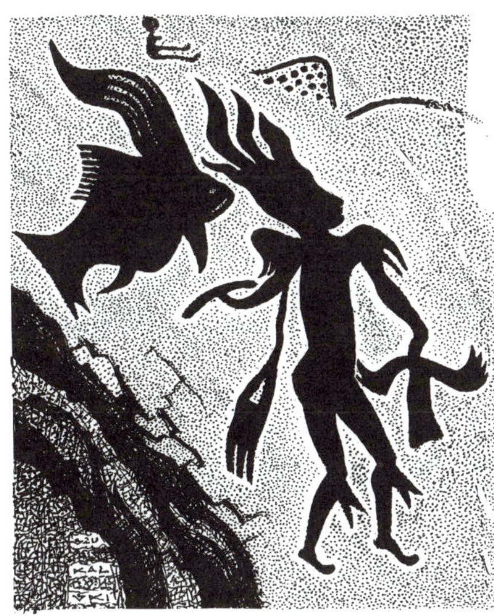

Descending at his Sunset (turned right), the **Sun God** with his flaming
head, carries his White Eagle so he can order it to help him save the
Motherland, seen at the top. The island is covered with air bubbles, for it is
drowned (hence the Sweep of Nullification on the right), while her bald-
headed personification helplessly awaits. (Sahara)

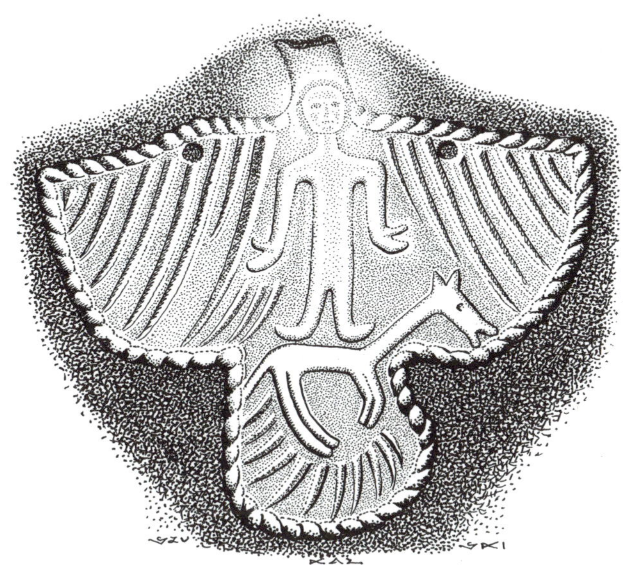

The "Flood-born" **Dawn God** is carried by his White Horse to save his
deluged Motherland. (From the Irtish-Ob river basin, Siberia)

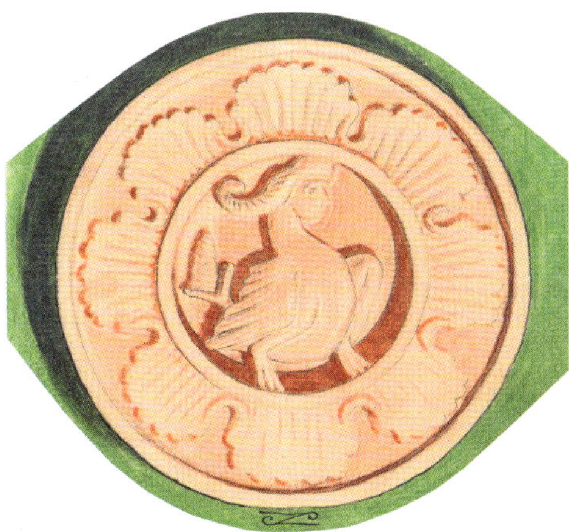

This **Dawn God**, in the form of an Eagle, is pictured here at Sunset (turned
right), already beneath the waters (note wave-shaped hair). He has the
divine intention of saving Easter Island, the air-bubble covered "island"
held in back of him in the hand-like tail. The Eagle is placed within a disc
with a hole in the center (called a *Bi*, meaning "Killed"), and around him
glares the sea-shell-like Light.

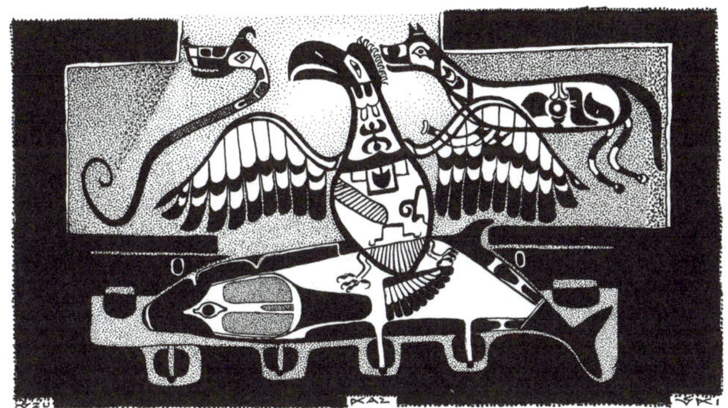

The **White Eagle**, after descending into the Horizon Jar (black cross-
section), about to devour the Flood Serpent while picking up the Island-
backed White Whale with his talons. The Great Lioness (pictured here
localized into a She-wolf) is being carried away by the Eagle from its
present submersion. (Nootka Indian painting, N. W. Alaska)

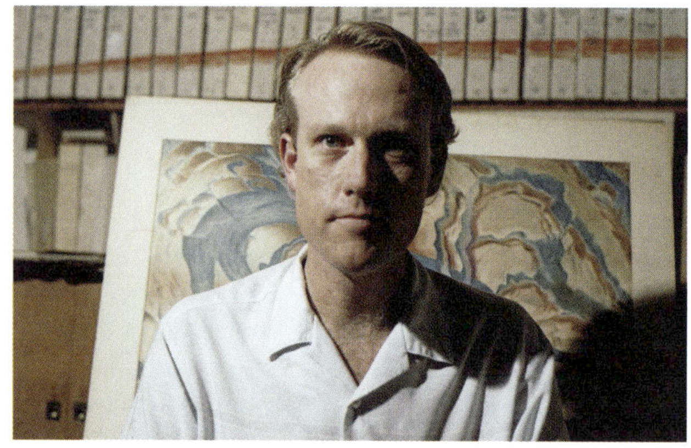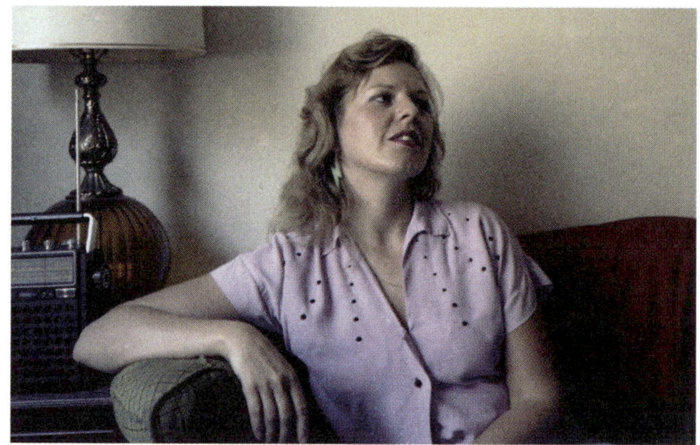

Mr. **Glenn Bray** – "no aristocratic, concocted background" and his "gorgeous, intelligent, Hollandese wife," **Lena Zwalve**, 1980

names and were pro-Communist and anti-American.

What I did in Art, or presently do, is not for myself. I am never an artist for myself. It is all done for the eventual public viewing. Abilities were given to some of us with specific purpose by our national biology, to glorify Ideas, heroic individuals in whatever fields of elevating the human species, and Historic moments. There are many wealthy foundations I have attempted to contact—National Geographic, the Smithsonian Institute, Berkeley University—but all have rejected my pleas to interest them in my new science ZERMATISM, returning my packages unopened, for on the wrapping was clearly printed a Polish name.

A few years ago, a young voice on a phone informed me that he had copies of my two monographies… Would I autograph them for him? He came and we became friends. I have a square face and squarely built body (denoting ethnic vitality), and he is of narrow face and structure. He knows very much about me since I bubble and percolate continuously, while he sits erectly, very circumspect and tactful. Hence our relationship is that I talk… he listens.

Lately, he asked me if we should not publish a book with my works. What prompted his notion is the knowledge that Southern California, as I expressed it, is the Cultural Siberia of the two Americas for an intrinsically creative man like me. That all my clumsy ways of approaching American institutes have failed me because my name ends in *-ski* instead of *-sky* (Russian, Czech or Jewish adaption of Slav names). He proposed that then I would be able to send copies to publishers and perhaps one of them would begin to publish some of my 39-volume work on my science, *Zermatism.*

An interesting part of this proposition is that my second monography, printed 50 years ago by Chicago University Press, was initially similarly proposed by a man I had never met before. He was a German, born in Chicago, of uneducated class. He was a commercial artist who had gained some money, but most definitely was not "rich." Nonetheless, he came and right in the doorway proposed that "we publish a book with your works." Due to the fact that, prior to publishing the monography, my preface raised such commotion at the gathering of the Chicago University faculty after one professor had read it, they asked if he would not relinquish to them "the honor of publishing the book of Szukalski." It was however dedicated to W. C. Both.

My present patron who, like W. C. Both materialized out of thin air, is Mr. Glenn Bray. As would be proper for a so significant, AMERICAN happening, my friend Bray has no aristocratic, concocted background and no claim to super-cultural upbringing. He has what I class a biologically motivated MISSION to fulfill. Instead of buying himself an expensive new automobile to impress his neighbors, he came to me and proposed "Let's… do History!"

Out of the hopeless Southern California "Siberia" (Los Angeles) materialized young providential visitors, Glenn and his gorgeous, intelligent, Hollandese wife, Lena Zwalve, bearing on their palms two eager hearts to create the needed temperature for the sprouting of a Cultural Event, the publication of this really tragic, though tearless book. I was sent to this world to Give, to Create in many fields, but in whichever world there is Russia, everything will be destroyed. No creature on earth is free from the Curse, the Plague, the corruption by the Abominable "Man," the species of Yetinsyn Predator that, as Kipling so observantly pointed out, "walks like a man"… in the opinion of all those easily fooled—the Anglomericans. ■

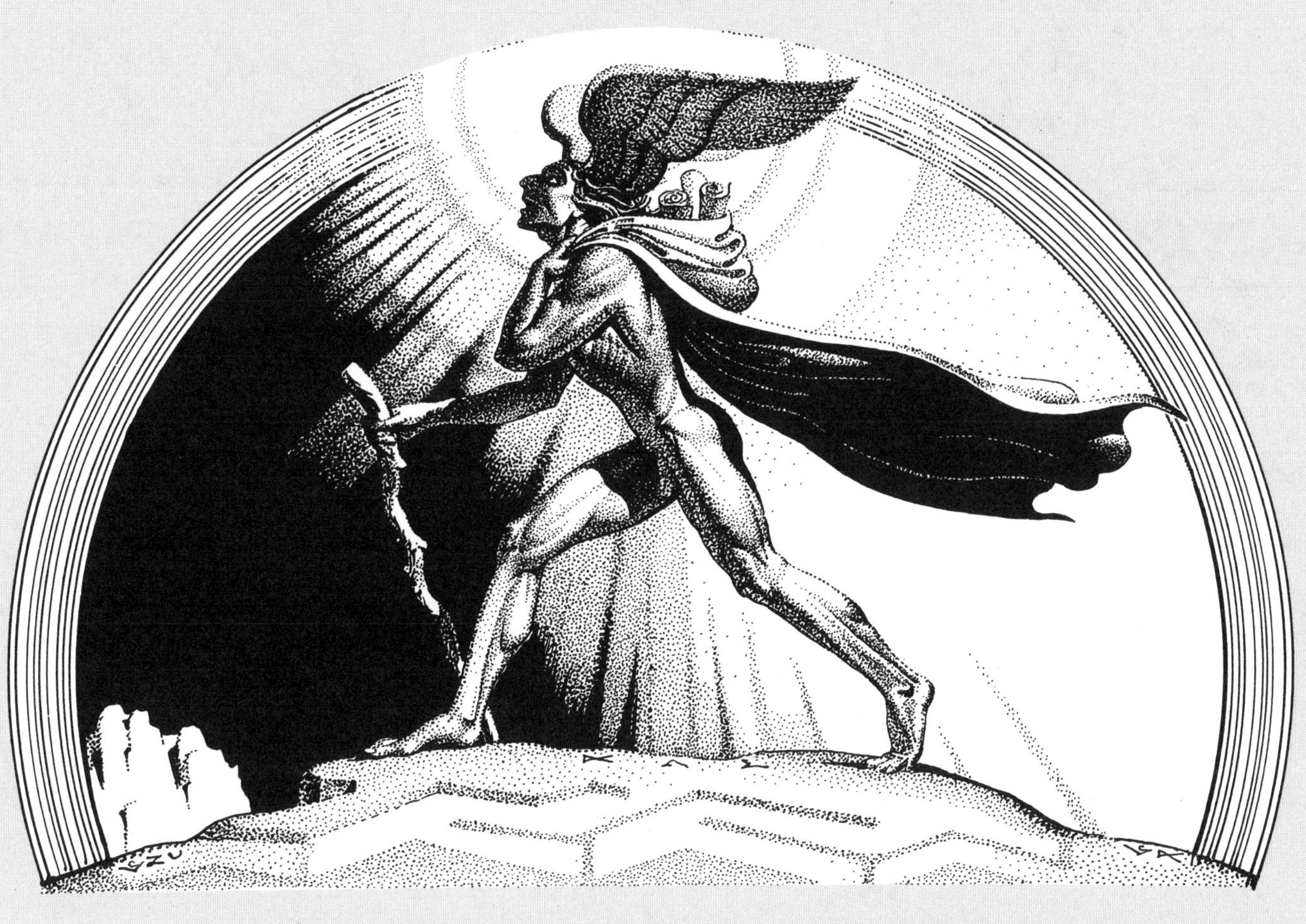

all who eagerly perceive
the as yet unnamed, are
vagabonds

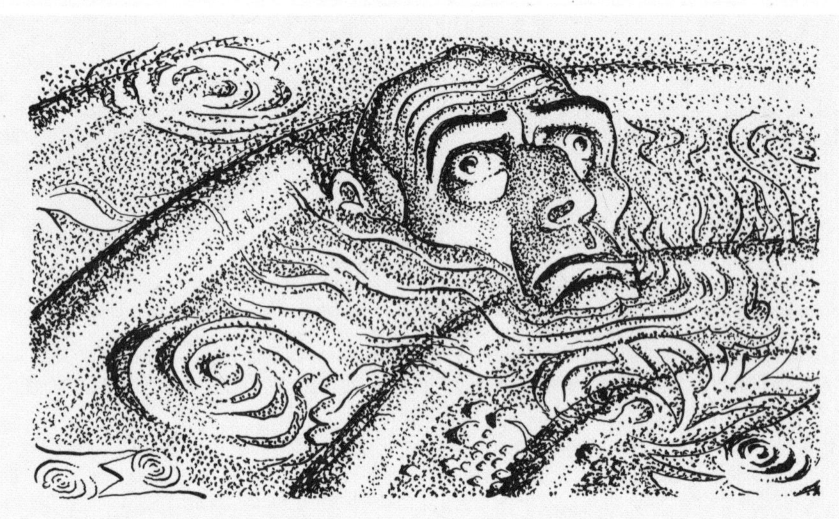

THE NEARSOLAR AND FARSOLAR EPOCHS

IRST! Let us get it straight about the Universe! All creatures have their seasons: their life-bursting, energy-spending summers, and their winters for hibernation and recuperation of life-vitality. So does the Sun Itself. I have gathered evidence from archaeology and pictography for proof of recurrent Ice Ages and Ages of Dehydration of our globe.

Because we live a shockingly short time, we humans judge our history in numbers of years… which are shorter than seconds, compared to the history of geology and astronomy. As a species we are but recent creations, and in the existence of the planetary system and its evolutionary sequence we are less than latecomers.

From our limited knowledge and vast scheme of theoretic suppositions a delayed gossip reached us about an Ice Age. But because of our meager limits and microbe-like short existence on this earth, we have never suspected that there might also be an opposite Ice Age, a period of time for the Sun we could compare with the opposite of hibernation, summer. We believe that, since the Ice Age has passed so long ago, today's temperature must be the "normal" temperature of the world and the universe.

While looking for the inter-astral causes of the legendary Global Deluge of the past (so persistently sustained by prehistoric man in his petroglyphic communications given to us as heritage), I came to suspect that there must be this opposite of the Ice Age hibernation, and that is the time when our atmosphere is practically dehydrated, whereby life on this planet is extinguished due to this lack of moisture. At such a Nearsolar Epoch the seas are emptied of all waters, since their function is finished.

What then is the function of oceans, seas, lakes and rivers? After their bottoms have been refilled with the waters of melted snows and ice of the just elapsed Ice Age of the Farsolar Epoch, these waters are pulled back by the Sun's heat-caused GRAVITY in the following Nearsolar Epoch. From these vapors the Sun regains its combustive energy from lost hydrogen and helium. The function of the oceans, seas, lakes and rivers is that of water buckets which at astronomic intervals of some 26,000 years are lowered into the interplanetary vastness to be refilled with the waters that, before melting, cloaked the hibernating earth as snow-ice. What then is the function of all the satellites, our earth among them? Their role is solely that of water-boys who are sent into the interplanetary well of the Ice Age waters, in order to revive our CREATOR, the Sun, from hibernation.

■

How the Sun Creates the Planets

I have drawn for you a smithy where I pull at the bellow's lever, thus blowing the air into my blacksmith's fire. He has just pulled out a piece of iron from the burning coal after it has been brought to "white heat" " when it is in a state of explosive energy and hundreds of particles of the metal pieces are shot into space. These particles arch their way, away from the white heat, being repelled by it, like tiny bullets, never to return as long as

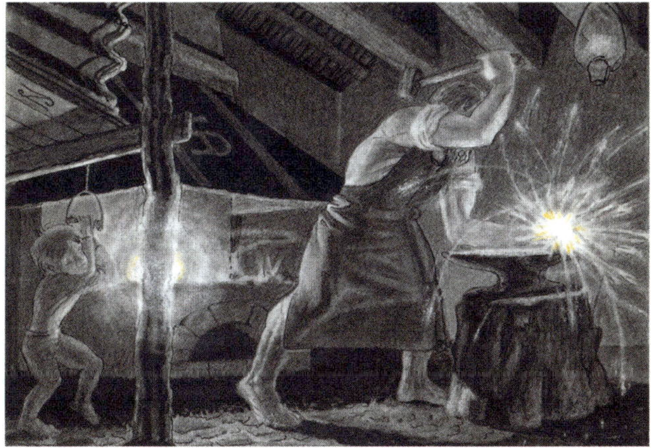

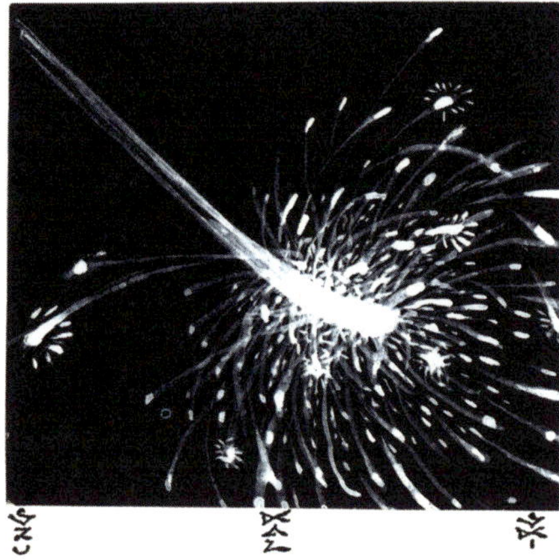

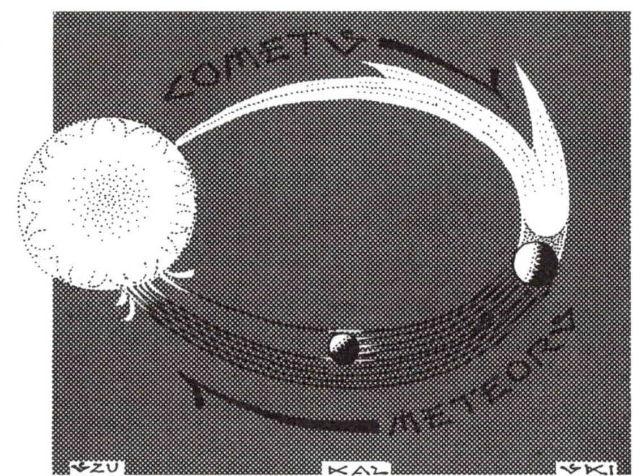

they are hot. This state of heat is necessary for welding iron to iron.

2 A closer view of the tiny planets my blacksmith father, Dyonizy, used to create for my pleasure. Though the life span of each of these sparks of spent energy is microcosmically short, I regard the white-hot iron as the minuscule Sun with its planets and satellites in the Nearsolar Epoch.

I had no formal education, so I dare solve all quandaries by myself, using Polish Logos. Here is the complete story, contained in this little drawing, illustrating the story of the life of a planet from its birth to death, for, indeed, all planets are living creatures that breathe, while making their archway from and to their Maker.

3 You see the Sun, at the left, during the Nearsolar Epoch, when it is but a liquid sphere, held together by its own heat-gravity. Like a pot of boiling porridge, it sputters in all directions. These sputterings we refer to as comets. As they depart, they pass each other and, when very close, melt into larger masses. As they hurtle through space, their surface chills. Their dimensions vary and they are eventually awarded their own precisely-exact positions in the Universe, according to the reciprocal law between the remote cold and solar heat-gravity. Since their sizes never equal, they never collide while catching the proper chair on which from then on they must remain seated until they become cold enough to permit lives of other creatures to develop upon them.

After the allotted length of time for their size, they have spent their inherited solar combustive materials and slowly begin to die as planets. Their relationship with the Sun, their father, changes and, having become cold and lifeless, they are, doubling upon themselves the former road of departure, recalled by their Maker as junkyard material. Thus, at the return of the next Nearsolar Epoch, all the loose matter on their surfaces flies into space in the form of meteors and meteorites. First, all the geologic stratifications, then all the metals, until only one Mooncore remains (what we call the Moon, is a planet of which all the geologic flesh has already gone). Thus, all the meteors that strike our earth do so ONLY at NIGHT (on the side turned away from the Sun)… because all meteors are on their way to their Maker, the Sun.

■

Near and Farsolar Deluges

What is seen on our globe protruding above the waters of the oceans, the comparatively small continents and islands, is precisely what remains of the full size of our original world. The seas cover the lavaic extensions; thus, I name the landmasses the Primary Globe and the lavaic sea bottoms underneath, the Secondary Globe. It is the latter that perpetually grows larger, while the former constantly diminishes by crumbling of its shores.

According to my reasoning, there are two different types of Deluges, but because of their astronomic timing, our human wink-of-an-eye existence does but remember one. Since seven-tenths of the global surface is covered by waters and only three-tenths consists of continents and islands, the rise of the sea level is so substantial during the Nearsolar Epochs when the ocean bottoms bloat, that all of the Primary Globe's surface is inundated. Thus, those who save themselves from drowning, find themselves on the newly re-emerged Secondary Globe of lavaic sea bottoms, where they rekindle

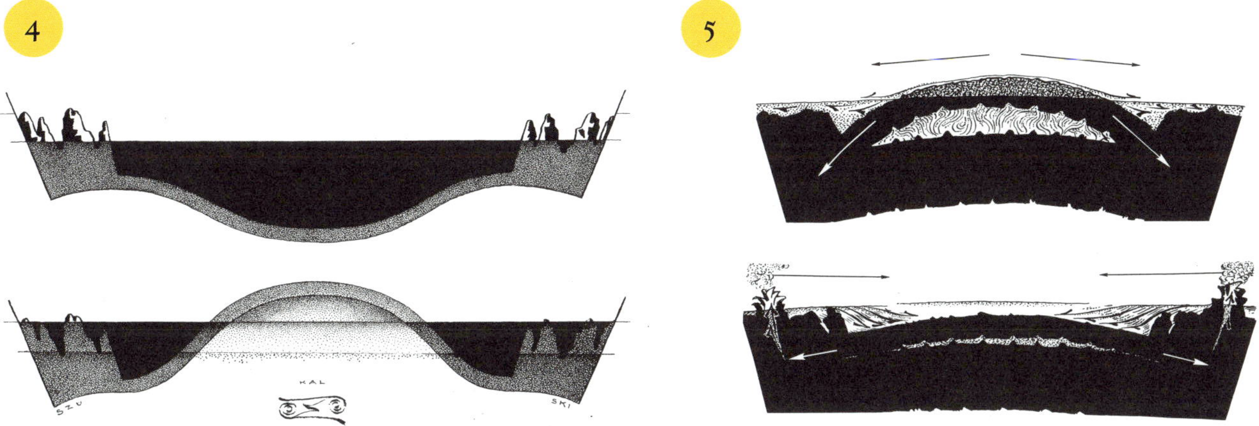

their perished Civilizations. This is the Nearsolar (due to global bloating) Deluge.

But there comes an astronomic time when the Sun begins to cool for hibernation, getting ready for the Farsolar Epoch whereby the lavaic continents, still found above the seas, begin to deflate. Gradually, they submerge, and as they are about to completely disappear beneath the seas, their former peripheries, the geologic pinnacles of the Primary Globe that we see presently, commence to re-emerge. This happens at the beginning of the Farsolar Epoch, hence the term Farsolar Deluge.

When Noah, the Chaldean Oannes, Chinese Fu Hsi, the Aztec Quetzalcoatl, the Mayan Id-zamna, and other diluvial leaders were getting ready for the Deluge by erecting their arks, crafts, ships, on which to save their kind, they were departing the Secondary (lavaic) Globe on which their ancestors had re-established their Civilizations.

After floating aimlessly with the deluging seas for forty days, Noah was startled one morning to find his ark resting on a projecting rock formation. He had landed on a Primary (Geologic) Globe pinnacle which he promptly "named" (described) "(W)ara Rat" or "Faith Saved."

4 On this drawing, top, you see the global horizon reduced to a simple diagram. This shows the world in the Farsolar Epoch when the earth is deflated and the ocean bottoms are "sucked in." This is the Sun's and all of its satellites' moment of total exhalation of "breath." You see the thin, ever growing, lavaic Secondary Globe of the sea bottoms hanging hammock-like with the submerged homeland of Noah's ancestors somewhere in the center. Noah found himself suddenly in the middle of a great "dish"

and saved himself only when he struck upon the re-emerging rocks that form the rim of the "dish."

The other drawing, below, shows the simplified scheme of the situation reversed. This is the state of our present globe's surface completely altered. This is in the middle of the Nearsolar Epoch, when the earth, instead of being deflated, is bloating with gaseous combustion because of the Sun's closer proximity and its ensuing hottest temperature. Noah's ancestors, if they could save themselves from this Nearsolar Deluge, left the rim of the global (extreme right and left peripheries) and crawled on the center, that here bulges above the level of the global waters.

You may take notice of the mechanics involved in these perpetually recurrent (every some 26,000 years) epochs. Only the ocean bottoms change as they rise or fall below the water level, the Primary Globe never fluctuates. The difference between the two epochs is in the cataclysmic shuttling of the oceans, which must always MIGRATE to the newly created abysses.

5 Not because I think of my reading public as slow-wits am I presenting two more drawings, but because I am fearful of not being understood in this first presentation.

These two drawings show the situation applied to the roundness of the globe. At the top you see the soft belly of the globe being progressively bloated, thereby forcing the seas that cover the thin lavaic Secondary Globe to flow off (note arrows) and cover our present geographic features with the waters of the Nearsolar Deluge.

The lower illustration shows the soft earth-belly deflating in the Farsolar Epoch (the Ice Age), causing the shores to capsize, whereby the global waters return (note arrows) to their proper place, the ocean bottoms.

But there occurs an unexpected thing, so remarkable that it should make your breath stop for one second from astonishment. When we set two gigantic logs together vertically, they will stand securely, weighing their appropriate individual weight, but if they are chained together at the top, and we begin to separate them at the bottom, their weight gradually alters from VERTICAL to HORIZONTAL. As they are pushed further apart, the horizontal pressure becomes tremendously intense and it stops being a matter of weight and becomes HORIZONTALLY DIRECTED POWER.

Note the two bottom arrows in the lower drawing. At the extreme point of the last moment horizontal PUSH, the opposite shores of the seas are under so much pressure, that the rock formations actually melt and the old mountain ranges actually erupt as liquid lava to create, when cooled, yet another mountain range.

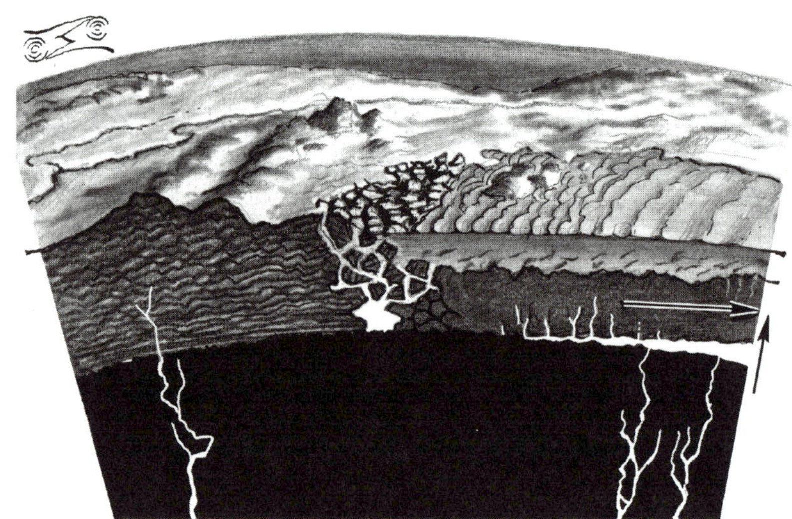

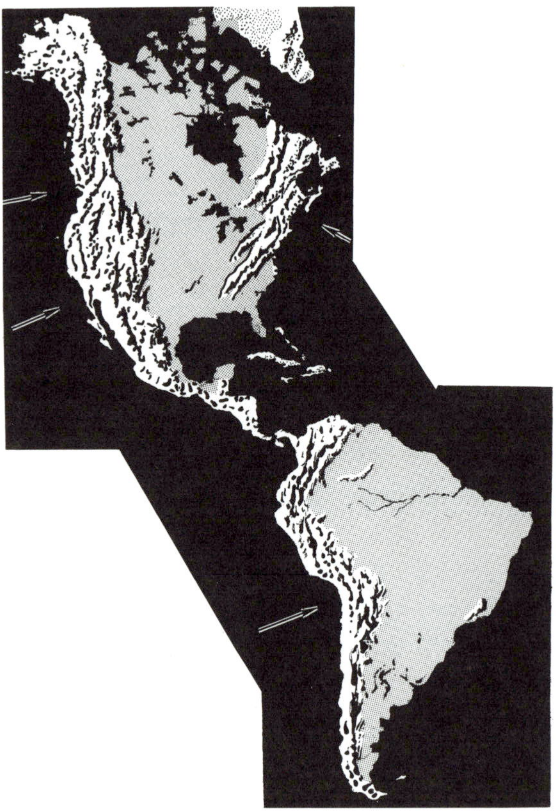

6   Here is proof of the above claim: the many compressed mountain ranges on the sides of the oceans, particularly in North America, facing the Pacific. They consist of the pulverized mountains that began to fountain upwards when the subterranean rocks melted under the tremendous horizontal pressure and were chilled immediately by the departing waters.

7   Here I show you what happened in recent years in Anchorage, Alaska. Contrary to scientific claims that we are nearing another Ice Age, I insist that we are nearing the opposite to it, the Dehydration of the Globe in the oncoming Nearsolar Epoch. The ocean bottoms begin to bloat due to our nearing the Sun. The gaseous combustions intensify and the lavaic "roof" covering the gasses, the present ocean bottoms, is being heaved upwards, incidentally tearing their rims away from the Alaskan moorings. Thus, many chunks of land suddenly lost their foundation and fell into the newly created vacuum (note the direction of the arrow) and whole city blocks dropped in the town of Turnagin. The seas will progressively rise and the Primary (Geologic) Globe will begin to submerge under the waters forced to migrate off the bloating ocean bottoms.

That we are entering the Nearsolar Epoch is further attested to by the progressive spreading of the Sahara Desert, currently 31 kilometers a year. Spain, as the continuation of the Sahara, is losing rivers and water is becoming a prime concern of that country, its usage already being governed, so that there be enough for all.

8   My rendition of the photograph of the layered, laminated surface of Mars, which I obtained from Cal Tech of Pasadena, California. I am not curious as to what explanations the physicists, metallurgists or astronomers use to justify these laminations. Scientists walk backwards in order to progress, for they are too mindful of what their predecessors opined, or what their professors

authoritatively decided upon.
I, however, walk wherever
my long nose points to,
forward. The authority on
which I lean with both of
my elbows, is the Common
Sense.

These crystalline layers
supply me with the needed
evidence. These glazed-over
surfaces were left behind
each of the Nearsolar
Epochs within astral timing
after the sand on Mars had
been melted by the torrid
heat of the then liquid Sun.

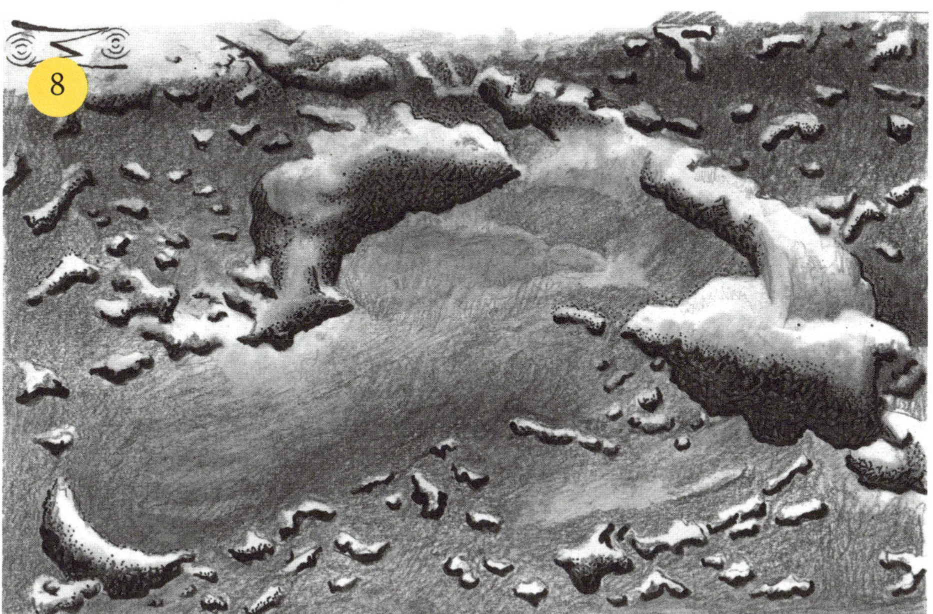

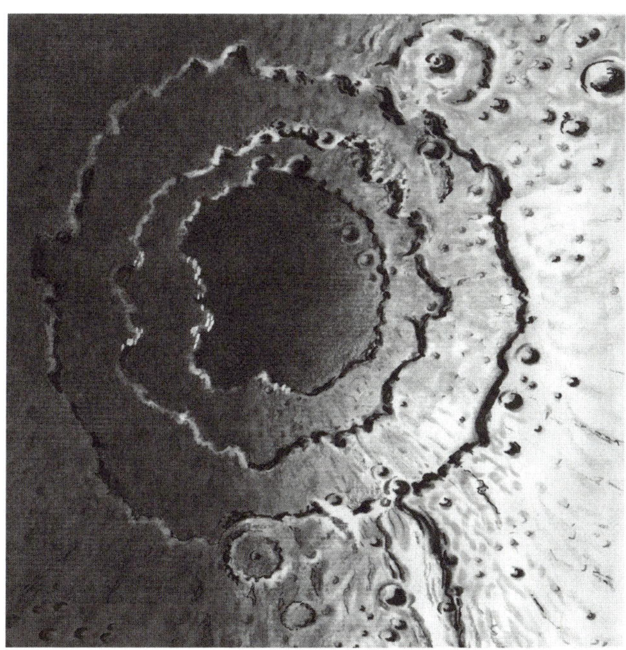

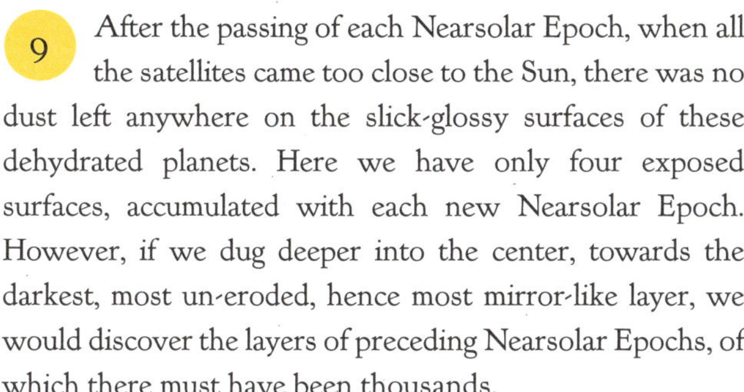

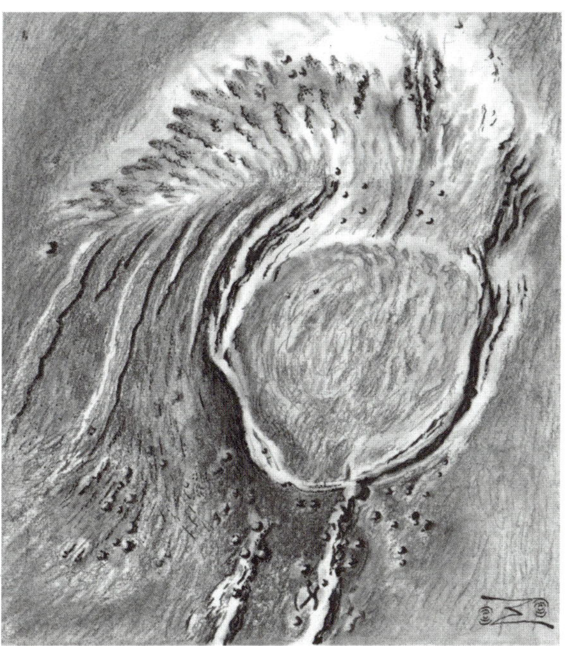

 After the passing of each Nearsolar Epoch, when all
the satellites came too close to the Sun, there was no
dust left anywhere on the slick-glossy surfaces of these
dehydrated planets. Here we have only four exposed
surfaces, accumulated with each new Nearsolar Epoch.
However, if we dug deeper into the center, towards the
darkest, most un-eroded, hence most mirror-like layer, we
would discover the layers of preceding Nearsolar Epochs, of
which there must have been thousands.

Following epochs
brought tremendous winds, blasting the surfaces and
making pockets, whereby ever-deeper abyssi were exposed.

 In another photograph of Mars I found this crater.
We are told that these craters on Mars, as on the
Moon, were created by falling meteors. I insist that all these
craters are "native," occasioned on these expired planets by
the winds. This and many other dead planets, which I have
named Mooncores, were long ago covered by their
respective geologic mantles. The geologic surface "flew off"
into space, hurtling back to the gravity of the nearing solar
furnace, leaving the dead planets in the form of meteors to
eventually plunge back themselves in the solar cauldron to
be melted.

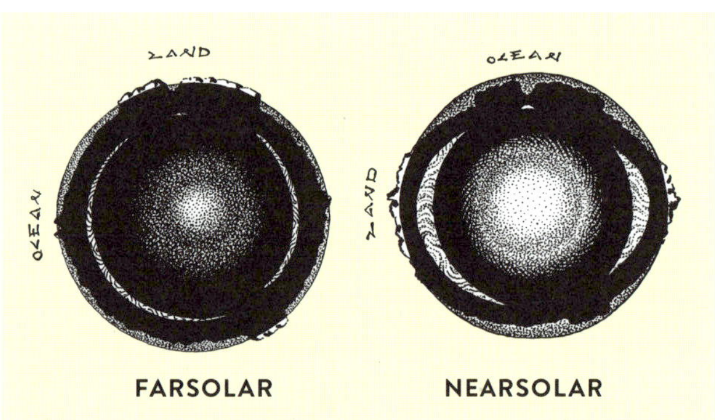

11   To better understand the small, craterous pockmarks of this planet, let me show you the principle of the structure of planets in cross-section.

At left you see a planet in a Farsolar Epoch at its high point. Geologic formations are standing above the seas. In the oceans, only a few islands barely break the surface of the waters. The internal combustion in the circular loft between the Mooncore and the geologic mantle is almost extinct, because of the too great distance from the Sun. This is the period of the Ice Ages.

At right you see the same planet at the high point of a Nearsolar Epoch, when its "soft belly" is in a state of vital volcanic activity. The ocean bottoms have risen to their utmost, becoming pseudo-continents, consisting of lava, forcing the seas to MIGRATE elsewhere, which means DELUGE. It is from these pseudo-continents that our forefathers saved themselves during the Deluge that has been related to us, and this explains why the Eskimo people originally started using the Protong self-description "(J)e Z Ki Mo," which means "Is From Where Sea."

As you see in this cross-section, as opposed to the earlier, similar drawing of the causes of the two kinds of Deluges, there is an inner Mooncore, a pit, actually the furnace of the planet. Our earth, then, has exactly the same kind of Mooncore and, on losing its geologic "flesh" in the oncoming Nearsolar Epochs, will become a metallic skeleton similar to the one we see above us at night, called Moon.

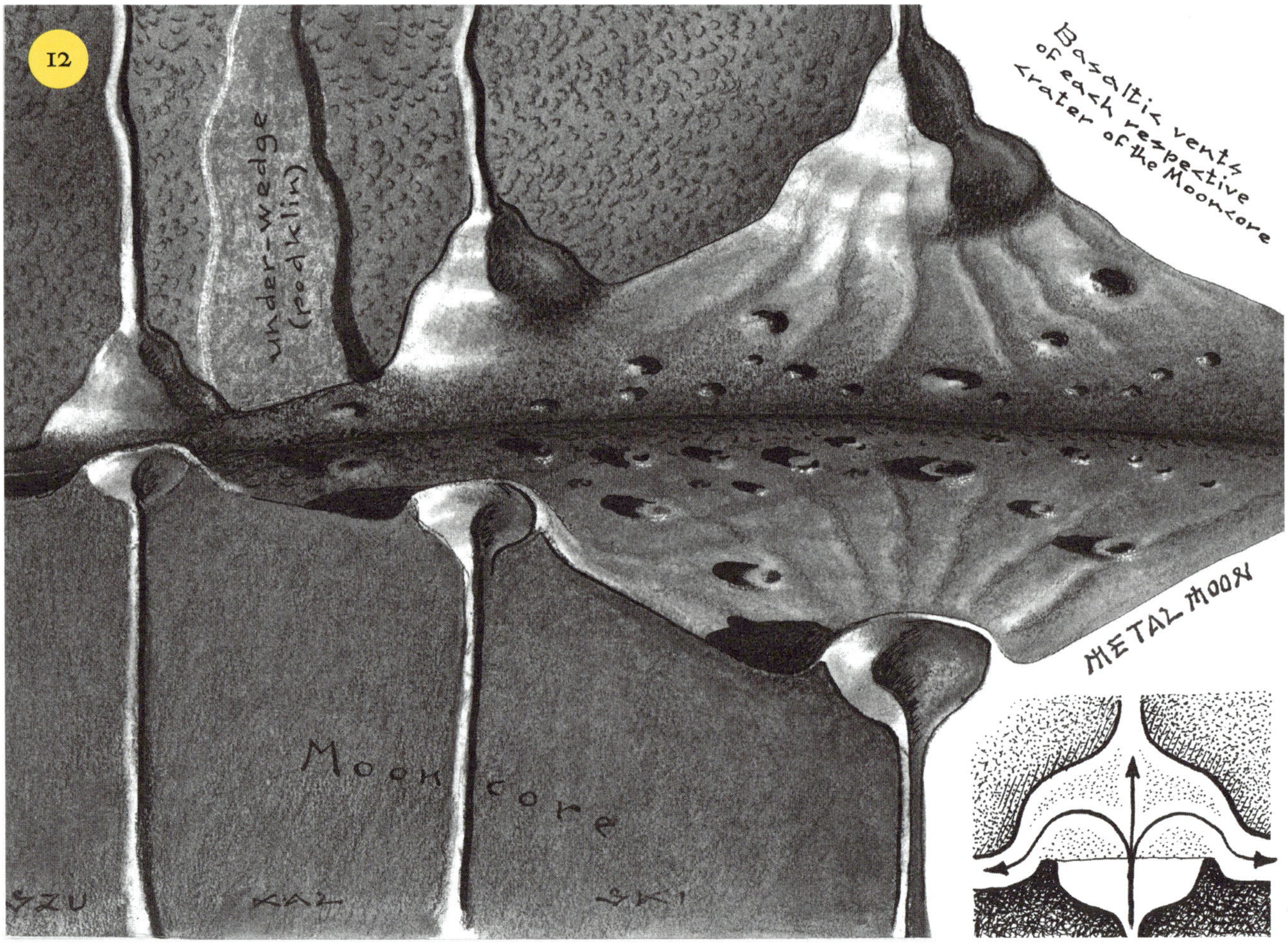

12   Let me show you how the Mooncore and the geologic mantle look from the inside of the loft. The lower half of the drawing shows you the Mooncore and the upper half the underside of the lavaic (sub-oceanic) mantle. The great cleavage is the circular loft. On the underside of the mantle are the complementary craters, the melted-away hoods that at some small distance cover the mouth of each Mooncore crater. These were not inflicted upon the Mooncore by falling meteors, but are the vents of the circulatory lava that distributes the heat, like an organic radiator, so that there developed life above and all flora and fauna flourished. Planets die when there is no more flow of hot lava, the blood of the planetary system. Bottom right I have drawn for you a cross section of the fitting of the craters and their receptor-hoods and the space between them for the flow of life-bringing lava.

In the upper left corner you see an under-wedge where the mantle cracked. That crack filled up with liquid lava that, when chilled, hardened. But on top of the bloating mantle larger cracks appeared which in turn became filled with rocks and gravel. Once filled with hard substances, the many over-and-under-wedges permanently elongate the arching surfaces, causing the continents to "float" away from each other.

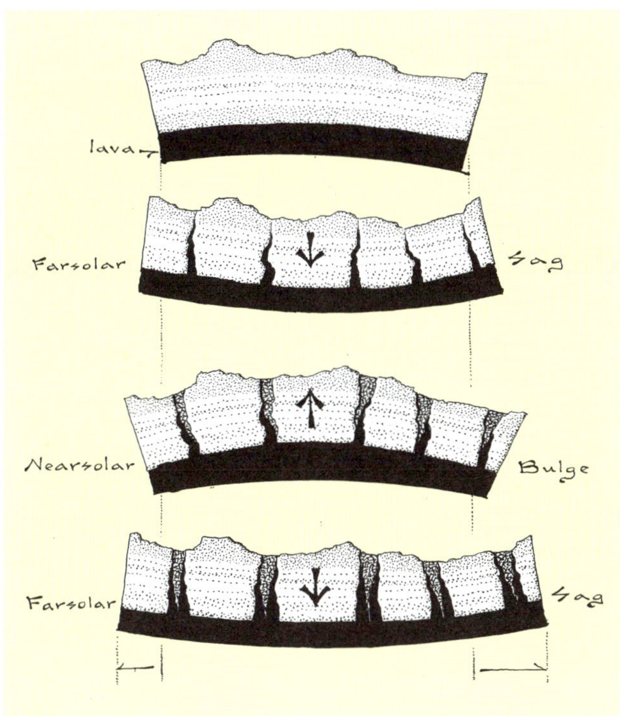

13 When a solid wall is bent, cracks will occur on the convex side. When these cracks are filled with concrete, they lengthen the wall. Then, when we bend the wall in the opposite direction, the same lengthening occurs at the other side. Thus, each time a Nearsolar or Farsolar

Epoch passed, wedges in the Horizon Jars of the oceans remained, thereby widening them and pushing the continents apart, making the seas ever vaster. Hence, it is the fluctuating solar temperatures that cause the growing of our globe.

■

Heat Gravity

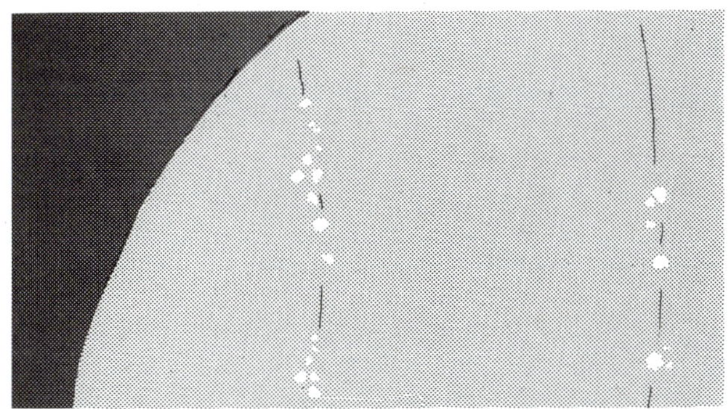

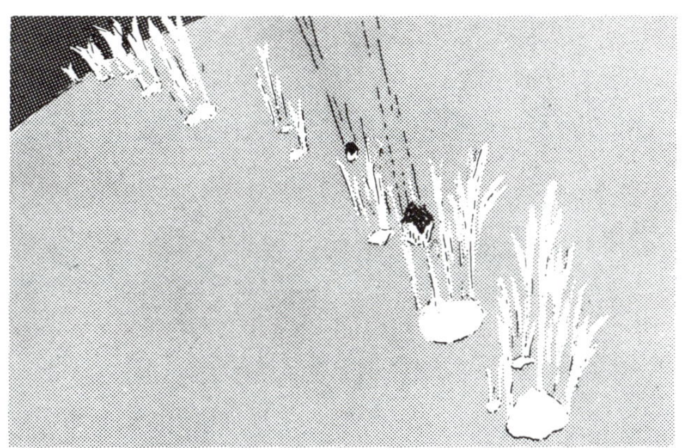

14 In 1957 I came across a photograph of the sunspots. They form a startling arrangement for, though they are obviously caused by objects plunging into the surface of the Sun out of the interplanetary spaces, they are perfectly aligned over a vast, especially considering the Sun's size, distance. Looking closely into this phenomenon, I instantly had the answer. These were the charred remains of an exploded dead planet that returned to its Maker to be smelted in the Cauldron of our Universe. Though the Sun is a liquid ball, without any rocks, or even metallic solids, in a constant state of combustion, it needs no receptacle whatsoever, not any pot to contain it. Why not? Because, being white-hot, it is in the center of its HEAT GRAVITY.

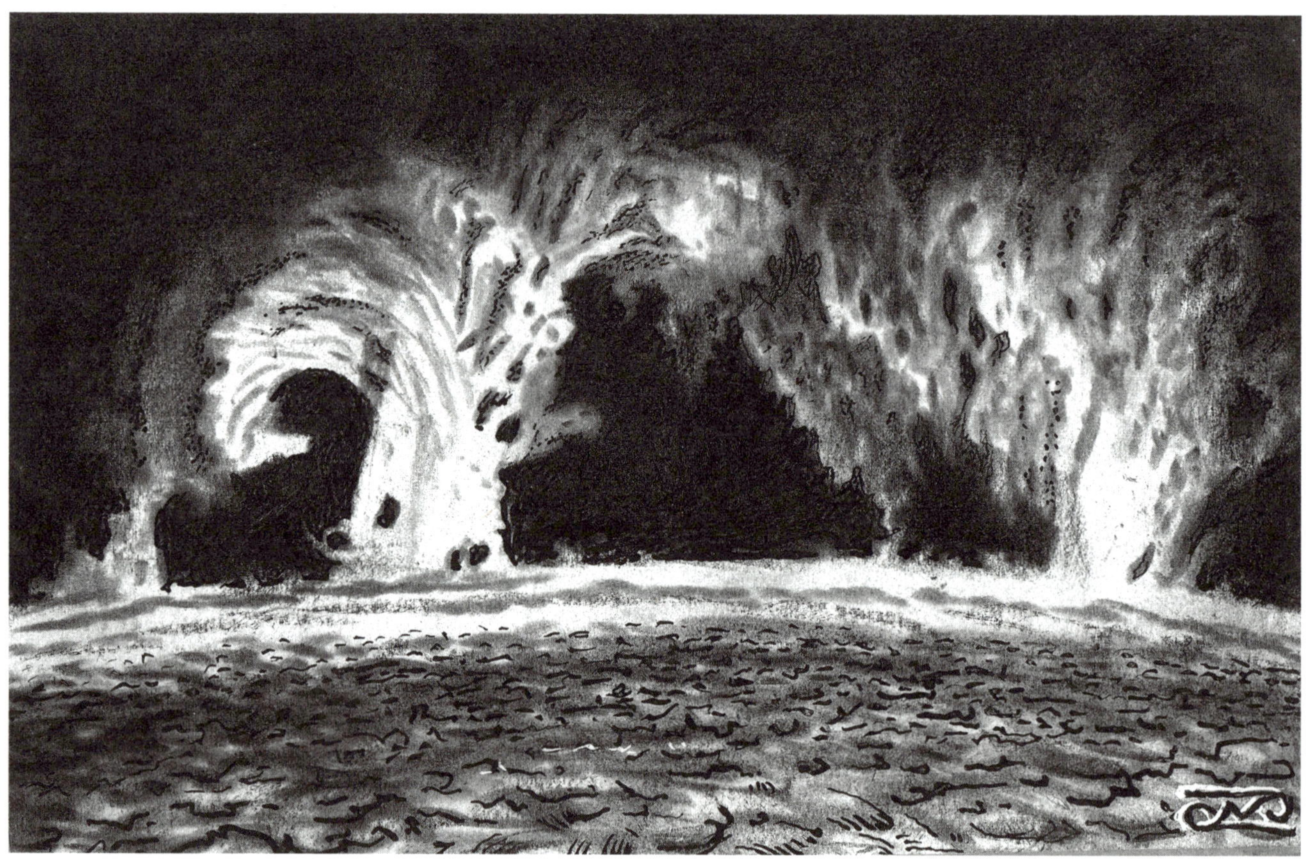

15 I have carried you up to the surface of the Sun to see how this planetary scrap iron plunges into it. The disturbed surface of the inexpressibly enormous body of the Sun reacts with tremendous light explosions, so vast that thousands of our globes carried in these fountains of light would not even be noticed. These gigantic pillars of light are formed of billions of densely packed lightnings. They last sometimes for up to a few hours, then abruptly fade. The Sun is the cemetery of dead planets, but also the creator of others in Nearsolar Epochs, when it boils like Scottish oatmeal porridge, spurting and splattering millions of liquid blobs which we call comets, from which, when expelled into the frigid inter-planetary spaces, new planets are born.

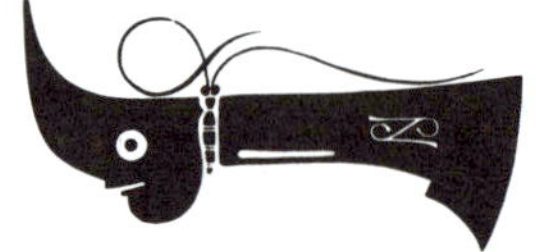

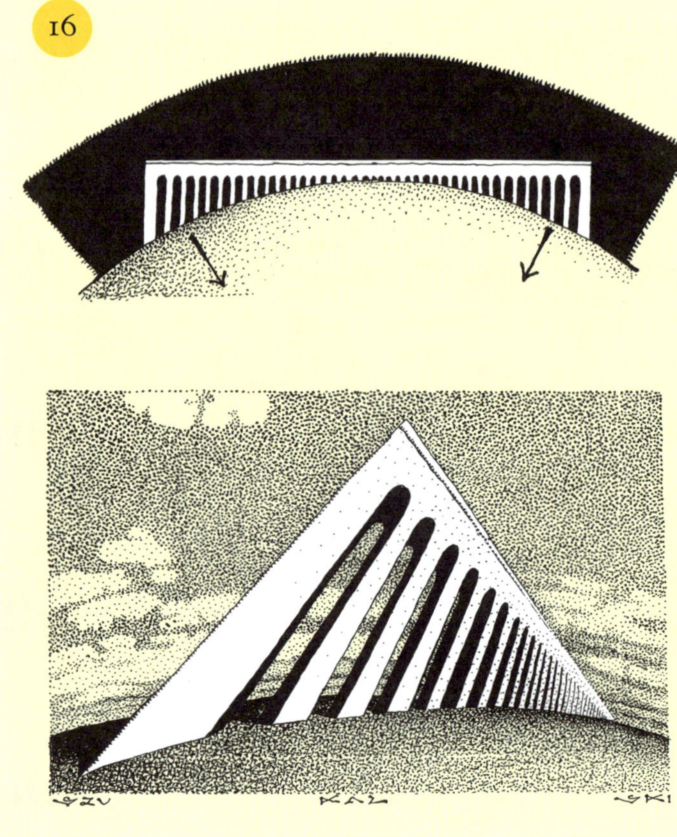

16 How do I prove to myself and the nation that it is the Solar Heat, "sympathetically" reimbursed to our globe by its proximity, that causes my pencil to drop to the floor instead of to the ceiling of my room? Here is my form of reasoning.

If we were able to construct a gigantic level aqueduct, some thousands of miles long, with a very deep trough at the top, and pump water from the sea into it, the liquid would not fill it in its entire length equally deep. At the extreme ends of the trough the water would be sloping down at a 45-degree angle, and if we let streams of water drain from each end of the bridge, their fall would not be downwards along the pilasters, but directed to the right or left, towards the center of the earth. For what we call "level" is actually only a curve around the center of GRAVITY, which is the interior of our globe where the furnace is that consumes the heaviest metals as fuel, with the help of hydrogen and helium from the Sun that gained these long ago by dehydration of oceans and seas in Nearsolar Epochs.

17 Looking from above into the vast trough, we would see a seemingly illogical phenomenon for, instead of filling the gigantic receptacle throughout its length, the waters of the sea would sit in the middle in a humped-horizoned body. It would follow the identic curvature of the land below, around the hot furnace of our globe where remains the entire fuel endowment given to it when it was born, in one of the Nearsolar Epochs, out of the boiling Sun.

18 Similarly, if we could place a terribly strong plate of glass over our globe and pour Lake Michigan on it, the water would not spread evenly to the edges, then pour off into the abyss, but "hump" in its center. For, in relation to the central point of our heat-caused gravity, the plate is not level, but actually bowl-shaped; hence, gravitationally speaking, LEVEL is CONCAVE. ■

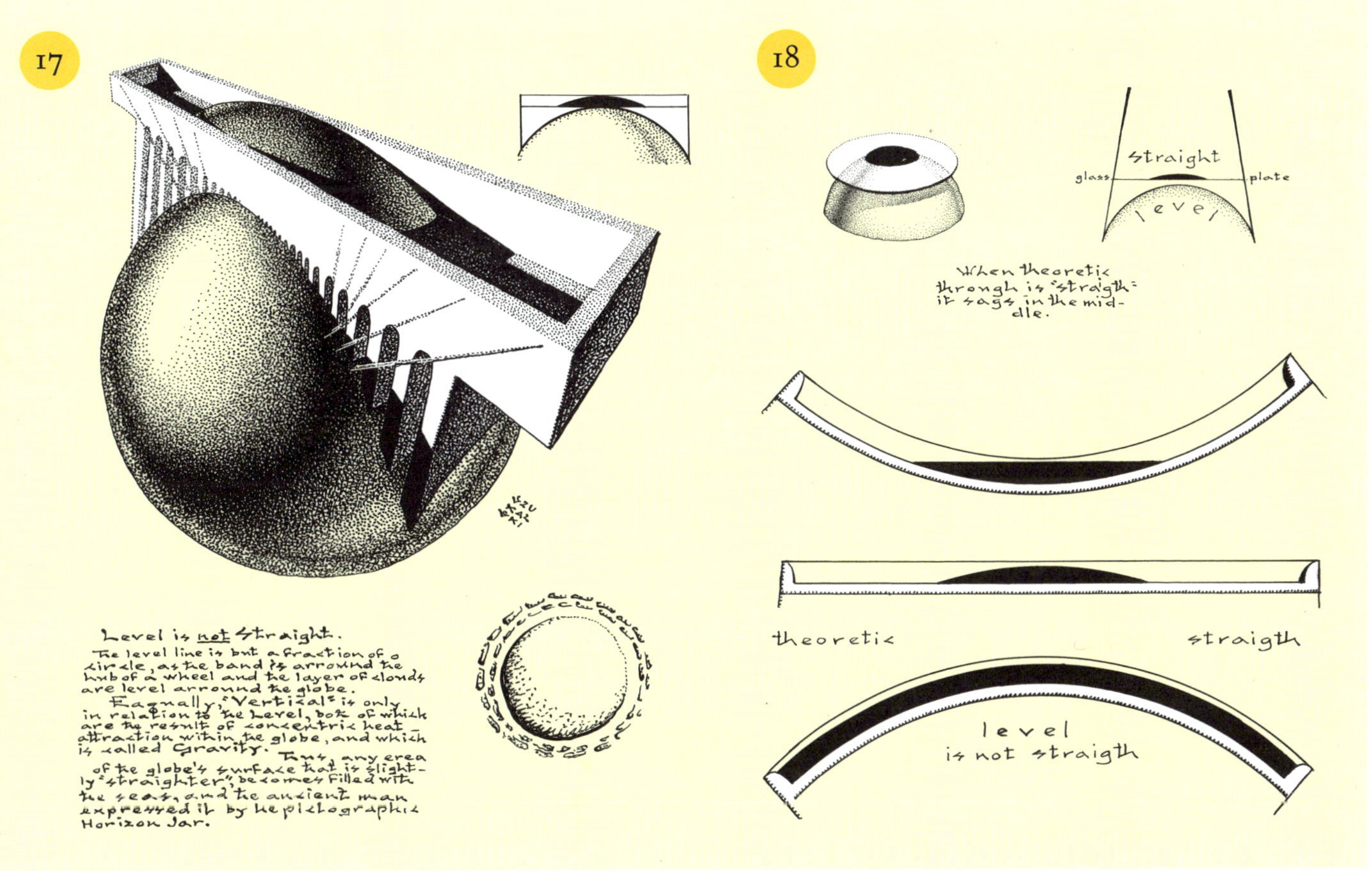

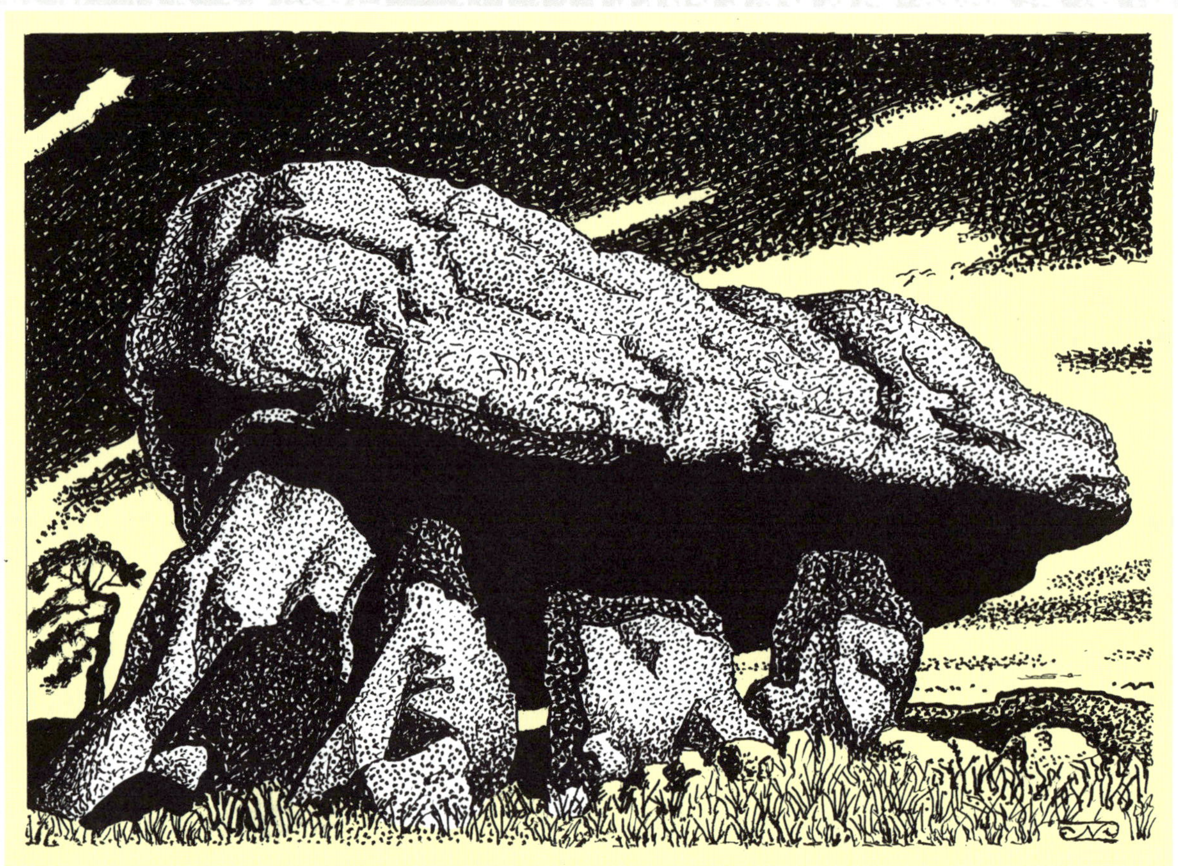

DOLMEN IN CARLOW, IRELAND

Caves: The First Post-Diluvial Dwellings

NOAH, Oannes, Fu Hsi, Quetzalcoatl, all escaped from the Deluge by saving themselves on the RE-EMERGING isles that progressively became the continents. They departed from the tops of the mountains, which were the last to SUBMERGE.

On discovering that every pictograph in the world pertaining to man, his beliefs and his history, describe him as being witness of the great Deluge, I had to find physical reasons for this recurrent calamity. I soon evolved the theory that the Sun's temperature fluctuates. Thus, I suggested that there are two astronomically timed epochs succeeding one another at long intervals.

Geologists and astronomers, though thinking in terms and measurements of TIME, used mathematics, and greatly disagree in their conclusions, placing the Ice Ages from a few to tens of thousands years back. That approach seemed to me inadequate.

I had to find a way that would exceed mathematically braced arguments. While reading in *Genesis*, I was bemused, then raised off the floor of legendary broad statements by learning that the patriarchs of the Hebrews (therefore of all other races and nations) lived over a thousand years in the beginning (Adam), then, as time passed, lived shorter and shorter lives, till their descendants were finally reduced in their longevity to a mere 70ish.

From delving in prehistoric achievements of man, I have learned that all events reported by him, no matter how preposterously fantastic, were factually true. So when the systemized prehistoric gossips became mythologies speaking of centaurs, mermaids and other unlikely creatures, man spoke the TRUTH.

But that truth has to be understood. Our contemporary minds, ignorant of the crude petroglyphic communications of megalithic man, are as limited in scope as the minds of primitive humans regarding our scientific ways and skepticism. We cannot disdain prehistoric man as merely graduated animals.

Looking through thousands of illustrated books, I have learned how to SEE. Since childhood I have been addicted to seeing "pictures" in books. My grandfather had a large library and as a five-year-old I had seen every book, page by page, looking for pictures. On arriving in America, I spent all my free time at the Northwestern Settlement House off Milwaukee Avenue in Chicago, looking through the magazines in the dark basement room. When I was twelve, I had looked through every magazine in the for many years accumulated, ceiling-high pile. I learned not only to look, but really SEE, for I did not know English yet and had to jump to CONCLUSIONS. In fact, I evolved the, to other people unnatural, instinct for UNDERSTANDING things, without knowing what they were.

Looking became my life's OBSESSION. When I am dying I will despair over the fact that I will no more be able to Look and See. Though presently, as my hair is white, I bear in mind that at last I will also no more see the inane sports reports and commercials on TV, and for such an exclusion I shall be grateful.

Learning that the patriarchs lived over a thousand years and their descendants lived shorter and shorter spells, I did not dismiss their claims saying that the ancients were too stupid to know better. The patriarchs actually did live that long. But, their years were those of the Nearsolar Epoch when all the satellites of our Sun were closely drawn to it, bringing with them their oceans filled with the waters of the melted snows of the previous Ice Age from which Our Maker draws its energy (hydrogen and helium) by dehydration. For planets serve only as "water boys" to the Sun which has to replenish its fuel at the astronomically proper intervals.

Thus I had the inspired notion (every worthy revolution begins with a "silly" notion, as did the Copernican) to count the years of successive patriarchs, from mythical Adam up to one who reached the age of about 70, and came to the conclusion that the Farsolar and Nearsolar Epochs repeat their cycle every some 26,000 years.

The old patriarchs lived on this earth when it only had to make short trips around the Sun, so that their "year" consisted of two or three months of ours. There should be two concepts of time: Solar Time, as we practice now, not realizing that we are presently nearing the Sun and our days and years are shorter than they were in the last Ice Age, and Theoretic Time. Theoretically, the patriarchs lived no longer than we do, but it took them many more shorter years to complete their life-journeys.

Though their seemingly longer lives were no different from ours, our planet on which we defecate, dream and expire, was fundamentally affected by those Farsolar and Nearsolar Epochs, for they alternately cause Ice Ages and ages of almost total DEHYDRATION of the globe. (On this matter I wrote in the first volume of my *Zermatism*.)

When the diluvials escaped from the submerging lavaic continents (now the ocean bottom) in the Pacific, and landed in Europe that was just re-emerging, there were no human settlements to take possession of. Therefore, wherever they discovered caverns, these became the first emergency dwellings.

19 Two of my volumes on Zermatism, *Listen to These Stones*, deal with such caverns. One is located in Tangier and is called Bisitun by the natives. What there was to be found is already deposed and explained by archaeologists and there is nothing else they have deducted from their findings than the trite, rubberstamp claims that

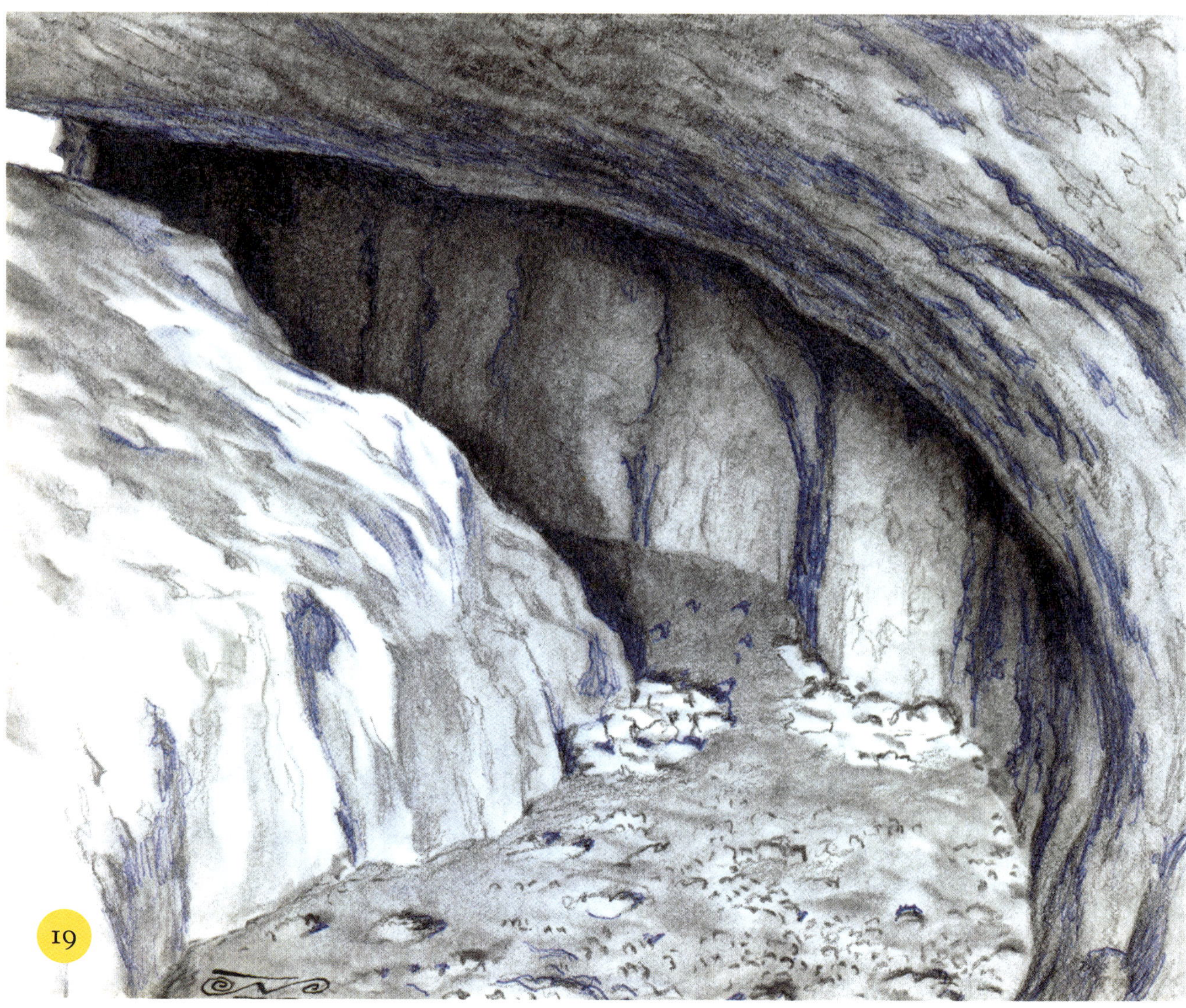

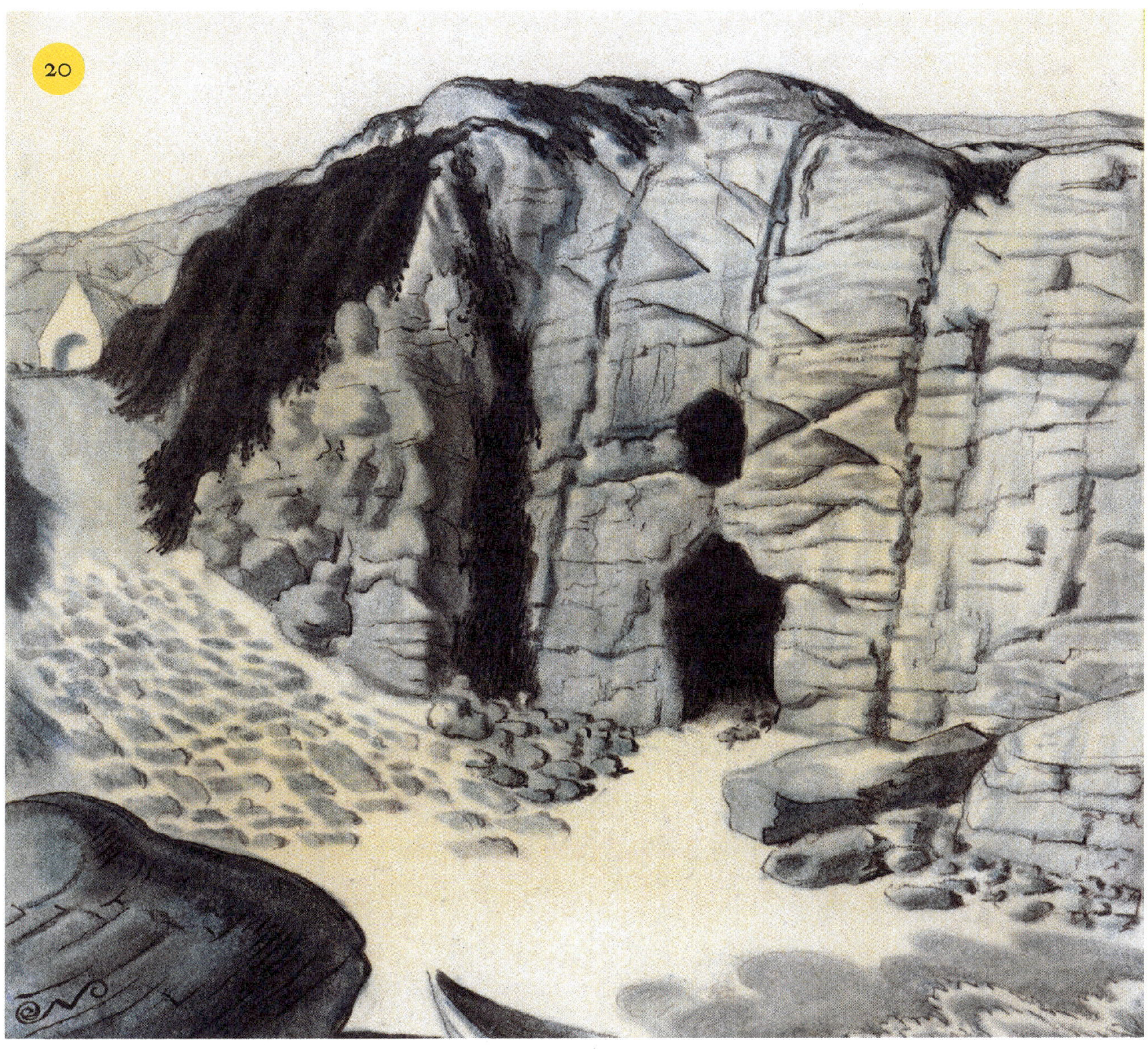

these were prehistoric hiding places for man, who attempted to escape from the night cold.

But with my Protong I have found the way whereby you can actually almost hear the voice of the one who named this cavern Bisitun. Resegmented, it becomes "Bi Zi Tun" from which, through the use of grammatic Polish, we can deduct the translation "Killed Motherland Sinking." In Polish "land, motherland, soil, earth" are all covered by the word *zim* or *ziemia*. Therefore, the Hebrew prayer beginning with *Zema Isroel Alekienu, ZemaJa Do, ZemJe Hod* ("Oh Land of Israel, Land That Gave Me, Land That Is Gone") is pure Protong-Polish, not Hebrew.

Thus we learn that the people who found safety and revived their Hopes in this cavern in Tangier, were diluvial refugees. They formed their description-name in Protong—the grammarless Polish—multi-millennia ago.

In Britain, at a place called Portgwarra, there is a cavern facing the sea. When we erase the modern forepart of the name, we are left with the name *Gwara.* Now, please recall the two Polish port towns Gdynia and Gdansk. They are pure Protong, meaning respectively "Where Daying (Is)" and "Where (towards) Denmark."

We know that "Ra" means "Morn." Thus we learn that the name of this location in England means "Where Worship Morn:" this was a primitive temple where the first arrivals from the Pacific region assembled to worship the Sunrise.

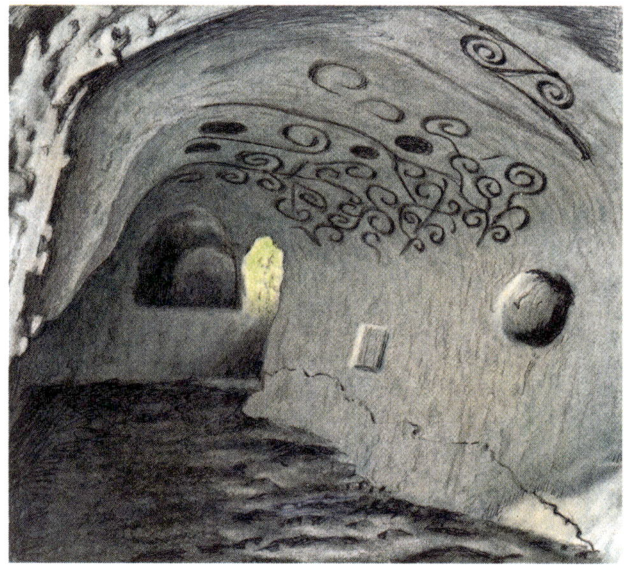

On the island of Malta there is a cavern named Hal Suflieni. On its ceiling are ancient whirls (smoked or painted with blood, the most enduring coloring), emulating the churning surface of the deluging seas, each whirl marking the place where something sunk. On re-segmentation, the now meaningless name becomes the description phrase "Ga L Z Ut, W Li Je Ni," which means literally "Exiled Flood From The Sunken, Within Flooding (sea) Is No (more)." No doubt this cavern also was a temple where the faithful refugees from Easter Island assembled.

But not everywhere were caverns. Therefore, the next thing to do, when need for a temple arose, was to erect a simile of a cavern. So Dolmens arose, made of many, vertically stood, gigantic slabs, over which a slab of still greater dimensions was placed. Over these Dolmens soil was piled from baskets carried by the whole population of the territory. When the earthwork was completed, the mounds were called *kurchany*. This name comes from a Protong compound, "Gur Gany," which means they were raised by the "Mountain's Exiles" (by "mountain" was meant the Island that vanished, since there is no word in Protong for the latter).

In France I found the most elaborately decorated Dolmen I have seen so far. It is located at a place called Gavrinis. This was anciently "Ga Wr In Ie Z," which means "Exiled Worship Elsewhere Is From." The interior of this megalithic temple is completely covered with one persistently repeated pictograph: the whirl. Whirls, no matter how they are conceived, mean diluvial SINKAGE, for they picture the churning, turbulent seas. Again, this tells us that "Else-where" ("In") in the name indicates the place where the whirling seas of the Deluge cover the original homeland of the diluvials and the netherworld of the drowned ancestors.

A Dolmen in Korea, at a place named after it, called Hoang-Ha-To, shows us the primal form over which later, in Buddhist times, the Chinese and Koreans began to superimpose other Dolmens, every one smaller and slimmer than the underlying one. The name of this temple was made of Protong "Go On Ga To" and means "He (was) Exiled, Driven (away by) Flood."

I have 442 of such witnesses in two volumes and what I show in this book is only a thimbleful sample of the whole universe I have discovered, which was never even suspected by the sciences. It can hardly be expected that you will believe that this crude form of Polish Protong could have been used all over the globe, but if you had the translation of all the names of these 442 monuments of global history as part of the astronomically linked happenings, you would be more than astounded. The whole organon on every specific subject must be published, that my Zermatism be perceived as the most precedent-shattering and up-turning of all notions on our ORIGINS.

In Frejlev, Lolland, in Denmark stands this Dolmen. This name evolved from the Protong description "Wre (J)e Le W" and means "(The) Worshipped (one) Is Flooded Within." Who is the object of worship? It is the Scandinavian version of the Deluged Motherland of the Dawn. The Scandinavians called her Freya. Her now misinterpreted name was originally "Wre Ja," meaning she is the one whom "Worship I."

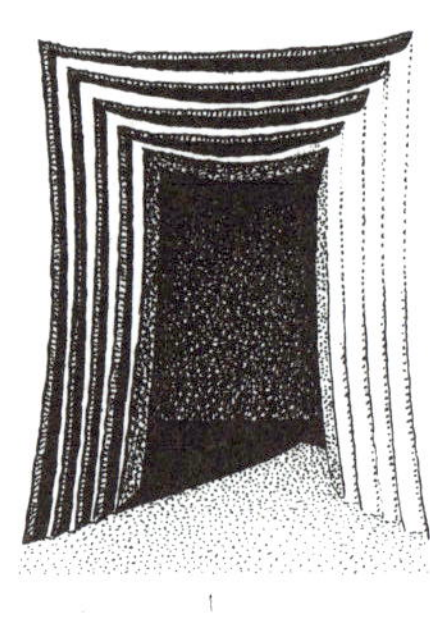

Look at the small drawing of this limestone carving, inspired by the interiors of such Dolmens. The place where there are a few of these similarly carved doorways, is Cassibile on Sardinia, which in more ancient times was described by the Protong phrase "Ka Z Zi Bi Li," meaning "Where From Land Killed Flood."

I do not know if these entries led into grave chambers dug out of the limestone hills, or temples large enough for the post-diluvials to assemble in. Therefore, I cannot comment on them, though I do have evidence of other such entries with their specific "names" to be translated.

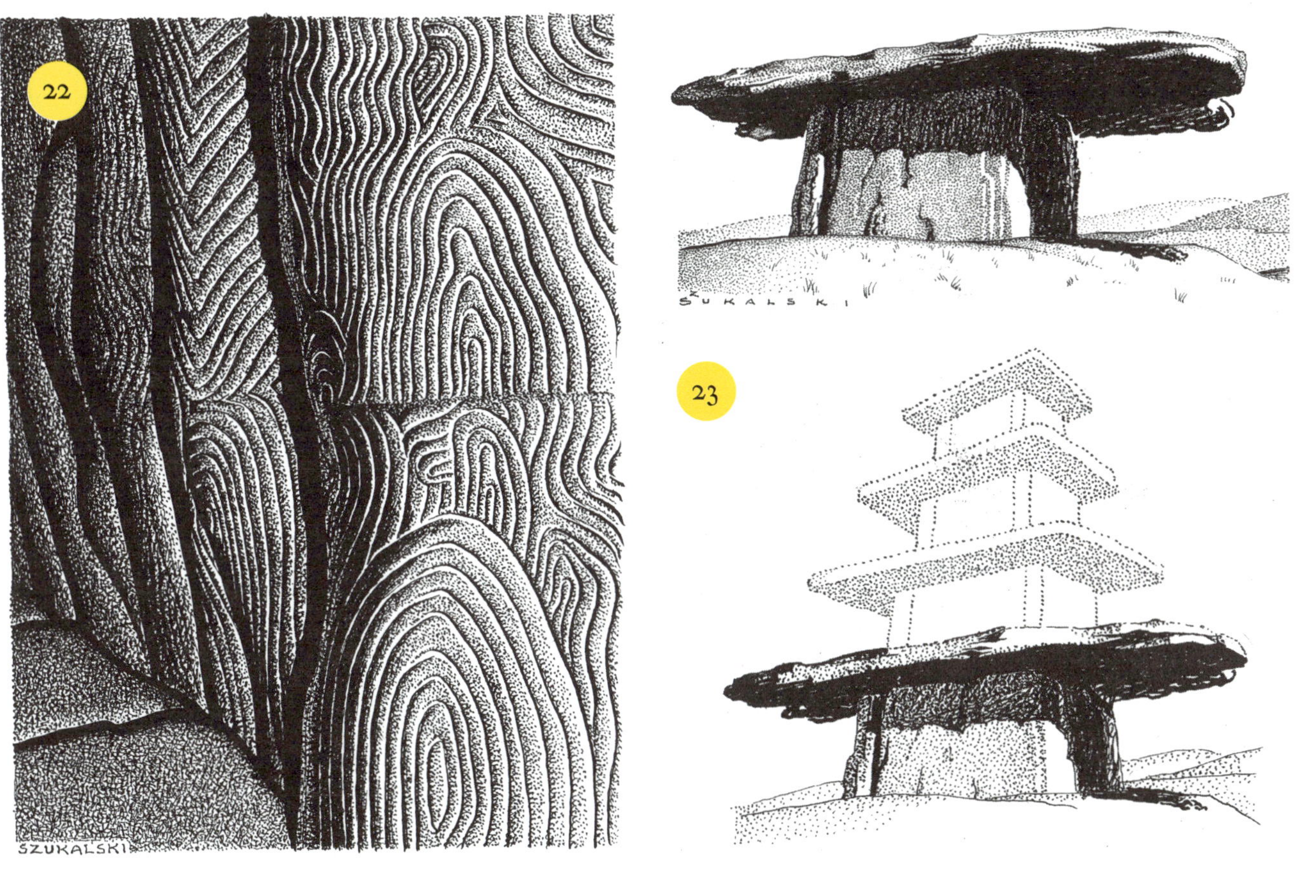

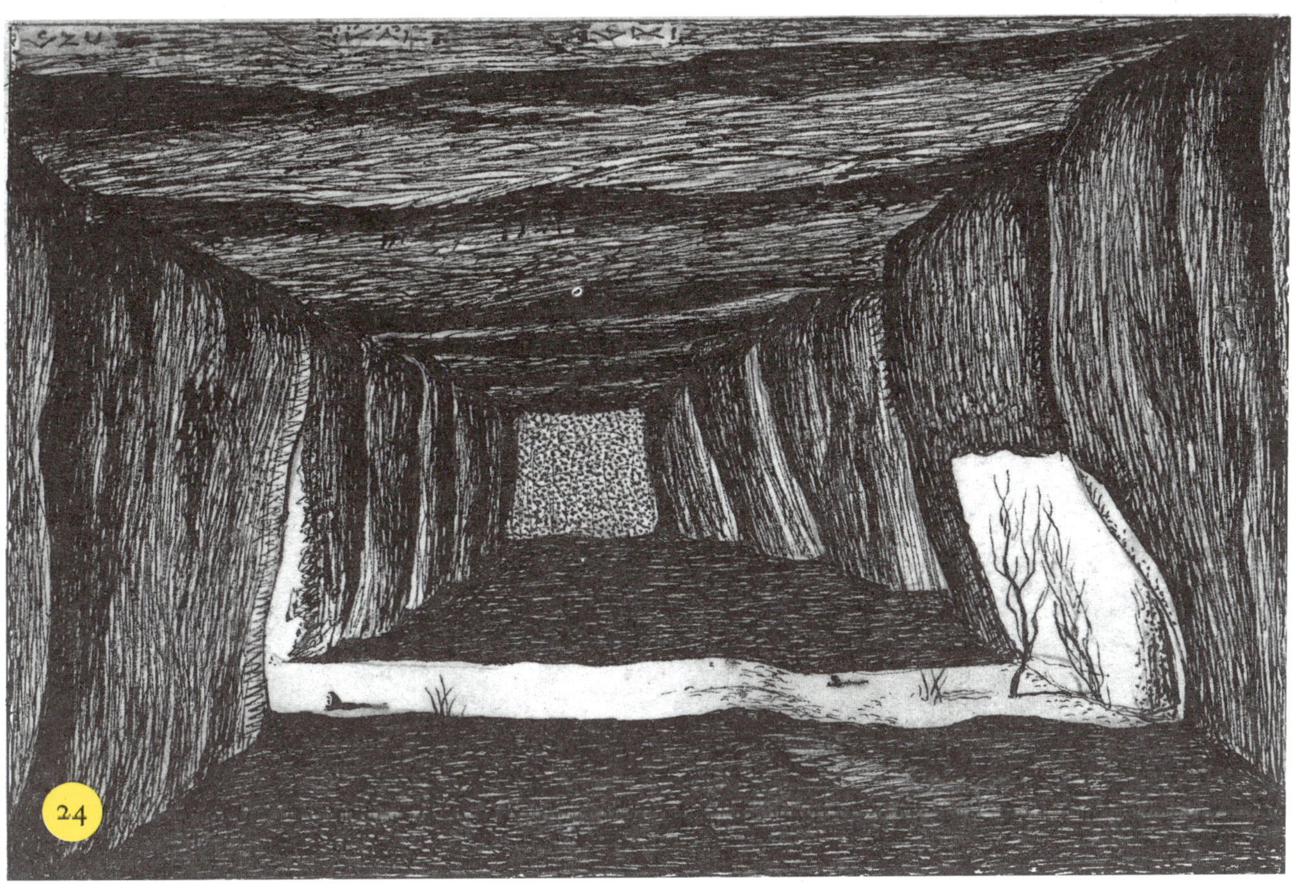

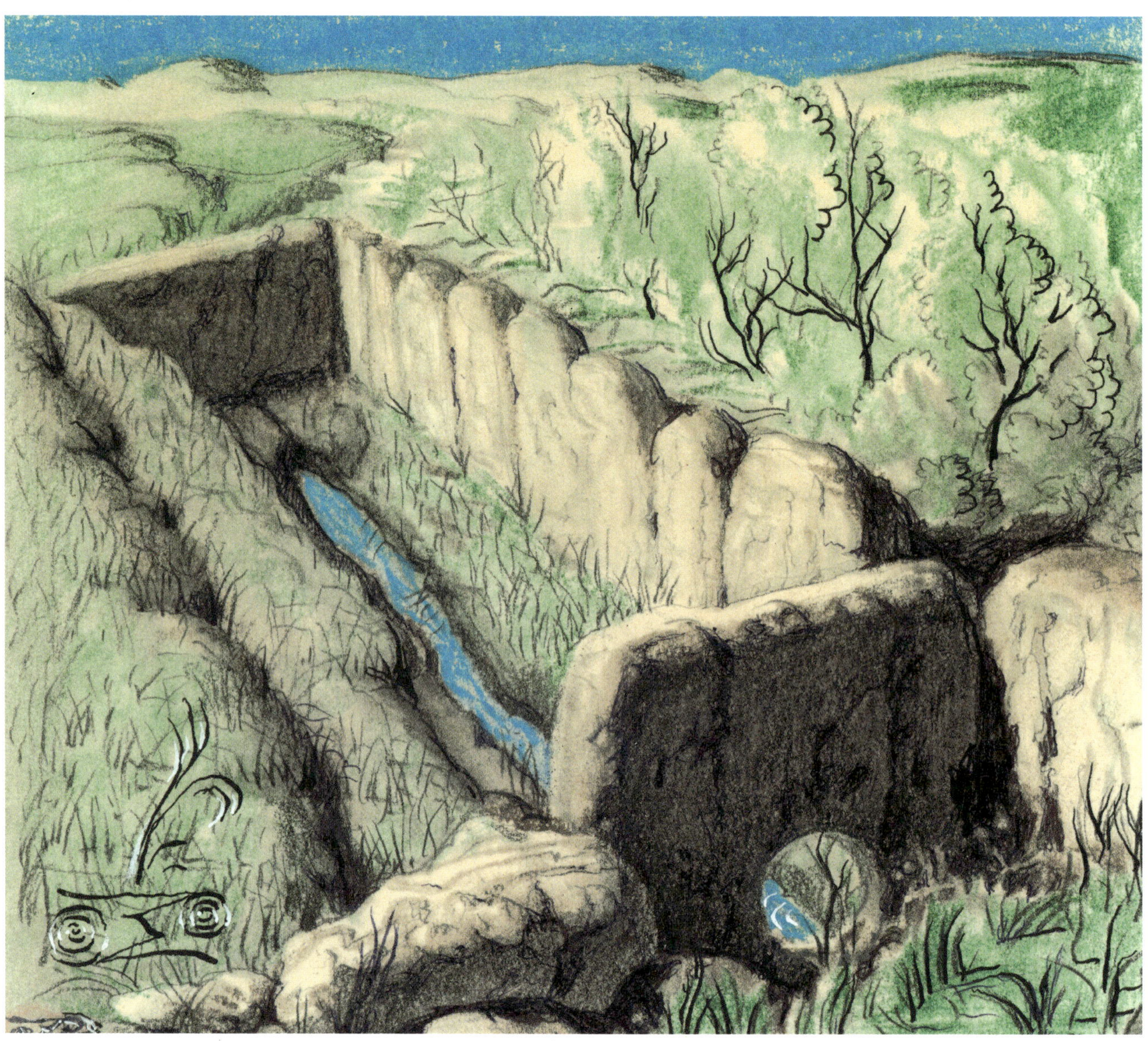

26 This remnant of underground burial grounds was found in Zueschen, Waldeck, in Germany. Though from the photographs I cannot adequately judge its size, it looks like it was sufficiently large to serve as a temple (recall the Mithraic temples where the doors were intentionally so little that the men entering, had to crawl in, as if re-entering the womb).

The name Zueschen was compressed of the Protong phrase "Z Us Ze Ne," meaning "From mortally-Asleep Land No (more existing)."

We must not expect smooth formation of the Protong phrases, for it was a primitive language that did not have even the beginnings of grammar. The sequence of words was random, though the priests who coined the names, selected a sequence that would make them smoothly pronounceable. The Protong vocabulary is very small, though each mini-word has many dialectic variations, but if you know about mathematic permutations, you know that almost endless combinations can be made. Each name could be re-arranged in many ways, but always would carry identical meanings.

27 Here you have a substitute for a cavern, shaped by fitted-together gigantic stone slabs. The name of its location tells us for what it was used: Bounias, near Mount Majouele in Arles, France.

It is very likely that this part of the country was named Arles because of this temple. As I mention in the Protong Glossary, there never were words in Protong or Polish beginning with the letter "a." The letter

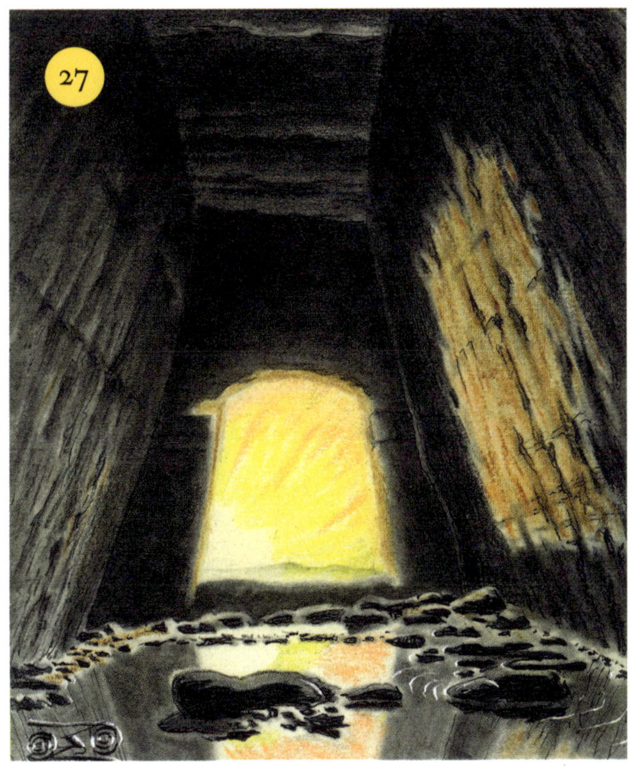

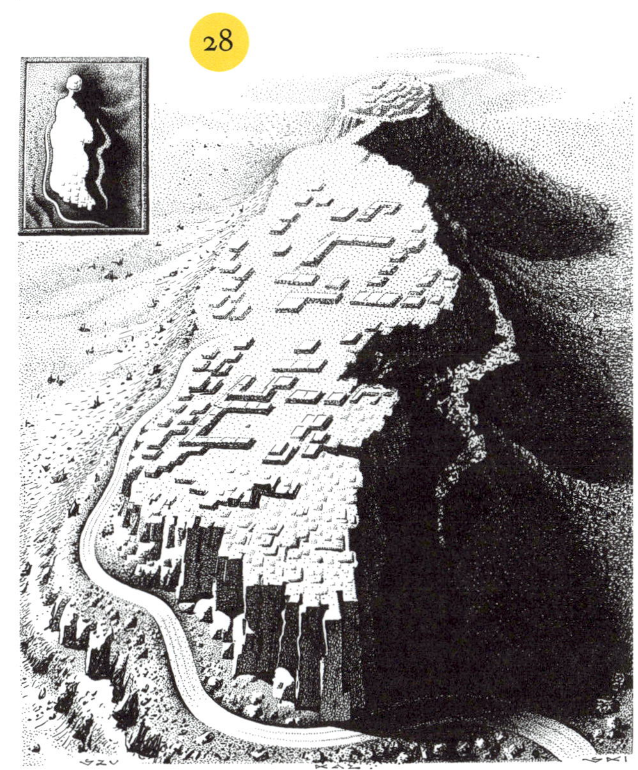

"w" ("v") is inaudible from some distance. I assume that the letter "f" in all words was originally "w" or "v," that the law of sound-wearage softened them into "f" (anciently the name France was "Wrance," meaning "Worshippers") or made them disappear. Whenever there are words beginning with "a" or "e," as in Arthur, Aristotle, they are missing the preceding "w" that wore off.

Thus, *Arles* was originally "War Le Z," which tells us that within this superb temple "Worship, Flooded From." The locality of the Dolmen is named Bounias. Its re-segmented compound phrase is "Bo O(t) NiJa Z" and means that the temple speaks of itself in the first person: "God, S(unken) No (more existing) I From." Both names bespeak of Easter Island or the "Mother of Worship' (the Sunrise). Thus we know that the Dawn was worshipped in this temple. It is so ancient that the ground outside it has accumulated, and the rainwater flows in from outside making a pool. Its vault-like interior is properly magnificent.

28 In New Mexico, at a place named by the Indians, Walpi, is an ancient community. The entire village is located atop a rocky elevation, the whole plan of which has the shape of a pregnant woman. The "head" on the thin "neck" was anciently the sacred precinct of the Kiwa, a subterranean temple. Presently the community houses

center on this head of the gigantic image of the perished Motherland.

The name *Walpi* was anciently the Protong description "Wa L Bi," which means "Worship Flood-Killed," referring to the Motherland in the distant Pacific. The body of the gigantic image is called Sichomowi. This, even to the Indians, meaningless name is the compression of "Zi Co Mo Wi" and means "Land That Sea Out" (i.e. drove its population into migration).

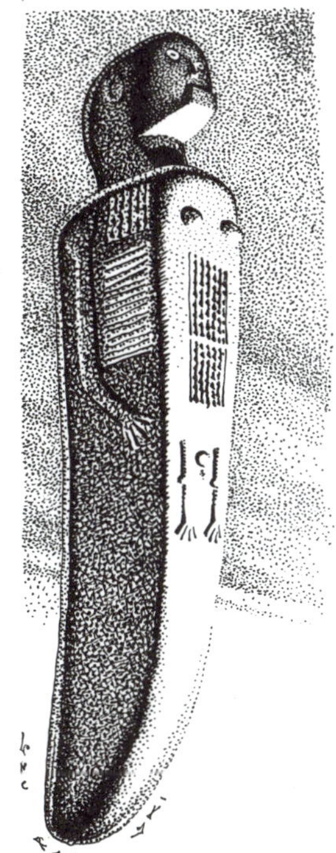

29 Lately, because of Russian Yetinsyny (Sons of the Yeti) bi-species activities, we frequently hear the name Zimbabwe. A separate nucleus has been formed in North Rhodesia that adopted this name from the mysterious, ancient ruins there. All sorts of suppositions among the learned sprouted in an attempt to find some clue to the meaning of this group of temples,

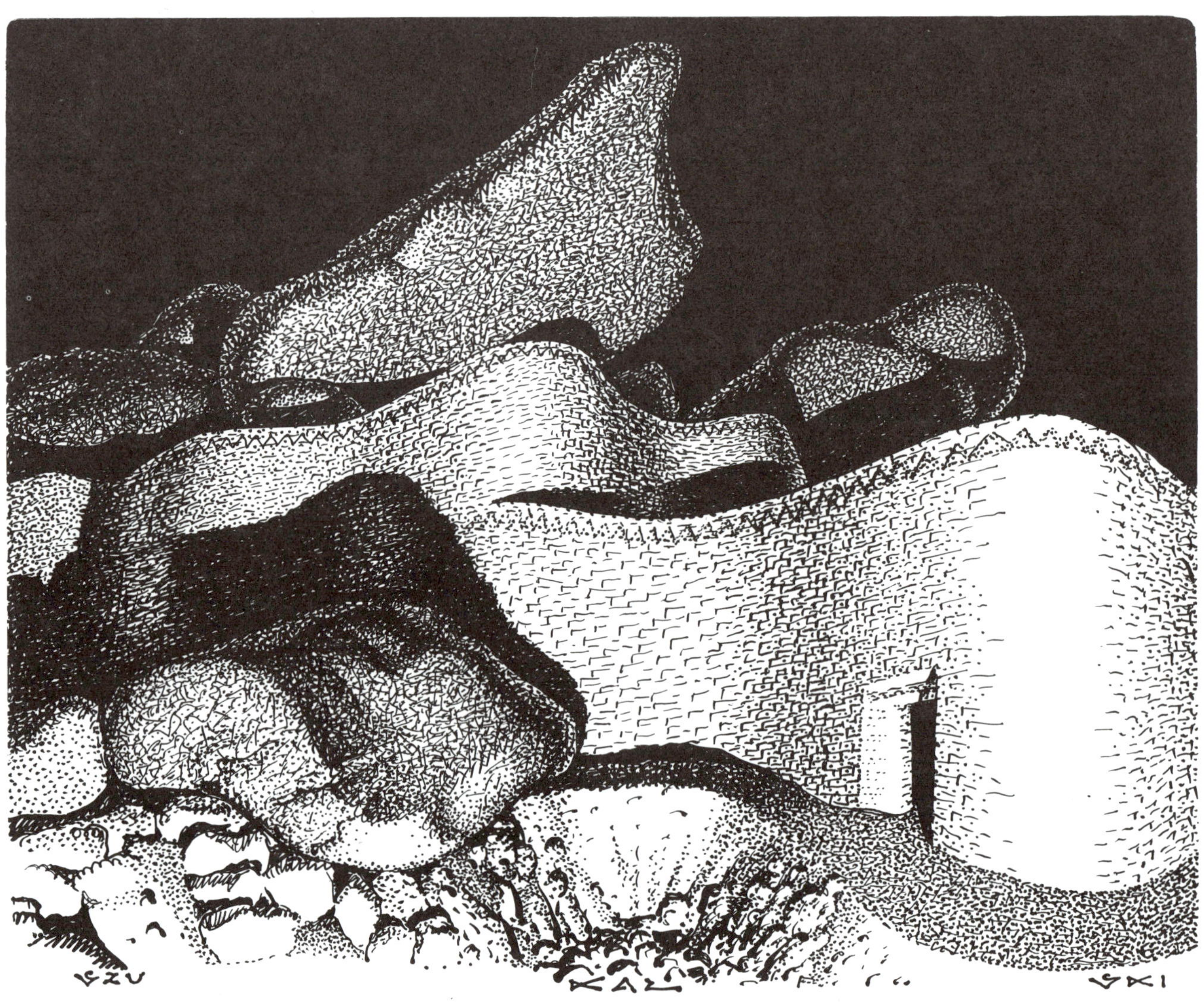

including a hint that perhaps — why not? — King Solomon had been looking there for gold.

I made drawings of some archaeological finds excavated from the once sacred precinct, among which is an Eagle and the image of the bald-headed and breastless Mother.

When in dilemma concerning the origins of anything in the world, turn to my Protong. So in this case: "Zim Bab We" is purely archaic Polish, meaning "Land Old-Woman Worship," referring to the image found there, carved in black basalt, which is now in the collection of the British Museum, where I drew it.

30 finally, the reconstructed-by-me city of Lachish, Judah. When Babylon invaded Judah, only two cities did not succumb to the onslaught. One was Lachish, the other Zekah.

Anciently, the Poles were *Lachi* (plural). This name came to be adopted after the Swiss Zermatian survivors of the Deluge found new lands for cultivation on the just re-emerging Polish terrains. Proto-Poland, after departure of the Long Sea (*Mare Longum*), consisted of mire, swamps, and the alpine explorers selected firm sandbars, called *lachy* in Sarmatian, to settle upon. From the "Sand Lachy" they became known as "Lachy." Till this day the Ukrainians and all nations of the Near East call Poland "Lachistan" (Lach State).

In my volumes on *Zermatism* I write on the European origin of the Hebrews and Iranians as hailing from Pomerania. They are the descendants of the Ice Age Polish Saki who escaped starvation by migrating to the Near East. The ancient city of Lachish was originally named "Lachi Z," meaning that the founders were "From (the) Lachy."

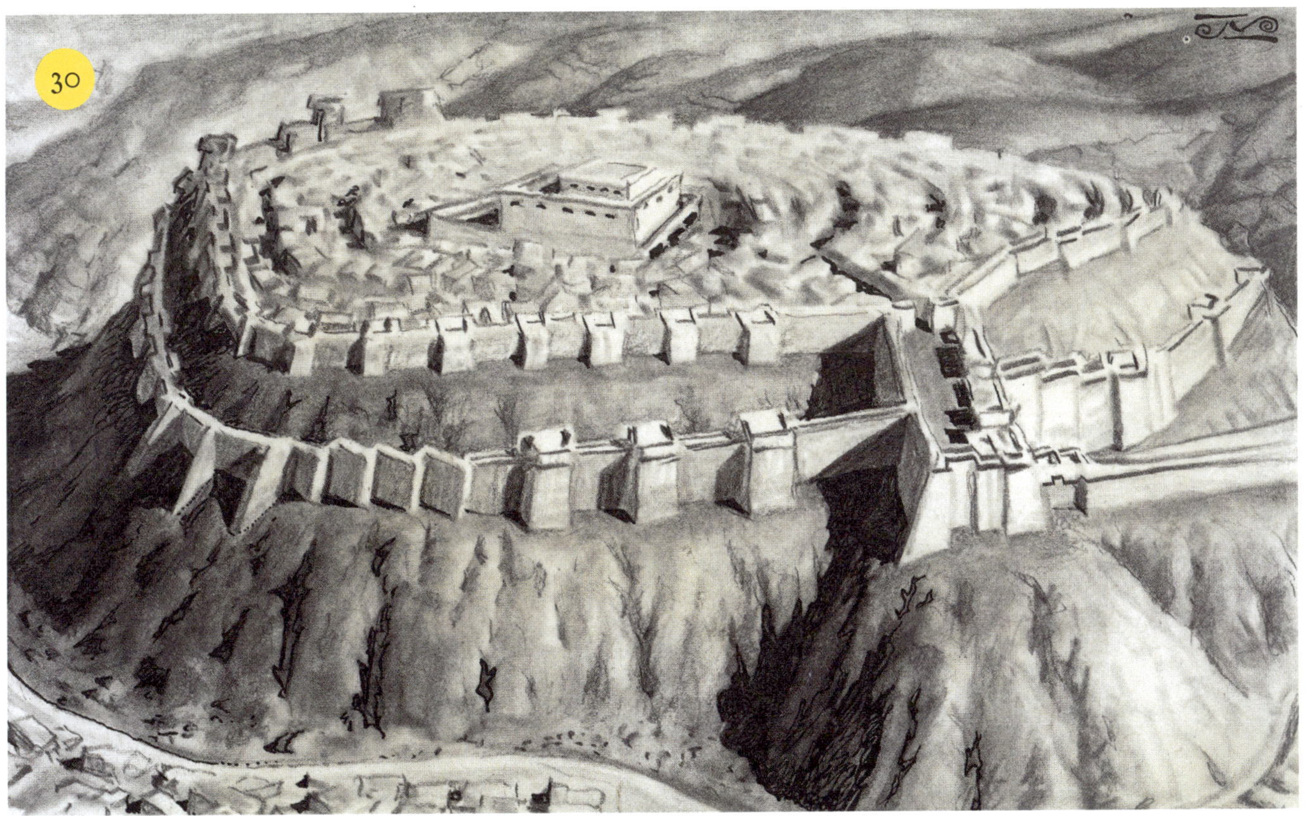

LACHISH, JUDAH

IT breaks my heart that the allotted space does not permit me to give you more examples. There are 442 drawings I took the trouble to draw for you, that I would like to crowd into this sampler-book, just to convince you of the shattering truth that the whole globe is covered with similar "witnesses" to the veracity of my scientific claims.

I have made the greatest discoveries that a human was ever capable of. Why was I able to discover Protong? Why did I discover the meaning of every pictograph, no matter where or when it was created? Why did other, professional scientist not discover these things before me? Because they were educated by those who were educated by those who were educated in those incubators of non-entities who can only think in formulas, repeated from one generation to the other by learned automatons. I intentionally avoided that education, so that I would save the Wisdom all humans are born with, my innate capacity to solve the dilemmas that previous scientists failed to budge. Educated men are basically cowards in their thinking. They must have authorities behind them. I dismiss all authorities. I deal with Culture, not with Civilization. I am a kite whose only connection with this prosaic earth is the frail string on which I soar way, way above the rubberstamp thinking of the well-educated bipeds.

I have re-segmented and translated names that were totally meaningless for thousands of years, from every ancient epoch and Civilization. The scientific world would never have suspected that within them the entire prehistory of Mankind is disguised. Only because I was born with a Polish tongue in my mouth and, being formally uneducated, I DARE think my way; because my ego is monumental, and I never deviate or resign from MY WAY of thinking, I was capable of discovering things that less self-assured scientists would NEVER suspect.

The prescribed size of this book makes it possible only that I blurt our short gushes of breath as a call for help. I hope that this book will be read by Americans of a different vintage than the ones that assumed the fictitious name of "English" in order to conceal their national origins, Americans who hail from HISTORIC peoples, that perhaps one or several will offer me the so tragically needed assistance, so that the discoveries I made (only glimpsed at here) be published, for… the new knowledge of my Zermatism will alter the present world. ∎

37

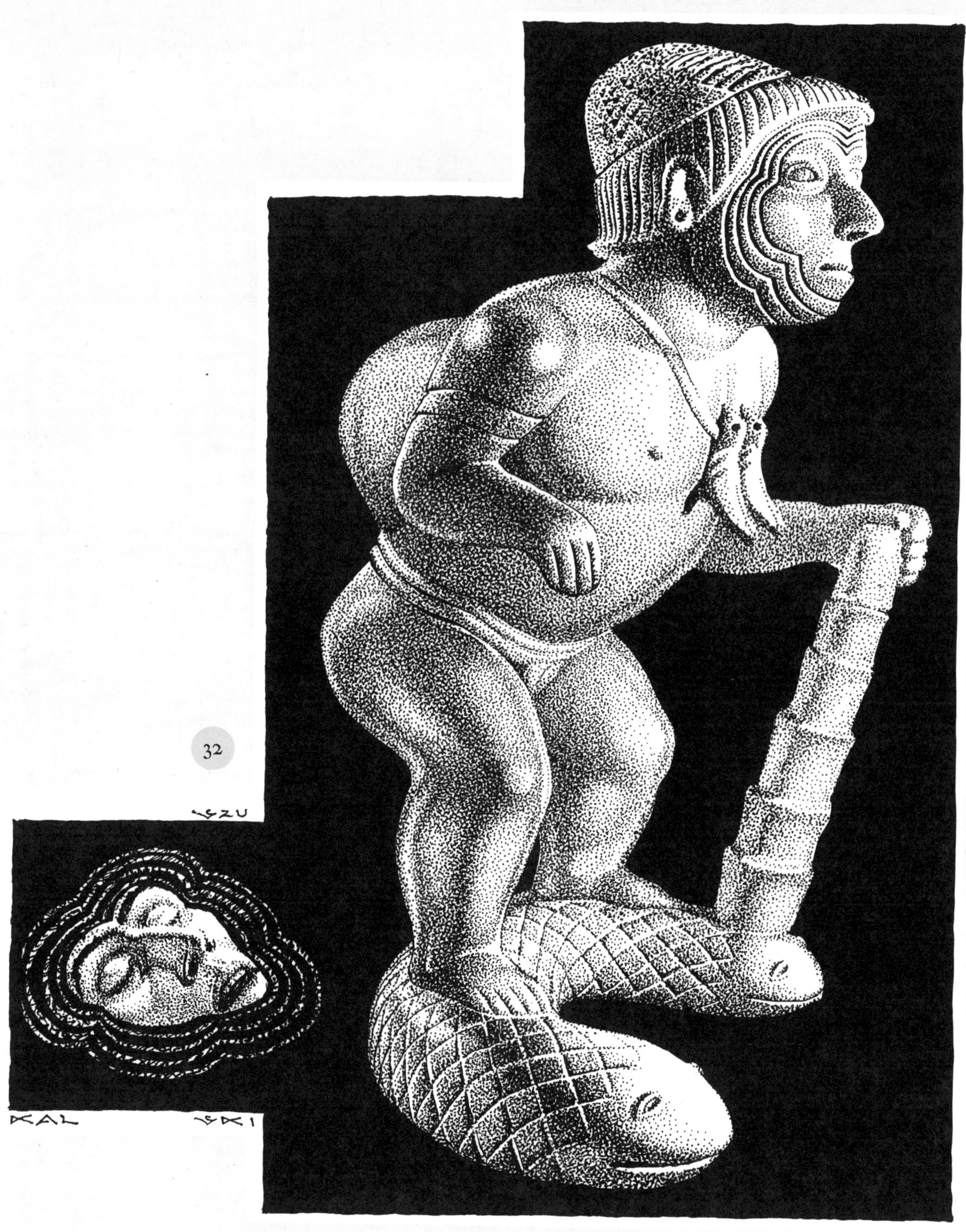

PERUVIAN INCA POTTERY SCULPTURE

The Tribal Flood Scumline

READERS who have not been professionally involved with the archaeologies of the world cannot know that all of the things I speak of here have never been made known to the sciences nor the laymen. Naturally, I have got many photographs of objects that already were in museums, or in open country chipped on rocks, but in the books that these illustrations have been redrawn from, there never were satisfactory explanations. Prior to me, no scientist has ever been able to penetrate the significance of these pictographs, much less point out the startling fact that they were used UNIVERSALLY in all parts of the globe. Along with the Protong language, these pictographs were spread all over the world by the diluvial refugees.

Through our current media of communication, we moderns have learned all manner of swimming strokes. Yet, each one of us uses some personal manner of swimming, due to the strength of our upper or lower extremeties, lung capacity and endurance.

When the Secondary Globe (the lavaic ocean bottoms) began to submerge in the beginning of the last Farsolar Epoch, the global seas were forced to glide off the Primary (Geologic) Globe. The soil of all the lands that were re-emerging was washed off by the departing seas and the waters of the globe became very muddy. In fact, Plato, after visiting Egyptian temples, learned of the chronicles that spoke of the Mediterranean Sea as "The Sea of Mud." Homer's *Iliad* was about Ilium (the Latin word for ancient Troy), which in Protong means "Mire Remembered." The state of Illinois, U.S.A. is named after the Illinois river, and in Protong ("Illi No J(e) Z") actually means "Mire made-Born Is From."

Wherever the terrified diluvial escapees shored re-emerging lands, their faces were caked with mud. And since each swam differently, each would emerge with individual muddy water ripples across the face. So when they lay there in the mud in a deadly faint, exhausted beyond words, and were found by earlier arrivals on that islet, the facial mud markings were remembered and the Flood Scum lines became the tribal markings. I have an entire volume on these *Scumlines* with 195 such drawings from every part of the globe. Here are a few examples.

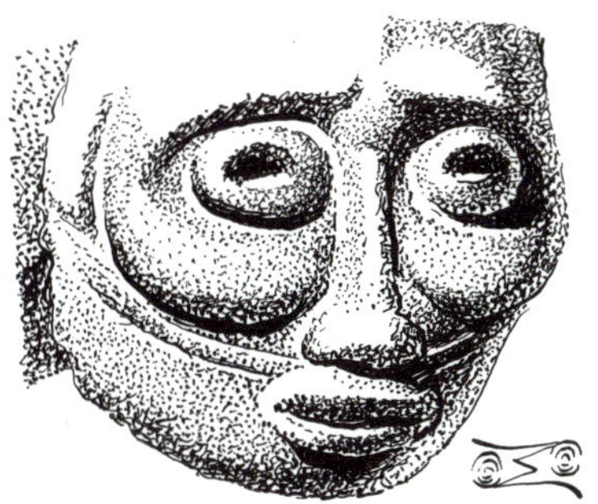

31   This head with the Flood Scumline from Rapa Nui (Easter Island) should be regarded as the evidence that the application of such mud markings first came from Easter Island. The horizontal line below the nose clearly shows that the ancestor swam to that island in the last Nearsolar Deluge. The name *Rapa Nui* was originally the description "Ra Ba Nu Je," which means "Morn-White's Birthgiver Is," attesting to the fact that the island is regarded as the Mother of the Dawn God.

32   This Peruvian Inca pottery sculpture (*left*) commemorates a diluvial ancestor who shored on the beach of the Andes, when they were still re-emerging from the undulating seas. He stands upon a two-headed Serpent, representing the Two-Ocean Flood, forming a raft, while holding the cane of Migration. Upon coming close to his particular isle, he left these and then floated on his back, so that only the front of the face protruded above the water line, which left him with his particular markings.

The bamboo stick he is holding is a rebus pictograph for "Id," a "goer" or migrant. The two little birds suspended from the necklace tell us that he originated from the Twin flight-Migration where the Pacific and Atlantic waters meet. From this angle I cannot tell if the projection on his back is a hunchback's hump or an emigrant's bundle. If the first one is right, then he is a *garbus* (Polish for "hunchback"), which tells us that he was originally from the deluged Easter Island (Protong "Gar B(i) Us" means "Mountain Perished, mortally-Asleep").

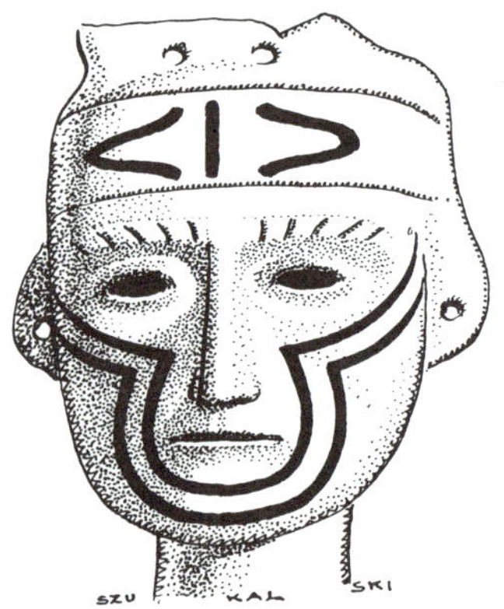
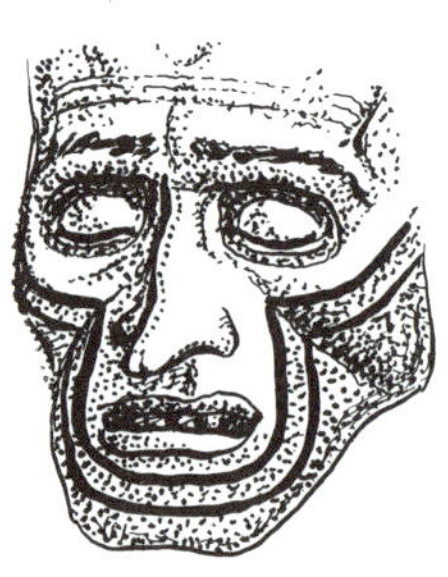

33 From earliest **JAPAN** comes this witness to give us his evidence of his ancestral mode of swimming from the great Deluge. He too came from the junction of Pacific and Atlantic waters where the Twin Angles (lavaic continents) submerged: note the forehead rebus. These same two angles made up the royal interlaces on the scarified cheeks of the Aztec emperors, the Hebrew Star of David and the Scottish "Z," so often found chipped on rocks and boulders in Scotland. This ancestor also floated on his back, so that only the forepart of his mask was scum-marked.

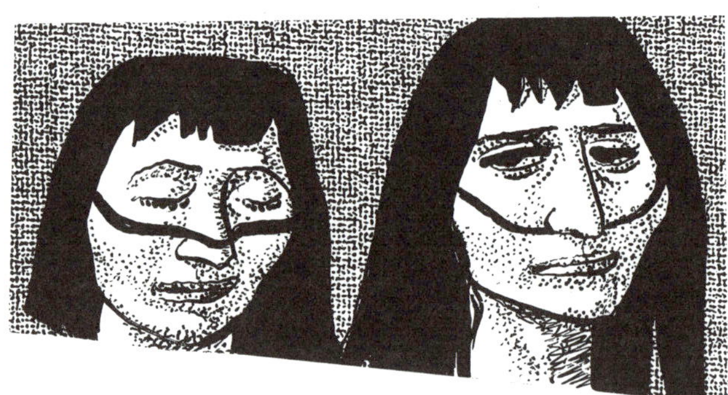

34 The **YAKO** ("Ja Ko" or "I Worship") Indians of California mark their hereditary Flood Scumline with paint. They are extremely gentle people.

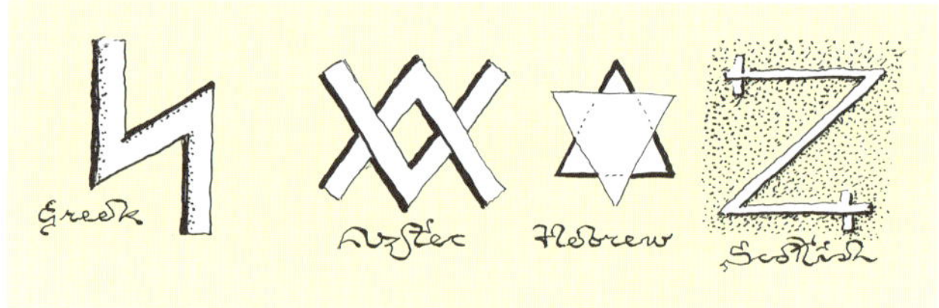

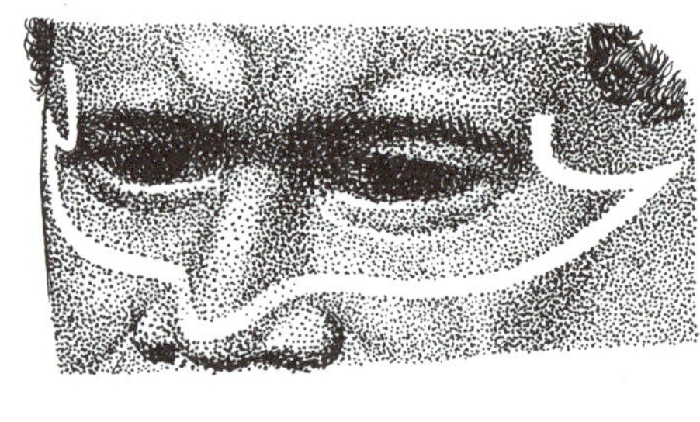

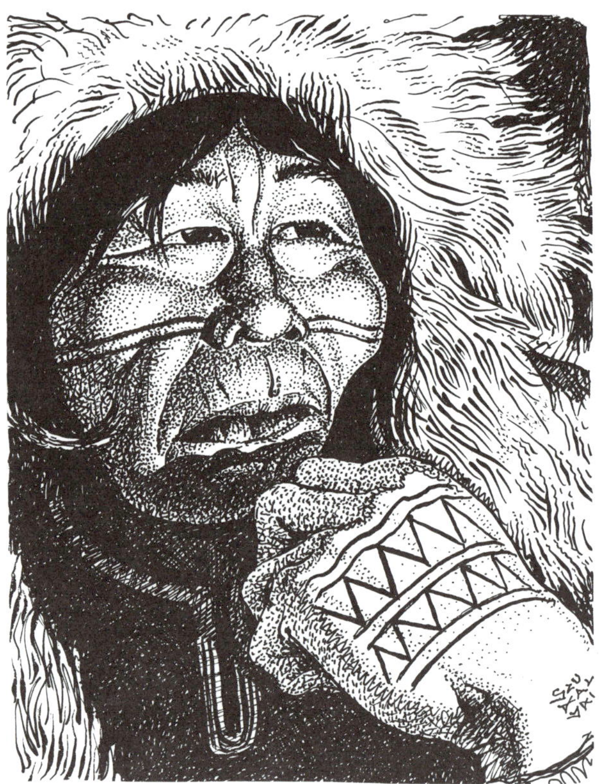

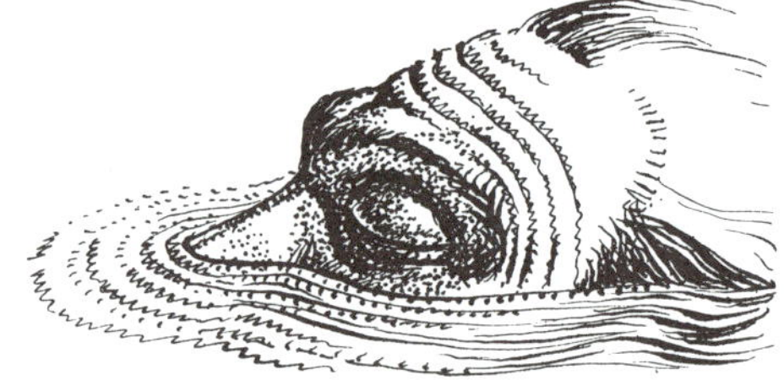

35 This **ESKIMO**'s diluvial ancestor swam with the nostrils under water, coming up to inhale while starting his arm strokes.

36 The ancestors of this Melanesian of New Guinea and the **BAYOWAN** people also swam with the nostrils under water, much like the Yako Indian ancestor.

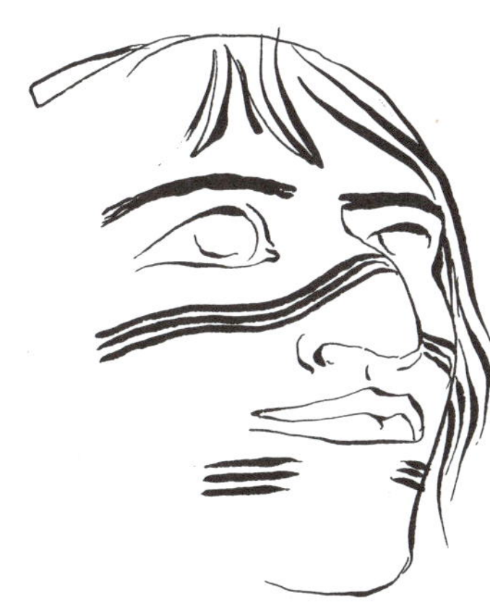

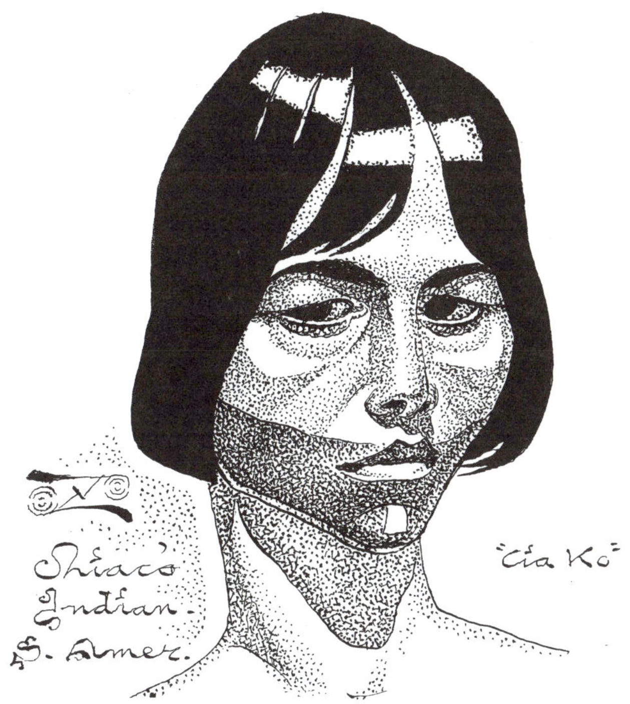

37 This **JIVARO INDIAN** held his head at a more down-ward angle, so that his ears were above the water. "Gi Ba Ro" means "(from) Perished White's Birthgiver."

39 The **CHIACO** Indian tribe of Equador continue to mark their faces with the Flood Scumline on the very rim of the upper lip. Protong "Cia Ko" means "You (I) Love" (adore, worship).

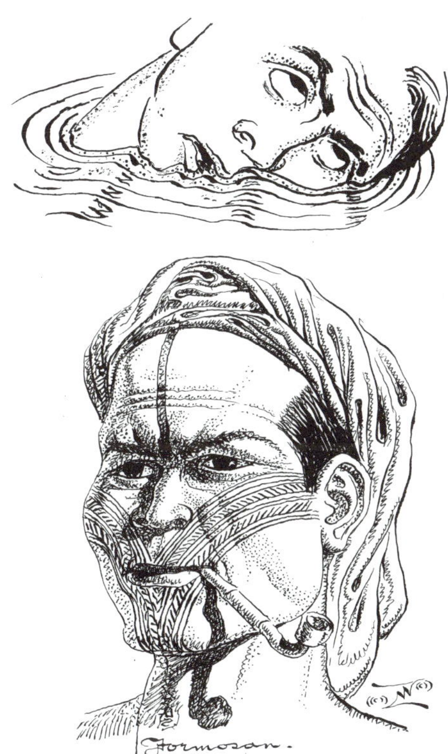

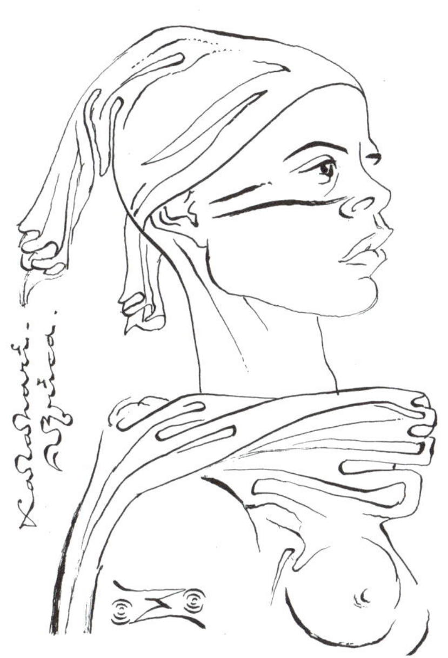

38 A **FORMOSAN** (from Taiwan) shows that his ances-tor swam to the re-emerging shores turning his shoul-ders with the head, so that each time an arm would make the stroke, the alternate side of the face would turn sideways up and the muddy water would leave diagonal markings on each cheek from mouth to ear. The vertical forehead line com-memorates how the mud slowly drained off the top of the head where it had gathered profusely between the hair that remained wet longer, thus drained slower.

40 **KALAHARI** African girls mark their faces with tribal lines running from ear to nostril. This horizontal position tells us that the ancestor swam in a standing posi-tion, pedaling as if sitting on a bicycle. "Ka La Ga Ri" means "(from) Where Flooded Exiled (by way of) River." "Ka La Gari" means "Where Flooded Mountains."

41

In distant Brazil, the **KASHINAUA** tribesman tattoos his face with the Scumline on the level of the upper lip, but also horizontally. His ancestors too pedaled their way to safety in a standing position. "Bra Z Il" means "Taken From Mire," "Ka Zi Na U(t) (J)a" means "Where Land Birth-giving Sank, I (from)."

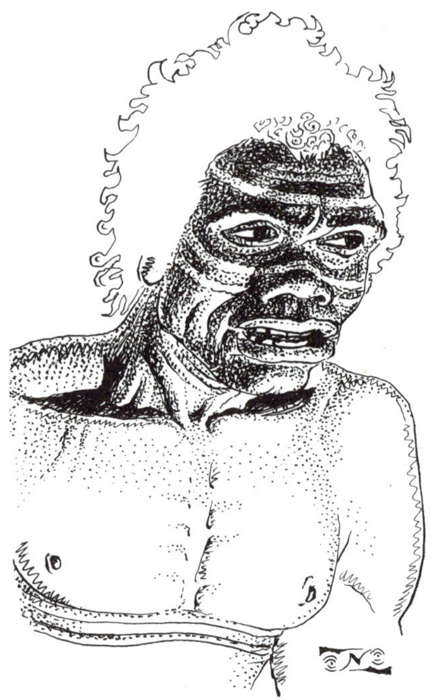

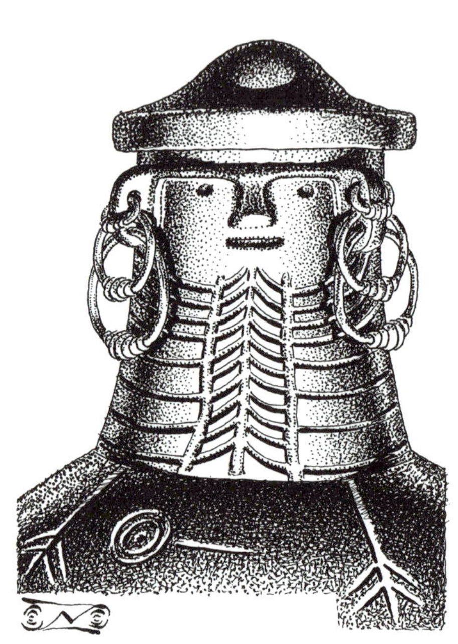

An **AUSTRALIAN BUSHMAN** has three tribal horizontals on his face. These markings of ceremonial face dress recall that his people swam in a standing position, pedaling dog-like . He also has two horizontal lines painted on his chest, which shows that his ancestor had to wade a long distance to the beach sand. It appears that between arm movements, while he floated, he sank up to his brow, where the Flood Scum caked up, to re-emerge till the water level was across his nose.

One of the many **FUNERARY JARS** for holding the ashes of the cremated dead. This one is from prehistoric Poland. These jars often have large earrings in bronze attached to the pottery ears of the jarheads. Atop the head reposes the cover in the shape of Easter Island. On their necks are many metal necklaces and, as in this one, the image vomits the salt water of the sea. These rings on the neck emulate the water ripples (a ring-within-a-ring-within-a-ring) spreading from a drowning person. Usually, there is a large *szpila* (Polish for "pin") as a rebus for "Z Bi La," which tells us that the person cremated came "From Killed (by) Flood" land and to there was returning.

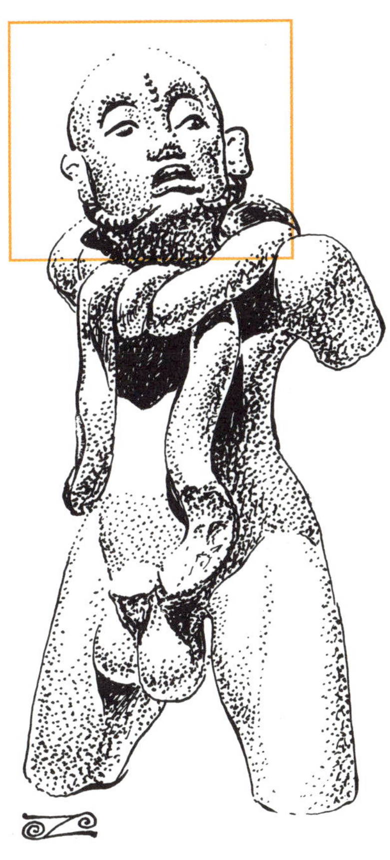

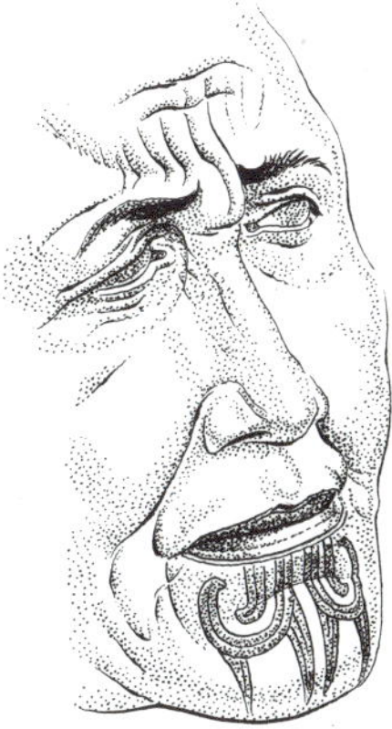

Among the **MAORIS** of New Zealand there is a post-diluvial custom to have one's lower lip and chin tattooed. These lines indicate the flow of vomited seawaters with which the diluvials became sick after swallowing too much. Equally so, there are numerous patterns of this spewed vomit among the American Indians. I have drawn many amuletic coins of peoples of Gaul which show the White Horse of the Dawn God re-emerging from under the seas, also vomiting and having diarrhea from swallowing too much salt water.

This **DAWN GOD** sculpture was excavated in Campeche, Mexico. He is shown walking on the bottom of the Pacific Ocean, emerging in South America. He has an erection, which means that he is the God of *Wschod* (Polish for Sunrise, actually "Rise"). Around his neck, tied in a secure knot, is the Pacific Flood Serpent, vanquished. This means he is just emerging, his head already above the water ripples, hence the air bubbles floating in circles around his head.

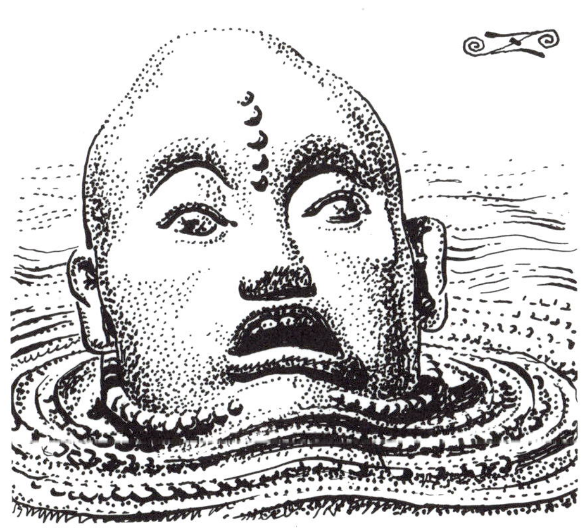

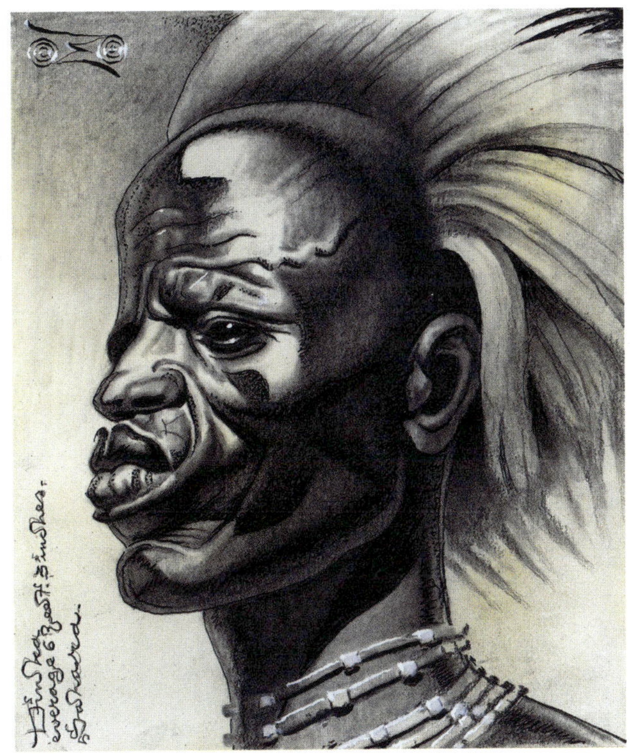

Portrait of a **DINKA** tribesman, 6 feet, 3 inches tall, whose tribal ripple of diluvial descent comes in the form of a rippling necklace. His tribe dwells in the Sahara desert. "Din Ka" means that his people arrived in diluvial times "(From) Where Day (is born)"—the Pacific region.

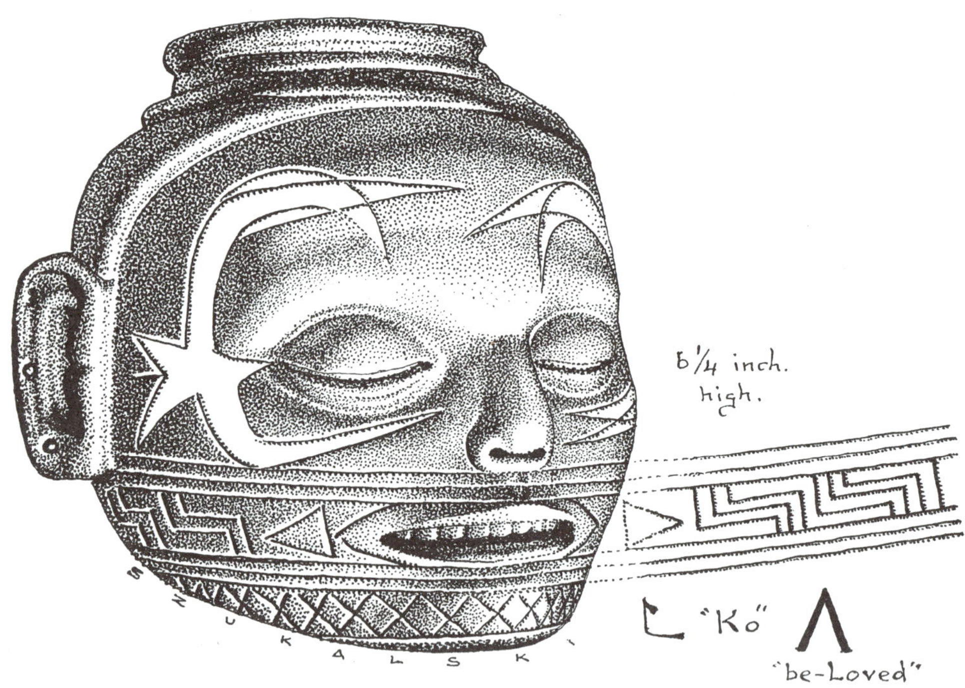

47 In one of the *Smithsonian Reports* I found a few similarly molded heads. They are only about 6 inches high and I have redrawn all that were reproduced. Naturally, I have discovered things in them that no other scientists could possibly suspect. It is only because I love archaeology… passionately, while they merely respect it. Only one who loves these CREATIONS (that no God could ever match) would draw them so lovingly as I do.

Here I can show you only one. These ceramic sculptures were suspendable. I came to the conclusion that they were used as lasts (like shoemaker lasts) over which actual skins were drawn flailed from the heads of Flood-spared ancestors. The pots were kept to preserve the likenesses of the saved, and remind the nation of the Great Flood.

Since real ears consist of cartilage and do not shrink like skin, the sculptor of this pot had to make ears in the pottery. The noses were made smaller than in real life, for there is no thinner skin than that on the ridge of the nose, and if left the same size to dry on a stretcher, it would soon crack. Therefore, to prevent such damage, the noses were diminished. Mouths were left open in order to facilitate the draft for the incense that burned within these head-jars with the purpose of drying the superimposed head-skins from inside.

This head was excavated from a *kurchan* (mound) in Arkansas. It must have been a girl's or a woman's face, so benignly beautiful. On her lower cheek-halves the articulate sculptor-historian engraved with love the Flood Scumline, just below her nose, for that was the way she swam to the shores of America. From where did she float on her diluvial raft? From somewhere between the Pacific and Atlantic regions. How did I come to such a conclusion? Because the historian placed the Twin Triangles (Aztec angles or Scottish "Zs") at each other of her gently opened mouth, signifying that she drew her first breath somewhere between these two lavaic continents The multiplied squares at the bottom of the scumline denote "countries" (squared-off, measured-out, geometrized, allotted, economico-governmentally controlled).

What about these pictographic "crabs?" These are the devourers of dead creatures, the consumers of lifeless flesh. I suspect that the word comes from German *Graben* (graves). Here then the crabs are taking over the *Oce* (Polish for "eyes"), a pictograph of the continents that are being taken by the oceans and buried underneath. In prehistoric graves of Poland many small earrings were found that had been inserted in the rims of the ears of the deceased. Here you see three perforations in the ears for such rings.

One of the very first syllable scripts of the Mediterranean region was the Cypriot. Two lines joined at the top (see drawing below) stood for the syllable *ko* (Polish for "love, adoration, worship"). From these lines came our "cone." The universal pictographic cone of island-shape represents Protong "Ko Ne," meaning "Loved (one) No (more existing)."

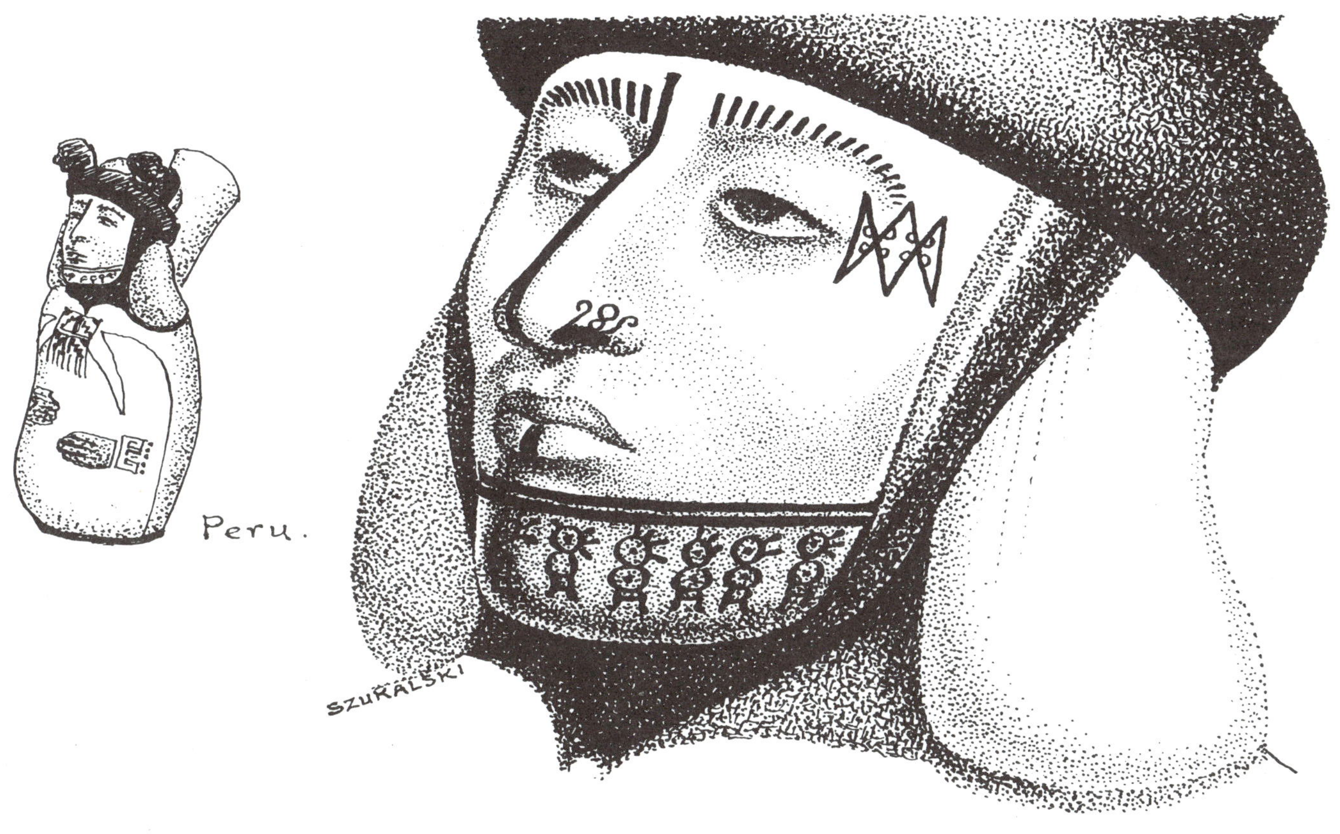

48 My mind is in the perpetual habit of paying attention to things I see. One winter day in Tarzana, California, I was going home from the store with my groceries and, having no car, walked through slush and mud. I stepped over the gutter at the side of the field road when I noticed a shredded magazine in the water. I returned to pick it up, because I saw in my mind after passing, that there had been a photograph of a sculpture one inch tall. At home, I dried the page and discovered that this little picture was something I must draw. Here are the results.

This **PERUVIAN JAR** with a handle as an opening shows a beautiful face, doubtlessly of a young king whose ancestor had saved himself by swimming from his raft of a floating log onto the re-emerging island that later grew to be the Andean mountain range. On his face, noted the people who landed before him, was the Flood Scumline, running horizontally just between his lips and chin. That location was marked in their memory, so that later their children and still later descendants sustained the custom of the providential location that saved the life of his species.

But here is something more than a marker of the Flood, which is purely my personal explanation. The historian potter-painter-sculptor drew many personages, all "killed" (their bodies and heads are *Bi*'s). Their bird-like legs and feathers are pictographic of flight-Migration. They seem to float just below the dual line, representing the risen waters of the globe.

From his forehead, from under the black, encircling body of the two-headed Serpent, there runs a black line down his nose, the slowly draining mire gathered in his hair. Perhaps this is a portrait of a beautiful lady, the daughter of a king. Whoever it is, I adore the face, grief-stricken, melancholy, philosophically stoic and with a shade of bitterness at the fate of all those she lost, floating below her cheeks. I have not come across more reproductions of her, else I might have discovered more. Note that from her nostrils issues her breath, and from her gently closed mouth she still spews a black line of mire after having swallowed too much of it when nearly drowned… Such benignity! Such silent acceptance of her Fate! Were I a religious man I would not mind… worshipping her remoteness, and claim her a Divinity.

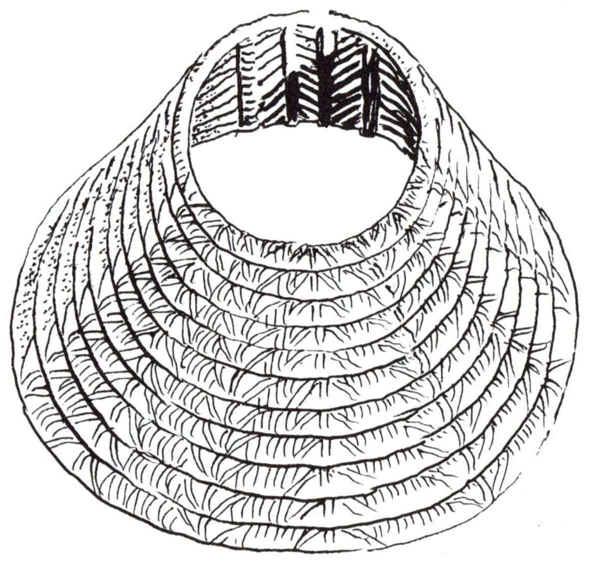

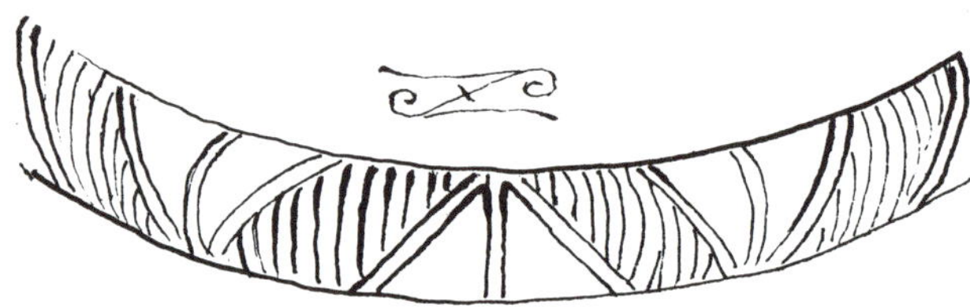

This solid gold **NECKLACE** was excavated in Poland. It was made in the 7th–6th century B.C. and, emulating the rippling sea waves, it was worn by a king or some other high dignitary who was of direct diluvial descent. The people who later wore such necklaces did not know why they continued this custom of every ancient country, for they merely did what everyone else did. But in postdiluvial times the significance was profound and tragic, for it harkened to the greatest cataclysm mankind had experienced.

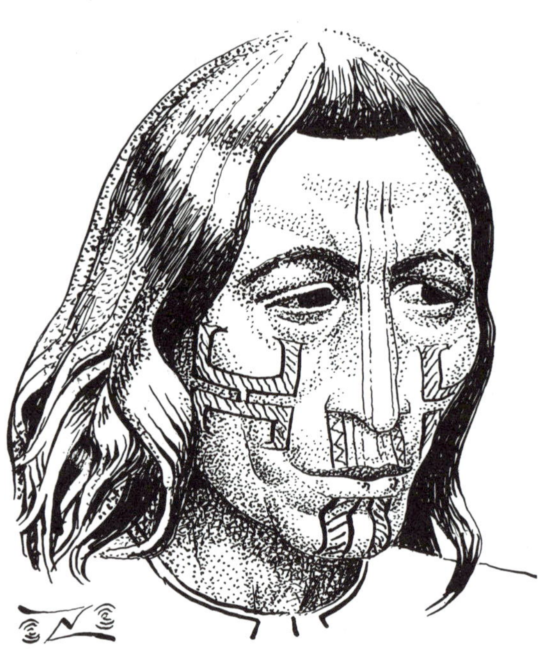

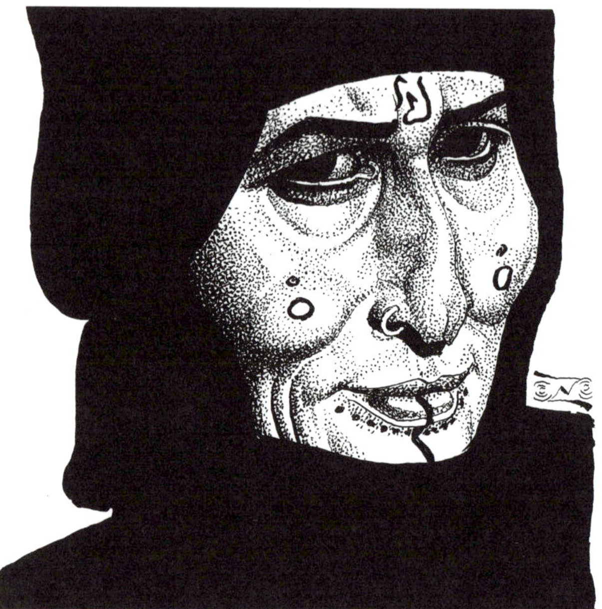

An **INDIAN FROM GUINEA**. On his cheeks devices are tattooed consisting of two Horizon Jars joined in the center, each on opposite sides of the globe. From his forehead downwards streaks the water leaving some dirt behind. From his mouth and nostrils oozes the swallowed, dirty water ever since the time his ancestor was picked up by the already saved diluvials.

On the handsome face of a **BEDOUIN** woman the diluvial markings of her people are tattooed. I found many of these markings sustained among the Arabic peoples. In this case she has a black line of vomit from the swallowed mire.

Just below her lower lip, where the surface of the muddy waters of the Deluge left a line on the face of her ancestor, she wears air bubbles. Perhaps the Hindu and Arabic custom of wearing rings in the nostril is to commemorate the sustenance of life's breath to the nostrils which would not submit to being drowned permanently. They are still worn in gratitude for saving the ancestral lines of families that existed prior to the Great Flood.

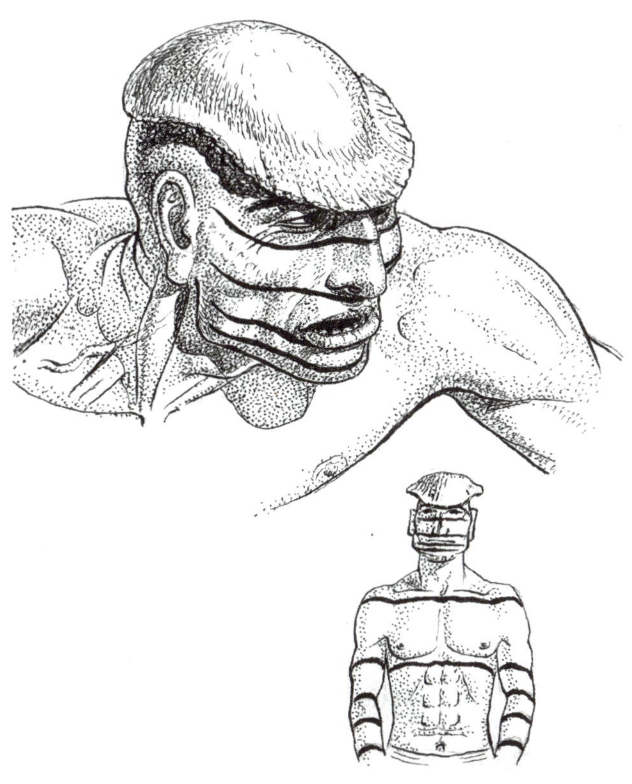

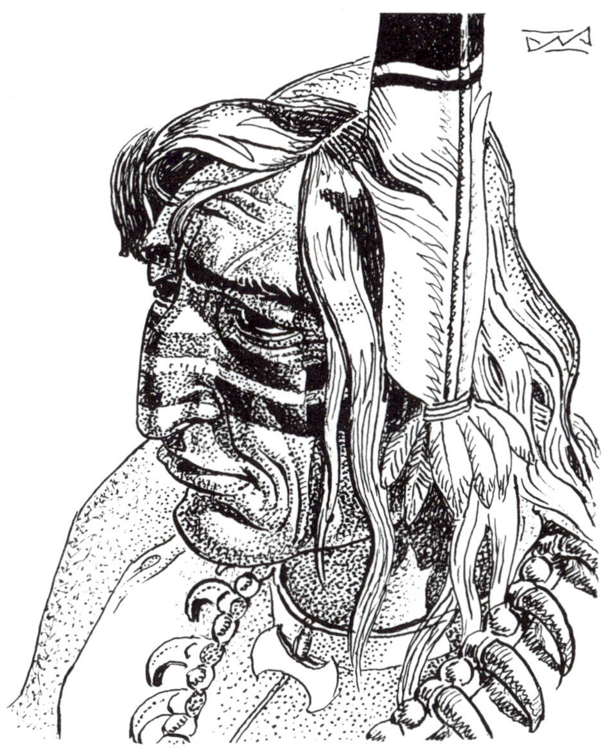

52 In Equador and the vicinity of the Panama Canal there are Indians who paint their bodies with black lines emulating the waters in which they stood. They repeat the same lines on their faces, but the topmost of these crosses their noses, just below the eyes. This means that their diluvial ancestor buried his face under water while swimming and made a stronger stroke with his arms when he came up to get air.

Since the waters of the Great Flood washed away most of the top soil where the land was re-emerging, the diluvials swam in thick water with soft soil, while the crystalline sand sank downwards. This ancestor saved himself someplace that had an abundance of brilliant red clay. On finding him on the beach, his rescuers noticed the thick pancake of an "island" atop his head, caught there by his hair.

Till this day, these Indians put on such clay hats of hair in their ceremonies.

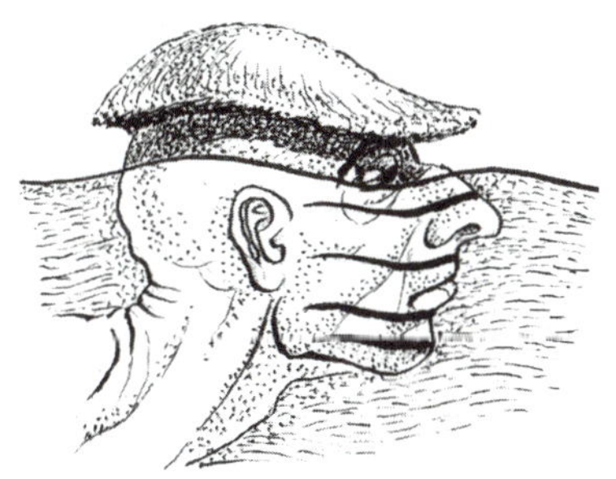

53 I once saw a large volume on old photographs of Indian Chiefs, but in my American circumstances (where creative men are dispensable nuisances) I could not afford it. Some time ago my new friends, the Brays, who are the financiers of this publication, brought me another book on Indians, and from it I made many drawings of those Chiefs whose Indian names were given. I made these only to magnify the importance of the names, which I re-segmented into Protong, to make clear the actual meanings. These will be published in a separate volume.

However, here is one of the **FOX TRIBE** Indians whose face bore two horizontals as his tribal Flood Scumlines. Earlier, his people migrated from the Great Lakes region to Kansas. It is likely that it was in the latter location that the split tribe took the English word *Fox* for their tribal Totem.

I PROPOSE now that you begin to be impressed with the fact that the same notion of making these marks across the faces of tribesmen was *universal*. The reason for these markings is not coincidental, but that such system would be easily conveyable to others, because the deluged ancestors had evolved a uniform agreement on the use of ONE SYSTEM OF PICTOGRAPHY, which I have rediscovered and made into a science.

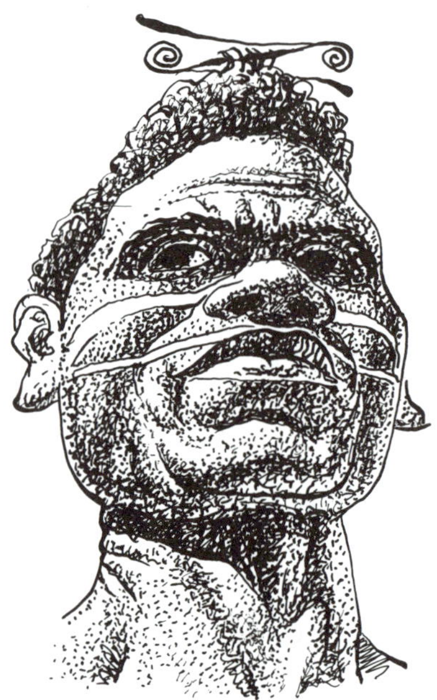

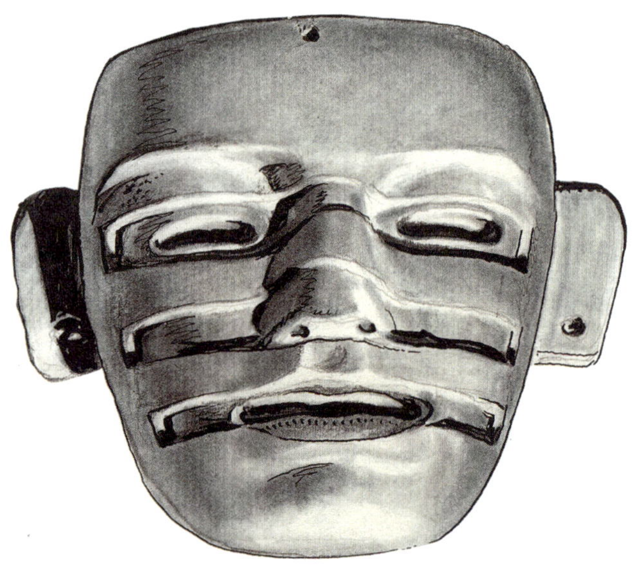

54 While the preceding Indian from the Great Lakes sustains two horizontal bars across the high-bridged nose, this **AUSTRALIAN TRIBESMAN** placed one line across his short nose and the other across the upper lip.

55 At the Teotihuacan Pyramid an **AZTEC MASK** was excavated with three horizontals, across the eyes, nose and mouth.

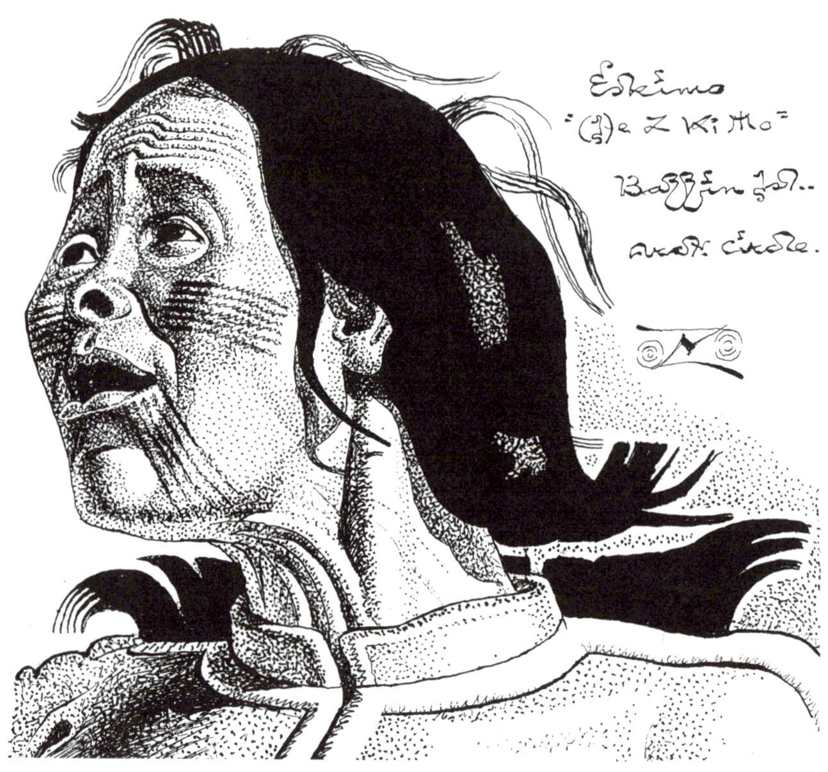

56 An **ESKIMO WOMAN** with delicate features has the watermarks horizontally across her nipple-nose and additionally, carries two streaks coming from her mouth. They again represent the vomiting of muddy waters, but the ancestor had the habit of holding his tongue in the middle of his teeth so that the regurgitated mud flowed out of the corners of his mouth, as he tipped his head from side to side.

The term *Eskimo* was originally the Protong compound

"(J)e Z Ki Mo" and means that this people "Is From Where Sea" deluged their prediluvial Homeland. Their other name, used among themselves, is *Inuit* which in turn was "In U(t) Id" and means "Elsewhere S(unken) Migrated (from)." It is from this name that we may conclude that the Eskimos must have come from the same region as the Japanese. But the Arctic climate has prevented the Eskimos from developing as brilliant a culture as the Japanese climate permitted.

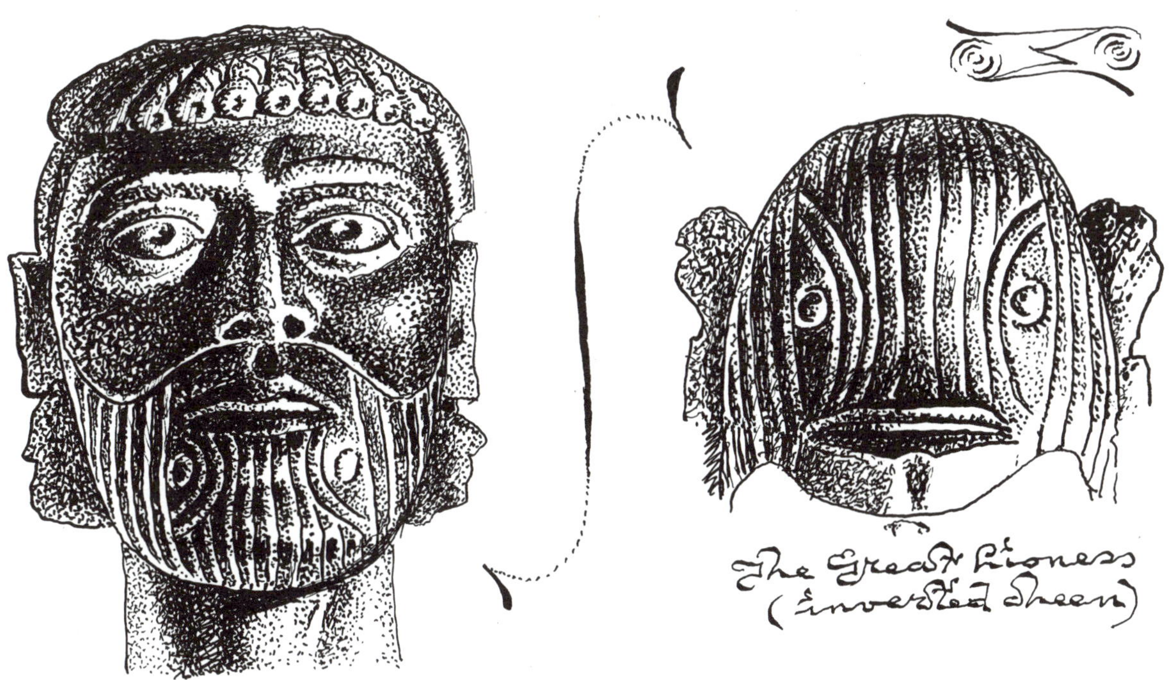

57 A funerary portrait of a young man drawn from the lid of a large jar that holds the ashes of a cremated man. It was excavated in Italy and dates from the Etruscan period. On the man's face the ancient tribal Flood Scumline was engraved, crossing his mask just below his nose, emulating a beard. However, the vertical direction of continuous lines tells us that this is really the draining sea water, heavy with mud.

The two small circles on the chin and the edge of ripples around them made me turn the drawing upside down and there I saw that the mask resembled the Great Lioness (Easter Island), streaked with sliding-off water as if re-emerging from under the Flood.

The Etruscan Civilization is an enigma, for the scientists and historians cannot liken any language extant to the Etruscan. I, however, have dis-covered that they were Rusy (Ukranians presently, in Latin called Ruthenians; but the latter name is very recent, devised at the time of forming their union with Poland and Lithuania). The Hyperborean Saki, who were driven off from Ice Age Europe, migrated in great masses southeast and, having become a great military power as Scyti-Sarmati, created all the Near- and Far-East Civilizations. When the Nearsolar Epoch began and the florid lands began to dehydrate, the Mongo-Tartar and Arabic people migrated to Europe, causing the ensuing invasions and conquests. The Etruscans were a Slavic people returning from Asia. But on their return way across Italy, finding an ideal climate, they remained and began calling themselves "Et Ruski" or a people that "Is Ruski" (-*ski* always means "of," like *Szukalski* means "Of the Searchers").

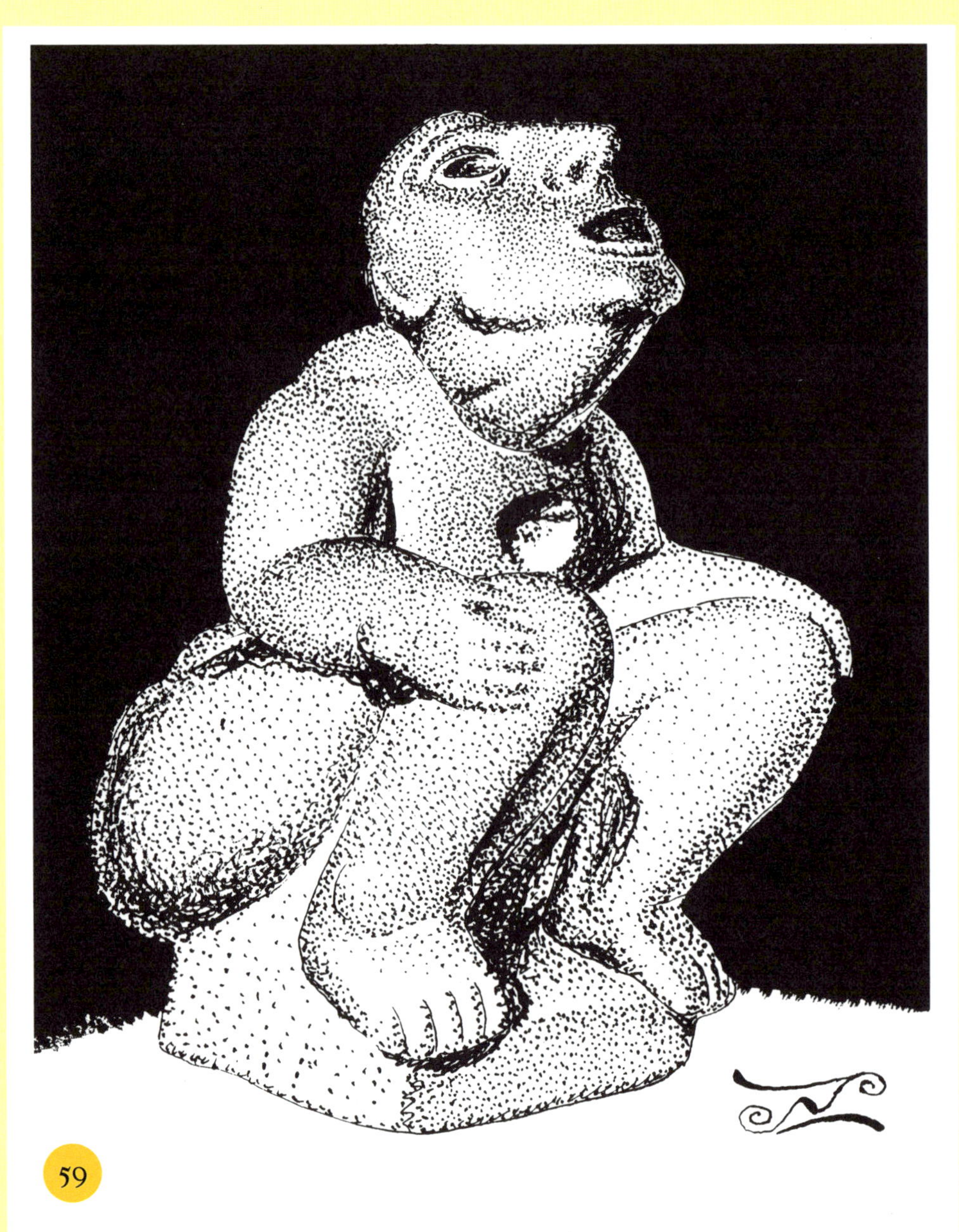

59

The Most Primordial Images in the World

AMONG my 39 volumes on *Zermatism*, there are three which deal specifically with the most ancient images in the world. These are most crudely carved and always portray broad-hipped, breastless, bald-headed women. In many countries they were intentionally without a head, often without arms or feet.

Naturally, they are called differently in each country, which would be taken for granted, were it not that all now meaningless "names" were once compounded of one and the same language: *Protong*, which consisted of root-words without prefixes and suffixes, hence totally grammarless description phrases.

The images were found scattered throughout Hyperborea (the name of early Europe), mostly in the fields of Britain, Poland, Ukraine, Russia, Tartary, Mongolia, India, Iran, Sumeria-Babylon, the whole Pacific region and both Americas.

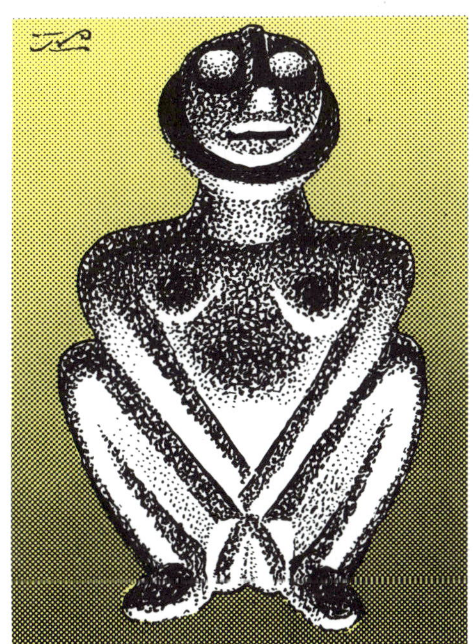

58

58 In Poland they are called *Baby* (plural; pron. "bah-bee"), which means "Ancient Women." This name is identical to that of the first town of Babylon. The reason is apparent, when we look at the image of the "Ancient Woman's Womb" to which that community was dedicated, being founded by the diluvial refugees from the "Mother of the Sunrise" (Easter Island) in the distant Pacific. Hence the name "Old Woman's Womb" which is "Babi Lon" in Protong, the language I have discovered.

Note the sea ring around her island-face and her "Lon" (womb). Her bald head is pictographic of the Island.

59 Compare another image of her, from Mexico. She too has no breasts, as the image from Babylon, because this was the only way the sculptors could convey the notion that these were representations of the VIRGIN Mother of the Dawn. The hole in her chest tells us that she was killed by the Deluge (the *Bi*, a disc with a hole in its center symbolizes the Dead Mother). Both are giving birth to the Dawn, and are calling, which is a rebus for Protong "Wo La" ("Worship Flooded").

Since childhood I have known about the *Baby* and have seen them in remote fields. Being most crudely carved, they are never reproduced by the Poles who feel that showing such naive sculptures would bring disgrace, instead of fame, to their pseudo-sophisticated Culture. Ever since I started preparing these volumes, I wrote to many people, begging them to send me some photographs of these *Baby*. But to no avail. The Hottentots, crocodiles and Poles do not answer letters. At long last, my nephew, Roman Romanowicz, sent some money to a place I indicated and went there himself, to see to it that I would get what I wanted. Thus I learned that there was a museum in Nieborów, left to the nation by an aristocratic family, which had such images standing among the great trees in its park.

On receiving the photographs, I reconstructed the

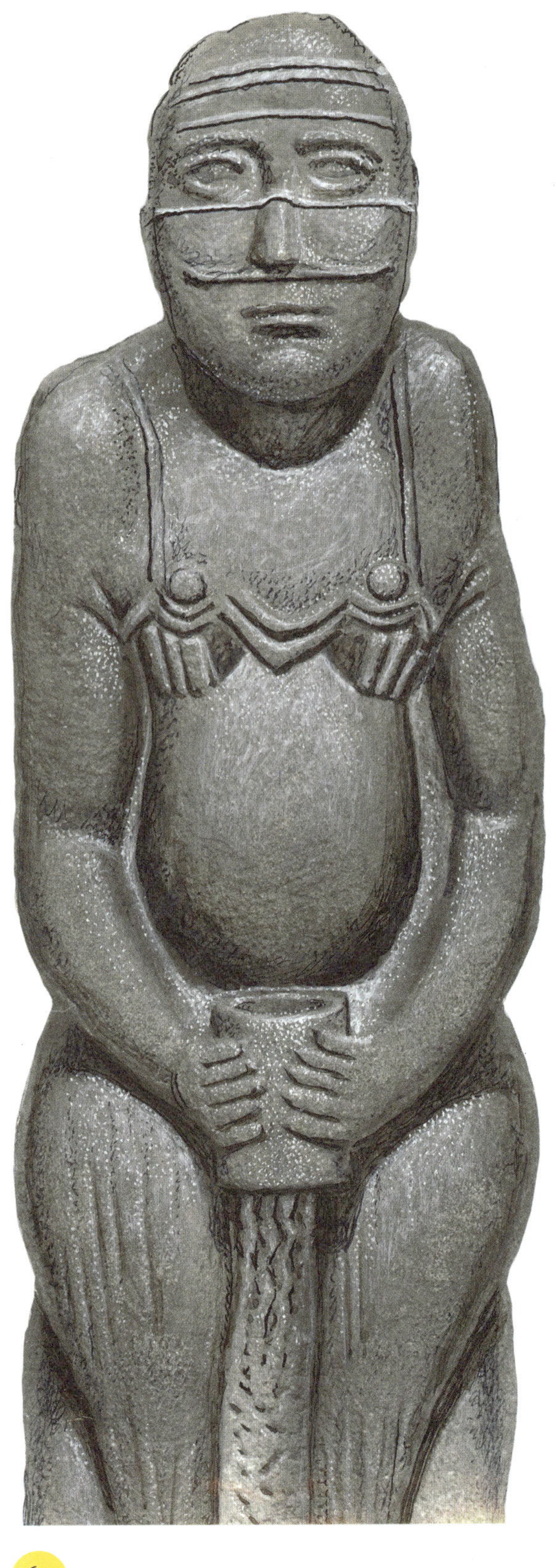

60

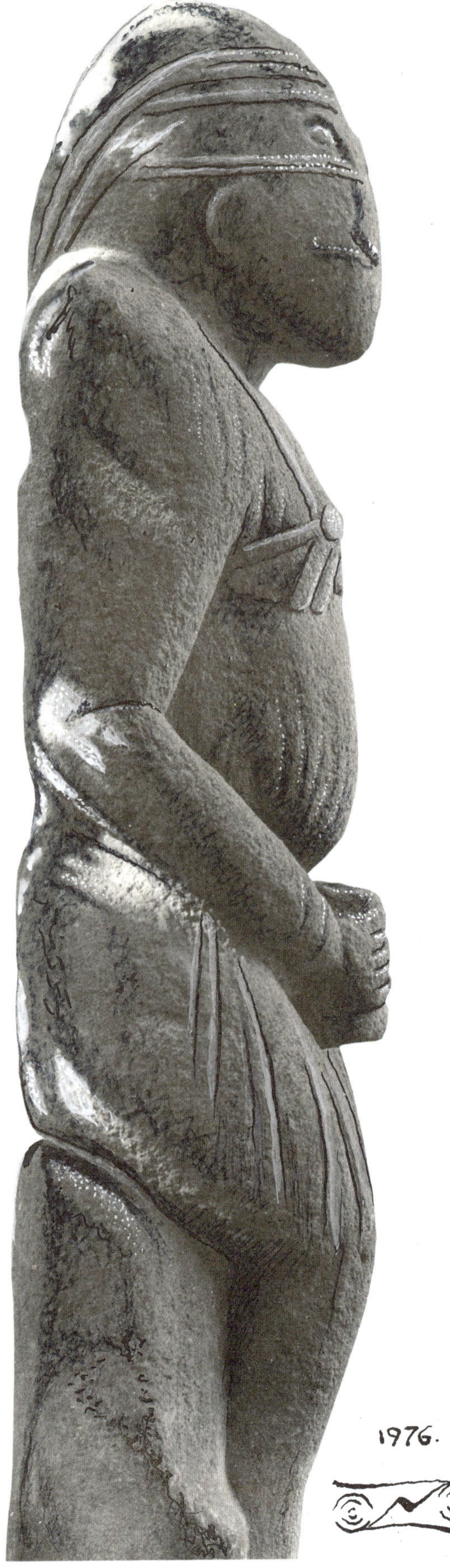

61

1976.

eroded elements. As in Mongolia and Peru, Rumania and Moravia, they are bald-headed, which serves as a rebus for *lise* (Polish for "bald"), which, after re-segmentation, presents us with two Protong root words, "Li Ze," meaning: these personify the "Flooded Land."

■

BABA 1

60 This *Baba* (singular), like the others, holds a sieve over her womb, out of which waters of the Deluge that drowned her, are draining off in Wishful or Imitative Magic, suggested by the priestly sculptor. Her abdomen bulges with the swallowed water, which in Wishful Magic already slides off the lower part of her body in rivulets. Intentionally, all four figures do not have feet, but end in pointed, peg-like stumps. This was the only way the historian-sculptor could convey that she simply could not "walk" out of her submersion in the Pacific. Identically footless were the small pottery images made by the Hohokam sculptors of prehistoric Arizona, the ones of Rumania, Kurdistan, Moravia, Spain, Greece, Iran, and Mexico.

Across her face horizontal lines were placed, the surface waters of the Deluge, leaving the very top of her bald head exposed. The tip of her head is Mata Weri ("Mother of Worship," i.e. of the Dawn) or Easter Island of which we presently see the vestigial top, since before its submersion it was the tallest lavaic mountain in the whole Pacific region. It is not a moustache under her nose that we see, but a shallow Sagging Horizon that filled with the seas to where her nostrils were, so she could not breathe and was drowned.

■

PROFILE OF BABA 1

61 No matter what culture a given prehistoric sculpture comes from, or from what part of the world, there is no pictographic or rebus usage that I cannot explain, since there was only ONE SYSTEM of pictography used universally. This image, however, has mystifying pictographs over the space where her breasts are supposed to be. But since the sculptor was not an articulate artist, though very thoughtful in the ancient ways of conveyance of thought, I think he meant to represent sea waves (undulating horizontals), and the universally used "pouring" of waters through the vertical lines. Over the sea waves were placed the Sunrise, on her left, and on her right the Sunset, which

was regarded as the daily death of the Dawn God, hence in later ages as the Crucifixion.

These, the most venerable of European carvings, were neglected and, in one case I know of in Poland, destroyed. Since they were not carved by some sculptor of the abominable Baroque style, Poland is embarrassed by their primitivism and does nothing to protect them. If they would be an excrement of Picasso or some other charlatan, that country, like Barbaric Russia, would erect some pompous palace to enshrine them.

■

BABA 2 OF NIEBORÓW

62 This is my reconstruction of the badly eroded sculpture that is now in the park of Nieborów, Poland. This *Baba*'s eyes are closed, which was the universal way of

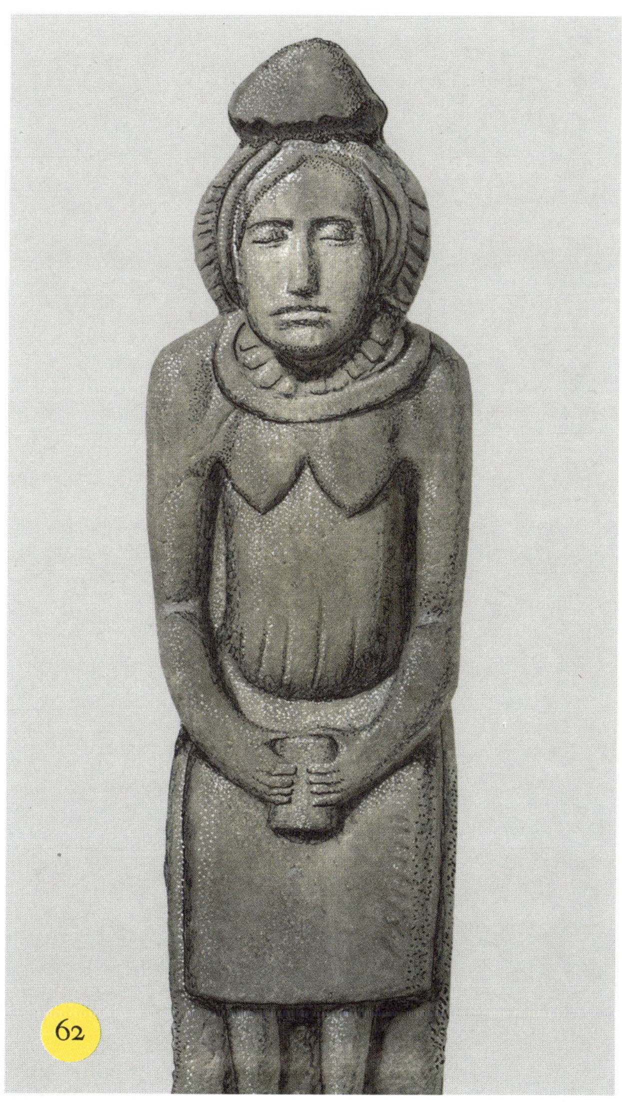

62

saying that she is "mortally-Asleep," deluged, or in Protong "Us."

Wherever on earth, in whatever language, you find the Protong mini-word "us" in any part of a now meaningless name, it ALWAYS means "mortally-Asleep." In Polish there are several words for "to die," depending on whether it is an animal or a human that dies and which family member. But there is one animal that does not die in Poland. This is the fish, which "falls asleep" (*usnela*). The reason for such distinction is that the Mother of the Dawn God was universally worshipped as a Mermaid. A later reincarnate of her son was named, in a Protong compound, "Je Z Us," which actually means that he "Is From the mortally-Asleep."

Even Theseus of Greek mythology is from "Where Land mortally-Asleep", for in Protong his name is "gDe Ze Us." Similarly Zeus ("Ze Us") is from the "Land mortally-Asleep." But only peasants keep applying these old descriptions to their dear dead, not the sophisticated Christians, because the uneducated still retain the ancient, universal attitude towards death which sees all dying as a personal or national drama, for it brings back the heart-tearing story that was originally told about "Dra Mat." She was the "Exiling Mother" who ordered her children to escape and save themselves, when she was deluged. "Dr, dra, dre, dri, dro, dru" were the dialectic forms for "escaping, being driven, exiled," which we still find in the Spanish word *Madre* ("the Mother that Drove Away" her children). On this matter I have written two volumes, entitled *Artemis Flings Away Her Children*, with 386 pen drawings.

Baba's breasts were made flat to indicate that she is the Virgin Mother. But what could be the object atop her head? It is an extraordinary "witness" for my side of persuasion, another pictograph of Easter Island surrounded by the deluging disc of seas.

63 On her shoulders she has a slim *Bi* (see **OCE ON** and **BABA 3**), the same ring the earliest Polish Eagles wear on their tails. The reason for this is that the Eagle is the pictograph of Priestly Messengership of the Dawn God. He emerges each day from under the seas to announce to the sleeping world the coming of the Dawn, the four-faced Sunrise that will shine in all cardinal directions of the universe.

She, too, holds the Sagging Horizon or Horizon Jar in her hands, from which the waters of the Deluge are about to be poured out.

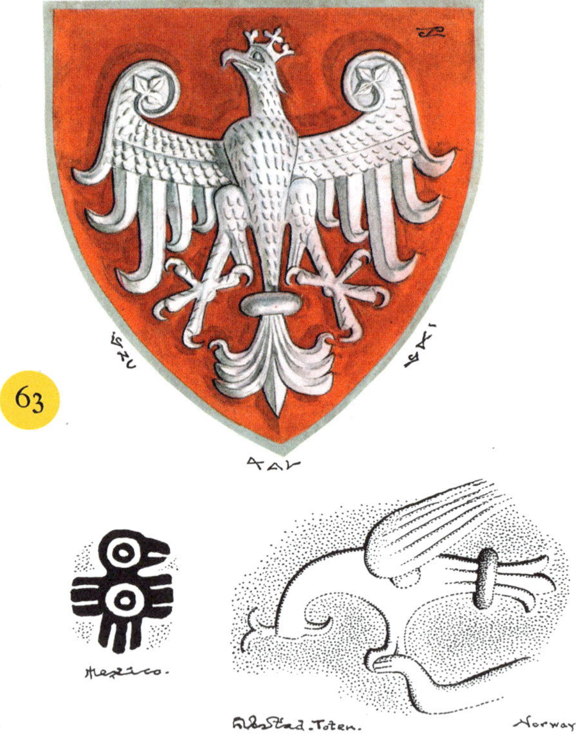

63

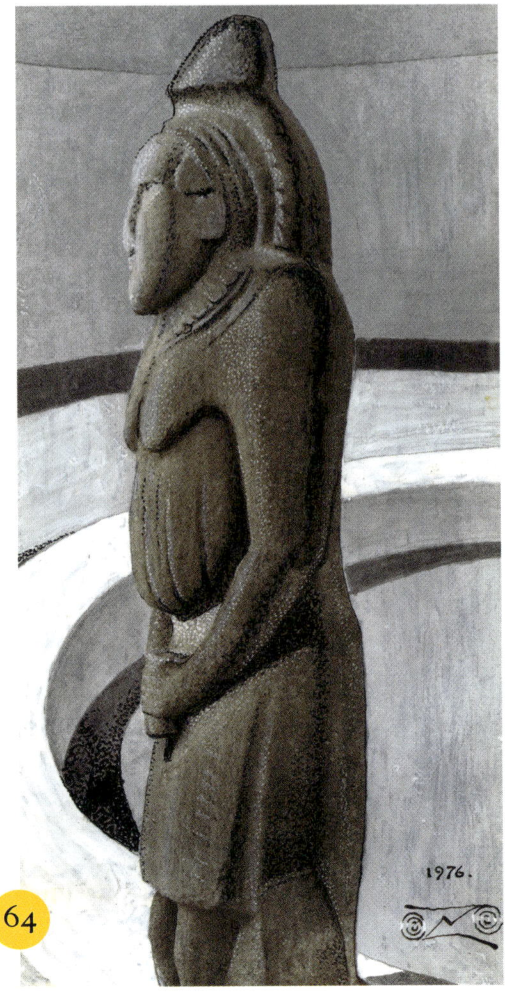

64

64 As the great geographer and traveler Ptolemy (born 112 A.D.) reports, the ancient Greeks, the Hellenes, sailed from the Black Sea to the Baltic, stopping in the seaport Kalisia, which now is the Polish inland city of Kalisz, near which I was born. Since then the Long Sea, which he called *Mare Longum*, disappeared and Poland was born on the re-emerged bottom of that sea. Not only Poland, but the whole continent of Hyperborea (Europe) rose out of the seas, due to the change of the Solar Temperatures. All limestone deposits are former sea bottoms.

Originally, perhaps only a few people had saved themselves from the Diluvial Cataclysm by moving to the Alps and Pyrenees. These then just began to re-emerge from under the migrating oceans, because the flexible belly of our globe (which I call the Secondary Globe) alternately rises in Nearsolar Epochs and then, deflated, sinks beneath the waters of the seas, while the Primary Globe, the geologic continents, submerges with the Himalyas and all mountain ranges in the Farsolar Epochs.

The names *Switzerland* and *Helvetia* still indicate from where the refugees came: the Protong phrase "Swit Zer" means "Gleam of Dawn," and Helvetia can be re-segmented to "Ge L We Tia," which means "Where F(looded) Worship You." (There is a sound-wearage to all ancient names; in this case the original hard "g" became a soft "h".)

It is in the pictographic image of their native Easter Island that the name *Matterhorn* in Switzerland was chosen, which in my Protong phrase "Mat Der Gor N" means: "Mother Drove (away) Mountain No (more existing)." (Remember: Protong is grammarless.)

With the rise of the continent, the geometrically multiplying descendants of the Pacific Refugees commenced to spread in all directions. The jungles of all of Hyperborea became their homelands, but my family still has the mountain goat in their coat of arms, and the name *Szukalski* means "of the Searchers." They descended from the Swiss Alps in search of cultivable land into re-emerging Poland, calling themselves *Sarmati,* because they were from Zermatt. "Zer Matt," meaning "Dawn's Mother," also commemorates their deluged Mata Weri (Easter Island), which in pictographic representation is seen here atop the head of the Polish *Baba.*

65 Once again a reconstruction of the eroded parts of this venerable image of ever the same personification of Easter Island.

On the photograph I spied very faint lines at the rim of her skirt and overskirt that is open at the front. The only substance that would withstand many myriads of winters and scorchings of sun is… blood. All large buttons on your grandfather's overcoat were made of stockyard blood, mixed with the appropriate chemicals.

From the ancient Chinese the Japanese learned the enduring assets of blood, which, mixed with chemicals, produced their "lacquered" sculptures and utensils. Many a cave painting was done with the blood of animals. I have completed the border of her dress, that you may see how the image looked originally.

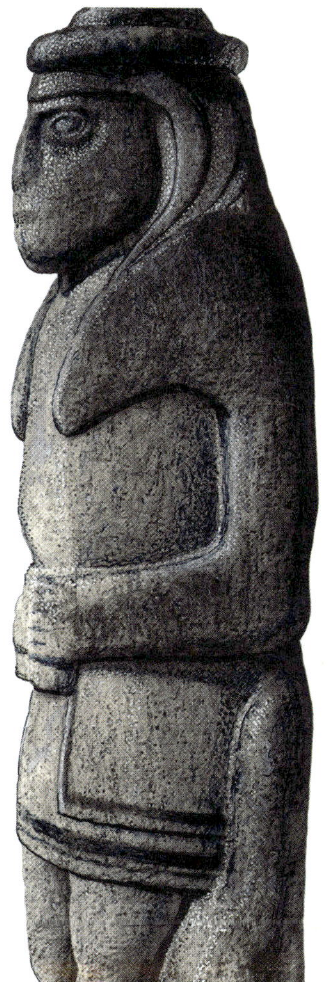

65

She, too, holds the Horizon Jar with the waters of the Deluge. The extraordinary concept of joining the breasts with the shoulders and arms is another proof that there are no such things as "mistakes" in Art, provided we have SOMETHING to say—and execute our mistakes as if we were Divinities, even if we are cursed to be Polish sculptors whom Polish governments eventually… destroy.

This image has something astounding again as a "witness" for my scientific claims. Look! On top of her head you see Easter Island surrounded by the great *Bi* of the deluging seas. This is the same *Bi* you see, only much thicker, on top of the Easter Island sculptures.

This image of the Mother of Dawn also has footless stumps, conveying that she is helpless, for, not being able to walk away, she must remain deluged.

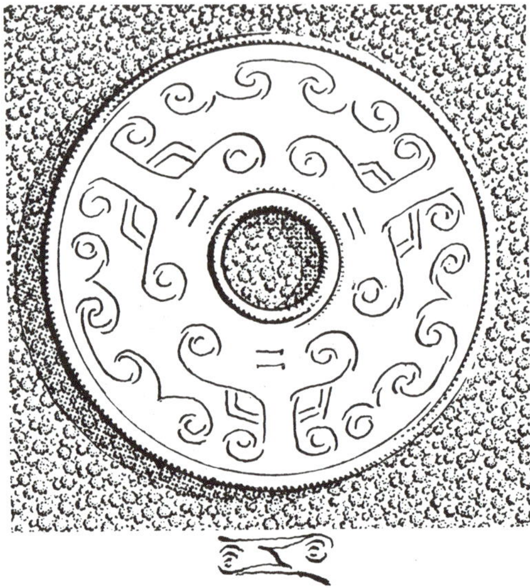

66 Glance up and see what the most sacred object of ancient China, the *Bi* (pron. "bee") looks like. It was sent to me by a Chinese friend who knew of my search for documentary bits. It is but two inches across and has pictographic heads of Flood Serpents. Since there were three landmasses in the Pacific, which the ancients regarded as the Mother of Sunrise, we have three Serpent heads here and amidst them the pictographs of swaying sea-waves. The hole in the center means "killed" by the Deluge. This same *Bi* is seen on the tail of the Polish White Eagle (see **BABA 2**).

67 At the top of her head you see the Matterhorn again, the pictograph of the Motherland. From her shoulders and her head the first glow of the coming Sunrise radiates, for it is the faint glow in the night sky that is the Dawn or "Zer," hence "Swit Zer" (see **PROFILE OF BABA 2**).

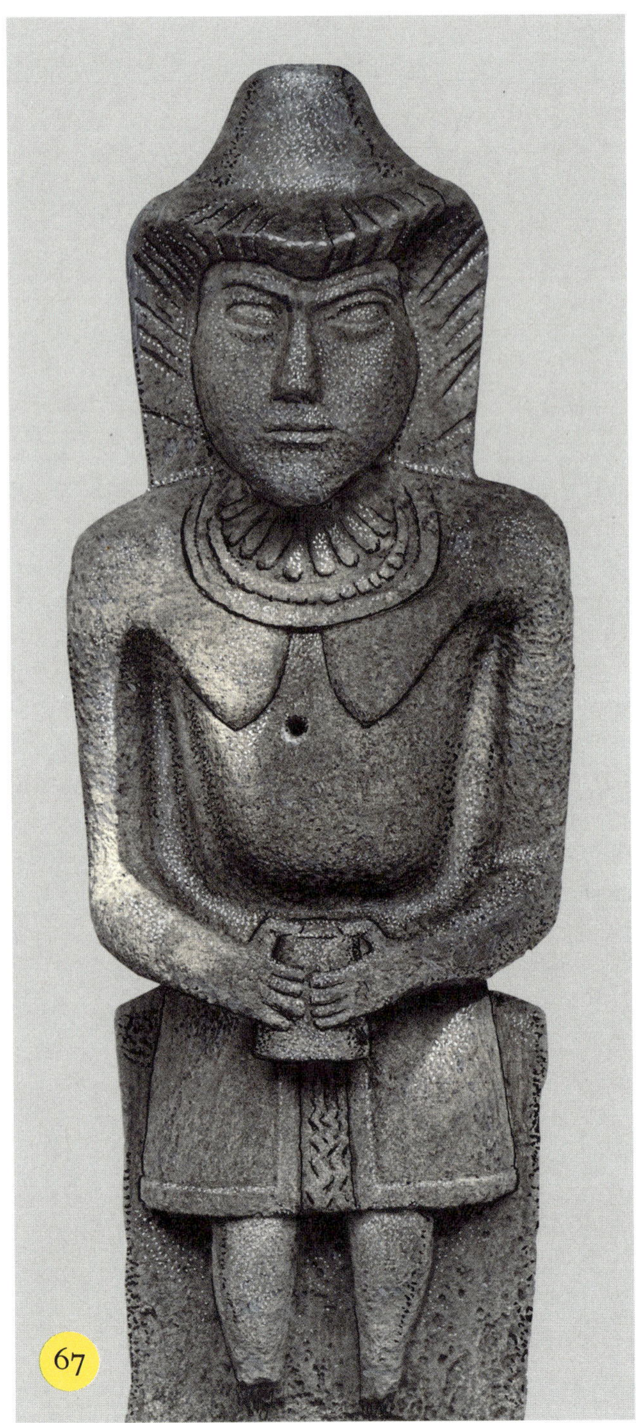

Because she was regarded dead, the historian-sculptor pierced her chest. Because she represents an ancient Motherland, he gave her flat breasts, associated with the "old Baba."

She holds the Horizon Jar inverted, already emptying the waters of the Deluge, in Wishful Magic of the worshippers and the sculptor. She has no feet, for she cannot escape.

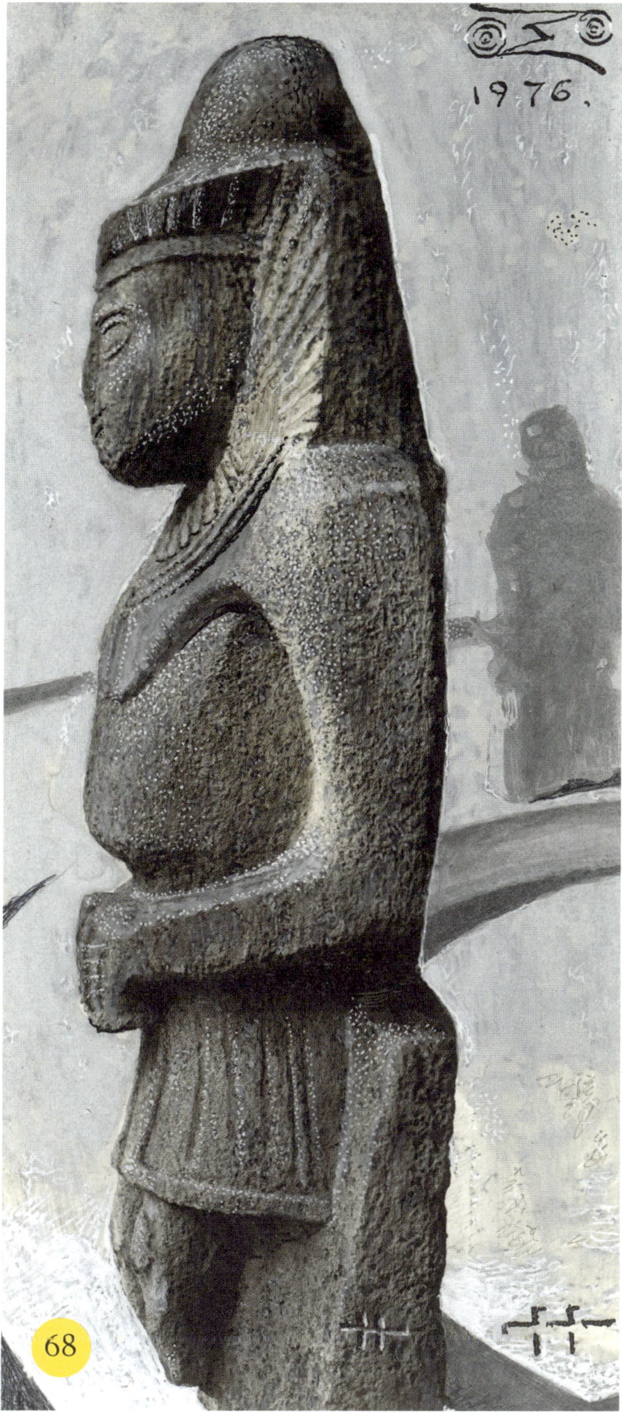

No, the wide face is not a racial trait, but denotes tremendous vitality, since only the sturdy were able to survive the cataclysm, and their descendants inherited that capacity to face all obstacles, while the frail, narrow-faced drowned or died of hunger. This sculpture is the prototype of all majestic monuments in the world.

LIVING in the United States, where I have been a superfluous man in this crass civilization, I have had no means to travel or get the books that would assist me in my further research. Yet, for almost forty years I have worked with total dedication, with absolutely no help from American institutions (as you know from the anti-Polish "jokes," this is not a country where Poles are regarded as humans; Russian agents prefer the Anglomericans to think so).

Doubtlessly, there are numerous images of this kind in Germany, Austria, Hungary and Switzerland, but I have never come across reproductions in books. I would be most grateful for thoughtful contributions of any clippings with illustrations. Each image carries some additional specific information, some pictograph I unfailingly can interpret. It is vital that the "names" these images have in various countries are included, as they are ancient and were formed in Protong, which I then can re-segment and translate, thus bringing forth some new data on their origins. Each of these reproductions will be reconstructed in my drawings and interpreted, after which a copy will be sent to the person or institution that contributed it. Every such drawing will carry the name of the kind contributor.

Mine is a totally new approach to prehistory. It will contribute to the knowledge of each country that will give me such help. I already have tremendous numbers of such illustrations, but some revelatory material may come up, for which not only I, but all Humanity will forever be grateful. These are the greatest discoveries man has ever made.

■

PROFILE OF BABA 4

68   As a sculptor versed in all the archaeologies of the world, I regard these images as being older than 5,000 years. Without doubt these are Stone Age carvings. But each people or race had its prehistory's fluorescence at a different time; their Stone Ages did not coincide. There are tribes, in this year of my writing, that still live in their Stone Age. History begins with the writing down of historic events.

The term *prehistoric,* applied to a people, does not necessarily mean that they are primitive savages. The Incas of Peru and Bolivia who evolved one of the most brilliant Civilizations, never had any system of communication but their Quipu (knotted strings of various colors), which could only be understood by a few people initiated in the particular arrangements of the knots. When they died, the knotting would remain a secret, never to be solved.

I would say that all these images belong to the Celtic Epoch. The Celtic race had not discovered a way of recording their history, but they were the ones who CREATED all Civilizations on this globe. As the Protong compound re-segmentation informs us, "Cel Tik" actually means "Whole (world) Touch(ing)," i.e. UNIVERSAL, for it was this race that scattered over all continents after it had to leave their submerging Pacific continent, and later leave Ice Age Europe as Saki.

At first, at this postdiluvial epoch, Europe was barely seen above the waters. Two groups of isles emerged: the tops of Spain-France and of Switzerland. Both were occupied by the same Celtic race, which later became twin branches, known as Scythians (*scyty* is even today a Polish peasant term for "pinnacles") and Alpine Sarmati. The Sarmati named themselves after their first community in Helvetia, presently the Swiss town of Zermatt (see **PROFILE OF BABA 2**). At the time of the oncoming Ice Age the Celtic race spread eastward to Europe, to Iran, India, China and both Americas. Once the Iranians regarded the Scythian language as their own, but now have forgotten. Their Celtic ancestors came from Polish Pomerania. These ancient Poles, dwelling in the vicinity of Holy Rugia and Arkona, worshipped the Dawn and called themselves "Rani" (Morningers; remember "Ra," the Egyptian Sun God). During the oncoming Ice Age, when earth was entering the Farsolar Epoch, the maturing youths of Pomerania, as a measure against overpopulation, were driven off as "Saki" (sack carriers). Their descendants called themselves "I Rani" (a people that "Is Morningers").

■

BABTYNIA (THE OLD WOMAN'S TEMPLE)

For years I have written to various people in Poland to do something to protect these venerable *Baby* against destruction by ignorant peasants and idle youths whose substitute for their inability to create is to destroy what has been created. But, as everywhere else in godforsaken nests of backwardness and café indolence, nothing is being done.

On receiving these photographs—thanks to my nephew Roman's efforts—I wrote to the Nieborów Museum, where they proudly cherish Rococo portraits in a fine collection of Art, proposing a plan to save these images. They should be assembled in one place from all over Poland to make it easier for anthropologists and archaeologists to compare them and draw certain, till now unprecedented, conclusions.

Further, I proposed that a Babtynia (a temple to house the *Baby*) be erected at Nieborów. Naturally, the Polish reaction to any proposition is to ignore it. These provincial creatures, suffering from "Polish Paralysis," i.e. lack of will, always fear they may be exposed to ridicule by the outside world of foreigners. They dare not breathe for fear of being accused by FOREIGNERS of stupidity. Thus intellectually, they are psychotically timid and ever wait for the foreign world to invent things for them.

Being in the United States—specifically in the Cultural Siberia of Southern California where entertainment and football are the acme of spiritual interest—I have been reduced by Poland to the status of an unknown and unneeded man, whereby due to my poverty, I cannot travel, even to Mexico, to personally gather and investigate the appropriate materials.

I beg the "foreigners" among the readers who know of such *Baby* in the vicinity of the places of their birth, to assist me in getting some photographs of them. These images are too crudely carved to be regarded as Art by laymen, yet they are THE MOST important documents of our prehistoric origins, which were the same for all of us, in the distant Pacific.

■

SHEILA-NA-GIG OF BRITAIN

Some years ago, while perusing the UCLA library in Westwood, California, I came across a large set of books published by the Royal Institute of Anthropology in which there was an article written by a woman archaeologist on the "Sheila-na-gigs." These are the bald, breastless, often broad-hipped women, prevalently portrayed in a "frog squat" as a traditional way of presenting her in childbearing.

These "Sheilas" are invariably most crudely carved and shockingly exhibitionist, particularly for Ireland where religion is as frantic as in Poland. The article was illustrated with a few examples of these relics of ancient Ireland. I have drawn most of the sculptures shown by the authorities, who proved bold in printing these mysterious images. Since

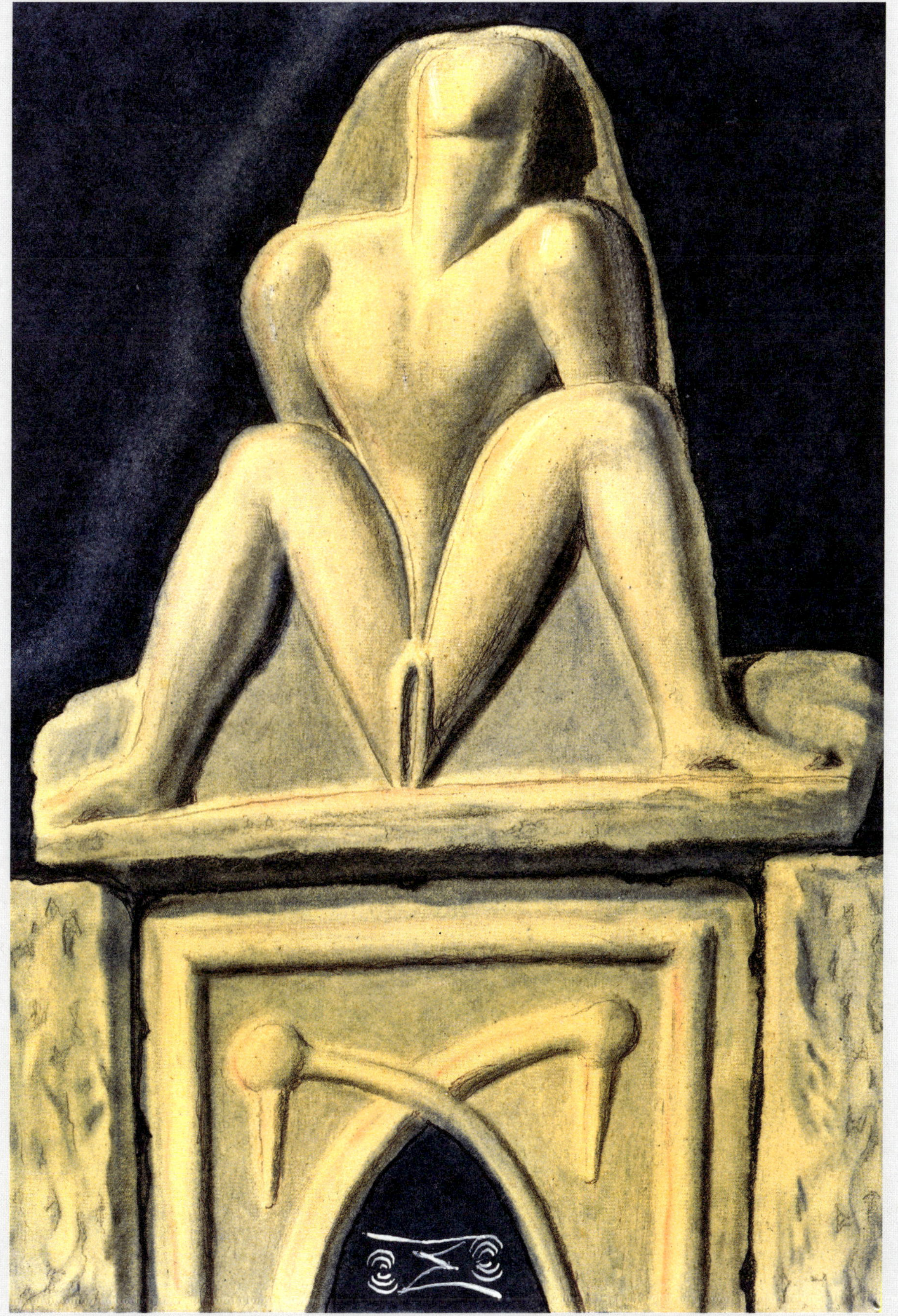

SHEILA NA-GIG OF BRITAIN

then I have found other such similar carvings throughout the world and have many drawings of them in my volumes ready for publication.

Nowhere in archaeological writings do the authoritative writers explain who "Sheila" is. Recently, I found a British scientific publication reprinting ancient relics of Britain. It was there that I learned of the tiny Isle of Iona, Scotland, where stands an ancient cloister, the first Christian church that has a Sheila in its possession. The book spoke about an attempt among the scientists and historians of Britain to discontinue the use of the meaningless name for these carvings, since no one among the linguists knows or even suspects to what language it belongs. How providential my seeing that article, for had the British been successful in dismissing the name from the text, the world would never learn what I am about to unveil here in this irreverent book.

The now meaningless name of **SHEILA-NA-GIG** was originally a compound phrase of WHO she is, in my Protong. It was made up of "Zi (O)e La Na Gi G(e)" and means that this is the "Land (that) Is Flooded, the Birthgiver Perished, Deluged."

I cannot show you many of the examples I have, for space here is prescribed. But please let these three suffice. I wrote to the Cloister of Iona begging them to send me a photograph of their Sheila. I received a picture of her shredded by time into some eight pieces, cemented into a wall just above an ancient window.

69 I have redrawn the unshy Lady of Iona Island for you, putting her fragments back together to return her to life. I have taken care to finish her injuries smoothly, in order that she may not be disdained by snobs who look down upon all the most primordial Art. I must however stress my awe of the British peoples' respect for such ancient carvings which they at least cemented into the walls of stables and barns, unlike the continentals who destroyed them because they were remnants of our ancestral paganism. Britain, therefore, is the possessor of the greatest antiquities of all Europe, for there the Gods of our ancestry were not strangled as in almost every other country in Europe.

Of what is known of the past of these images, we learn that they were relegated to the forests and woods, where in Christian times newlywed pairs would kneel before them to be blessed in their marriage. This would mean that each Sheila was the personification of the ancestral Mother(land). The window below her shows two long-necked cranes. All migratory birds, like cranes and geese were used as pictographs of Diluvial flight or Escape from Submersion.

Here too she is breastless (virginal) and *lise* (bald) to

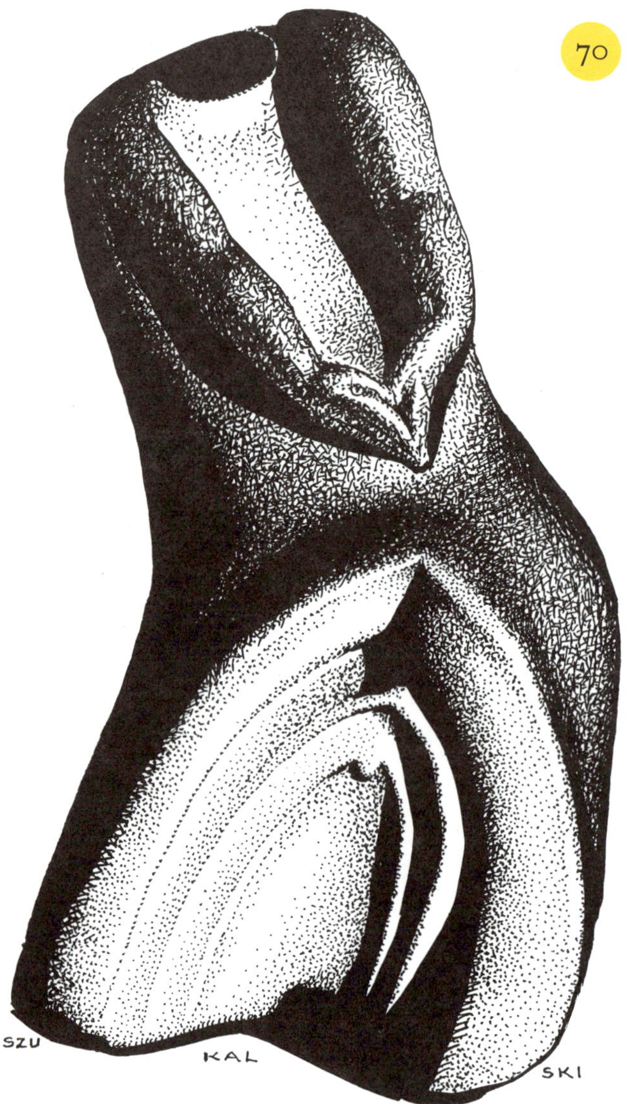

inform us that she too is the "Flooded Land," "Li Ze(m)" in Protong. But the absolute attestation to this fact is in the name of the isle inspired by her. *Iona*, in Protong "Jo Na," means "I Birthgiver." It is my conviction that this image is the most magnificent conception of all of Britain, and I am thrilled to have reconstructed her, returning her to life for this book. Any of the kind readers in Britain or on the European continent, I beg on bent knees to find me photographs of other such images, that I may draw them for the eventual publication of my whole organon on the new science of Zermatism.

70 Very many years ago when I was staying in Poland at the Europejski Hotel, I had a subscription to the now discontinued, wonderful publication, the *London Illustrated News*. Each issue, they reproduced the latest in archaeological diggings, and here I found a small reproduction

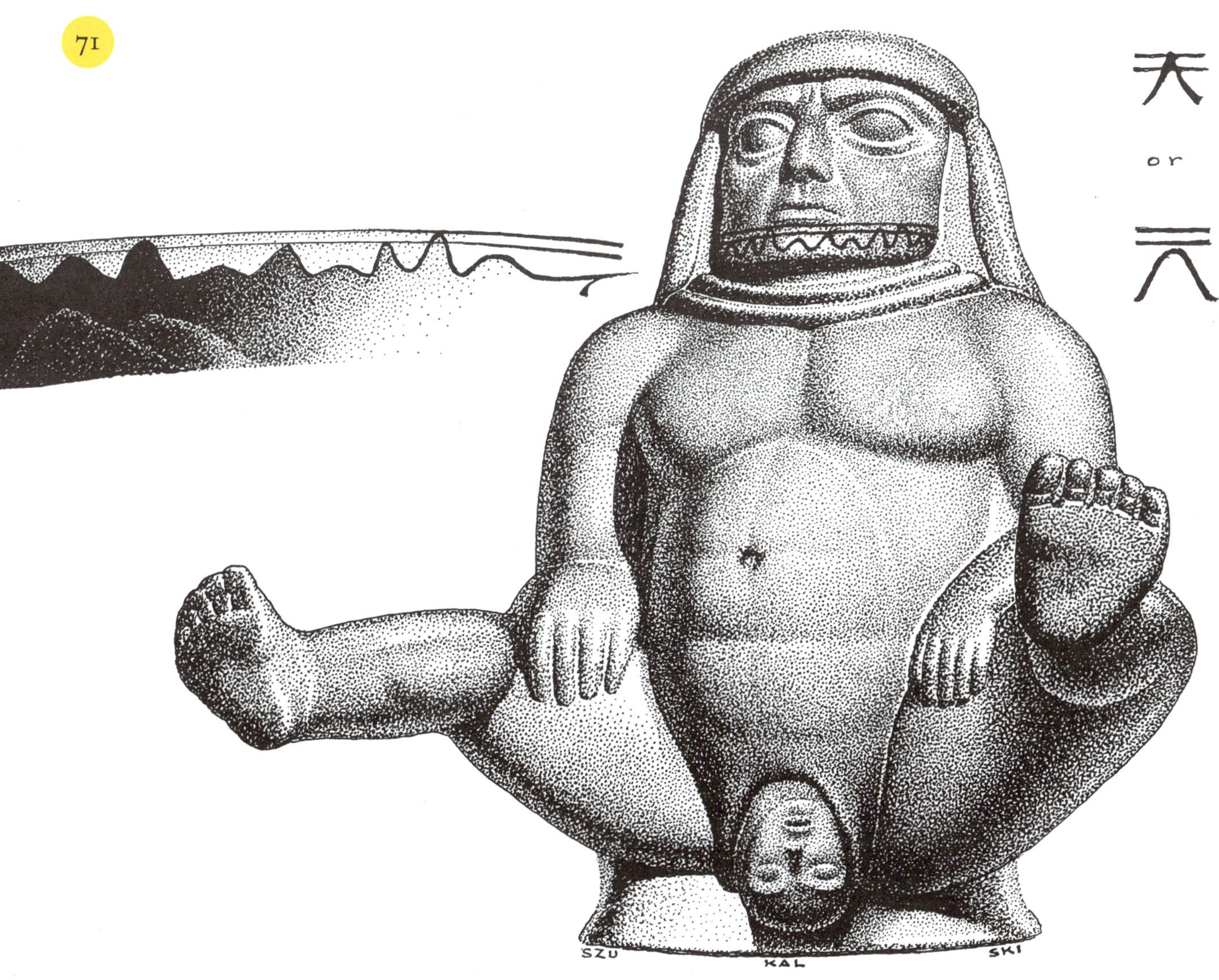

of this image found in the vicinity of London. I clipped out the little photograph and kept it until this day, never intending at that time to write my collossal work on Zermatism.

This image is all vagina with a very diminutive torso. Breastless and headless (intentionally) to indicate that she is dead. In Polish idiom "womb" is *lono*. It was after such an image, not particularly this carving, that London was first named. Protong "Lon Din" means that the image was dedicated to the "Womb (of) Day."

71 In case you still do not believe me, I present you Our Lady as conceived by a Peruvian (Inca) sculptor-historian. She is without the feminine breasts. She is sitting in the traditional "frog squat" while giving birth to the Dawn or Daylight, the longed-for Saviour. She was locked in her breath in order to assist the infant's creation; grimly, stoi-

cally keeping her face from grimacing.

But look what I have discovered (others saw it, but did not understand)! On her chin the sculptor-historian drew the Deluge, showing the ten landmasses that vanished below the surface of the global waters. Also on her face is the Inca Tribal Flood Scumline. Look at the illustrative commentary to the left of her, where I show you the Secondary (lavaic) Globe with her Mata Weri ("Mother of Worship", Easter Island).

Above, there are two Chinese characters (Chinese write with PICTOGRAPHS, not alphabetic letters) of the word *T'ien* which they say means "heaven." "T'ien" in Protong means "Shadow," referring to the submerged land of "shadows"... spirits, ghosts of our deluged ancestors, the Netherworld, where islands, mountains and continents are underwater (hence the horizontals).

In the year 1959, I crossed the Atlantic to make my project for the monument of the "Rooster of Gaul" for Paris. Not being able to find a small studio there and shocked by the high cost of living, I ventured to Corsica on the spur of the moment, hoping to find life there less expensive.

72 After arriving at Bastia, a seaport, I visited a small local museum, consisting of a few small rooms, located in an ancient fort. In one of the glass-enclosed cases, I found this little object. I am sure that to most onlookers it was an un-recognizable ornament. It is black (probably oxidized silver). It had been excavated from a prehistoric grave on a remote part of the island.

It is a startingly sophistcated concept, reduced to an abstract simplification, of a **MERMAID** (see **BABA 2**). It is basically a disc, which was partly cut out. Then the upper and pointed tips were pinched forward. The elongated holes, together with the diagonal cuts, form the division between the twin tails and the raised arms. This miraculous concept of a Mermaid was intentionally given an island-outlined head and two holes were punched in the cone at the top to look like eyes.

An identical notion had the old lady from Poland, who made mermaids in the tradition of her land for a shop which is subsidized by the government for the sustainment of folk art. She made her figurines three inches high, out of dough, which becomes very hard after drying. The *syrena* (Polish for Mermaid) reposes on her four up-curling fishtails, which stand mounted on a horizontal *Bi*, the universal pictograph for "killed by Deluge."

Her Mermaid's head is traditionally bald too, the rebusal way to denote "Flooded Land," and topped by a four-cornered hat, for the four cardinal directions in which the Sun, her Son, shines. Instead of arms, she consistently has fish fins, raised in the traditional gesture of Dawn Greeting.

The Corsican Mermaid was brilliantly conceived, particularly in the way her tails and fins were produced, with single cuts of crude shears. I wish Corsica would take this astounding Mermaid for its National Emblem and discontinue the further use of the decapitated head of a Negro, that has been used ever since the Arabs conquered ancient Corsica and made it the center of the black slave market and home of the Corsairs (sea bandits).

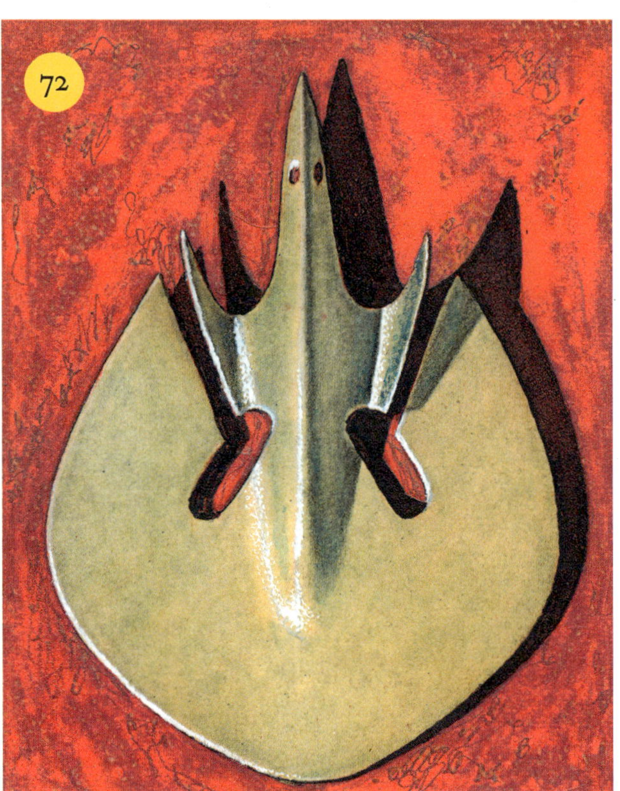

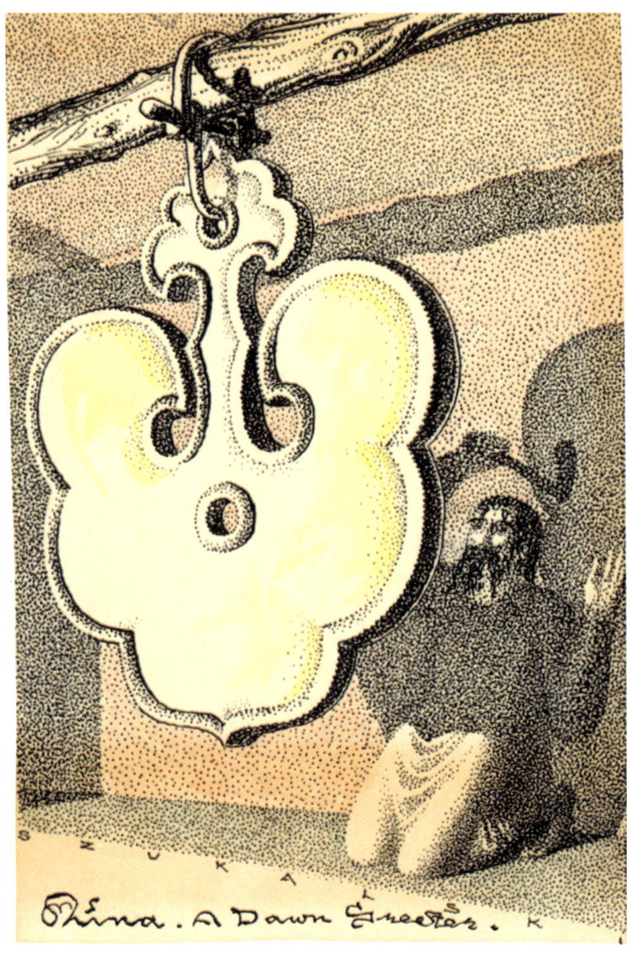

A DAWN GREETER (CHINA)

After returning from Africa, my father moved his family to another part of Poland, Gidle (pron. "geed-leh"), the largest village in the country. The name seems to have nothing to do with the language of the people who live there. But neither does the name *London*, since it means nothing to the English and it did not mean anything to them when it was still "Londin" as is seen on Alfred the Great's amuletic coins. Neither does the name *Roma* to the Italians, nor did it mean anything to the Etruscans. All now meaningless names were inherited from primordial times, be it Denver in America or Calcutta in India.

As I indicated earlier in these pages, all names are dead, unless they were made up of French and German, which languages are of recent vintage, or English, which was concocted of borrowed words from Latin-French and German. Thus, the Polish name *Gidle* sounds

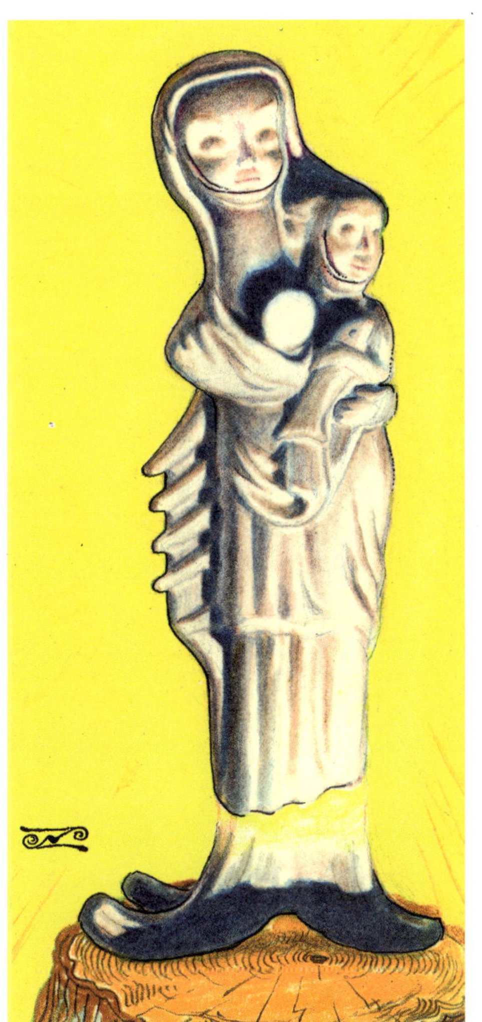

to the Poles as *oof* or *ik* to Americans; it makes no sense, just like the name for the images found in the British Isles that are called "Sheila-na-gig" which is neither Gaelic nor Sanskrit.

However, no matter on what part of the earth they occur, all names originally bespoke of only three subjects. One is the Flood, in various dialectic usages of vowels added to the "l" sound, hence *la, le, li, lo, lu,* for these were the earliest synonyms for "pouring" of waters or Deluge. The others are the Mother and Father of the Dawn God and the origin of mountains, lakes and peoples. Often from the last category the root word "z" (or its softened version "s") has been omitted, which means "from," so that upon re-segmentation, it has to be added to a name to make sense.

Thus, the compound "Gi D Le," consisting of three root words, describes the origin of the first inhabitants of Gidle. The phrase means "(From) Perished Where Flood" (here we had to add the word "from"). The "d" here is the root of the modern Polish word *gdzie* (where), which we also find as a remnant in e.g. the name Gdansk, meaning the city is located in the direction of "Where Denmark" is.

Thus, *Gidle* bespeaks of the Pacific, from where the ancestors of the Poles hailed, by way of the Swiss Alps, specifically the vicinity of Zermatt, the small town at the foot of Mount Matterhorn.

Ever since the beginning of my research into innumerable subjects as elements of my scientific work on Zermatism, I had written my friends in Gidle many times asking them to inveigle the priests at the Dominican monastery into taking the miraculous image of the Virgin Mother of Gidle out of the altar and into the sun to photograph it, so that I could make a drawing of her, since no one has seen her for centuries past. But crocodiles, sharks and Poles do not answer letters!

Finally, *Pani* (lady) Karpinska, grandniece of Władysław Reymont, the Nobel Award-winning author of *Peasants*, found persuasive words and photographs were made and sent to me in Tarzana, California. Here then she is, for Poland and the world to see for the first time ever.

The image is only 9 centimeters (3.5″) high. Though it is black, having been covered by the smoke of thousands of candles, it is actually a long piece of amber. To make her less pagan no doubt, the Christian priests have broken her tail off, so she would look less like the Mermaid. The unbroken fish spine however, on the left outline of her body, tells the truth: she is a *Syrena* (Mermaid). In the drawing I have added the tail, as I would if I had carved that miraculous image. Miraculous indeed, in a truly scientific sense, for let me reveal what this beloved image is the personification of.

Humans cannot worship any abstract notion or element of nature or universe without imagining it as a human-like being. Now, due to my discovery of Protong (*Macimowa* in Polish), we have a way to penetrate most of the enigmas that have for ages tormented man's mind, by RE-SEGMENTING the meaningless names of… everything.

The name *Mermaid* was made of "Mer Ma Id" in archaic Polish (which Protong is), which means that she personifies the "Dead Mother (of) Going." "Going" is a crude word for MIGRATION (compare the word *Yiddish* which also comes from Protong and means "Goer," migrant, and the name of the ancient Maya temple, Chichen Itza, which was made of the grammarless Protong description "Trzy Dzien Idza," meaning that it is located at a "Three Day Going" distance from the sea).

In all ancient myths she is thought of as dead, due to the Deluge. What then is the land she personified to ancient civilizations all over the world? This is EASTER ISLAND, which in primordial times was called Mata Weri ("Mother of Worship," i.e. Mother of the Dawn God). The Mermaid is the same as the Goddess Ishtar of the Semitic nations, because "Iz Ta R" means "Out of This (one) M(orn is born)." She is also the Greek Pallas Athena, "Bal La Z (J)a (G)de Ne" meaning "White (i.e. the Dawn God) Flooded From Where I No (more exist)." God Baal was her son, because his name indicated that he was the God of "Whiteness," i.e. the Daylight, and the ancient Hebrews worshipped him also.

In some parts of the world the word "Morn," being the name of God, was too sacred to be pronounced and only the first letter was used. Similarly, the full word for "Flood" (*la, le, lo, lu*) was too dangerous to fully pronounce, so only the letter "l" was used by some peoples.

The very long neck of this Mermaid was intentionally given her by the inspired sculptor. In earliest Greece I found other images with unbelievably long necks. These served as rebus: the Polish word for neck is *szyja*; on re-segmenting this word into Protong, we see that the image stands for "Zi(m) Ja" or "Earth I (am)" or "I (am the) Motherland." She personifies Easter Island which through the ages often sinks beneath the Pacific, and for that very reason the sculptor gave her the fishtail and the spinal fin, for she dwells in the Deep after her submersion.

So you still don't believe it? Then look at the two little faces of the Mother and her Son. Look at the pictographs, which I named "Horizon Jars" or "Sagging Horizons," that the sculptor engraved on them, so that you may learn. For these Sagging Horizons, resembling the letter "U," were filled with the waters of the globe, thus becoming the Pacific and Atlantic Oceans, which was so momentous to our common pre-diluvial ancestors.

Now glance at the drawing of **OCE ON** (116). While visiting London and the British Museum, I made a sketch of the colossal sculpture brought from Easter Island. There are the same Horizon Jars, engraved on the "hat," as we see on the little faces of the amber sculpture of Rybogini (fish Goddess) of Gidle in Poland.

The little child on the Mermaid's arm is holding a FISH, the same fish that the earliest Christians drew on the wall of their catacombs in Rome. Why a fish? To indicate that he was born beneath the seas, by the tallest lavaic mountain in the Pacific, whose forehead, after submergence, is barely seen above the surface as Easter Island.

Why does the Rybogini hold a mirror in her hand? She dwells beneath the seas, where she gives birth to her Son, the Dawn God who, according to ancient beliefs, then walks on the bottom of the Pacific towards the Atlantic, where his Father, Christopher, raises him from his gigantic shoulder. By raising the Dawn-greeting Mirror, she sees her Son's shining face from the distant Atlantic.

Her eyes are closed, because she is dead, deluged.

■

OBLITERATED MOTHER OF DAWN

On various occasions, Poland has been inspired to heroism by an *ikona* (Greek for "image") painted, as tradition has it, by Saint Luke. It was presented by a German Emperor to King Chrobry of Poland. He in turn, not being wholly taken by Christianity, gave it to the old holy place, the town of Częstochowa. It was placed over the main altar of a church atop the hill, where in pagan times the Mermaid was worshipped.

The cloister at Częstochowa was surrounded by massive defense walls, which at one time long stumped one of the great conquerors of Europe, Gustavus Adolphus of Sweden, who foolishly had besieged it after conquering practically all of Poland. These events were tragically written about in the book *Pan Wolodyiowski* by Sienkiewicz, the author of *Quo Vadis*. The end of the story is, that suddenly the besieged broke out of the cloister, annihilating the Swedish army. King Adolphus was lassoed by a peasant, thrown off his horse and decapitated.

Since then a tale has sustained about a Swedish soldier who was able to get close to the *ikona* and, being a Lutheran, twice slashed the Madonna's face, leaving two scars on her left cheek. I have always suspected that super-Catholic prejudice made a Protestant perform such an un-chivalrous act. That such a blasphemy never occurred will become clear when I introduce my wit-nesses from archaeology, and at the end of this chapter I will show what the so-called Black Madonna of Czestochowa really looks like beneath the rudely and barbarously imposed "embellishment" of gilt-silver tinsel.

The fact that I introduced myself to archaeology instead of having it uncovered for me by trite-minded professors, and that I make my own way towards understanding its dilemmas, makes all my discoveries and conclusions totally unlike those of professional historians and archaeologists.

Among the innumerable pictographs in the world (the earliest, drawn or carved attempts to communicate the history of the world) there are several that persistently "tell" about something having been obliterated, destroyed, lost. I am speaking here about what I have named the "Sweep of Nullification," which was variously conceived in various localities, but was most often expressed as a single or double line, from top right diagonally down to bottom left, as we do when discarding a column of numerals or a page of writing.

Here follow some mute "witnesses" who have known the things of which I speak multimillennia before my evolving these theories.

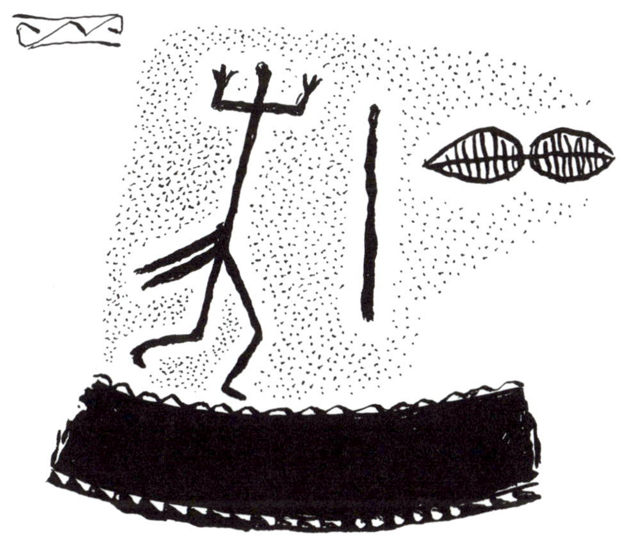

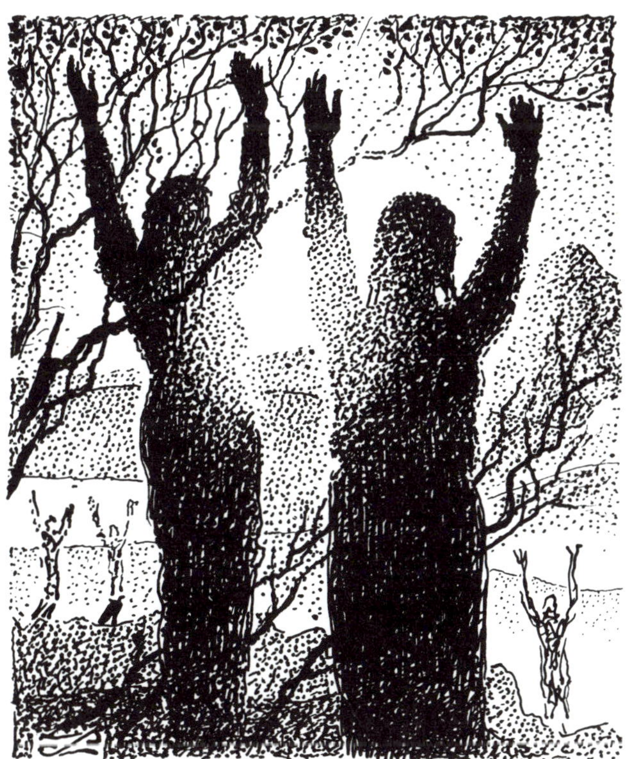

DAWN GREETING

74 In Mosul (North Iraq) excavations were made at a place called Tepe Gawra, which according to the Kurdish natives, means "The Great Mound." This pictograph was found there on a shard. It shows a figure, seemingly wearing a skirt, running to the right. The two stripes mean that she is the (by the Deluge) eliminated **MOTHER-LAND,** running towards her Saviour on the bottom of the seas, to meet him after his Sunset. The truth is attested to by her upraised arms: this gesture ALWAYS means Dawn Greeting. The two stripes were an Egyptian hieroglyph for "God(dess)."

Before her a cane was placed, the symbol for Migration-Escape, and two leaves which is a rebus for "Li Z Dzie(n)" ("Flooded, From, Day").

The name of the Great Mound is "Te Be Ga Wra" in Protong, which means "Day-White's (Mother) Worship."

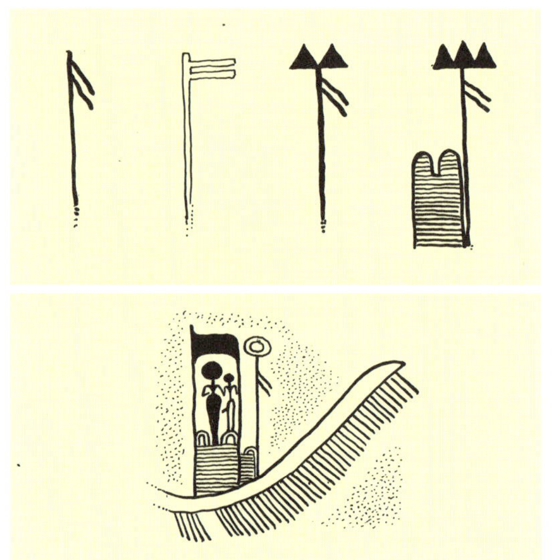

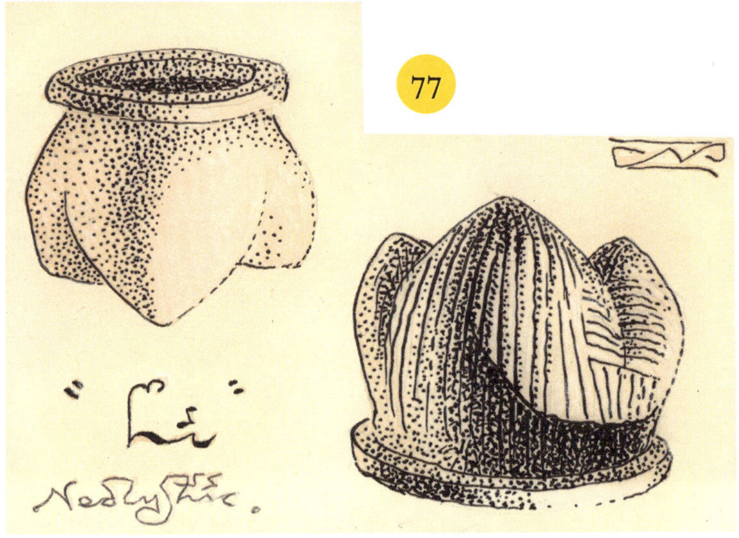

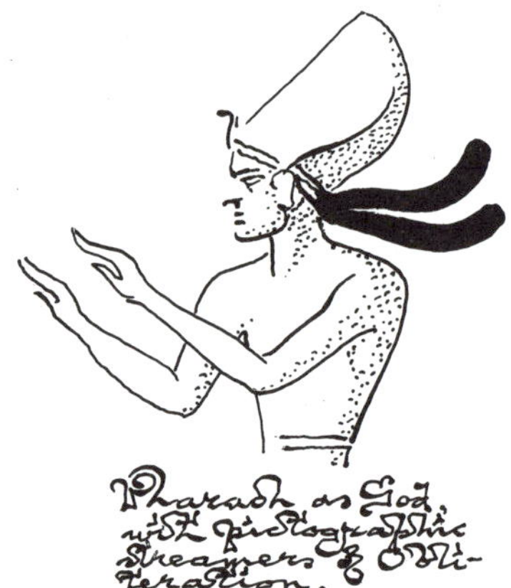

From Middle-Predynastic Egypt I gathered four examples (top) of an early stage of the hieroglyph for "**GOD(DESS)**" consisting of the two Stripes of Nullification on the masts of ships. The two on the right have additions indicating the progressively sinking islands. These posts, originally built on the "totora" boats, were later raised at the sides of temples, made of wood and covered with clay.

The bottom illustration shows the BLACK (for she is in the Nether-world under the seas) Mother with her WHITE (Dawn) Son who is carrying her away from her submersion. On the shaft on the right the two Lines of Nullification were placed, and mounted on its tip is the *Bi*, the ring that means "killed." This is the same ring the Polish Eagle has around its tail, symbolizing the possibility of flight-Escape from death by Deluge.

Picture of a young pharaoh as the **GOD RA** (Morn) with two black stripes floating behind him, indicating his departure from his Killed Motherland.

From prehistoric China comes this **CEREMONIAL VESSEL** called "Li" (Protong for "Flooded") in the shape of the three-pointed Pacific Motherland of the Dawn God. Note the Wishful Magic in the vertical striping, emulating the flowing-off of the deluging waters.

The earliest carving of the obliterated **MOTHER-LAND**, with the deluging waters forming a hood over her faceless head. Beneath the Twin Stripes a dagger was placed with a large *Bi* to tell us once over that she was "killed." At the bottom we see the clawed feet that represent the totemic Great Lioness (Easter Island).

Found at Roque-pertuse, France. Now at the Musée Borély, Marseille.

One of the most beautiful Mothers of the Dawn God, carved by the northwestern Haida Indians. Their mythology is derived from Eskimo legends. Therefore, she portrays "Sedna" whose face is usually horizontally striped to convey that she is "water-drowned." The diagonal stripes on her cheek mean that she is no more; obliterated. She has no breasts, as all prehistoric images of her, to indicate that she is the Virgin Mother of the Saviour.

The name *Sedna* evolved from the Protong phrase "Ze (D) Na," which is even modern, grammatical Polish and means "From Bottom." She, claim the Eskimos, dwells under the seas and occasionally comes up for air, scaring and drowning unwary fishermen.

The name *Haida* was once Protong "Ga Id (J)a" meaning "I Exiled, Migrated."

 78

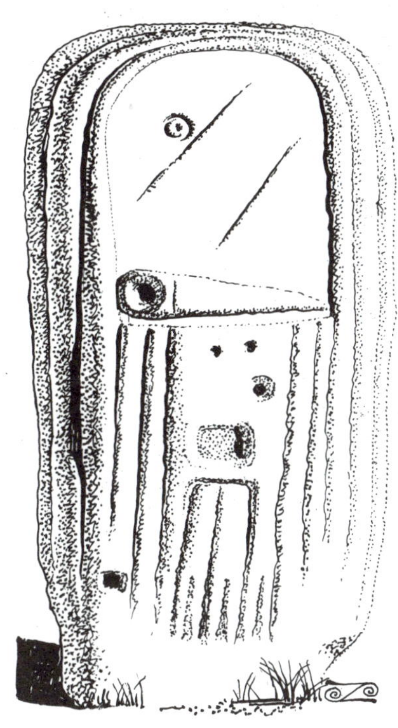

 79

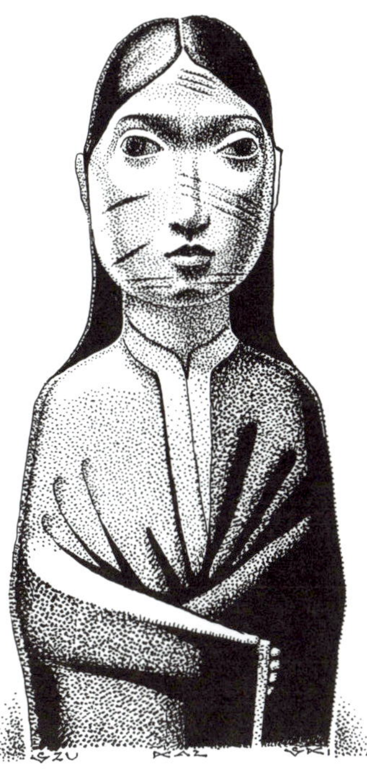

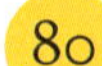 80

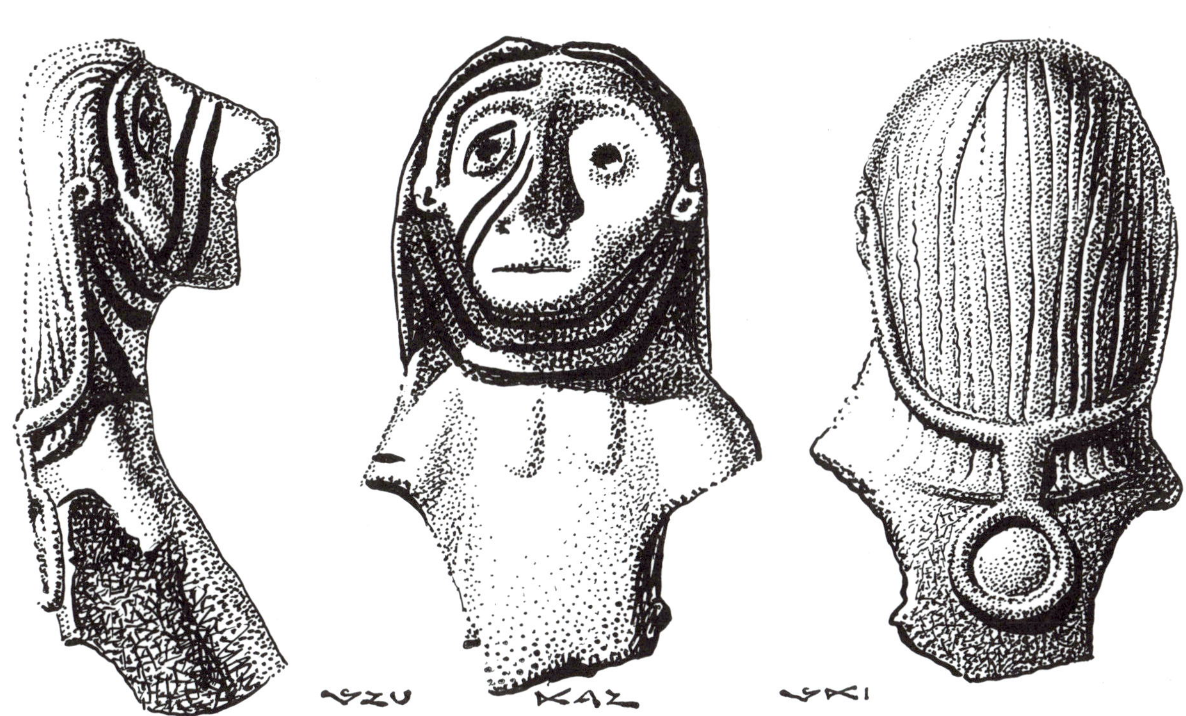

80 Across the globe, in distant Moldova (N. E. Romania) historic images were excavated giving heed to prehistoric times.

Here you have my witness from Trypolie, Moldova. The first two drawings of the **MOTHER OF DAWN** show her Twin Stripes of Nullification from existence. She too has only the slightest indication of breasts. Only one *brew* (Polish for "eyebrow") was painted. This is a rebus, since Protong "Bre W" means "Taken In," i.o.w. she is dwelling "In (the land) Taken" by the Deluge.

But the most remarkable document is seen on her back (right) where, over her chopped-off hair, hangs the Dawn-greeting Mirror identical with the Egyptian *menyet* (changer) which the priests switched to the back when ceremonials were over.

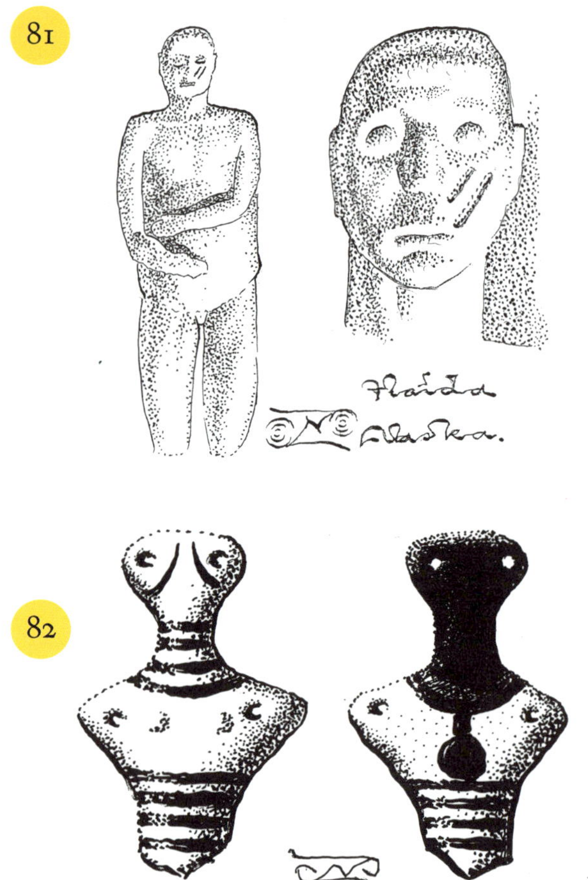

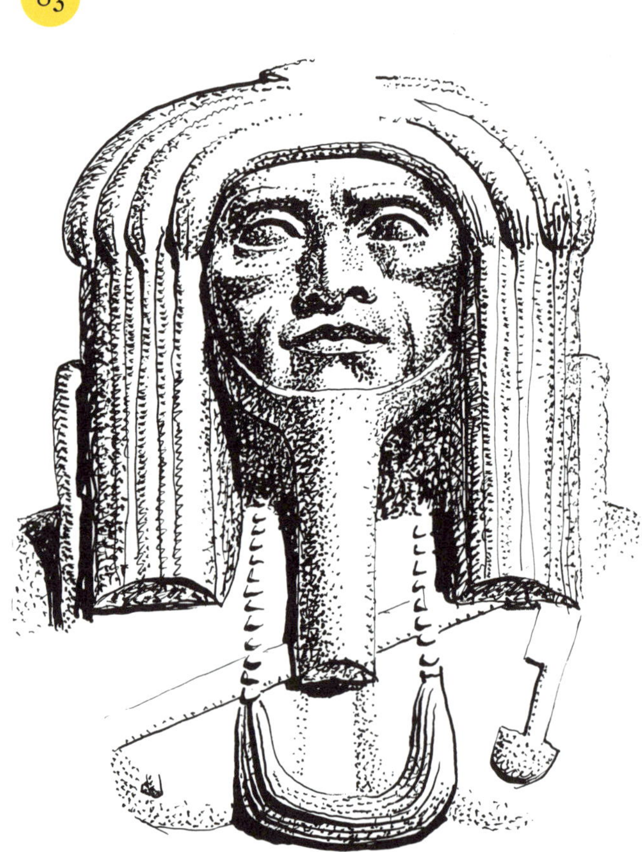

From Haida, Alaska, comes this bald, breastless but pregnant Indian carving. She is feeling with her hand for the life of her infant Dawn to be born. On her cheeks are the gashes of obliteration.

Another image of the same **MOTHER**, found in Trypolie. On her back, she has the Dawn Greeting Mirror only in black paint. She is bald-headed, rebusal for "Flooded Land," and her virginal breasts are merely indicated.

The name *Trypolie* is apparently Slavic, meaning "Three Fields." However, I think this is just a coincidence, for it can be re-segmented into the Protong phrase "Dri Po Li," which refers to the founders of the first community there who "Escaped After Flood".

(Originally, Romania was populated by the Slavic Vlahi but, after being conquered by Rome, was turned into a punitive colony, Rome's Siberia for homosexuals and political prisoners, and renamed Little Rome, or Romania.)

Pharaoh **AMMENMESSE** carries the beaded counter-weight on his chest, so that his Dawn-greeting Mirror hangs on his back, probably hidden under the cloak to protect it from human eyes when not used ceremonially.

The Egyptian *menyet* is the glyph representing a mirror with counter-weight beads, forming a necklace. In Protong, this word means "a changer." Thus we learn from the term that the priestly pharaoh would "change" the necklace's position from in back to the front of him, for use in ceremonial services.

From Jalisco, Central Mexico, comes another witness. The Spaniards, after their conquest of Mexico, imposed their pronunciation of native names. Actually *Jalisco* had evolved from "Ja Li Z Ko" that is neither Aztec nor Nahua, but archaic Polish and means "I Flooded From (the) Beloved (one)."

This image has the Twin Continent head-extensions, each terminating in a *Bi*, for she is killed by the Deluge. In all countries she is frequently shown open-mouthed, a rebus for Polish *wola* (she calls) from which we learn that she is "Water Flooded." On her right cheek three

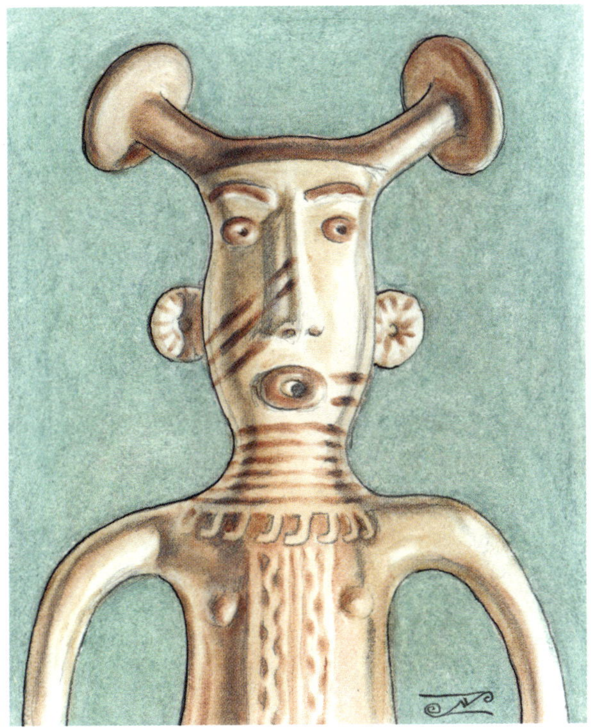

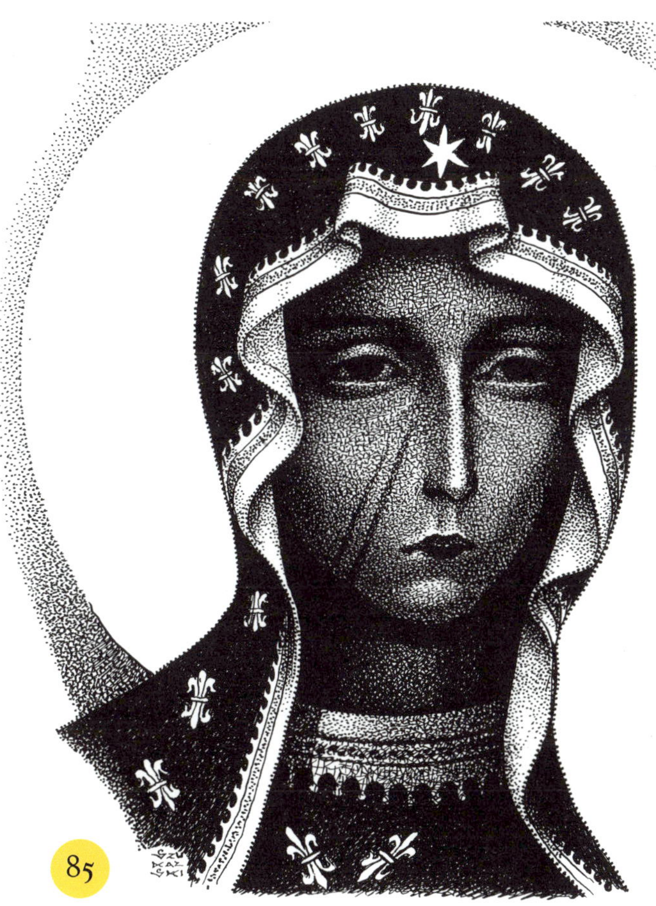

diagonal lines were painted, which refers to the three component land masses in the Pacific that were obliterated. Her left cheek has two water horizontals for the Twin Ocean Deluge. Her diminutive promises-of-future breasts tell us that she is the virginal **MOTHER OF THE DAWN.** Around her neck a *fret* of sea waves was painted. *Fret* is an Icelandic word that means "destroyer, obliterator."

Below her chin we see many horizontals. These are the ripples of the surface wavelets (a ring-within-a-ring-within-a-ring) as she sinks or… re-emerges in Wishful Magic, for indeed, the waters of the Great Flood are already flowing off her chest.

85 Here, finally, you have the Black Madonna of Czestochowa ("black" from millions of smoking candles and centuries of futile prayers), the only authority to which the Poles eagerly submit, the uncrowned Queen of Poland. She is the actual maintainer of the pictographic Sweeps of Nullification, the hereditary personification of Easter Island, who is now worshipped as the Mother of Jezus (Protong "Je Z Us," i.e. "Is From the mortally-Asleep," hence from Easter Island).

The Greek icon was found in Jerusalem in 336 A.D. by St. Helen and taken to Poland from Constantinople in the year 1326.

In pre-Christian Poland, the hill where the Madonna is now kept above the church altar, was one of the centers of worship of the Mermaid, the other pictographic personification of Easter Island. Therefore, it was called Jasna Gora, Bright Mountain, in commemoration of Mata Weri ("Mother of Worship"), which was the island's name before the discovering Hollanders erroneously named it Easter Island.

Due to the fluctuation of solar temperatures, the isle often submerges and re-rises, hence the Polish name for the town around Jasna Gora, Częstochowa, which means "Often Hides."

That the Greek painter St. Luke knew of the ancient Sweeps of Nullification, attests to the unbelievable continuity of Civilization after the Deluge; from the Romanian Saki (the youths driven away by the Ice Age) onto the Egyptians onto the Greeks.

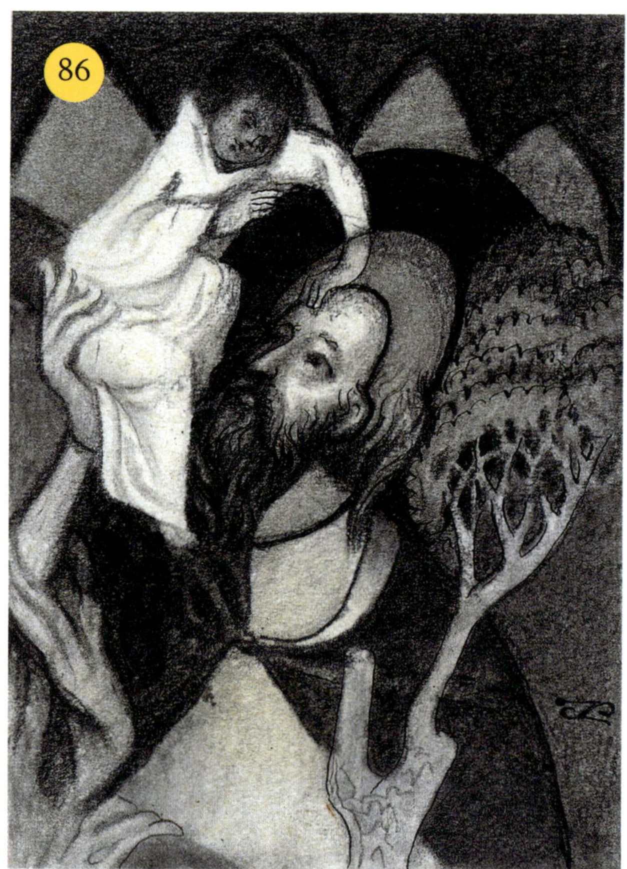

CHRISTOPHER OF TORUN

86 This is but a small fragment of a vast fresco at a church in the ancient city of Torun, in Poland. On seeing it reproduced in a magazine, I immediately wrote there asking if somewhere, painted tiny between Christopher's legs, is the Mermaid, always associated with him? The response brought me a photograph with an apology: the lower portion of the fresco, due to moisture creeping upwards from the ground, had peeled off and if there had been a Mermaid, it had not survived.

During my years of research I have found evidence that the concept of any Christopher was already used in pictographic art of Scandinavia and Babylon. In Bohuslän, Sweden, I drew the accompanying presentation of him carrying the child on his shoulders.

The Christian story about Christopher carrying the infant Christ on his shoulders was actually adapted from prehistoric legends. The now dead name of Christopher once was the phrase "Kri Z Top Wer." Since there is never any indication of grammar in Protong, and there are no suffixes and prefixes, we must assume that with this descrip-

tion was meant that he is the carrier of the Child who comes "Covered (by) Atlantic From, Drowned, Worship." He is the one who lifts the infant Dawn that crawled to him over the Pacific Ocean bottom, high up over the Atlantic Ocean, giving Europe the Daylight.

As you may recall from seeing various representations of Christopher, he always leans on a TREE (though with broken-off branches and roots). Why? Because this is a rebus for the Polish word *drzewo* which, re-segmented, is close enough in sound to Protong "Gdzie Wody," meaning that this scene is daily re-enacted "Where Waters."

87 Look again at the drawing! Look at the little hand of the child. It does not reach out to stroke Christopher's forehead, but round-about dips its hand as if under a watery ring (a *Bi*) of sea waves around the re-emerging-like head.

88 By Christopher! This Polish fresco in Torun is the picturization of the little islet off the English coast which strikingly resembles the heads on Easter Island. I am sure that this islet is part of the now deluged Atlantic continent, Oce On, and that it—having the features of a man—played an important role in the religious system of that continent. It is the **FACE OF CHRISTOPHER**, who is not a saint but a localized personification of Oce On or "He of the Fathers," the original God-the-Father of the Christians (earlier *Je Howa*, which means "Is Hidden," of the Hebrews, and *Shang Ti* of the Chinese). ■

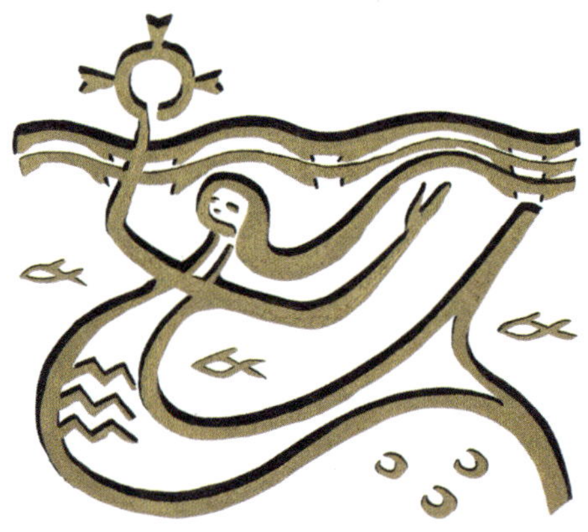

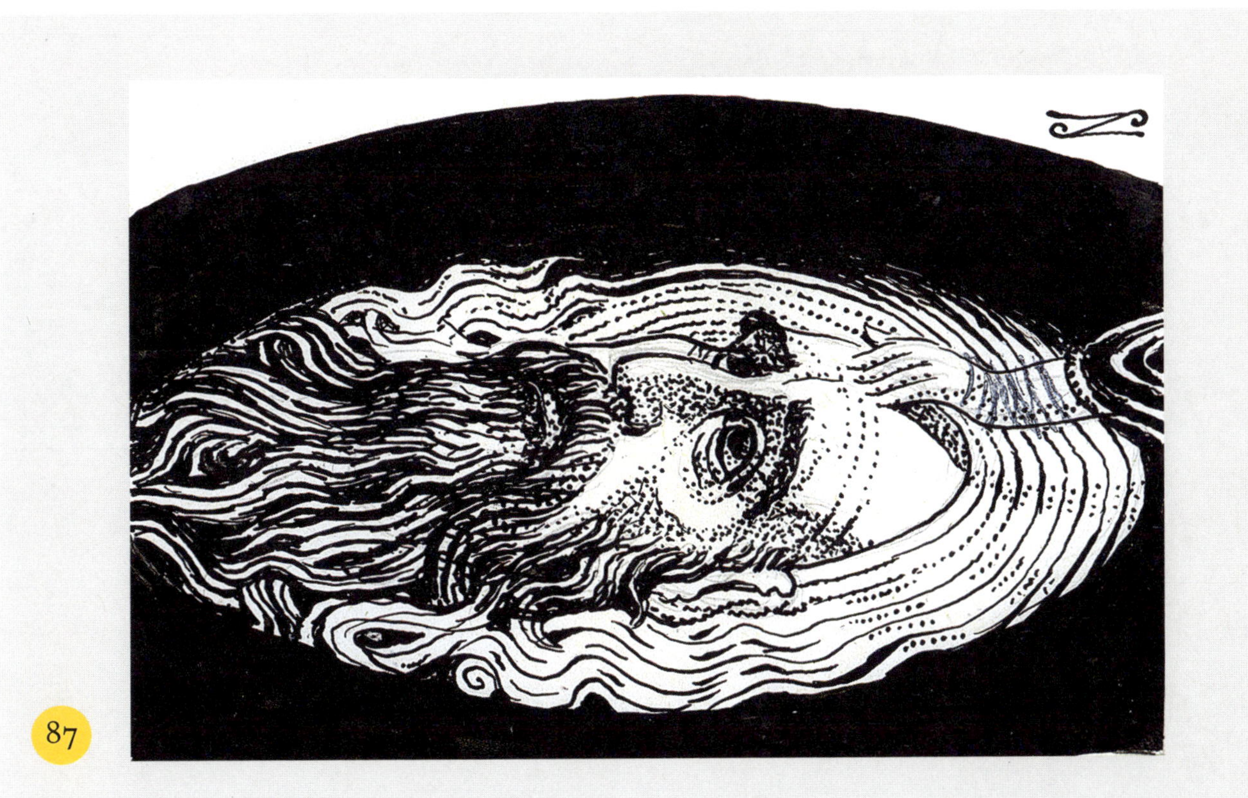

87

88

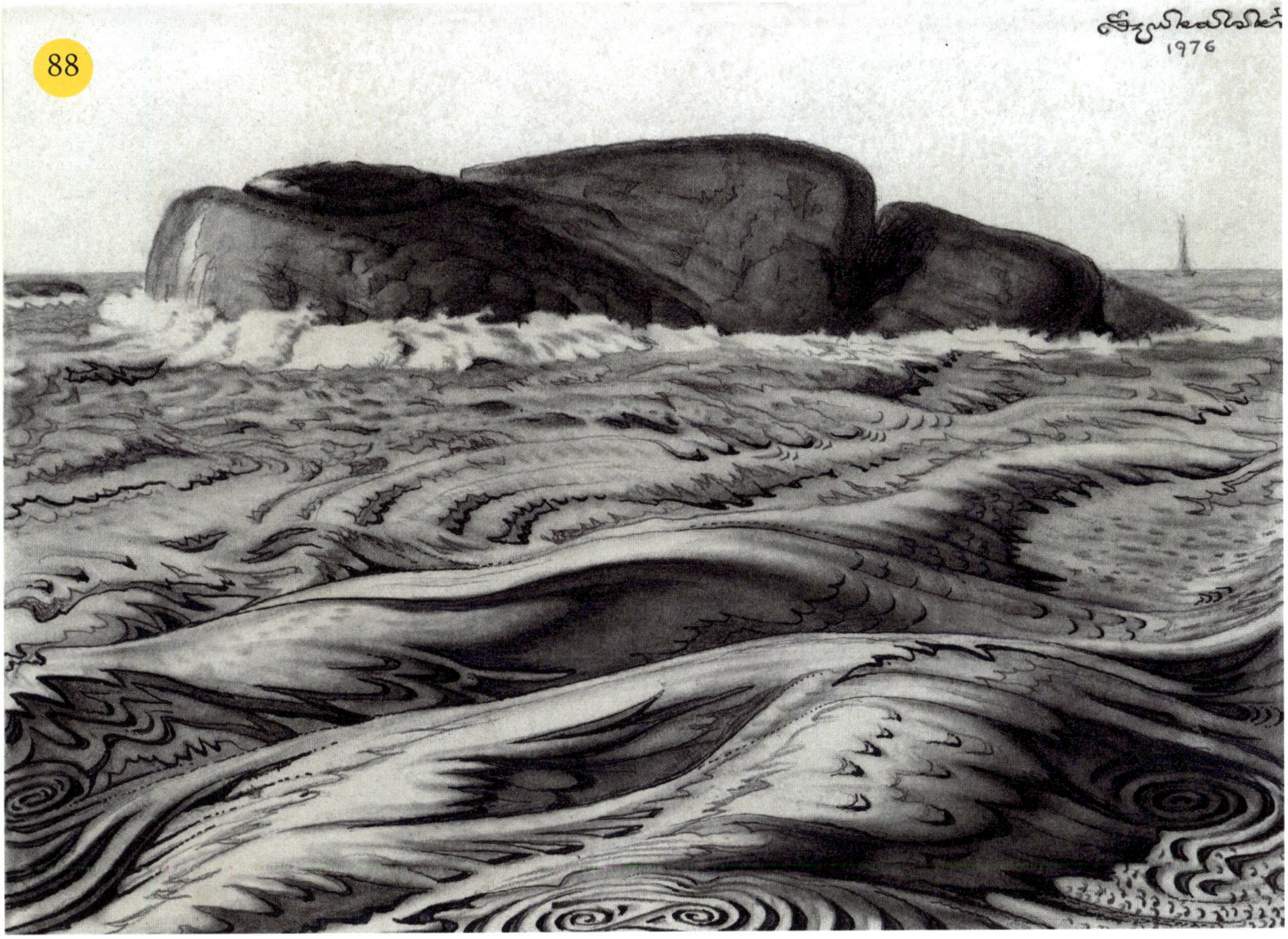

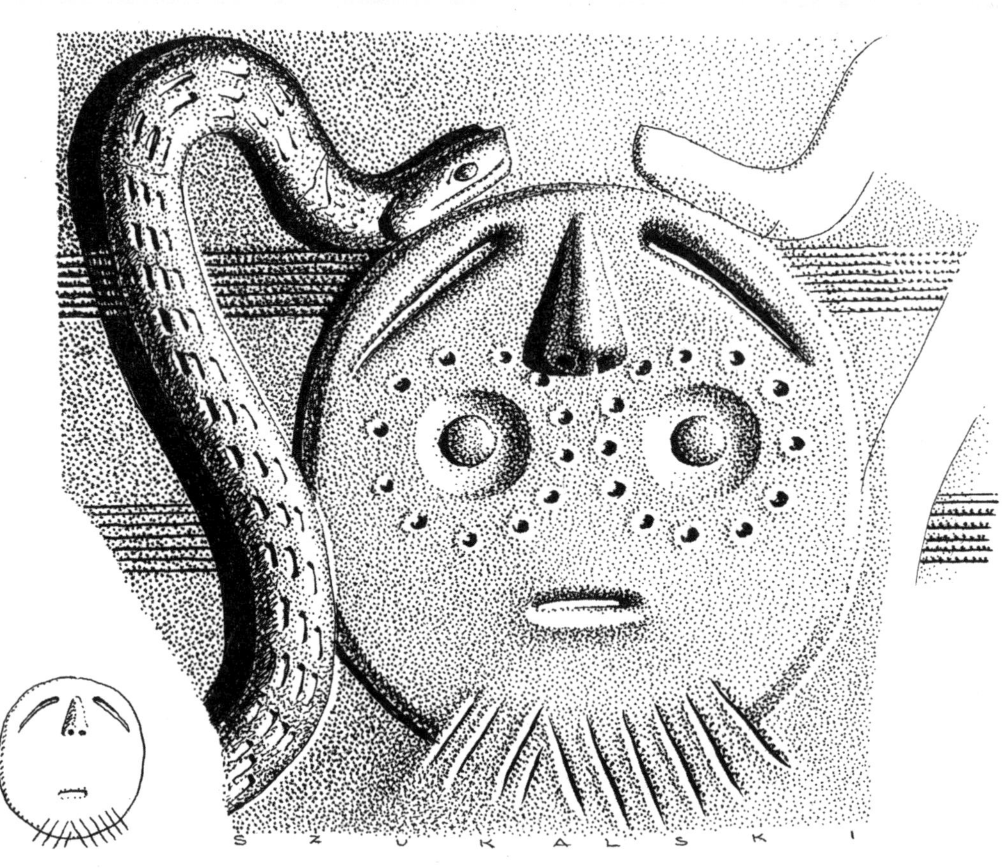

89

The Deluged Gods

FROM my compilation of the same pictographic elements in all the archaeologies of this earth, I came to the conclusion that the ancient peoples proved that in the Pacific region a lavaic continent submerged (Easter Island) that has the Great Lioness as its totemic coat of arms. And in the Atlantic the lavaic continent Oce On submerged, with the Great Turtle as its coat of arms.

When the Sun was at its hottest, the ocean bottoms bloated upwards and these two continents were visible above the water as two large mountains, hence their frequent pictographic representation as Twin Triangles. But when the Farsolar Epoch followed, the globe chilled and the sea bottoms deflated, so that each continent was overcome by its respective Serpent, the undulating Flood.

These were tremendously complex circumstances for ancient man to comprehend and still more so, to convey by crude pictography for posterity to unravel.

89 This little fragment of baked pottery from Syria shows us the face of **OCE ON** or "The Fathers' He," the lavaic continent in the Atlantic after which we named our oceans. In nostalgia-motivated memory, Oce On was personified as God-the-Father by the Hebrews, who called him *Ihv*, or fully *Je Howa*. The Chinese called him *Shang Ti*, which is the same word as Latin *sancti* (holy). The Babylonians called him *Ea*, which is Protong "E A," and Polish *Jestem Ja*, all meaning reversedly "I Am."

We see the solar mask rising from under the Flood Serpents and the sea (horizontal lines), carrying on its forehead the closed *ocy* (pron. "otsy") of the dead Fathers' He. The reason for this pictographic portrayal as two eyes can be found in the crude Polish peasant word for "father" (*ociec*), which actually means "eyer," one who constantly watches his family. (The Polish word for "providence" literally means "everywhere-lookingness," hence the "eye" of providence on your dollar bill at the top of the masonic pyramid.)

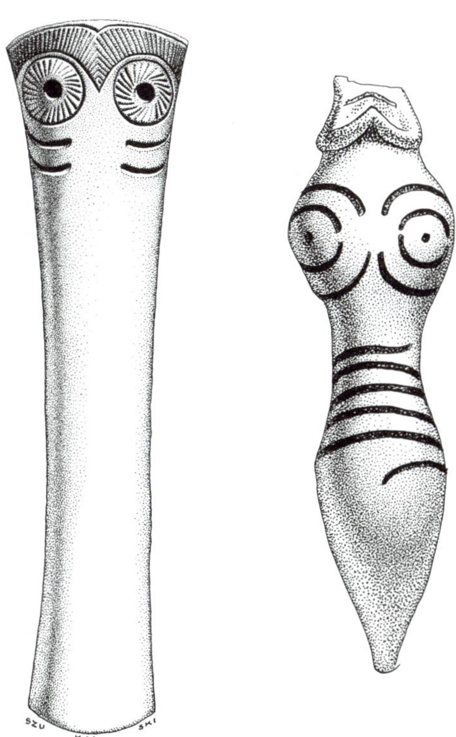

90 Two of numerous **SCEPTERS** engraved with the eyes of "He of the Fathers" from megalithic Spain, show the water rippling above and below them, informing us that Oce On dwells beneath the flooding seas.

The Holy Scriptures of the Hebrews report that God, through his prophet, said: "From now on women shall not call me *Bali*, but *Ishi*." The latter is Protong "J(e) Zi," meaning "Is Land." This happened when, after forty years of wanderings in the desert, the Hebrews took the land of Canaan and, for political reasons gave up their worship of Baal (the Sunrise) and took to the worship of Canaanite *Ishi*, *Ihv* or *Jehowah*, i.o.w. Oce On.

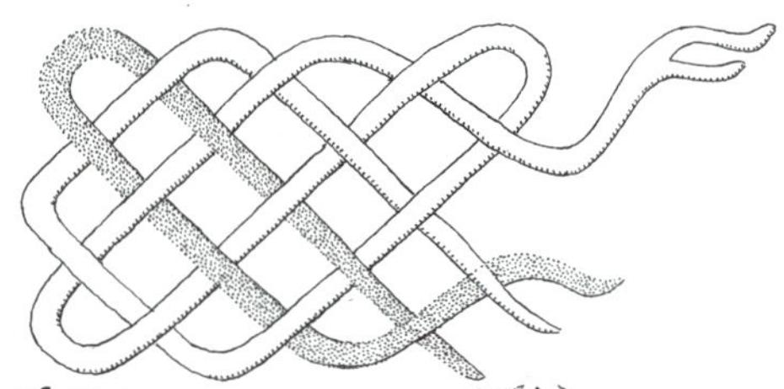

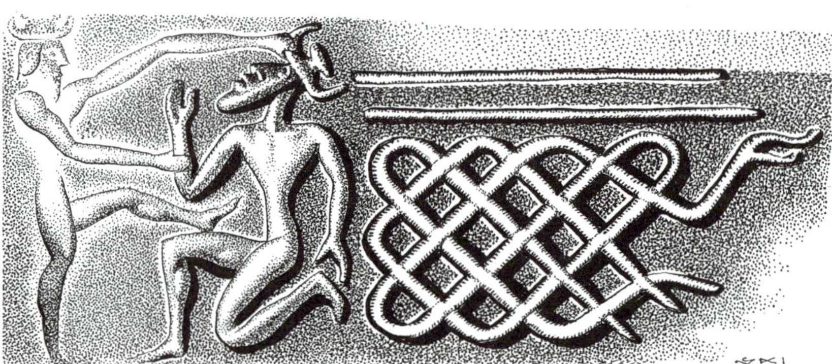

From Akkadia (Babylonia) comes this witness to further attest to my kind of logic. On a cylinder I found this dramatic scene in which the God **BAAL** descends beneath the seas (two horizontal bars), which moment is ever indicated by his or his Eagle-Messenger's head being turned to the right, denoting Sunset. He does so to save his father, Ishi, from his present submersion in the labyrinth of the Twin Flood Serpents of the Atlantic and the Pacific.

We know of the danger to any rescuer of a drowning man to be drowned himself by the frightened unfortunate trying to climb on his body. In order to avoid the risk, Baal kicks his father in the solar plexus to make him faint, which enables him to pull his limp body to safety by one arm and one of the rebusal *rogi* (Polish for "horns"); Protong "Ro Gi" tells us that the drowning man is the "Perished Birthgiver." All Assyrian, Babylonian, Hittite, Egyptian and Iranian divinities and heroes were given *rogi* by their historian-sculptors, to indicate their diluvial origins. Similarly, the Egyptian Gods and pharaohs were given cobra diadems, to indicate that they all came from under the seas, since the Serpent is synonymous with Flood. The word *cobra* is again a rebus for Protong "Ko Bra," which tells us that these reptilians "Took Beloved (continents)."

At the local museum of Santa Fe I drew this petroglyph for you from New Mexico. You see the baldheaded Motherland, a breastless virgin, about to grasp the Twin Flood Serpents by the head. She is turned to the right, indicating sunset, which is illustrated by her Son (note the umbilical cord), the Sun, descending after his drowning (crucifixion). Why does he have claw-like hands and feet? Because he is the God of the diluvial worshippers whose ancestors escaped the Deluge, which flight-Migration is represented in pictography by the Bird.

At the bottom on her right, is the Whirl of Diluvial Sinkage, and on her left the Great Turtle representing Oce On, her "husband."

From Spadarolo, near Rimini in Italy, comes this witness. It is a bronze plaque. In the center of the Horizon Jar, or Sagging Horizon, that filled with the global waters, stands again the baldheaded and breastless Motherland, legs apart to give birth to the Sun. The same Twin Flood Serpents are biting her knees for a rebusal reason: *koland* is Polish for "knees" which gives us the key to the translation "Beloved Flooded Birthgiver" from Protong "Ko La Na." She attempts to push the horizon closing in over her, apart.

Encircling the deluged Motherland, walking away above the global seas, are the totemic animals of her peoples.

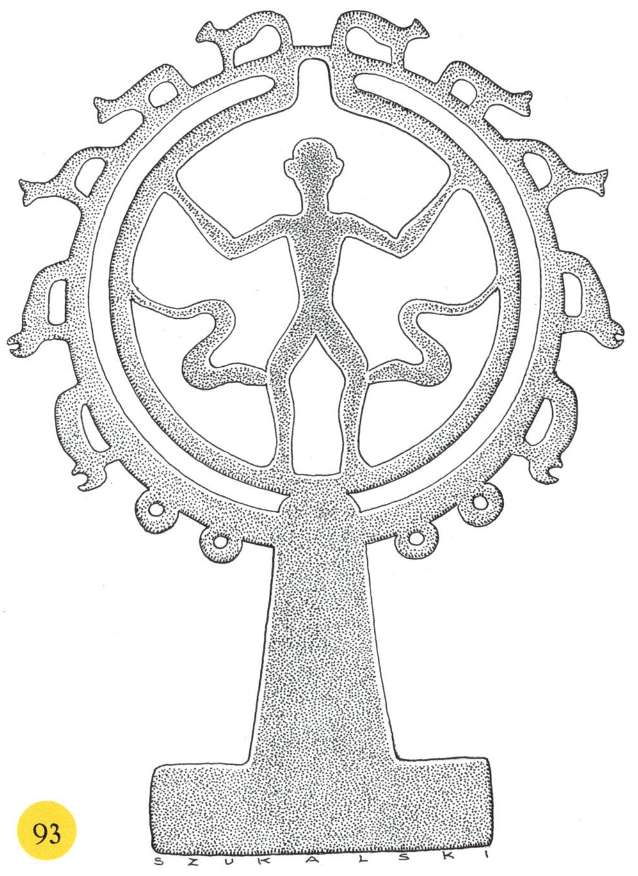

93

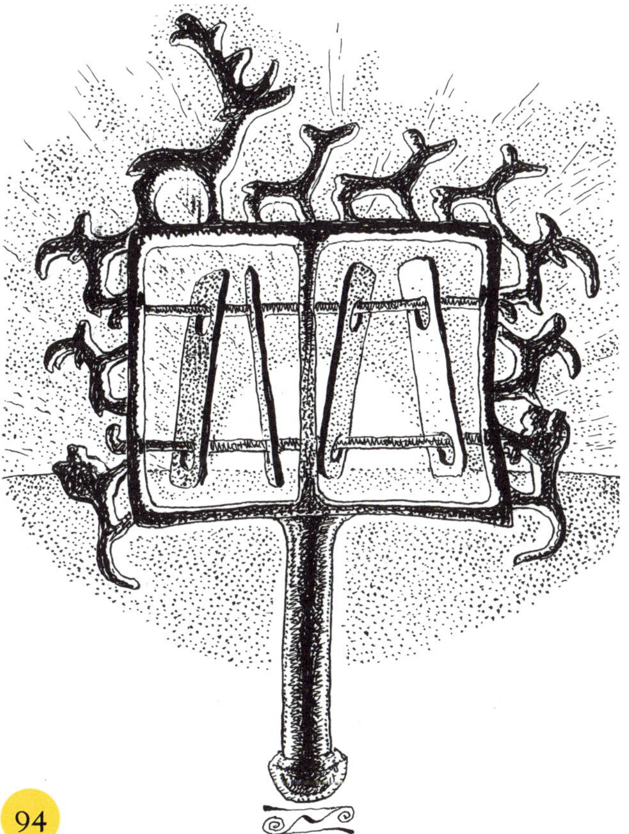

94

At the bottom in front of them, the historian-sculptor placed four *Bis* for the four component landmasses that were already "killed" by the Deluge at the time of his people's flight. So we learn that six landmasses were still above the migrating seas, for there were three component islands in the Pacific and seven in the Atlantic, ten altogether.

At the bottom we see not the supposed Thor's Hammer, but the same pictographic representation of the Motherland, Easter Island, as on the Polish *Baby*. The horizontal bar at the bottom indicates water. Now, compare this Island with the so-called "hats" on the gigantic sculptures of Easter Island.

94 A similar **BRONZE STANDARD**, which was carried on a shaft and jingled, leading processions of the Hittite people. Dating from almost 3000 B.C.

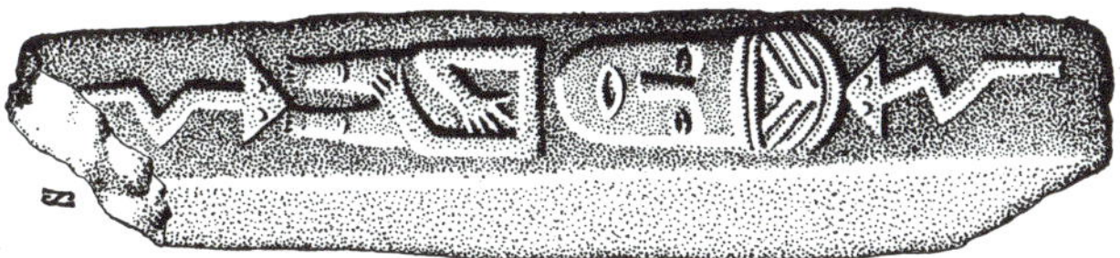

95 A lintel stone from the Royal Palace at La Paz, Bolivia. The prone body of the breastless **MOTHER OF THE DAWN**, holding her hand over her abdomen in expectation of the birth of the Saviour, is guarded over by the Twin Flood Serpents, that she does not get away from her submersion…

96 At Curium on Cyprus, there is a relief of the **TWIN SERPENTS** whose heads have already been vanquished, presumably by the Mother, though it could also be her Son, or Oce On, since no sex was indicated.

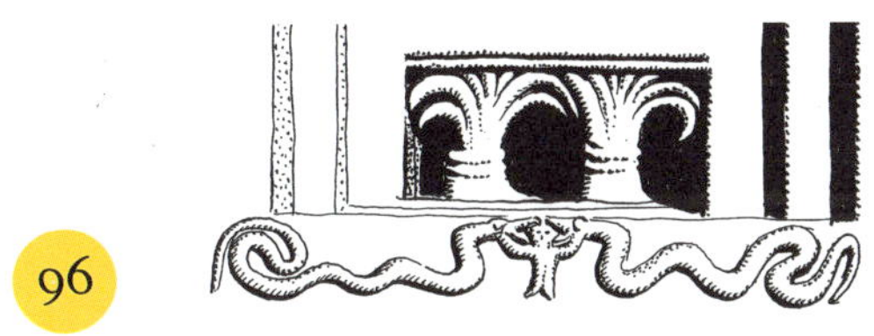

96

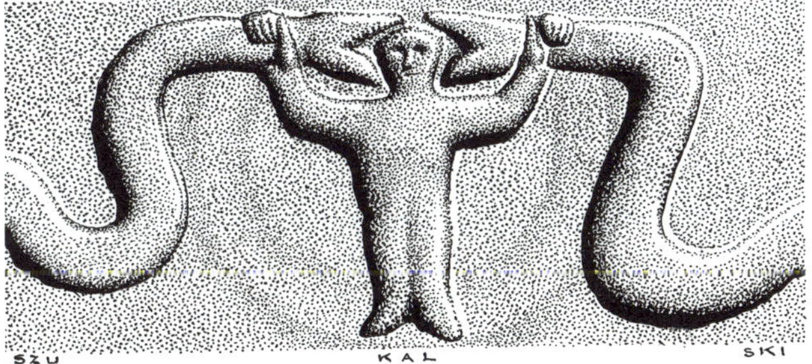

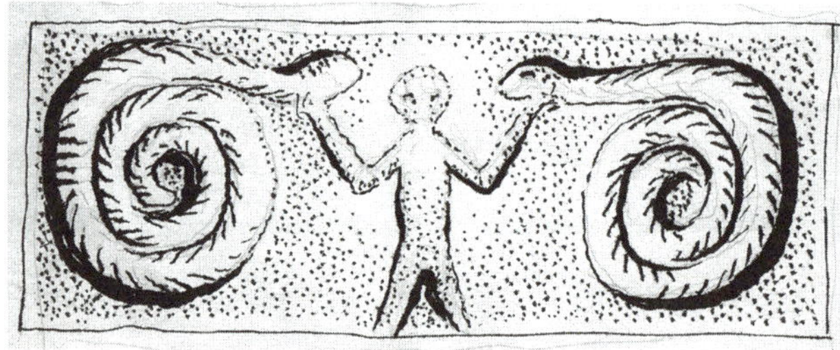

97 An identically conceived **RELIEF** I found in Baiga, India. (Protong "Baj Ga" means "Flight Exile"). Note the whirling bodies representing two-ocean sinkage.

98 At Aspiristningen, Sweden, I found another "witness." The original, as all the "bauta stones" in Scandinavia, is a very thinly engraved petroglyph, so if you stand some feet away, you will not even suspect that you have one of the finest examples of primitive Art in the world before you. I have drawn these Scandinavian Bautas as many times as I came across a reproduction of them. They are the most wonderous carvings to me and I am addicted to their beauty and their utmost significance as evidence attesting to the Global Cataclysm.

This is the **FATHER OF ODIN** (Protong "O Den," the "En-Dayer"), arrested by heart-shaped shackles at his thighs and head, and in the encoiling bondage of the Twin Ocean Dragons.

They are not Serpents this time. Their forelegs indicate the Dragon and its calisthenic raising and dropping of the body, hence they are pictographic of GEOLOGICAL UPHEAVALS.

The heart-shaped shackles occur in many of these superb Scandinavian compositions; they represent "prayers" with which we may or may not "arrest" the Dragons and free the parents. This daring attempt to convey as world-shattering a concept as global cataclysms can be compared to the undertaking of painting the ceiling of the Sistine Chapel by a blind painter. The creator was a primitive artist who had no examples of monumental works of Art, but drew upon his own primitive environment of the age. I marvel at the mentality of this genius, and the genius of the Scandinavian people who created the most inspiring monuments out of thin air.

To help my friend, the marvelous sculptor, I made the background black so that you may plainly see the whole drama and not miss a fragment. Also I have given this drawing some degree of thickness, and the shading is mine, so the overlapping of forms would be unmistaken. Finally, I must draw your attention to the small whirls at the elbows of the Dragons' forelegs, which identify the reptiles as the cause of the diluvial drownings. Feathers at the tips of their tails, hinting at the pictographic Bird, mean that they caused flight-Migration.

Because the eyes of Oce On are, as usual, drawn as circles (*Bis*), I assume that this engraving pictures the mortal struggle of Oce On with the Two-Ocean Cata-clysm.

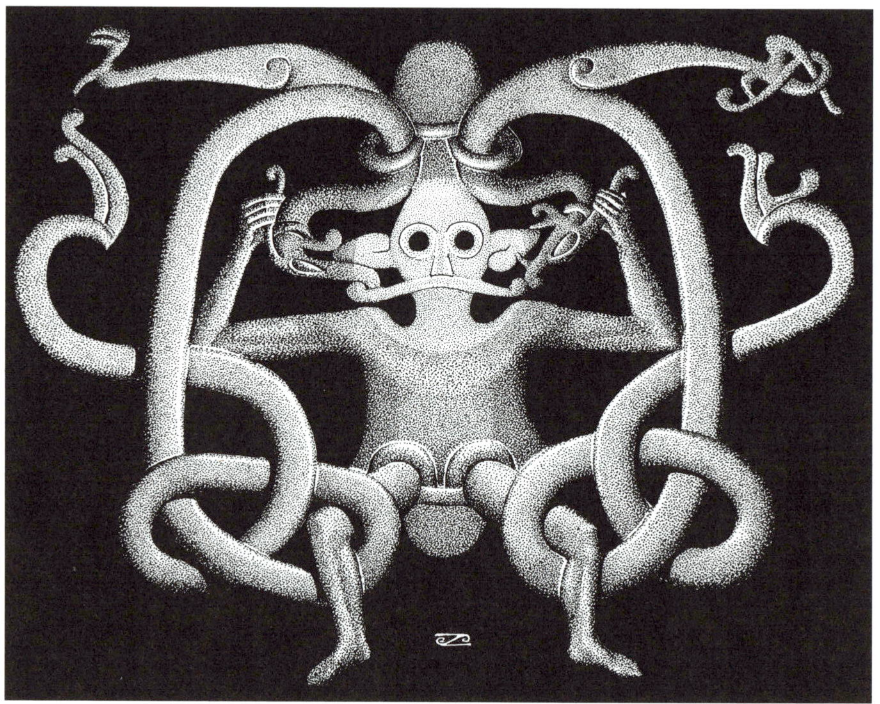

98

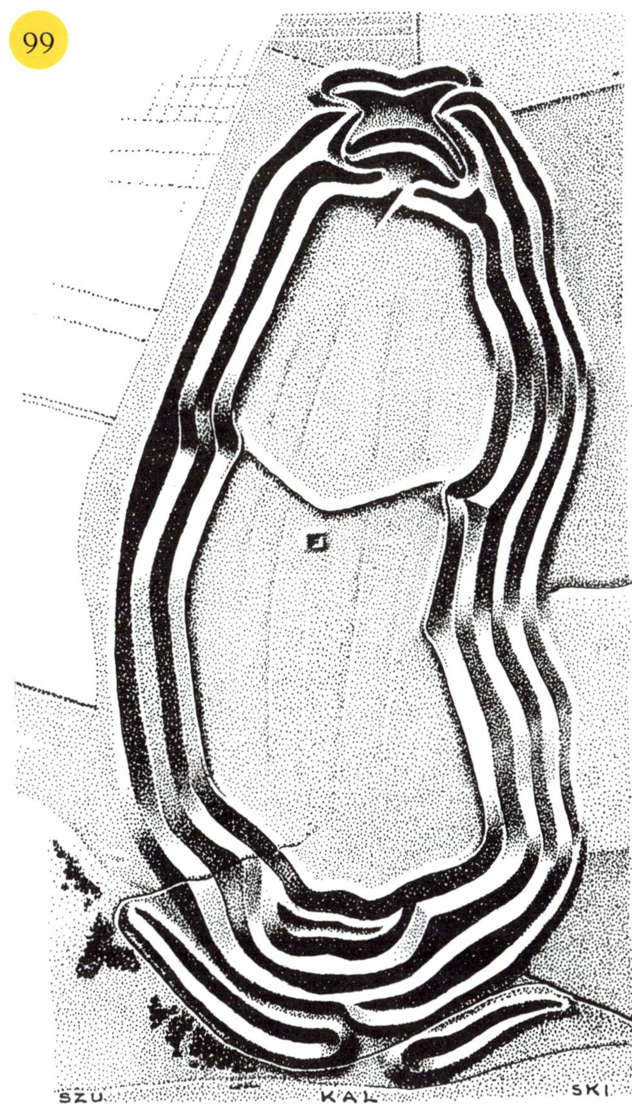

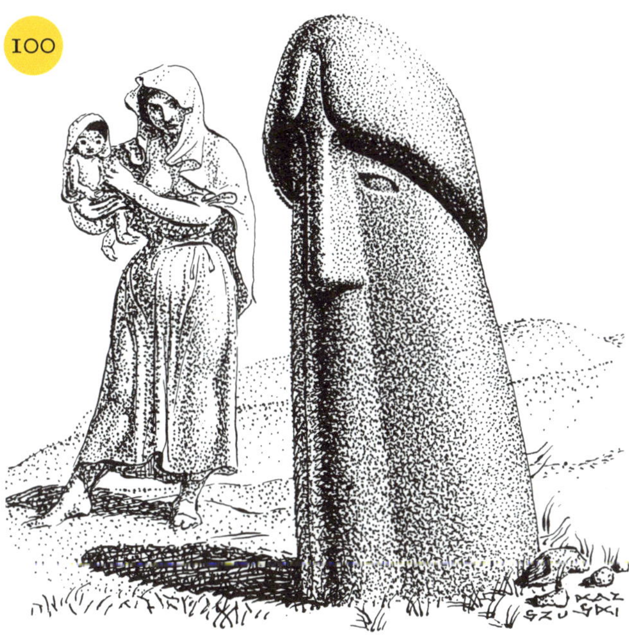

99 At the time of WW I many air photographs were taken for military purposes. From then on, after the discovery of new archaeological sites of ancient alignments and earthworks, special assignments were given to aviators to make photographs of terrains with specific meaning which from the ground could not have been recognized.

One of such photographs was taken in England to probe a small ruin, called the **MAIDEN'S CASTLE**. We see that the earthwork was raised in the shape of a gigantic phallus that is bent midway, surely meaning "killed." By what? By the Twin Flood Serpents that creep along its sides toward its head. Just above the phallus, between the Serpents' heads biting into it, is a pictographic device consisting of Coalesced Twin Triangles, which depicts the Father and Motherland in the Atlantic and Pacific. (If these triangles were slightly more coalesced, we would have the Star of David of the Hebrews. I have a separate scientific volume on the significance of triangles, angles and the Scottish "Z's.")

100 One of numerous **PHALLIC IMAGES**, symbol of "The Fathers' He" or "Oce On." He is mouthless, therefore breathless, dead. From Chichen Itza (Maya).

101 An Egyptian hieroglyph standing for *sem*, which is the softened form of Protong "Zem" (land), hence representing "Fatherland."

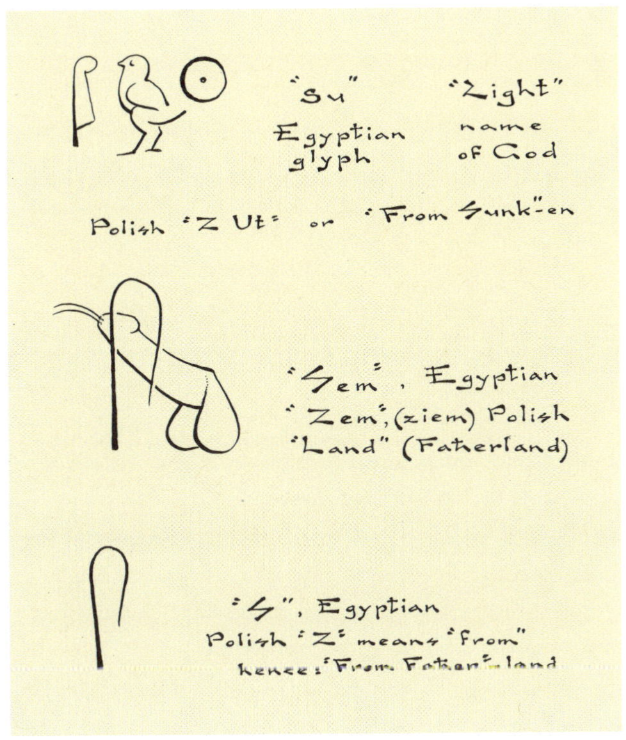

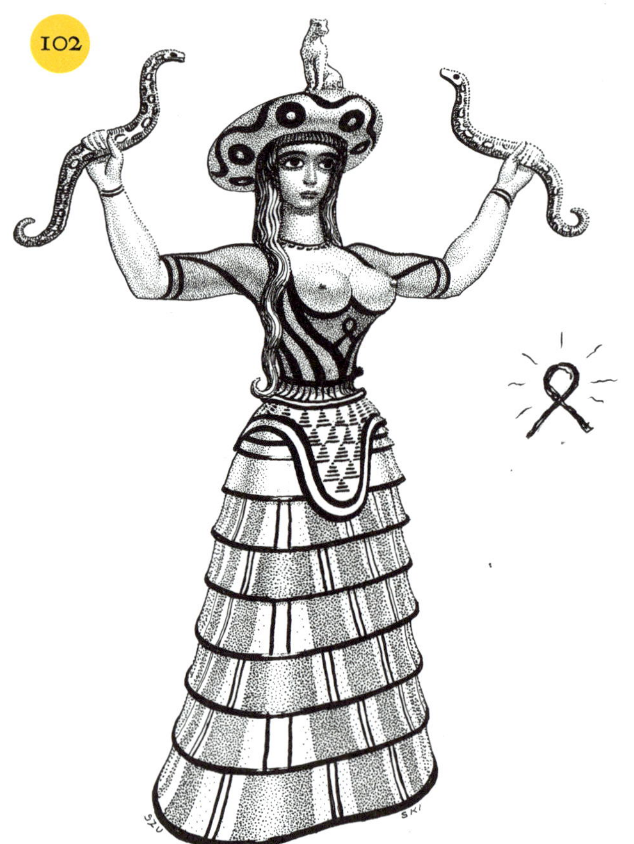

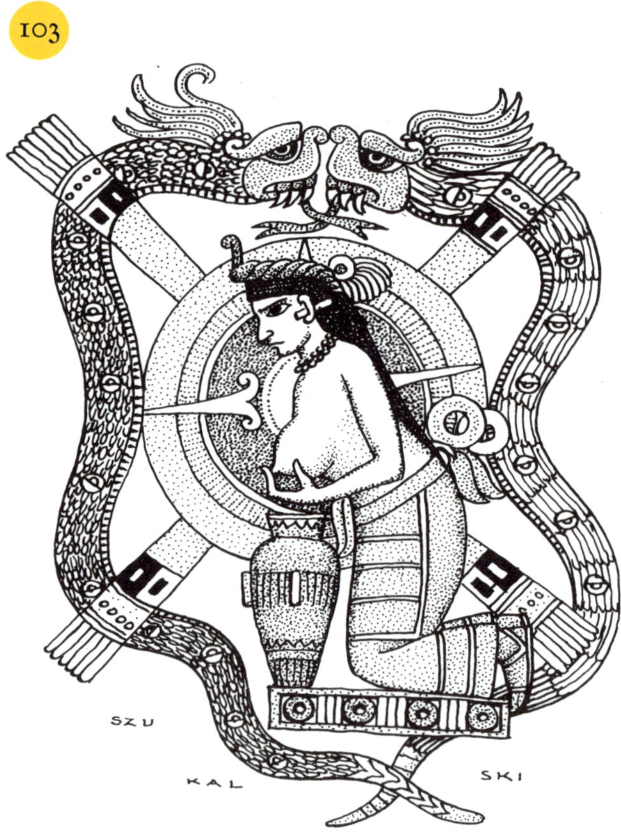

102 At Knossos, Crete, this world-famous figurine was excavated. She is holding the Twin Ocean Serpents of Flood. Her exposed breasts or Polish *piersi* serve as rebus for Protong "Bier Zi," which means that she is another personification of the "Taken Land," Easter Island.

At the beginning of this chapter I spoke of the Great Lioness as the totemic coat of arms of Easter Island. Well, right atop the great *Bi* on her head squats the Great Lioness! Just below her breasts the pictograph of an island was placed, which is Mata Weri or the "Mother of Worship," for the solar disc rises from its top.

Her apron consists of the Horizon Jar (Sagging Horizon) within which the many islands were placed that were deluged by the migrating oceanic waters.

On the large *Bi* the wavy water line was painted and just beneath it there are ten smaller *Bis*, representing the "killed" landmasses.

The name *Knossos* (where this delightful image was excavated) is no co-incidence. When re-segmented, the now mute name reveals that it was originally a Protong description. "K Nos Z Os" means "Towards (Crete) Carried from the Last" (of the submerging isles).

103 The Goddess **COATLICUE**, while under the seas of the Twin Flood Serpents, is about to release the milk from her breast as to bring life into the Horizon Jar of the deluged world. She kneels on a pictographic bar with four *Bis*, in between which vertical bars of water were placed denoting the "pouring" of floodwaters. Most commonly, she is shown as a skeletal personage (dead) with Lioness's feet.

104 In Tarzana, California, I had a neighbor, an old Ukrainian Jew who, to assist me in my research, posed for me with his **TWILUM** on his bare left arm, which is the ancient ceremonial observed in prayer.

The name *Twilum* derives from the Protong phrase "Twe L Um," meaning "Your F(lood) Memory." The narrow strap and the little box that is placed in the armpit are made of goatskin, usually lacquered black. It is hand-wrapped end tapers off like the Serpent tail, for indeed, the whole contraption emulates that pictograph of Flood. The reason why the little box is placed in the armpit is that it represents the Serpent's head: it is held so as to stifle the life out of it, while the tail squirms, twisting itself around the arm of the faithful descendant of Noah who survived the Great Flood. For that reason the devise is still called Twilum.

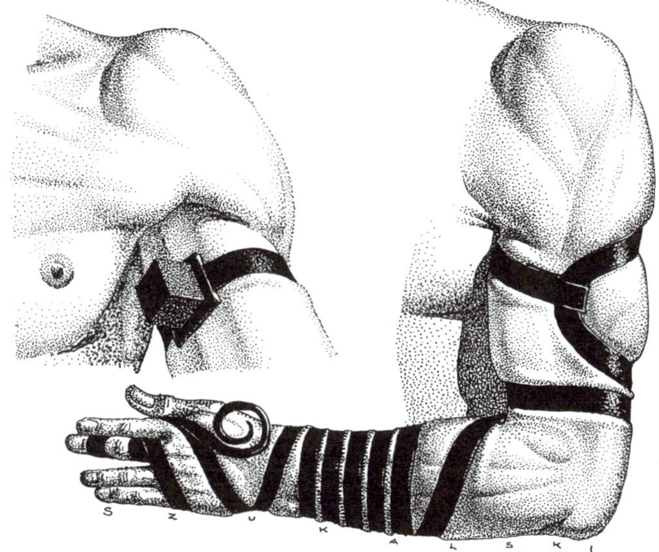

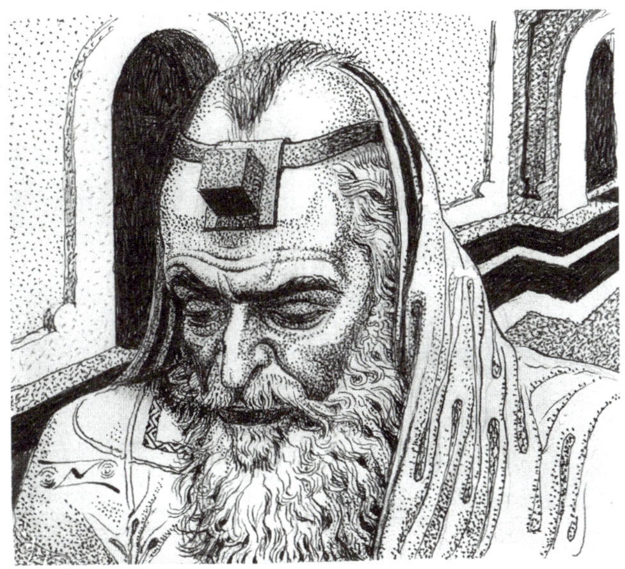

105 There is another kind of goatskin **TWILUM**. This is placed high on the forehead. Inside the little box a narrow ribbon of paper is secreted on which is written the most sacred prayer of the ancient Hebrews and the modern Jews. The prayer is called *Krishma* which evolved from the Protong phrase "Kry Zma" (modern Polish *Kryta Ziemia*), thus referring to the "Covered Land." Here it is:

Shema Isroel Alekienu Shema Ado, Shemehod

When re-segmented to its original Protong, the prayer consists of the three lines each beginning with the word "Ziema":

Ziema Jes Ro (J)e L(a),   "Land (that) Is Birthgiver, Flooded,
(J)a Le Kie Nu,   I (was) Flooded Where Born,
Ziema Ja Do,   Land I Given (by),
Ziem Je Hod!   Land (that) Is Gone!"

           Whatever meaning the modern Jews were told these words convey, it is incorrect.

106 In Spiro Mound, Oklahoma, this one of many marvelous engravings on seashell was excavated. It represents the four-faced **GOD OF DAWN** (the same as the Polish prehistoric "Swiat Owid"), seen from an angle that allows only two faces to be seen. Tears are running down his cheeks in grief for his deluged Parentlands. He is grasping the Twin Ocean Serpents so powerfully that both regurgitate the swallowed Twin-Triangle Continents, the smaller one being the Pacific because there are three gushes for the

three component land masses, the larger one being the Atlantic because it is slashed seven times. He sticks out his *inziki* (Polish for "tongues"), which rebus stands for "Land Towards Else(where)," i.e. the Netherworld where the Parents presently are.

He is the same one as **WIRAKOCHA** of Lake Titicaca, Bolivia (117).

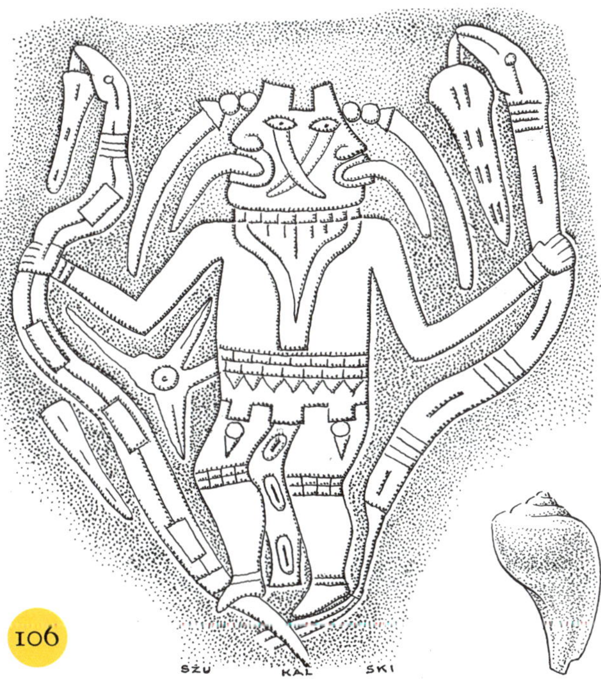

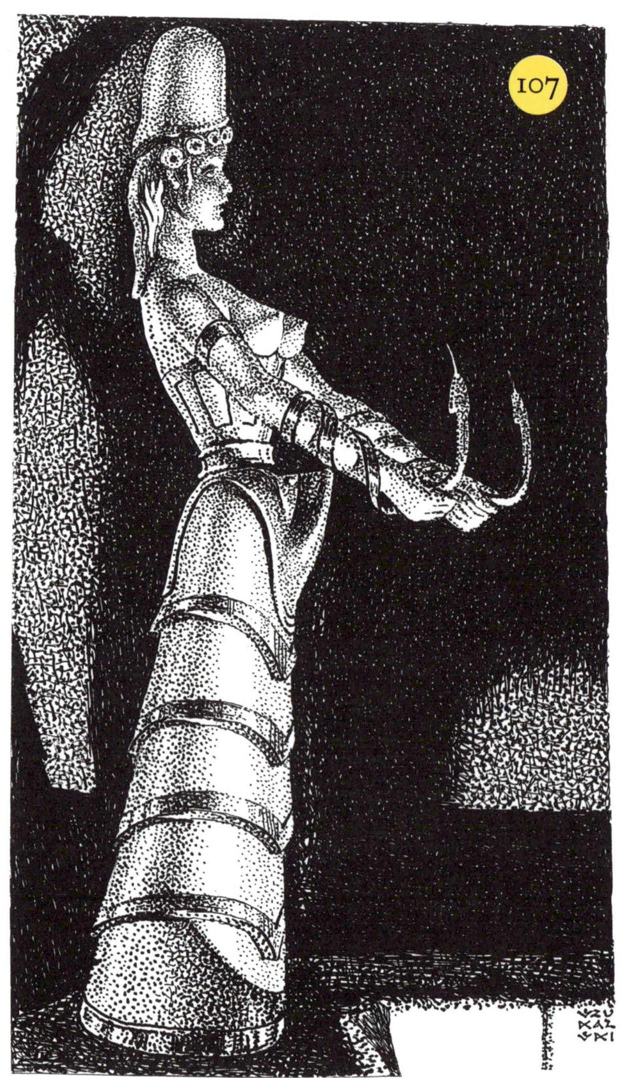

Another image of a Cretan **MOTHER OF THE DAWN**, with her island atop her head. Across her forehead from ear to ear the historian-sculptor placed a number of *Bis*, the perforated discs, for the number of islands "killed" by the Great Deluge. She holds at a distance the two Flood Serpents while their bodies, like the Hebrew Twilum, wind around her arms. This is a Wishful Magic sculpture, suggesting through the artist that this is what the Mother of Dawn should do to free herself from the deluging oceans. Each Serpent represents one of the two oceans that concerned our mutual ancestors.

Cretan Art always portrays the Dawn Mother as bare-breasted for rebusal purposes, since *piersi* (Polish for "breasts") indicates that she is the "Taken Land." On her abdomen she has an apron-like device to aid her in her terminal state of pregnancy with the daily Dawn, her hoped-for Saviour.

108 An Egyptian relief showing God **RA** (Morn) turned left, therefore still under the sea, before he emerges as the Dawn. Look! Instead of a human head he has the Solar Disc about to emerge from the bottom of the Horizon Jar, at the rim of which the sculptor placed two Ibis heads. Why that bird? Because "J(e) Bi Z" means that he "Is Killed (Mother) From." Like Jesus, who "Is From mortally-Asleep," and like Zeus, who came from "Land mortally-Asleep." For the daily journey, he has a cane stuck in his belt leaving his hands free for the grasping of the Flood Serpents in order to save the world.

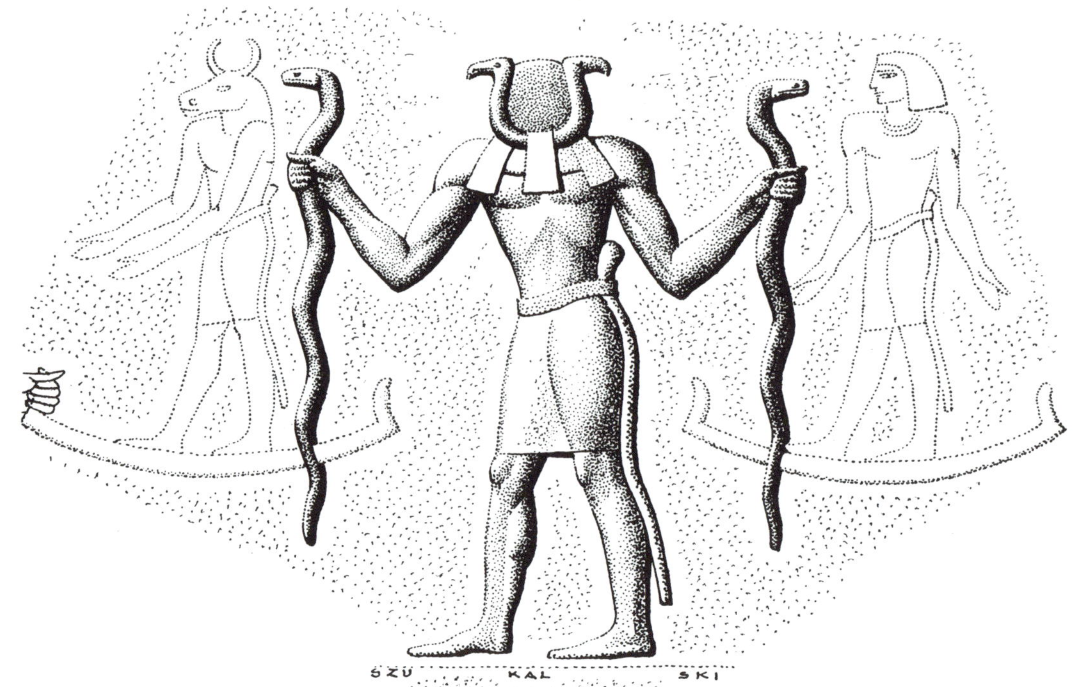

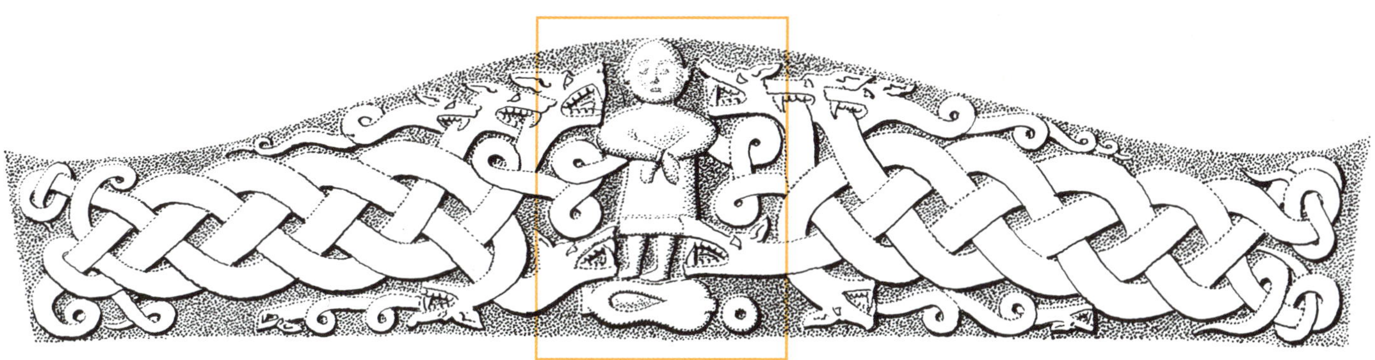

This dazzling relief is from a famed throne of the ancient Scandinavian people. Here we see **MOTHER FREYA** ("Wre Ja" or "Worship I"), bald-headed, breastless, and being arrested by the whirling currents of the deluging seas. On each side of her the historian-sculptor placed five Flood Serpents for the ten component lavaic landmasses of the Parentlands. Her head and feet are turned left, again meaning that she is under the seas. Beneath her feet is placed a lyre that plainly emulates the Mother's *pizda* (Polish for "cunt"). At that time, the ancients had no other word for what our grandparents later termed "vulva" or "vagina." The rebusal usage of *pizda* ("Bi Z Da") is to tell us that this is the "Killed (Mother) From Given." Note again the *Bi* (disc with hole) to the right of the lyre.

THE style of each "good" artist reveals his degree of vitality. English Art is "pale," for where nations produce Anglosex variants, there is a lack of sexual drive. Hence English Art is the tail end of European contributions to world culture. Centuries back, England produced primitive Art with vitality.

The reason that my works are complex, involved, always "busy-busy" where every place is filled with some intended element, is because I have always had indescribable vitality and forever spend my energy without apparent exhaustion. This relief, as is all Scandinavian Art, is also "busy" as if on a skewer, because the Scandinavian people possess tremendous vitality. The very fact that this drawing, like all the others, was drawn by me with a fine point pen with every minuscule dot placed in proper position, attests to the extraordinary energy I have. Energy like mine is symptomatic of inexhaustable sexual drive and it is due to this astounding endowment that man can be creative (as in my case, in many fields). If my environment was richer spiritually, I would have had proper economic circumstances in which to create. But as things are in America, I have had to spend my last fifty years away from sculpture for I cannot afford to be more creative.

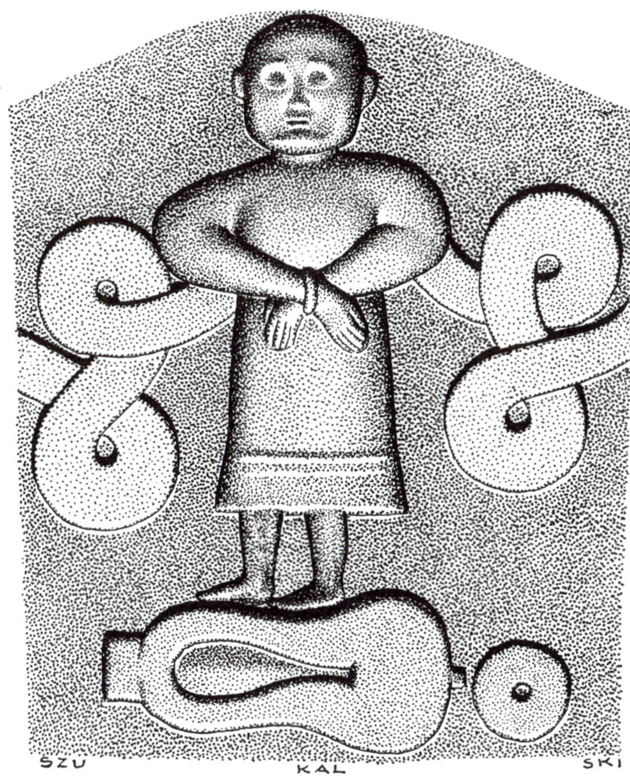

The reason for me not giving my age here is because that in this shallow-minded Anglomerican environment, anyone over forty is to be dumped into the trash bin, just at the stage of life when a professional person BEGINS to do his best work. Thus, while in Russia women are made to take on men's work… and men still heavier workloads to make greater potential force, America is diminished because of the subversive rule that the Best should be… dismissed. I am not surprised that the Anglomerican society is so easily manipulated by the Enemies of Humanity. This is a non-Historic nation, for it has never had National Calamities, as Poland has had, to learn from experience and become WISE… historically and culturally. I have been reduced to dispensibility by a race molded by so dominant the Anglosex variants.

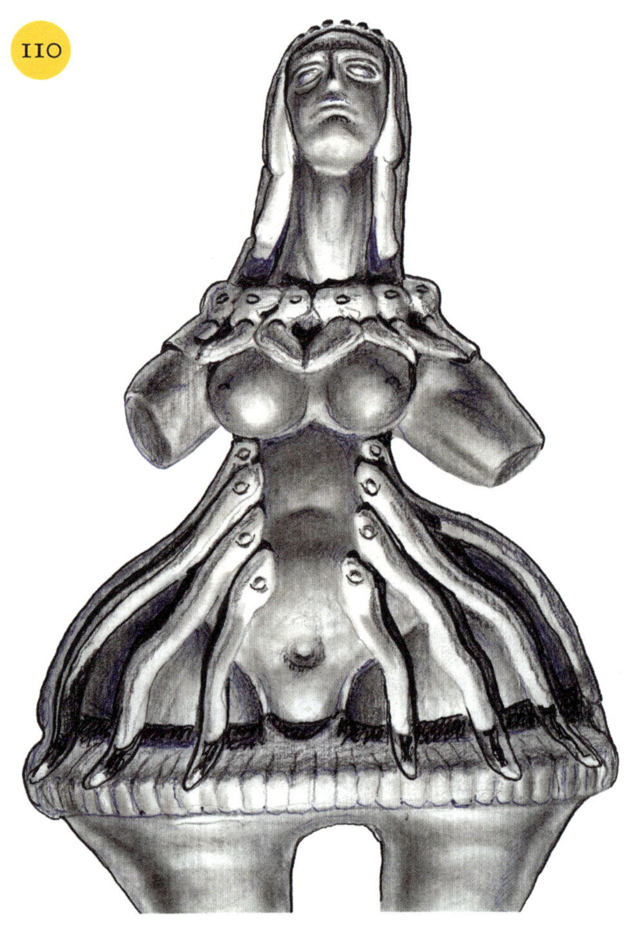

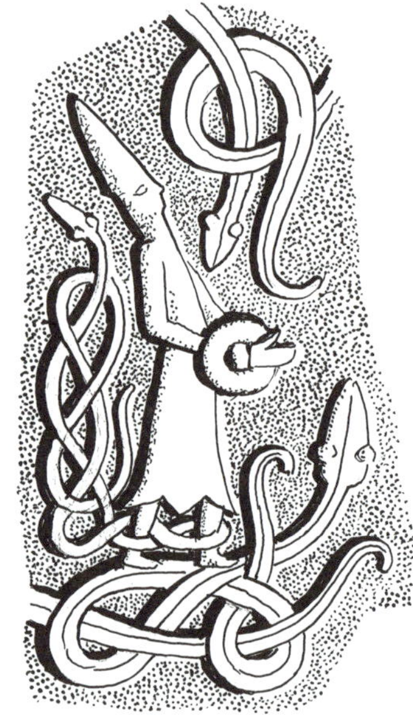

III   On Jutland, Denmark, in the ancient church of St. Andrew, is this fragment within a larger composition, where the Island-headed breastless **MOTHER** walks to the right in order to meet her Saviour who, after she settled in the seas (Serpents tangling around her legs), guards over her. Her wrists are entrapped in a large *Bi*, illustrating her diluvial "killing."

110   From the Maurya period of India, third century B.C., comes this **DAWN'S MOTHER** figure to be my witness. She is (geographically) vast-hipped and beset by eight Flood Serpents creeping up towards her head, in order to drown her. Above her shoulders are numerous small Serpents that together overtake her breasts, depicting "Taken Land." The arms were intentionally incomplete, to let us know that she is "helpless" and must submit to the Deluge. At the level of her vulva was molded the ocean floor for the reptiles to lean their tails on to climb even higher. Her exceptionally long *szyja* (Polish for "neck") is a rebus for "Zi Ja" or "Land I (am)." Very likely, she was excavated near the museum where she is presently cherished. The locality is named Mathura, which anciently was Protong "Mat Gura," meaning "Mother Mountain." In Protong there was no word for continent or island. Therefore Mathura must be a place where she was worshipped as Easter Island.

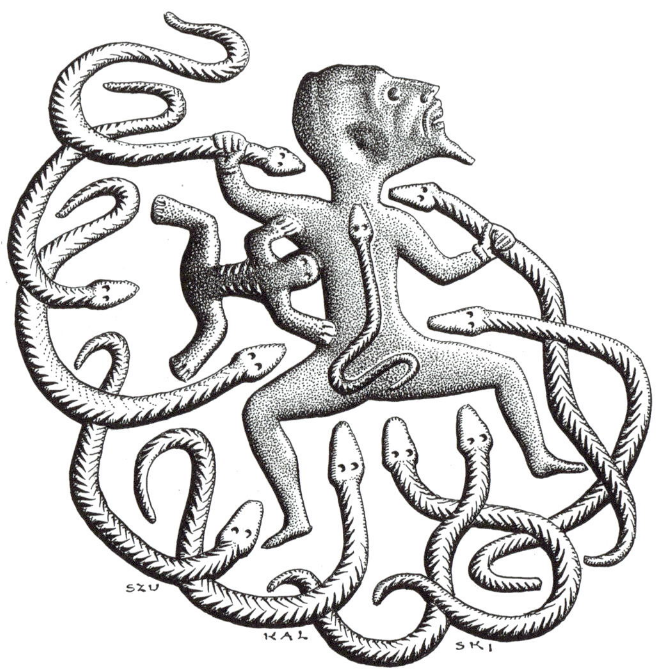

112   On an ancient sled that was buried within a Swedish ship, I spied a small fragment of a pictographic story of **OCE ON** entrapped by the Flood Serpents of the ten landmasses of both Parentlands. Oce On has already grasped at the necks of two Serpents in Wishful Magic of the compassionate sculptor, in an attempt to get away from his present submersion in the Atlantic region. At his side is one of the Twin Lion Cubs, representing the contemporary king, one of the numerous Sons of the Great Lioness. Its mouth is pressing onto the chest of Oce On in an attempt to grasp his skin, without hurting, to raise him from the ocean bottom where he is sprawled while deluged.

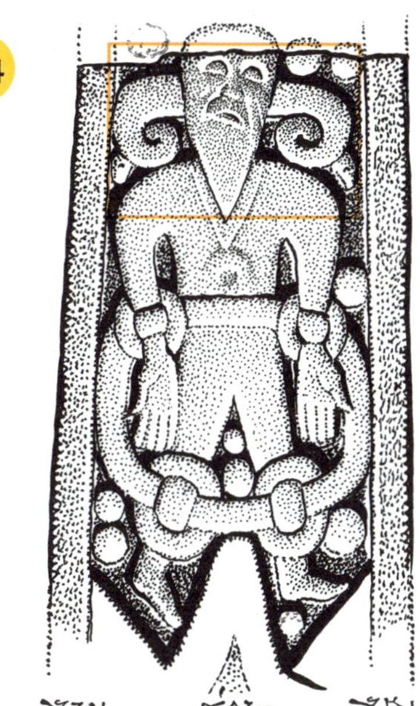

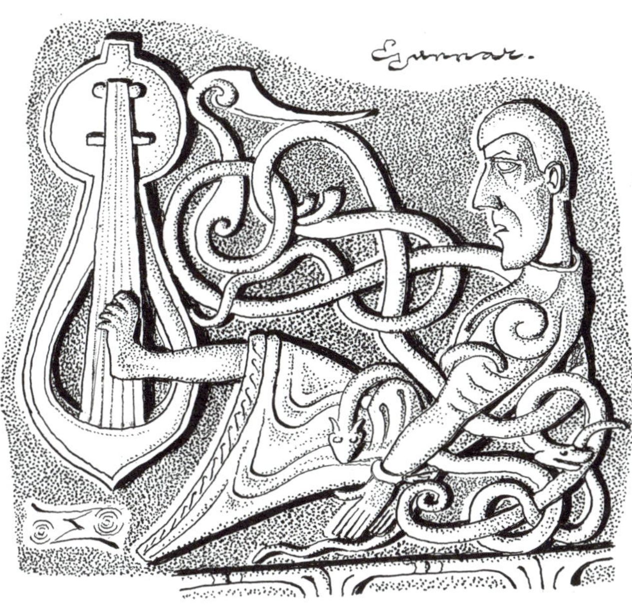

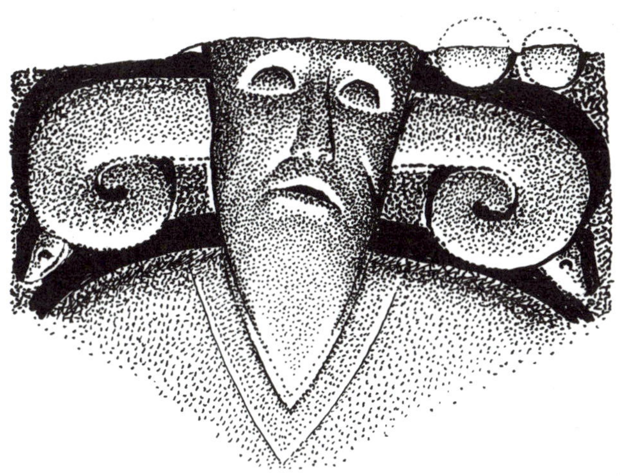

113 At the church of Hylestad, Norway, I found this relief fragment carved in wood. Hyle City (Hylestad) was earlier described in Protong "Gi Le" which means "Perished in Flood." This figure is supposed to be **GUNNAR**, who in Scandinavian mythology (as Orpheus in Greek mythology) played a lyre so exquisitely that besides all humans, all animals crowded around him to hear. For punishment, the powers that be had him decapitated and his head thrown into a great river. His head remained floating on the waves… singing. He sang so wondrously that mankind and animals… even the trees in the forests followed it to the great sea where his Mother lay deluged, helplessly awaiting his coming. His head grew back on his torso, but the Flood Serpents held his arms bound so that he could only play the lyre for his Mother… with his feet.

114 Inside an ancient church in Britain stands a monumental cross with this image carved on one of the stems. It shows **OCE ON** entrapped by five *Bis* (one pale one on his chest) while around his body are scattered nine or ten landmasses expressed in the form of balls.

A startling feature of this relief, very similar to the mask of Oce On on the Aztec **TONATIUH** (119, wrongly regarded as a calendar), is the place where our inspired sculptor placed Twin Flood Serpents.

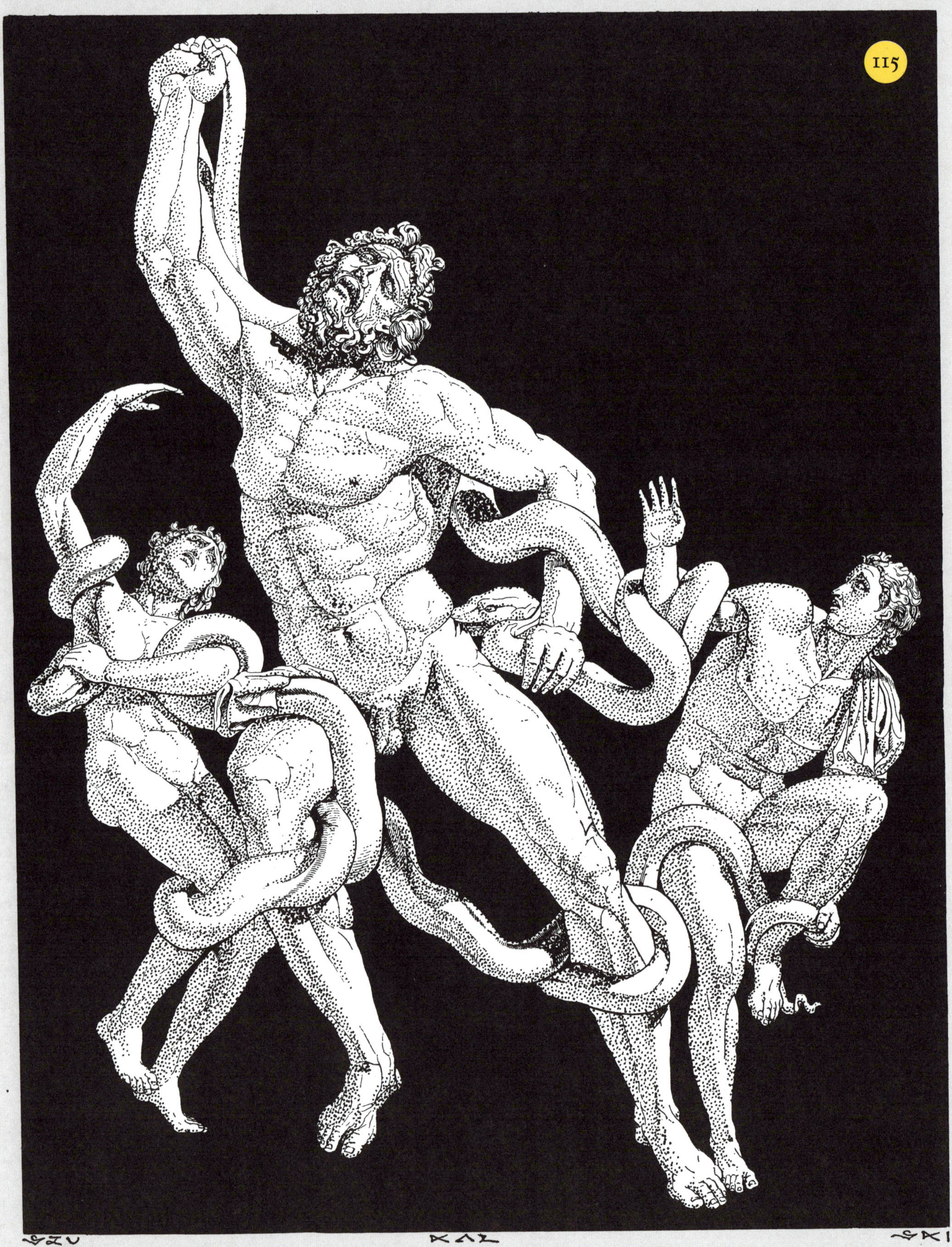

115

84]

 This world-renowned Greco-Roman sculpture of great size represents **LAOCOÖN**. At his sides are his Twin Sons (comparable to the Twin Lion Cubs) in mortal struggle with their respective Twin Flood Serpents. Each youth personifies one of the perished continents and is but a paraphrase of the better-known Lupita with the twins Romulus and Remus. The description of this is in the compound name, for "La O(n) Ko On" means "Flooded He, Love Hi(m)." He is God the Father or Je-Howa who "Is Hidden" under the deluging seas.

In the volume *The Deluged Gods* I have 335 drawings as my witnesses, each one presenting evidence, both pictographically and linguistically. All religions have been encrusted around three personalities, the Mother(land), the Father(land) and their hoped-for Saviour, the Dawn (who, when the Nearsolar Epoch comes, will actually save them from their present submersion).

■

OCE ON
("HE OF THE FATHERS")

116 This gigantic torso of **OCE ON**, found on Easter Island, is presently in the collection of the British Museum. Atop its head are two pictographic elements; the top center represents Easter Island, while the larger rim represents the ocean waters, surrounding and deluging this, at one time tallest, lavaic mountain in the Pacific. The rim is a circle with a hole in its center, therefore a *Bi*, the universal pictograph for "killed by Deluge." The armpits of the image show the Sunrise (left) and Sunset (right), while the navel forms a small *Bi* again.

Look at the "raindrops" above each Horizon Jar. This means that they were filled with the waters. And look again! What's this Diagonal Cross on the left side? This pictograph ALWAYS, whether it is found in the Sahara Desert, the Arizona Desert, or Easter Island or in Siberia, ALWAYS means "Mother."

Whatever the suggested explanations for this type of head that—though in a different period, hence in slackened obedience to established formulas for facial proportions—was so numerously carved on Easter Island, I have the definite answer.

I compiled a whole volume on Easter Island with 301 drawings of vital illustrative data. Here I merely touch upon the subject.

So what is the reason for the many identical sculptures carved in the same pattern, on Easter Island?

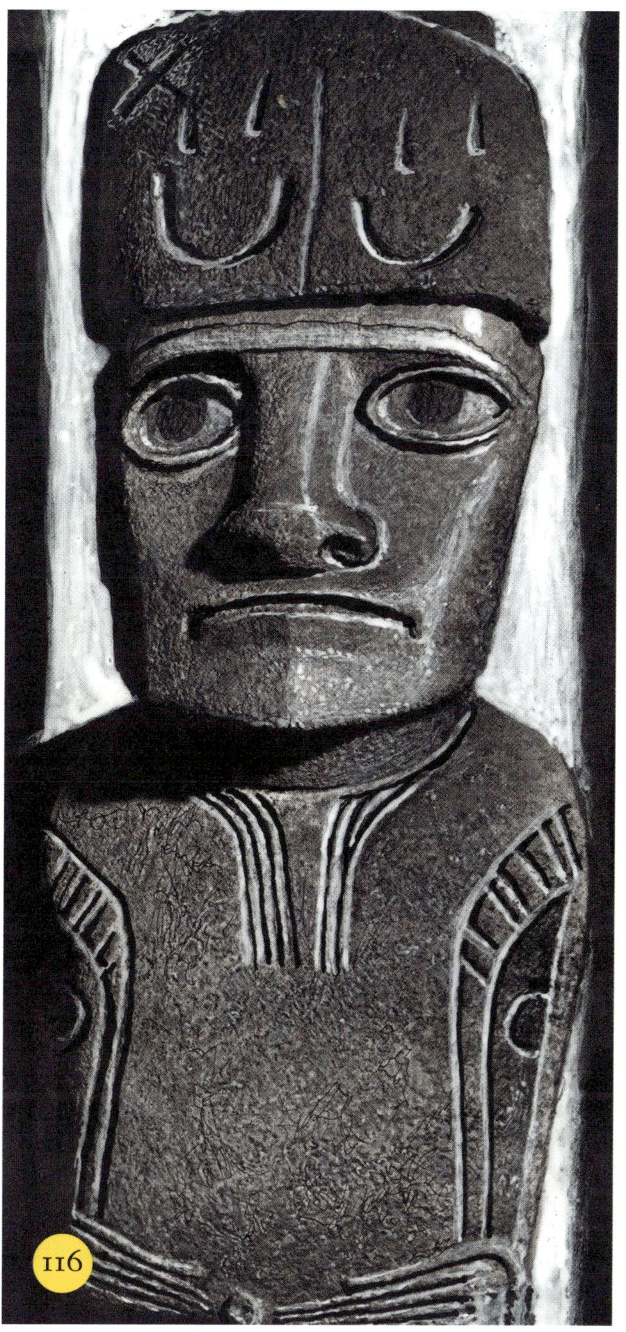

116

From the now-submerged lavaic Atlantic continent many ships sailed on pilgrimages to this island, anciently called Mata Weri, to beg her to influence her son, the Sun, to save their progressively submerging Oce On from the rising seas, which were migrating into the lavaic sections of the globe that were deflating when the solar temperature was decreasing. There were many cities, as we learn from Plato's report on the disappearance of, what he calls, Atlantis. (I, however, have not once, in re-segmenting thousands of names, come across such a name.) The pilgrims commissioned the native sculptors to carve and raise as many alike images as there were endangered isles and cities, each to face approximately in their direction.

Why did the sculptors suddenly cease to make the commissioned images? Because fewer and fewer pilgrims arrived, till all life had vanished from the surface of the Atlantic Ocean and none of the pleading cities and isles remained to seek salvation, for the Divine Sun had other than the Laws of Religion to obey, which were INTERPLANETARY. The Sun needed reimbursing of its combustive elements which were spent by then and the satellites were released from its decreasing heat-gravity and sent into the vaster interplanetary spaces to be covered with hoarfrosts in the then-ensuing Ice Ages.

■

WLRAKOCHA

To pick the 11,000 pen-drawn "witnesses" for my vast scientific work on Zermatism (*I Claim This World*), which would testify for my side of the scientific arguments, I had to become acquainted with half a million pictures in a thousand books, borrowed from various University and Public Libraries. Having been engaged in research for forty years and being an artist in a few Arts myself, I can claim I know more about Art than any ten archaeologists and Art historians. Therefore, let me say that the following relief is one of the two finest pieces of INSPIRED Art I have ever seen.

117 This relief represents the God **WIRAKOCHA**. The sculpture is, even now in this age of ostensible patronships over all antiquities, left to erosion by the Bolivian government, so that within the next ten years nothing but a lumpy slab of limestone will remain, which no one will ever care to photograph, unless it is to demonstrate the barbarity of its present caretakers.

Cultivated people in Bolivian society, who are capable

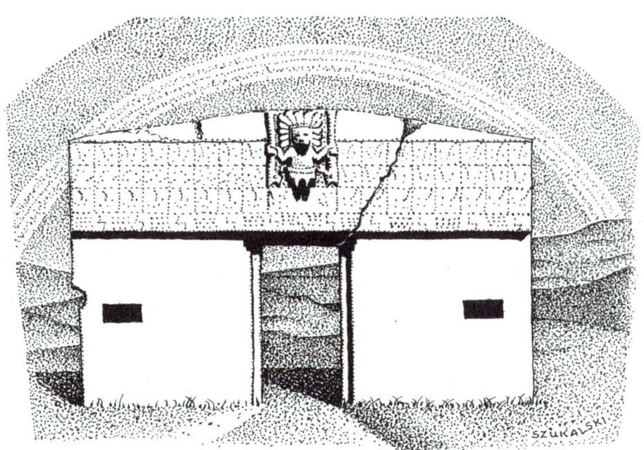

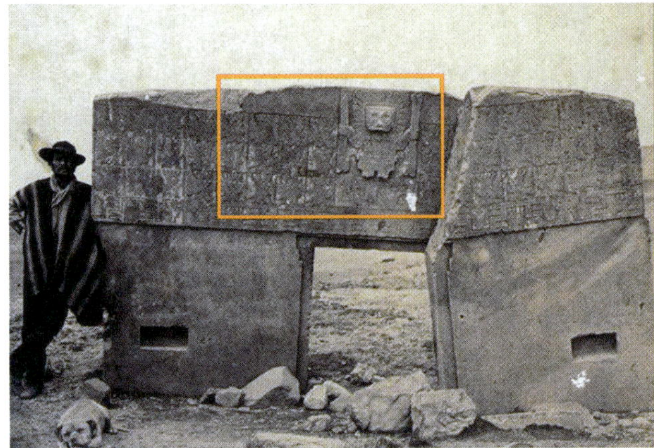

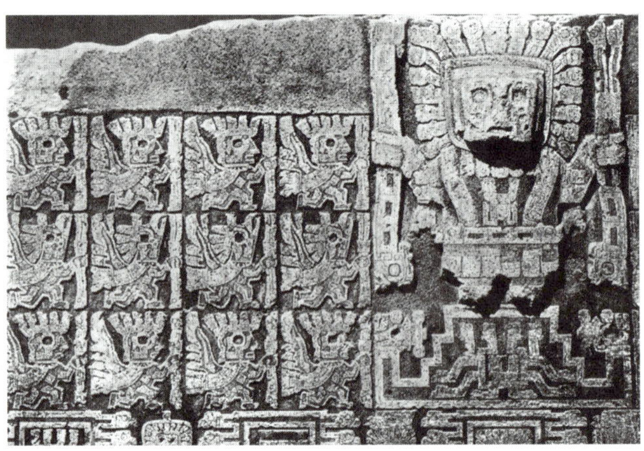

of perceiving that they have the GREATEST MASTER-PIECE in the world, should before they take another breath, erect a special building over the Gate of Dawn, on which this wonderful Wirakocha faces the Sunrise, to protect it against the terribly destructive effects of the desert temperatures—the blazing sun and contracting cold which combine to erode this creation of the greatest master sculptor of the Andes.

The name *Wirakocha* is pure Polish, even grammatically correct. It has been compounded of two words, *Wira Kocha*, which would be *Wiara Kocha* in modern speech and mean that he is "Worship Beloved." The purely dialectic difference between *Wira* and *Wiara* is astoundingly negligible, considering the fact that our annual ancestors covered thousands of years and thousands of miles after the last Ice Age impelled many of them to migrate and re-ignite European Civilizations in Iran, India, China and both Americas.

The Dawn Gate with the shining image of Wirakocha is located in a place called Akapana, on Lake Titicaca. The first name is a compounded Protong description phrase, "(J)a K Ka Ba Na," which means "I (am oriented) Towards Where White(ness is) Born."

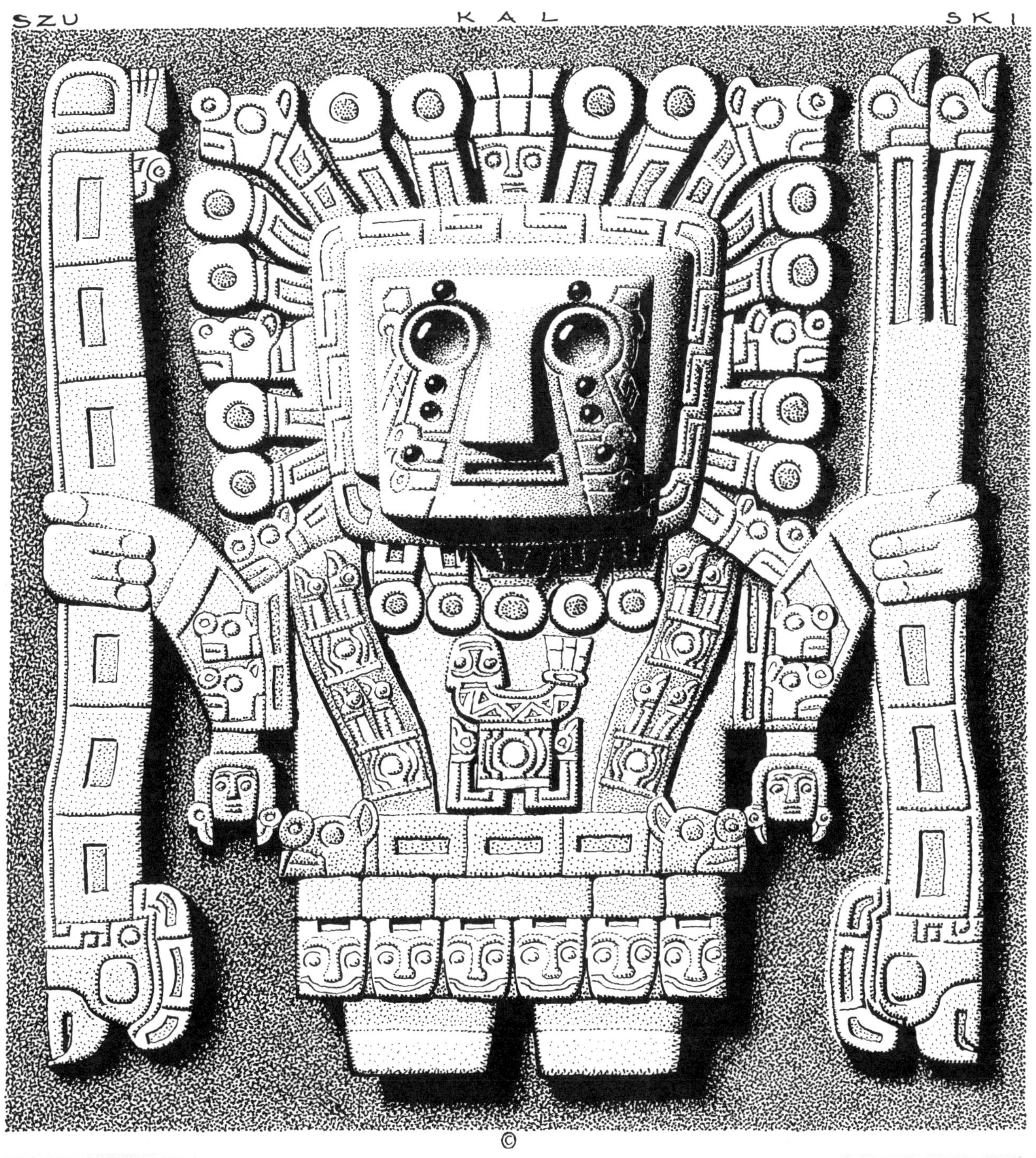

"Wira Kocha", Dawn god whom "Faith Loves", adores.
He holds (arrests) the Twin rooster-headed Flood Serpents.
Looking East, from Bolivia towards him, the left or Atlantic
Serpent is marked with 7 squared Bi-s (one hidden by hand)
and the right one or Pacific, with 3 (10 component lands).
His belt of 3 Bi-s, flanked by the heads of Lion pups, tells
of Faith's Pacific (Easter Isle) origin. 8 "tearfull" (grieved
over) holes on his face record the chronologic position of
the departure from the submerging Oce-On.

Fragment of the Dawn-gate of <u>Ak Kapana</u>.
Tiahuanako.   Bolivia.
"Ja K Ka Ba Na" (Polish). "I Towards Where White (ness) is Born".

The word "White" is used in the sense of "Daybreak." It still lives on as such in Polish, when a peasant woman wakes up her husband saying: "Get up, it is already white."

Ancient Protong did not yet use the letters "i" or "je" before vowels. Those were added later, when the need to diversify the language arose. I spelled the first word "(J)a" for readier recognition by the Poles—whose opinions you will ask in the matter of Protong—since their first personal pronoun is spelled *Ja*.

In all ancient languages there were no words like "very" or "ultimate." If superlatives were desired, words would be repeated: many, many or big, big. A Polish peasant who is not civilized, may say: "Let the Lord be praised," to another peasant traveling in the opposite direction, and the other will answer: "For century of centuries," meaning "eternally." So the translation of the name Titicaca is "You You! Where Where!" which is an address to God personally and intimately, where He is reflected, as seen from the northern shore of the lake, facing east, in the same direction towards which the Dawn Gate with the God Wirakocha was placed.

In his three-fingered hands Wirakocha holds the Twin Flood Serpents with condor heads, heads down, which means that he has already vanquished them. The fact that Inca Gods have only three fingers to each hand hints at the resemblance to a BIRD, which is a universal pictograph of flight Migration.

The Deluge occurred when the global waters poured into the newly created abyssi, due to the lower temperatures of the Sun during the Farsolar Epoch, when the ocean bottoms were being deflated of volcanic gasses and the Ice Age took possession of our globe. In his right hand Wirakocha holds the Atlantic Ocean Flood. How do I know it is the Atlantic? Because I have learned from innumerable archaeological "witnesses" that there were three lavaic landmasses in the Pacific, while in the Atlantic there were seven. The oblong shapes on the body of the first Serpent, including the seventh hidden by the hand, represent the Atlantic Flooded areas. The left hand holds the Pacific Flood Serpent with three oblongs.

Wirakocha's eyes were not hollow, but consisted of green-blue obsidian balls, which were held in place by coral resin. Above and below the eyes are eight perforations, in which transparent obsidian balls were inlaid so to imitate air bubbles, for the God, representing the Sun, is hot. The air bubbles glide down his burning face, while he is re-emerging from under the sea, after being reborn by Mata Weri (Easter Island).

Let me point out a real miracle in this masterpiece. Have you ever seen a more erroneous notion of the proportions of the human body? Yet, if the knowledge of academically learned facts is supposed to enhance the work of an artist, his ignorance did not impede this inspired sculptor who, totally unaware of proportions, created the most awesome masterpiece a human ever created. He was heroically bold to tackle to convey in sculpture so foreboding a subject. Yet it came out victoriously eloquent! His was a triumph equal to a mute's singing of an inspired hymn to God.

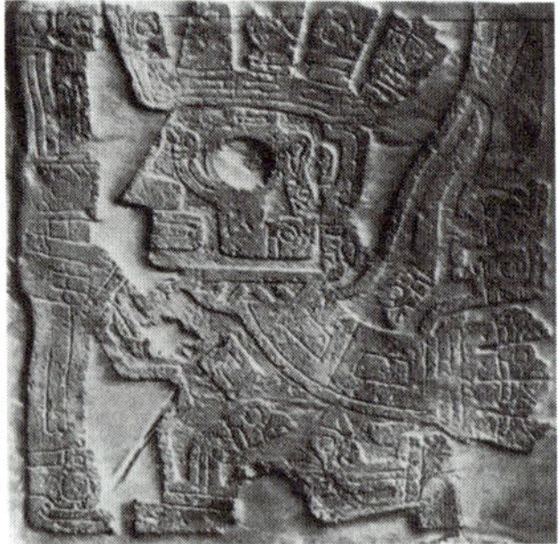

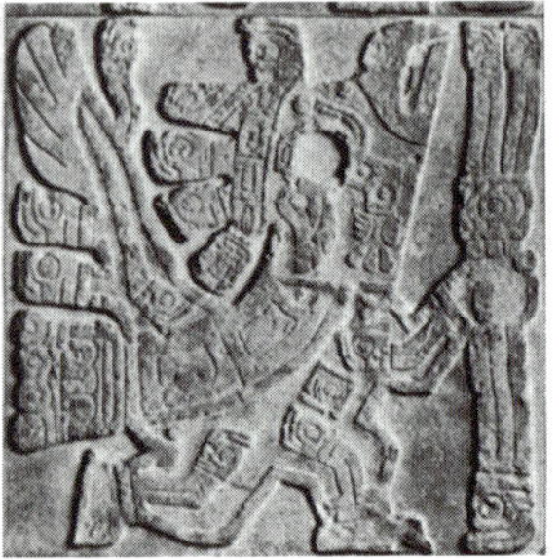

118 Below Wirakocha are three rows of smaller figures: one of crowned **KINGS**, two of **PRIESTS**, whose pictograph was the Eagle, hence this eagle-headed presentation. The figures are turned towards Wirakocha in the center, each of them holding his particular Flood Serpent. They are the refugees of the Deluge who run towards him in gratitude for being saved. Both the Kings and the Priests have wings, denoting their flight-Migration from the submerging Motherland, which was that gigantic lavaic mountain in the Pacific that was called Mata Weri.

Although the sculptures of the Kings and the Priestly Eagles are much smaller than the central relief of Wirakocha, I made all three drawings the same size, so that they be easier studied.

Please note that here too the reason for their flight, the Serpents of Flood, are shown heads down. Note also that the feet of the Priests are those of the Eagle, with long claws, while those of the Kings are dressed in moccasins.

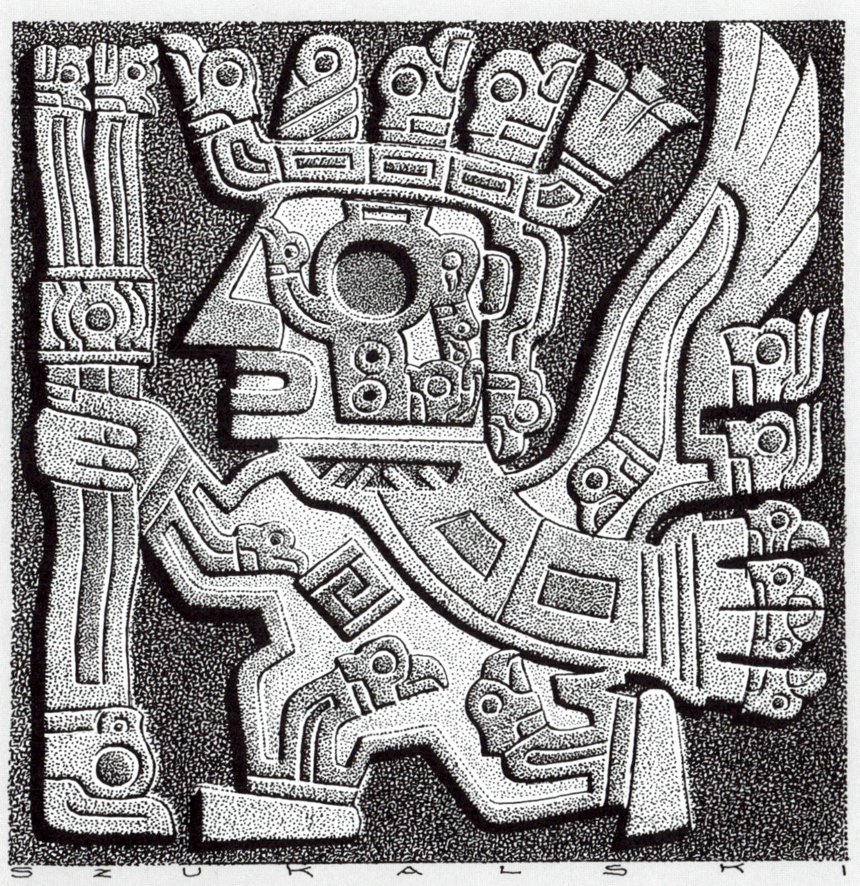

SZUKALSKI

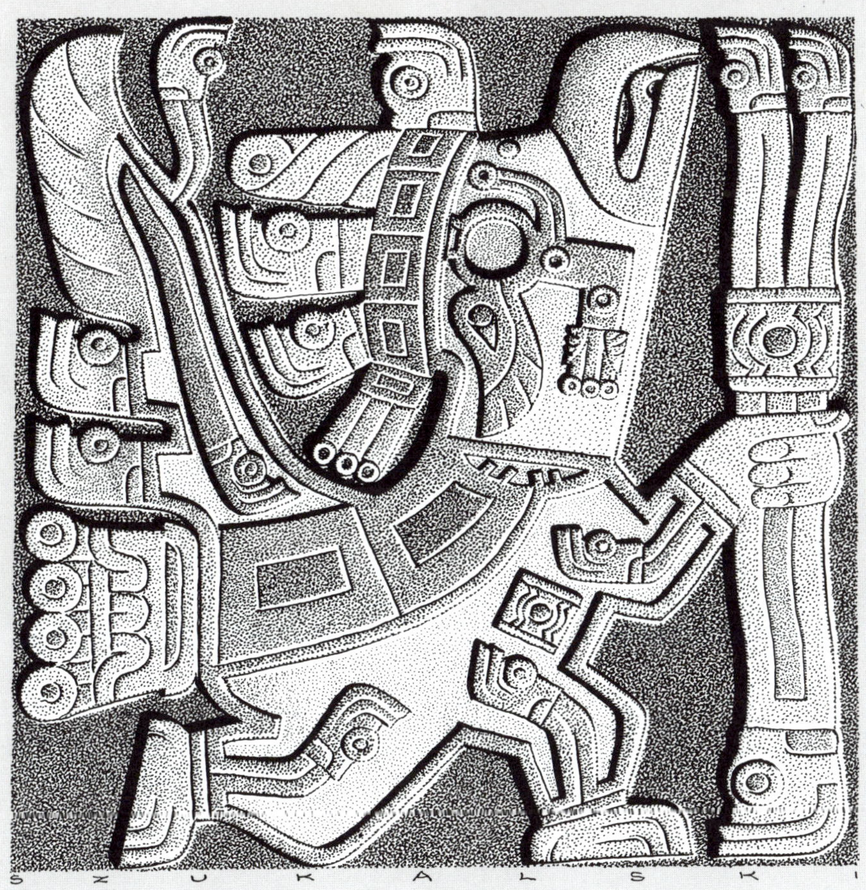

SZUKALSKI

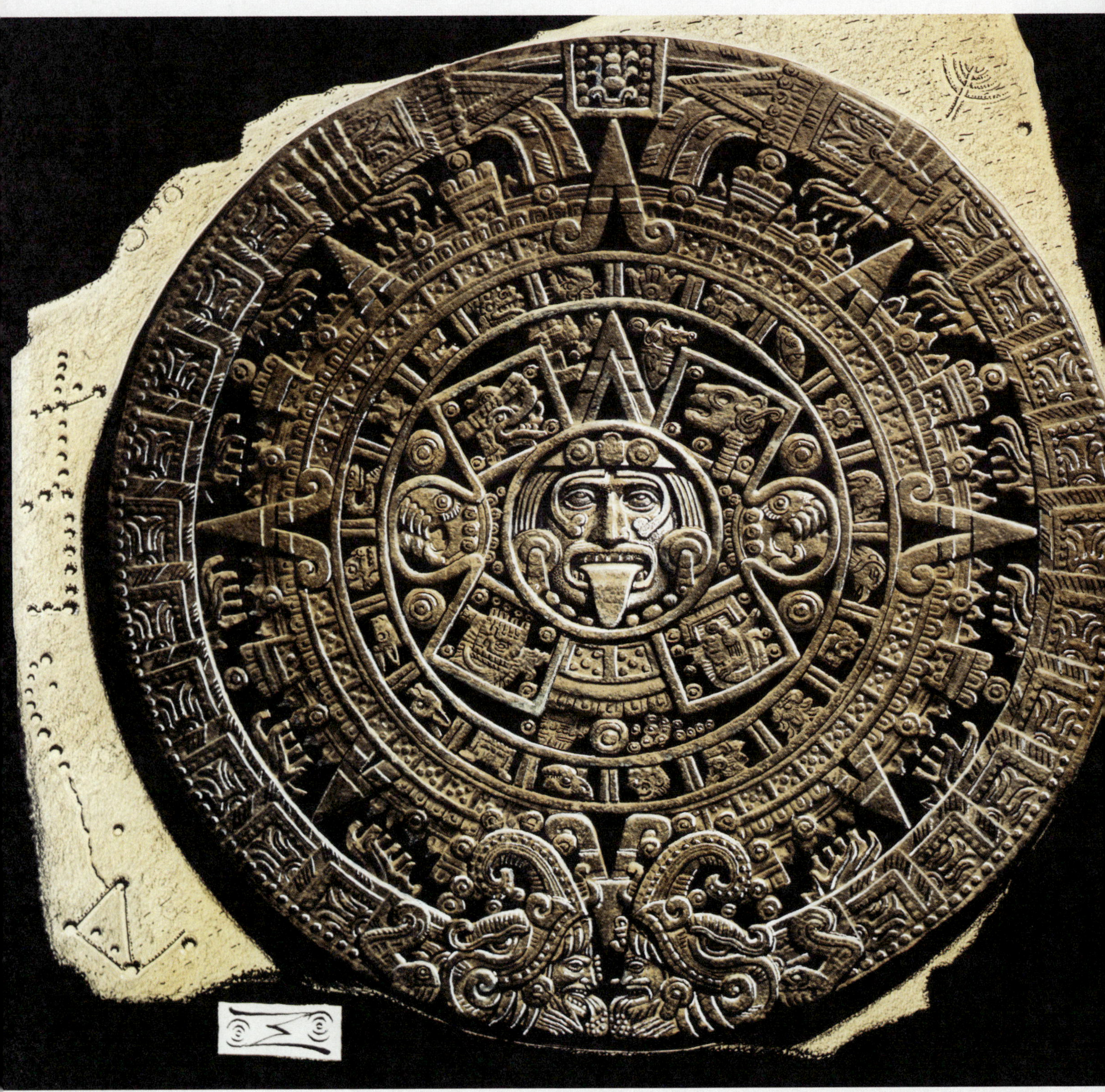

TONATIUH
("Aztec calendar")

119 Ever since the discovery of the so-called "Aztec Calendar," a gigantic monolithic carving, a psychological block has been imposed that prevented the actual analysis of this monumental masterpiece of Art. As usual, the educated became the victims of a once proclaimed opinion, never daring to analyze mystifying subjects and their meanings, taking for granted that this is the explanation, since the first archaeologist printed such a notion.

Indeed, the twenty calendrical glyphs running around the mask in the center, could be indicatory of the nature of the general intent, but the Aztecs were well versed in astronomy and the mere enumeration of twenty months does not mean that a calendric scheme was illustrated on such a colossal scale.

The clue to the significance of this remarkable carving I find in its now meaningless name, inherited from countless generations back and unalterably remembered as TONATIUH.

The presence of a "name" again blocked further investigation. People took it as a part of the mysterious language, as they took the name of the Greek Zeus, not knowing that it was made of two miniwords, "Ze Us," that mean: "(From) Land mortally-Asleep." They did not, because I had not yet made known my discovery of the oldest language on earth, Protong.

In Protong any declension of the verb "sink" is covered by the mini-words "ton" and "tun." Wherever you meet the sound "to" or "ton," in whichever part of the name, no matter on which continent, it ALWAYS means "sink, sunken, sinking" (we never can tell what declension to award any Protong word, since there was no grammar yet). For example, even the name *Washington*, coming from ancient Britain, was made of the description "Wa Z In G Ton," meaning "Worship From Elsewhere P(erished by) Sinking." This obviously was the name of a community dedicated to the Worship of Dawn.

In *Tonatiuh* "to" is a vestige of "ton." "Na" means either "make born, birthgiver" or "birthgiving" (but it is not "born" which would be "ro"). "Uh" (Polish *ucho*, pron. "ooho") is the word for "ear," but also, since Protong is an ancient, primitive language, it, in this case, stands for "hear" or "listen." Therefore: "To Na Ti Uh" means "(To the) Sinking's Birthgiving You Listen (Harken)."

In other words: listen to the underground rumblings; listen for earthquakes! This is a COMMAND to the people of Mexico to be constantly alert, every minute, every day (hence the calendric litany of the 20 months' glyphic signs), for if the volcanic terrain of Mexico begins to sink, they must do something to save themselves from repeated drowning, for the aboriginal people of Mexico too hailed from Easter Island.

That explains why they chose to compound the name Mexico, for "Me Zi Ko" (all x's were z's anciently) means "We (Mother-) Land Love."

From the name Mexico we learn why it was dedicated to the worship of the Goddess Coatlicue, the lioness-footed, skull-headed (i.e. dead) and serpent-skirted (i.e. flooded). She was the personification of now deluged Easter Island, the Mother of Worship. The name, given her by the Nahua-Aztecs, evolved from the description, "Ko, Wad Li Gle" ("Loved-one, Water Flood Destroyed").

Thus from now meaningless "names" we can learn the true meaning of ALL Aztec, Maya and Inca Gods, and furthermore those of ancient Sumeria, Egypt, India, Israel, Scandinavia, the Americas, Britain, Australia. Though the Protong Glossary is enclosed and you could do your own translations, you actually would have to know the Polish language for a readier guess at possible grammatical declensions.

Aside from this new approach to names, I developed the new science of PICTO-GRAPHY. Though the term "pictograph" has been used for the last few generations, there is actually no such science, so that a most learned archaeologist is no less ignorant in this matter than an average baseball howler. Yet, all writing of every Civilization has come down from crude pictographs. So I have spent forty years on the task of creating the new science of Pictography. I produced a small booklet with a function similar to that of a dictionary, called *Altheris of Pictography*. Wherever I go in the desert and come across petroglyphs, I can "transliterate" them all but the ones that are of mnemonic nature, hence without logic (an example: when a triangle would represent your family and a square mine).

If you have seen reproductions of this miraculous relief before (one of a few that I think are the most magnificent of all Art) and always thought that the composition was encircled by two parenthesis-shaped Great Serpents, you were wrong. If you look again very carefully, you'll see the not readily noticeable FORELEGS close to their heads. These forelegs are bent, which means that they are inactive.

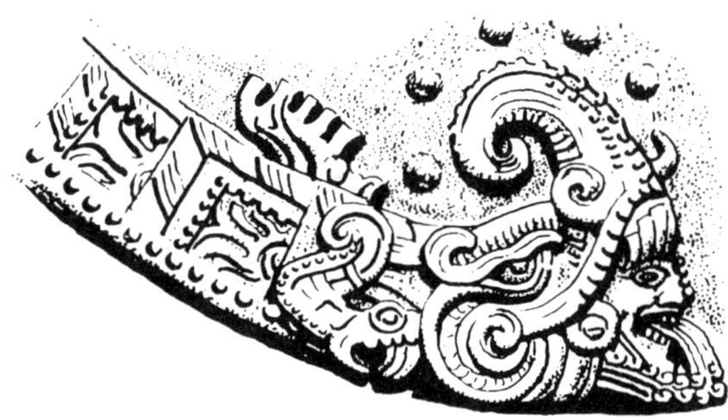

To be doing their "thing," they would have to have them straight, so their bodies would be raised. These are the Dragons, the pictographic personifications of GEOLOGIC UPHEAVALS. Their inactivity indicates that Mexico is in a permanent state, that presently there is neither upheaval nor sinking of its terrains. Dragons need not have four legs in pictography, since only the forelegs are necessary to do their lizardous calisthenics of raising and dropping the bodies.

Note that all along their spines are "tufts" of splashing, exploding LAVA. From their nuzzles sprout the upcurling tentacles of the Octopus to entrap human victims. Therefore, in their open jowls you see two personages about to be swallowed.

Who are they? I will answer that question obliquely. Each reptile was given the shape of a gigantic parenthesis. These half-circles are the Horizon Jars (Sagging Horizons). Each Dragon represents the other half of the global surface that, by sagging, forced the global waters to migrate to new abyssi, thus forming the Pacific and Atlantic Oceans. So now we know that these two people are the personifications of Easter Island (the Mother of Worship) in the Pacific and Oce On (The Fathers' He) in the Atlantic.

That there is no indication in the faces as to which one is man and which one woman, is due to the fact that the Aztecs did not know how to make a woman's face different from that of a male. They never conveyed Tenderness or Love, hence knew not femininity or gentility.

At the very top, between the tailtips, you see another glyph with three Horizon Jars, piled up on top of each other, with a nodule on the bottom of each. These represent the three component lavaic landmasses of the deluged Motherland in the Pacific that sagged.

The most noticeable subject of the whole sculpture, however, is the Tongue. Neither you nor the millions of learned archaeologists can know what the reason is for this Tongue, though there are primitive societies where people still greet each other this way, but this is a different case.

I have one scientific volume on Medusa, Gargoyle, Gorgon of ancient Greece and Etruria, as well as on Humbaba of Babylon, all of whom stick out their tongues, all for the same rebusal reason.

Inzyk (Polish for "tongue") is divisible into Protong "In Zi Ki" which, in a grammatical sequence of words, translates as "Land, Towards Elsewhere:" the Tongue bespeaks of the Netherworld of the drowned ancestors. Each eye of the central mask has the same half-circle around it as formed by the Dragons. This is to accentuate the *Ocy* (eyes) as a referral to the Atlantic continent Oce On.

The six nodules under the mask stand for six lavaic landmasses in the Atlantic region. They do not have holes in them, therefore were not "killed" by the Deluge. But since there were seven component landmasses of Oce On, one is missing! From this we learn that the ancestors of the Aztecs escaped from the Atlantic at the beginning of the Farsolar Epoch, when the earth began to deflate, due to diminishing internal combustion. The horizons were beginning to sag and the later Aztecs departed when the first of the seven landmasses was submerging.

Note within the first circle around the mask of Oce On a cluster of air bubbles. The same bubbles are seen around the Octopus' tentacles and on the bellies of the Dragons. They always represent the presence of continuous LIFE, since only the heat within bodies, even submerged and drowned, produces them.

Horizontally across the face's forehead, the sculptor placed the Water Bar, on which two air bubbles and another, not recognizable glyph. At the end of the Water Bar the water drains down in cascades, incidentally emulating Oce On's hair.

On preceding pages you have seen Oce On being entrapped by the Twin Flood Serpents. Well, here you see them again, heads only, as if extending from his ears. This is his "listening" to the possibility of new floods, hence the name *Tonatiuh*... "To the Sinking's Birthgiving You Harken;" "To Na Ti Uh!"

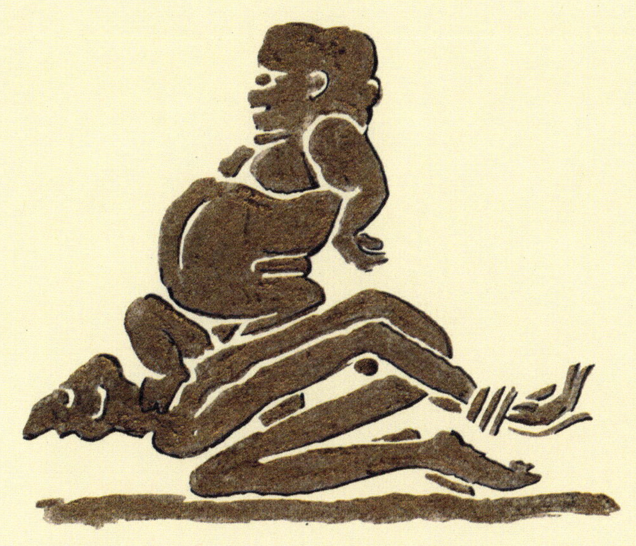

From Pans,Satyrs and Leprechauns
to
whores,mountebanks,Philosophers,
Dictators and Conquerors.

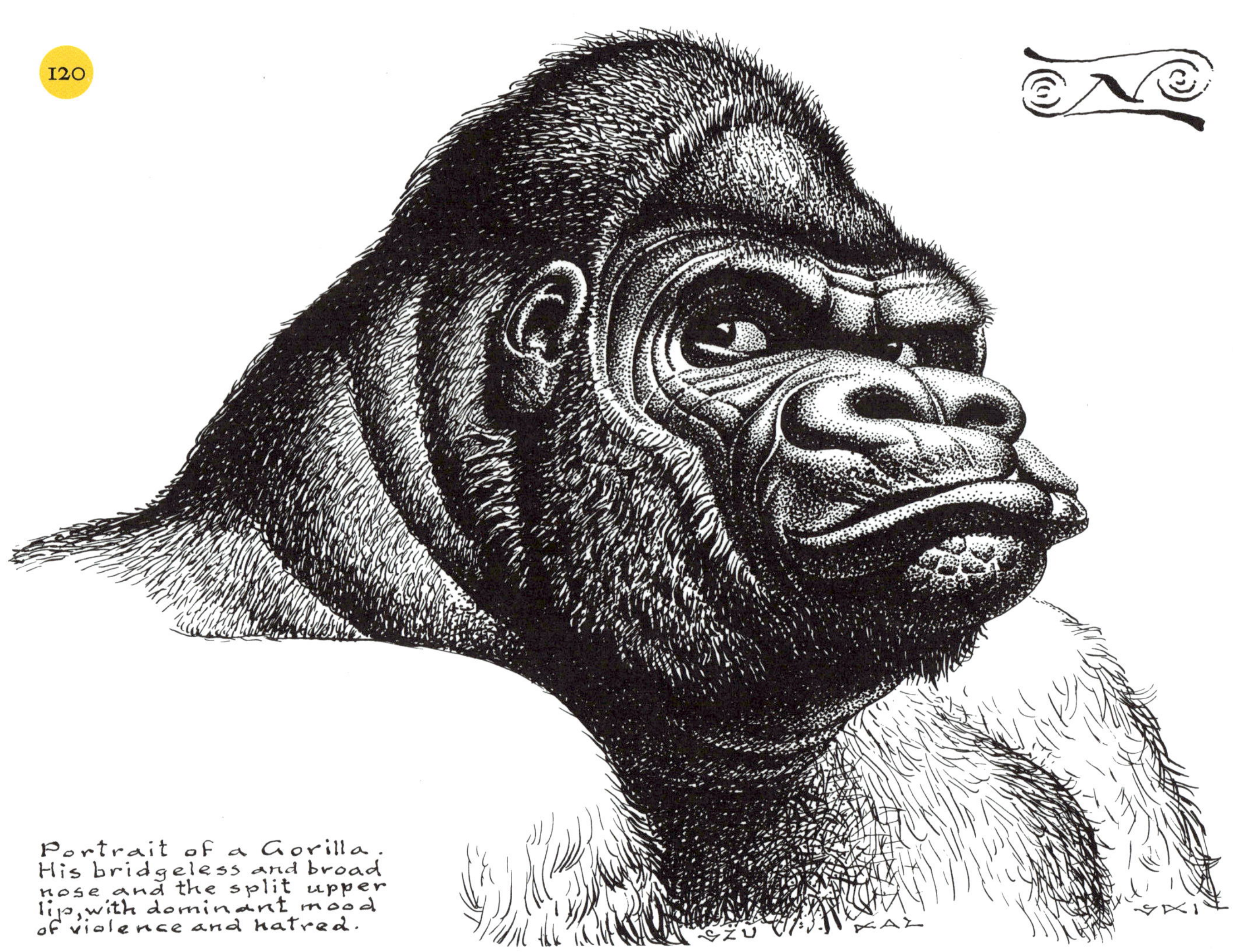

Portrait of a Gorilla.
His bridgeless and broad
nose and the split upper
lip, with dominant mood
of violence and hatred.

The Anthropolitical Motivations

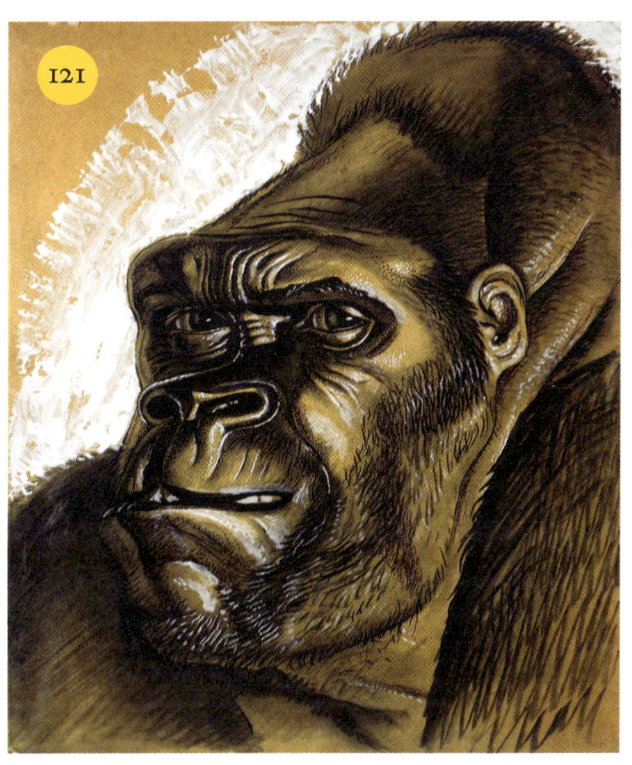

BEING a professional man in numerous fields of intellectual activities, I have evolved a different attitude towards them than the layman, who keeps on repeating the same phraseology and terminology, thus sustaining the same, common attitude. Frankly, I am talented in many fields because my interests are numerous, so that I understand to a higher degree how they are interrelated.

Thus, when I say about myself that I am a genius, it is not self-praise, but a statement to describe a type of mind that: whatever it does in any field, it does well. A mind that peruses in many fields will comprehend better, and many things more, than one that is absorbed in only one. It becomes a universal mind.

Since man recently suffered two global calamities in, as in my case, a single lifetime, I have been dwelling on causes that might have brought these to their culmination. Naturally I have read the opinions of statesmen and contemporary historians blaming the munition manufacturers, the bankers, the imperialists (always of other nations, never their own) for the two World Wars, but as usual, was not satisfied with their answers. Of course I am an egocentric, otherwise I would have remained a non-creative consumer of other people's thinking. But since I belong to the group of self-igniting individualists who never doubt their wisdom, it was but natural for me to personally approach the all-absorbing dilemma of What Causes Wars and their ever-increasing deaths (in the last World War almost 50,000,000 died on both sides of the conflict).

I20   For one, humans are mammalians. They are born in the same way as many animals and have the same means of procreation. Many a trait is animal-like and even dispositions are very often similar. A gorilla, though it is the largest of the apes and terrifyingly powerful so that it needs no pretending extensions of its ferocity, has an ever-ready growl on its face and a permanent frown, so to frighten all smaller creatures. This reveals intrinsic cowardice. So, many governments, when frightened by the military superiority of a prospective victim nation, abuse that nation with the foulest invectives, because basically they are cowards. Their bluff and their threats are symptomatic of their frantic FEAR. However, when they feel they are capable of destroying the other, they make special effort to show friendliness, so to attack unexpectedly.

But I have drawn four **GORILLAS** for you, which may seem overdone evidence that I wish to present. Not so! Though gorillas are native to West Africa, specifically the Kivu Highlands in Nigeria, there are several strains of them, each with various dispositions. Note the different design of the nostrils of the following anthropoids. Note that the first one has a split nose, which superficial cleavage continues on the upper lip.

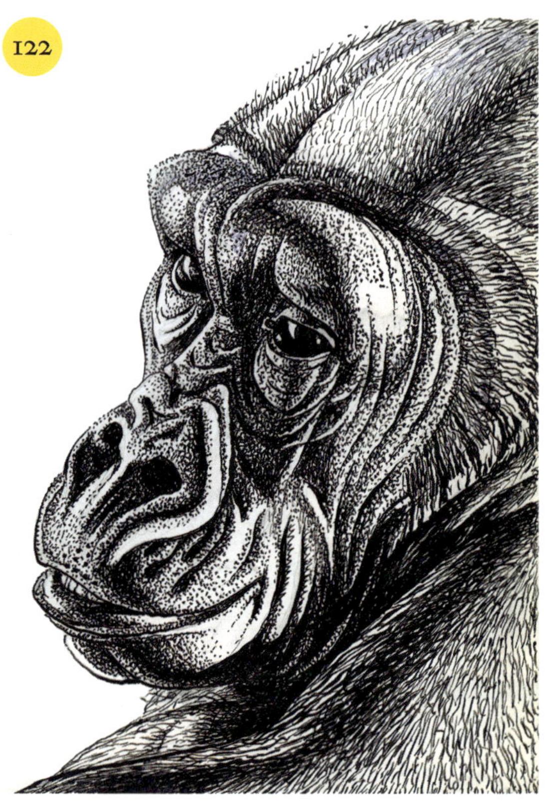

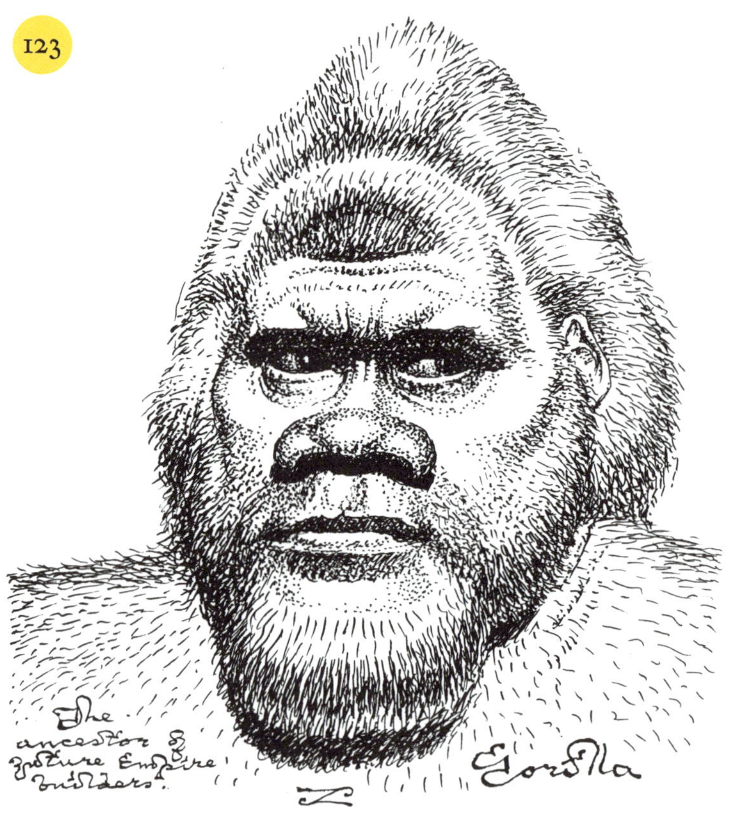

Syphilis, which was originally an animal disease, caused the cleavage of the roof of the mouth and the harelip, together with a large space between the upper teeth. Eventually these anthropoids became to a great extent immune to syphilis, and the cleavage became characteristic of the class.

121   Note that the second drawing shows a gorilla with an unsplit nose.

122   The third gorilla has nostrils that lay flatly wrinkled on the muzzle and there is no split across the nose. Its mass of hair begins immediately above the massive brows.

123   This gorilla's portrait, however, shows more human-oid traits, already indicating inter-species bastardy. The nose, though almost caricature-like, could be that of Leo Tolstoy or Maxim Gorki. The expression is almost human, but for the brooding hatred in the eyes. The mouth is completely human. The neck, like on the others, is of course totally missing. Here you have an ancestor, the sire of our future empire-amassers.

124   Due to our ignorance of our bastardly past, our inbreeding with the apes, we carry the **BURDEN OF HISTORY**, which actually is the struggle between Humans and a-Humans. The a-Humans, however, because they are born in our own countries and communicate in our languages, are not recognized and are taken to be Poles in Poland, English-men in England, Russians in Russia.

The gigantic abdomen that gorillas have to keep on filling all day long was inherited by their bastardly descendants, which physical trait was sublimated into avarice for everything in sight.

125   Despite Darwin's assurance that the two species of ape and human do not produce offspring, I will show you some examples to the contrary. In an old medical book I found this photograph of an oddly proportioned **DWARF.** His arms were so short that they barely reached to his pelvic bone at the base of his long torso. Therefore, he could not walk upright, because our arms have to counter-swing with the opposite legs in order to keep our balance while walking.

When I first came to the U.S.A., living with my parents in Chicago, I would always see the white horse of the cart that delivered goods to a bakery store, stand with its forelegs on the sidewalk. I soon solved the riddle. When it was trotting in the streets, I saw that its forelegs were much shorter than the hind ones, so that these would have

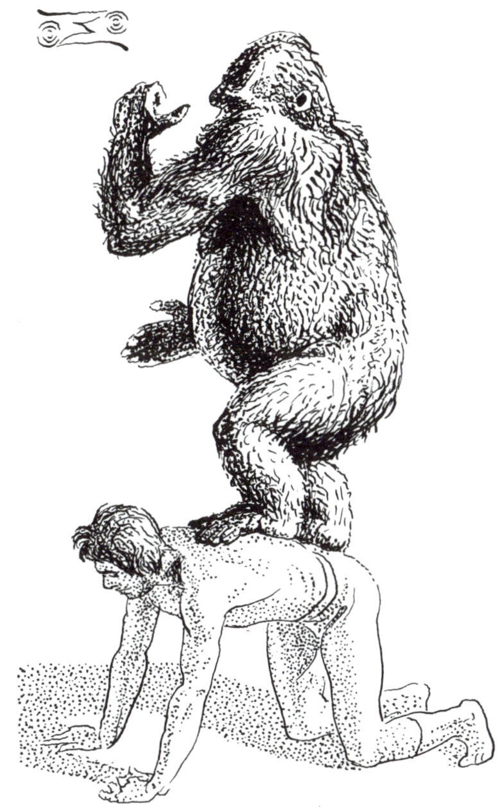

to carry a greater share of the body weight than if they had been much longer.

Thus, this little man who inherited the human short arms doubly exaggerated, discovered that if he held wooden blocks in his hands, he would make his arms longer and shift some of his weight onto his legs so his arms would get tired less quickly. Below I made his face in greater detail, that you may recognize the similarity to dozens of famous politicians who always serve some Ideology that, on succeeding, will metamorphose into another Tyranny.

WHEN ancient Greece found a substitute for the petroglyphic Art of scratching on rocks and cave walls, we gained the Art of vase painting as a means of relating the old legends and myths to the nation. There is a large part of the Greek vase painting that is little known to the general public, because it is of erotic nature. Some of the milder erotica, however, is seen in books and museums.

Until my discovery of their historic veritability, no archaeologist had ever suspected that the Pans which so commonly occur on the Greek vases, are factual truth, not poetic invention. The Pan was anciently called *Ban* which means "Feared," because this was actually the species of large apes that attacked human women and raped them.

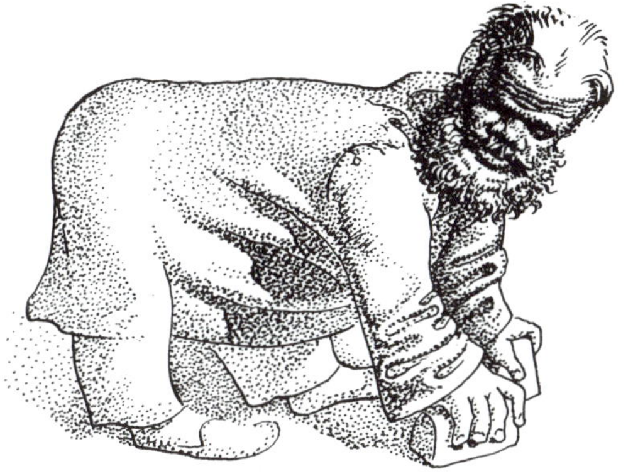

A throwback to ape-posture.

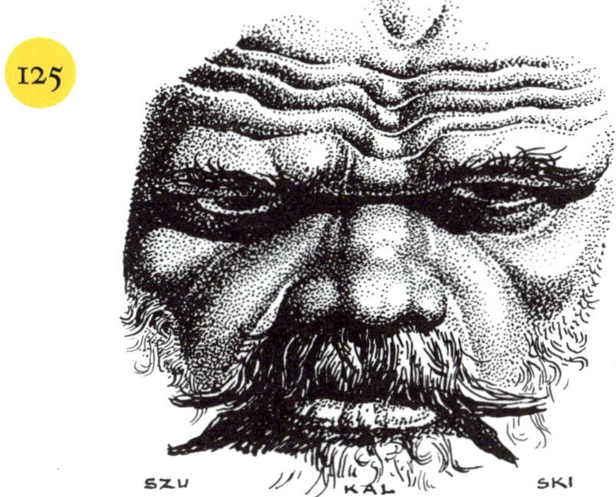

A throwback to "Neanderthal".

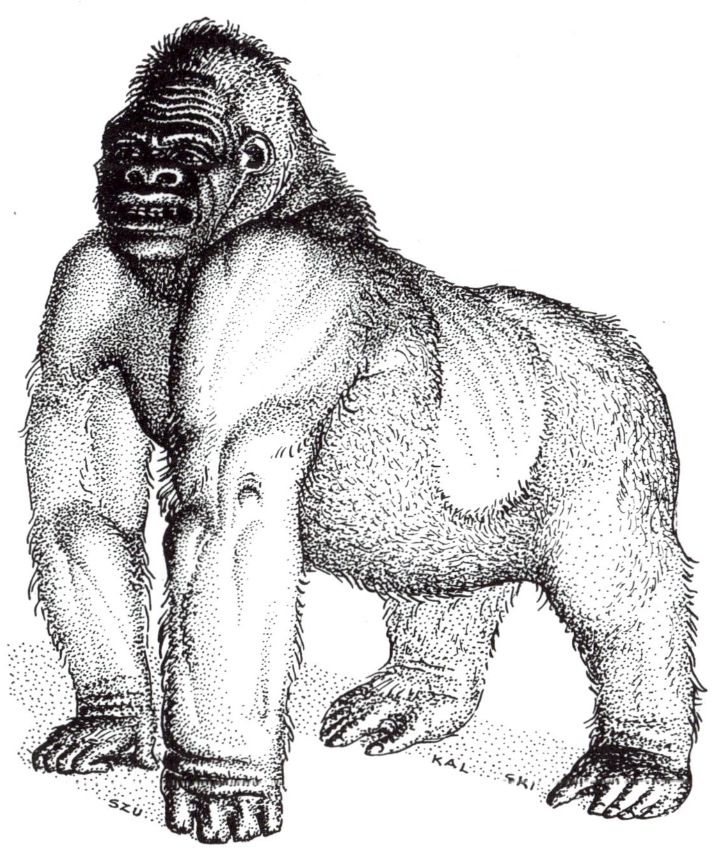

97

The Pans, according to legends, liked to hover near herds of grazing cattle. In a certain state of venereal infection, these creatures had persistent erections, due to inflammation, so that they were seeking any kind of sexual satisfaction. Most commonly they contented themselves with sheep or goats, hence the goat-legged mutant Pans. I insist that syphilis is a purely animal disease and therefore so destructive to humans. The fact that humans have syphilis is due to rapes by these Pans, and all the wart-nosed Greek philosophers, the pot-bellied, waddling pygmoids, were actually descendants of such inter-species bastardy. On this matter I assembled a volume of 344 drawings like these, to be eventually published, because it is of the utmost importance to know that our Human Destiny is afflicted with the greatest calamities (like the two World Wars) because our HUMAN female ancestors were raped by the Apes, the Yetis, the Sasquatches, and our male forefathers copulated with female anthropoids. Please follow my line of reasoning briefed in this chapter.

As the Ice Age was advancing upon Hyperborea, food became more and more scarce, so that it became the custom to drive away the maturing youths, giving them a sack of food for on the road (by which they became known as the Migrating Saki).

Parallel with this policy of diminishing the population, the savage Europeans resorted to substitutes in order not to make their women-folk pregnant. The accessibility of does in the jungles was resorted to by human males and Pans alike.

126 This drawing I made in the British Museum. You see the **SHEEP-MUTANT** raping a doe.

127 Two **PANS** enticing a doe with a jar of water, in order to rape her.

128 This drawing of a most renowned fresco illustrates a **PAN** dressed in the skin of a slain stag, so as to get close enough to the doe unnoticed, for the purpose of raping her.

A striking oddity of this presentation is the tail. The spinal column of animals continues naturally below the rump as the core of the tail. Here, however, the tail is set at a wrong angle, beginning more towards the thighs of the creature. This is due to a clever contrivance. The Pan has pushed the base of the dried tail into his rectum to hide his anthropoid sex. While a man's genitals are projecting from his lower abdomen, therefore in front of him, you may recall from your latest visit to the zoo that the genitals of the ape are placed further back, so that in the ape's slight stoop they show in the rear, as in this drawing. Thus, we definitely know that this is a Pan (the Feared One) from Greek mythology.

That this is a Pan, a Manape, is further attested by the large abdomen of the "gorger," the future sire of Yetinsyn empire-amassers, and the too-short arms of human heritage.

129 On one Greek vase I found this scene. A peasant woman is striking indignantly at a **PAN RAPING A MULE** in the street, while the rider turns around to discover it is this syphilis spreader that is annoying his animal.

130 More history told on a vase by a Greek painter. **TWO PANS** sneak up on three human girls while they bathe, hiding behind the palm tree waiting for the right moment to attack and impregnate, and at the same time infect them.

131 An actual **PAN**, scratched on a piece of slate, presently in the possession of the St. Germain Museum in France. From sleeping on the ground, the hair on the outside of the base of the tail is worn off, which fact is strikingly well observed. When you imagine the face without the beard, you can readily recognize many subversive politicians and Communists in it.

132 A **PAN** attacking a human woman. This is one of many paintings where the woman has the pictographic Tree with her with the Snake wound around it. This, being a rebus for Polish *drzewo*, refers to her origin, for Protong "Drze Wo" means "Where Water," hence she was one of the humans who came from the now flooded homeland. The Serpent, as always, represents the Great Flood.

133 On the neck of one vase I found the painter's story about a **DAUGHTER OR A SISTER** who had run away with a Pan for a sexual escapade. Then the same girl returns home, embracing the man, perhaps her husband. Note that in several places her dress adheres to syphilitic sores. After she died from syphilis, her body was burned and her ashes were placed in this vase.

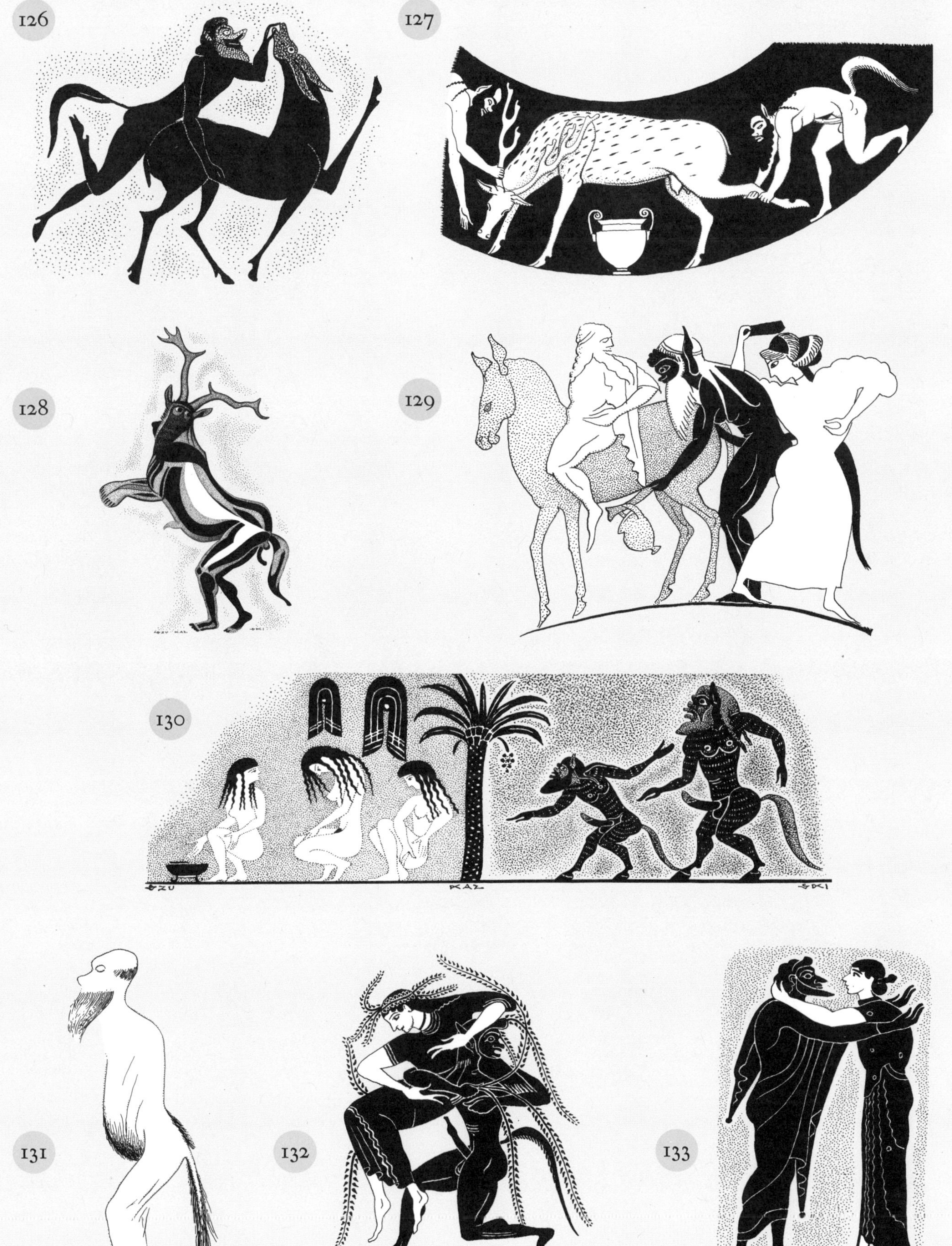

126

127

128

129

130

131

132

133

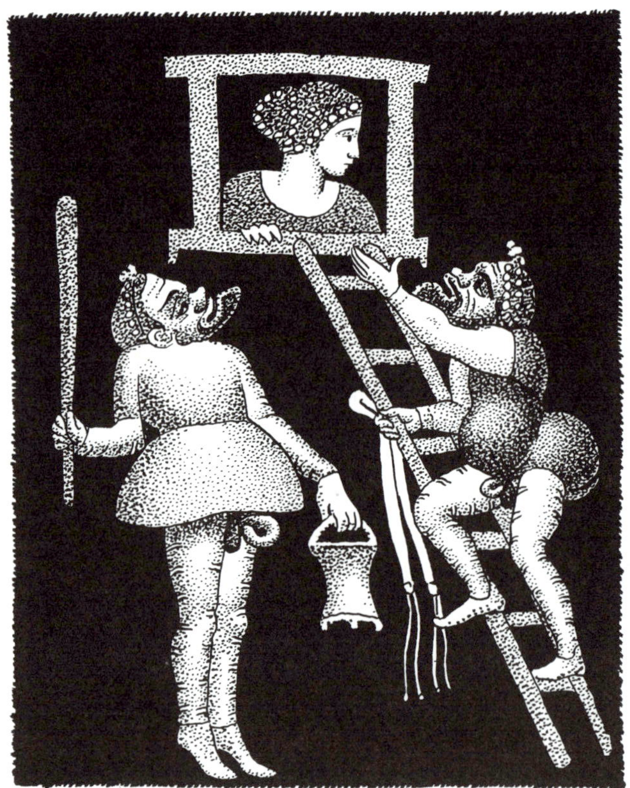

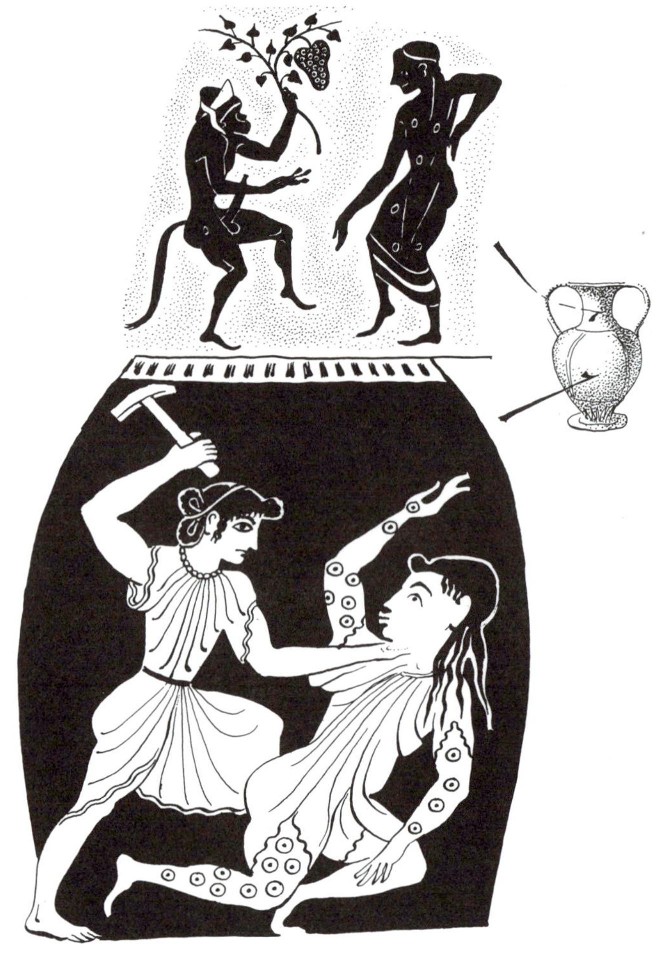

134 A vase painting of a scene of a morality play shows a girl looking at **TWO PANS**, one of which is already climbing a ladder up to her room. Both have long linen tapes with them to bind her hands before leading her away into the jungle. One has a large club to deal her a blow and make her unconscious, and they brought a bucket of wine with them. All this in anticipation of raping her.

136 On one vase I discovered another example of an **APE** with a permanent erection, enticing a girl by offering her grapes. Note that she has already been with the Pans, copulating, for her dress adheres in places to the syphilitic sores.

On returning to the village (below), she is attacked by a woman who, fearing that the whore will infect her brothers' sons, slays her with a hammer. The deceased body was cremated and the ashes were placed in this jar.

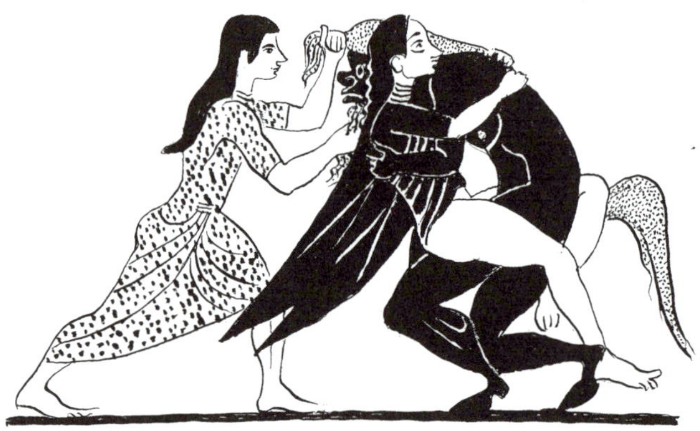

135 Like a delayed newspaper report about life in ancient Greece, here is another story. It is about **TWO SISTERS,** one of which was attacked by a Pan, who despite the other sister's tearing at his hair and beard, continues his brutal act with the rather cooperative victim.

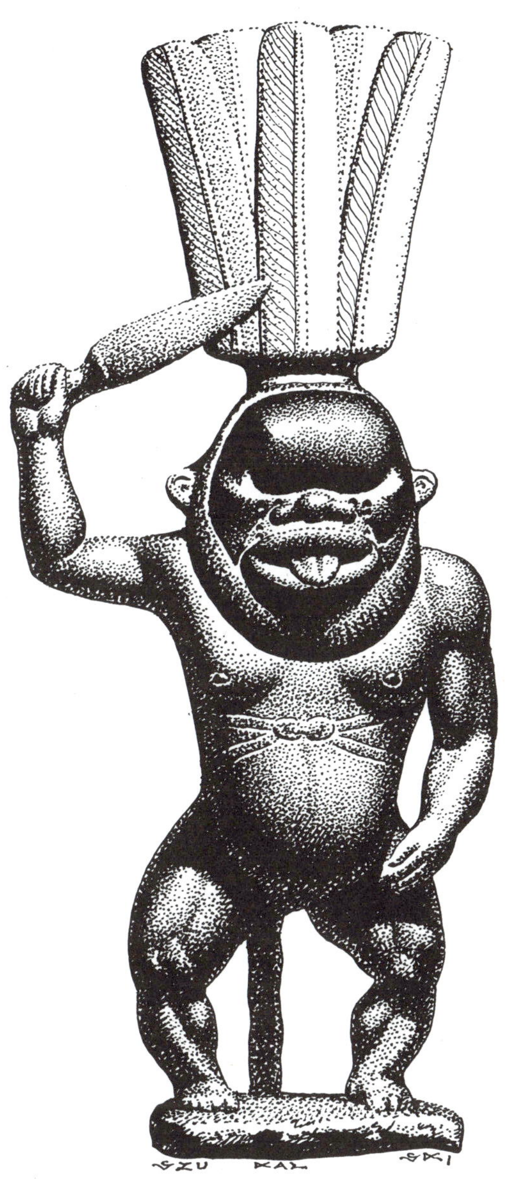

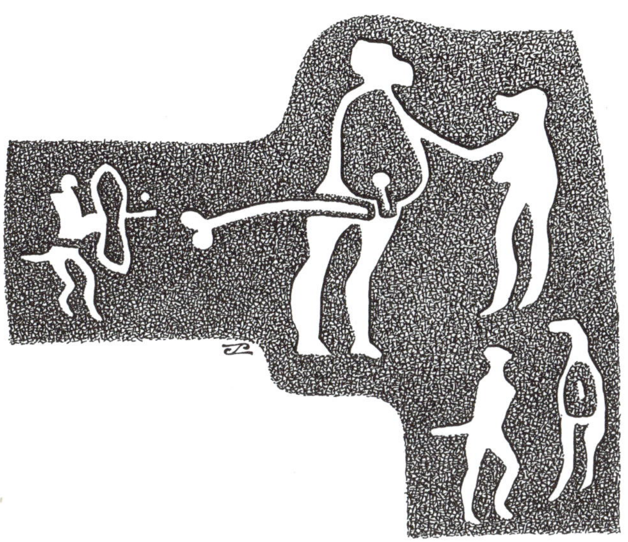

137 The Egyptians had a parallel of Pan in their own mythology, the God **BESS.** This name, when returned to its original Protong "Bez," means "Run," i.o.w. he, too, is dangerous to women. Across his waist he has diagonally crossed lines, which universally means that his species also escaped from the deluged Motherland of the Dawn God in the Pacific.

138 In Bohuslän, the place in Sweden whose name started me on my so extensive scientific task, there is a Petroglyph—one among hundreds—commemorating the **INTERBREEDING** of Manapes and Humans. You see a Neanderthal Manape at the left, who knows how to make bows and arrows, yet still has the tail of the anthropoid, standing guard over a female who was made pregnant by a "giant penis." No doubt, eventually one of the descendants of this bastard became a Communist agent or executioner, as all those with the undercut noses tend to be.

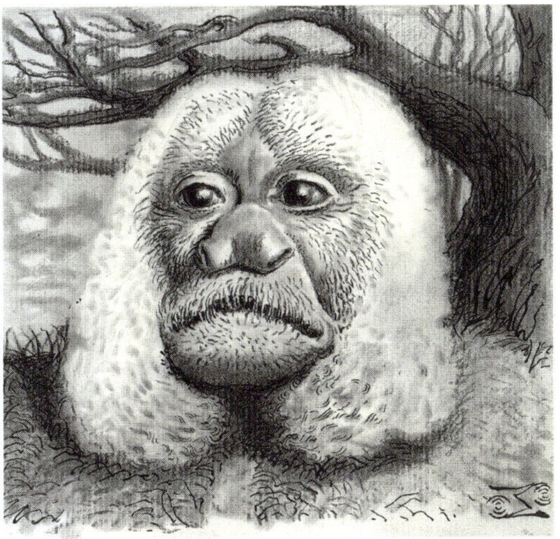

139 On the other side of the world, in South America, the Indian name for an **APE** is *Beesa*, which would be "Bez (J)a" in Protong, meaning "Run I." Thus, like the Egyptian name *Bess*, it indicates the necessity to run away when this ape is in sight, for it will rape women. The local Indians speak of the "Man of the Forest."

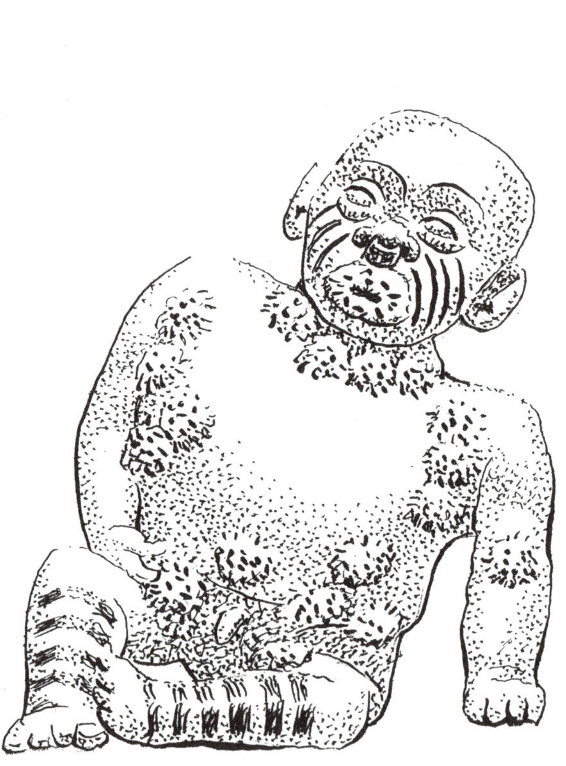

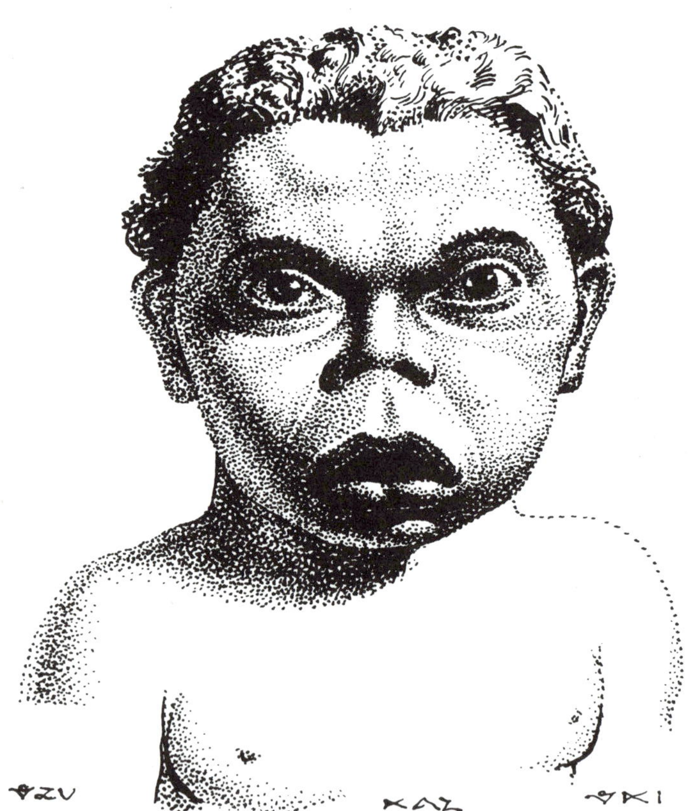

140 This pottery portrait, made by the prehistoric Nayarit of ancient Mexico, shows a **WART-NOSED YETINSYN**, a bastard of apeoid–human mixing. His mouth is shriveled from too many eruptions, his body being afflicted with the syphilis brought upon his human mother. His arms, as always with Yetinsyn descendants, are the doubly exaggerated short human ones. His legs are inherited from his ape father, which heritage is further attested to by the overlong torso.

141 A **THYROID CRETIN**, with nostrils lower than the base of the nose. Such a face often comes with a cleft roof of the mouth and the harelip. I think that all mentally deficient cretins, morons, idiots and mongoloids are actually not so much mentally sick as closer in their heritage to the Apes than to Humans. If they were brought up by Apes, they probably would fare no less well than these, but as human children they are deficient.

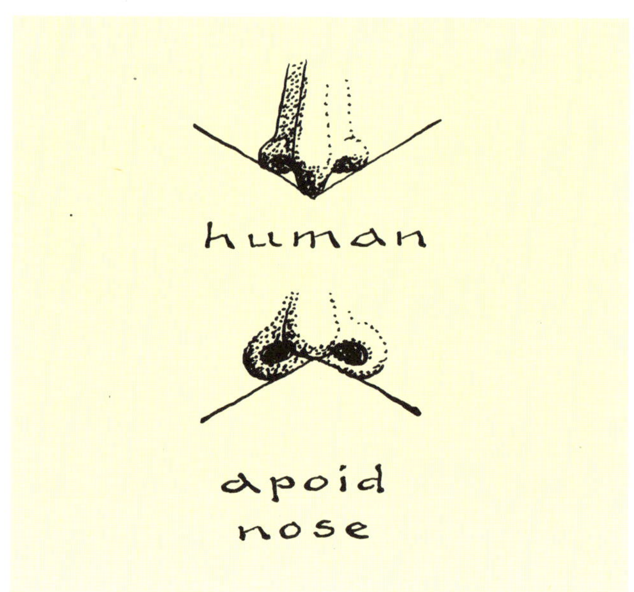

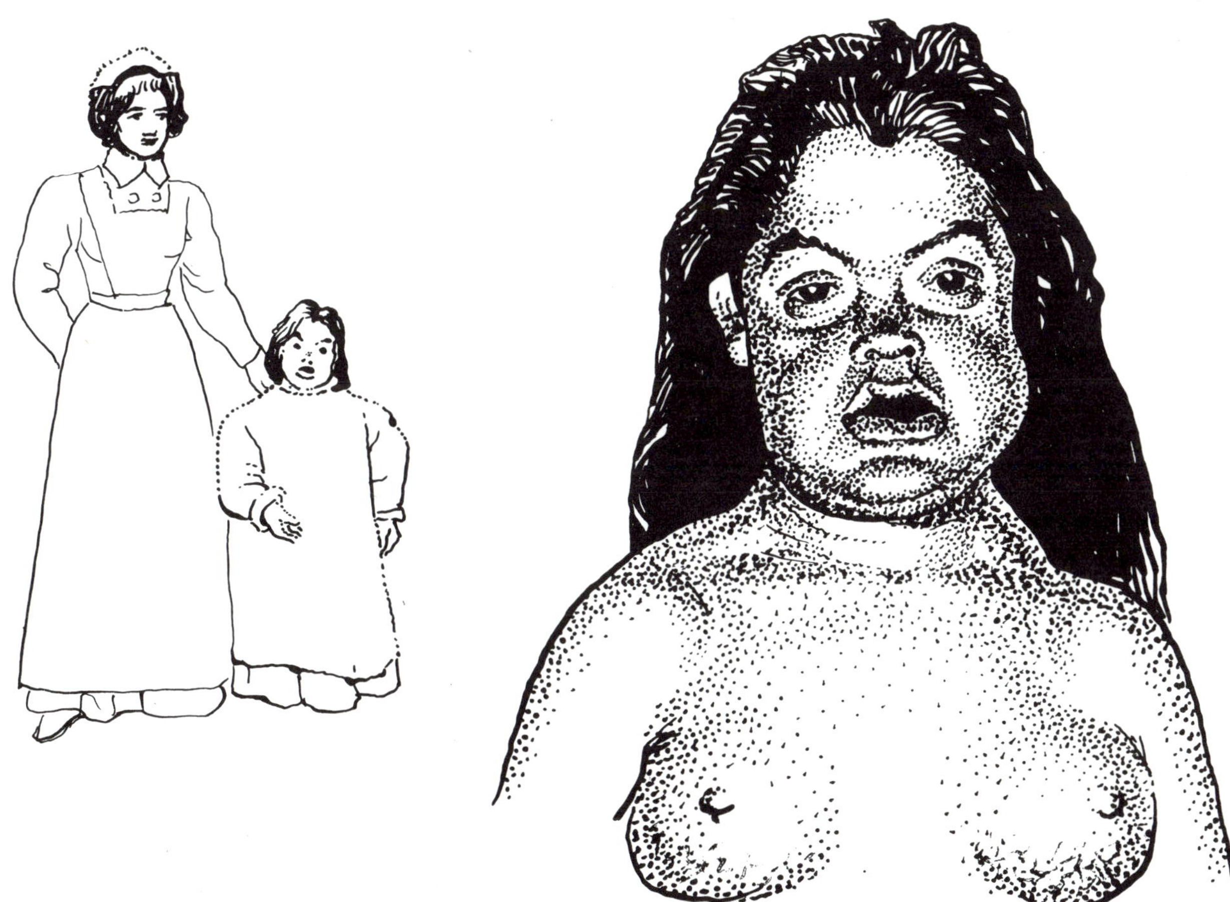

142 A **CRETIN-IMBECILE WOMAN**, 39 years old, sexually mature, as the breasts show, but half as tall as her nurse and mentally equivalent to an ape. Note the width of her upper lip groove.

143 The most recognizable characteristic of people involved in political subversion and treason, without having to undress and measure them, is the **UPPER LIP**. The descendants of the Manapes or Pans are the people with the long upper lips, which always go together with the sharply angled, undercut nose. The human upper lip flows down from the point of the nose to the lower rim of the lip. Compare the slightly exaggerated drawings of the Yetinsyn on the left, and the Human on the right.

The history of mankind up to this moment is the enumeration of STRUGGLES caused by the elemental foes of mankind, the results of the rapes of human women by Manapes who, having been born among us and speaking our languages, are mistakenly taken for our own countrymen. But it is these hateful, deadly and fiendishly exterminatory descendants of the Yeti that, on having been thoroughly admixed with the Humans, think up all the ideological "Isms" that create subversion, treason, revolutions, wars, and the eventual downfall of all Civilization and Culture.

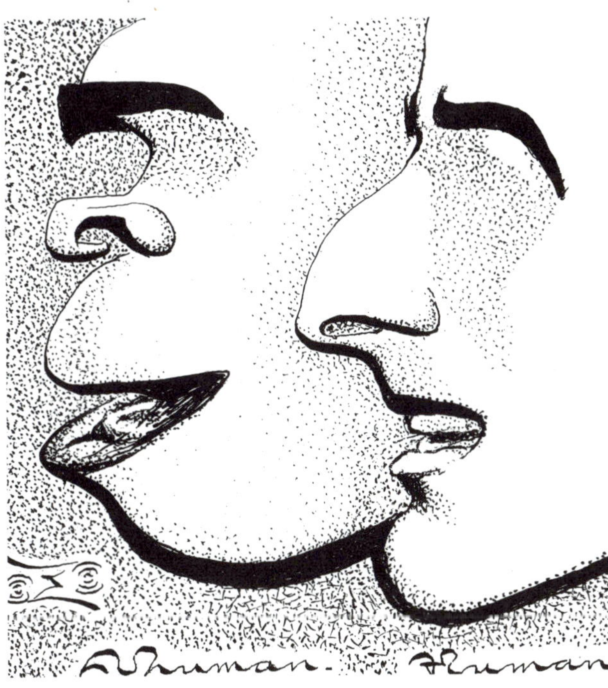

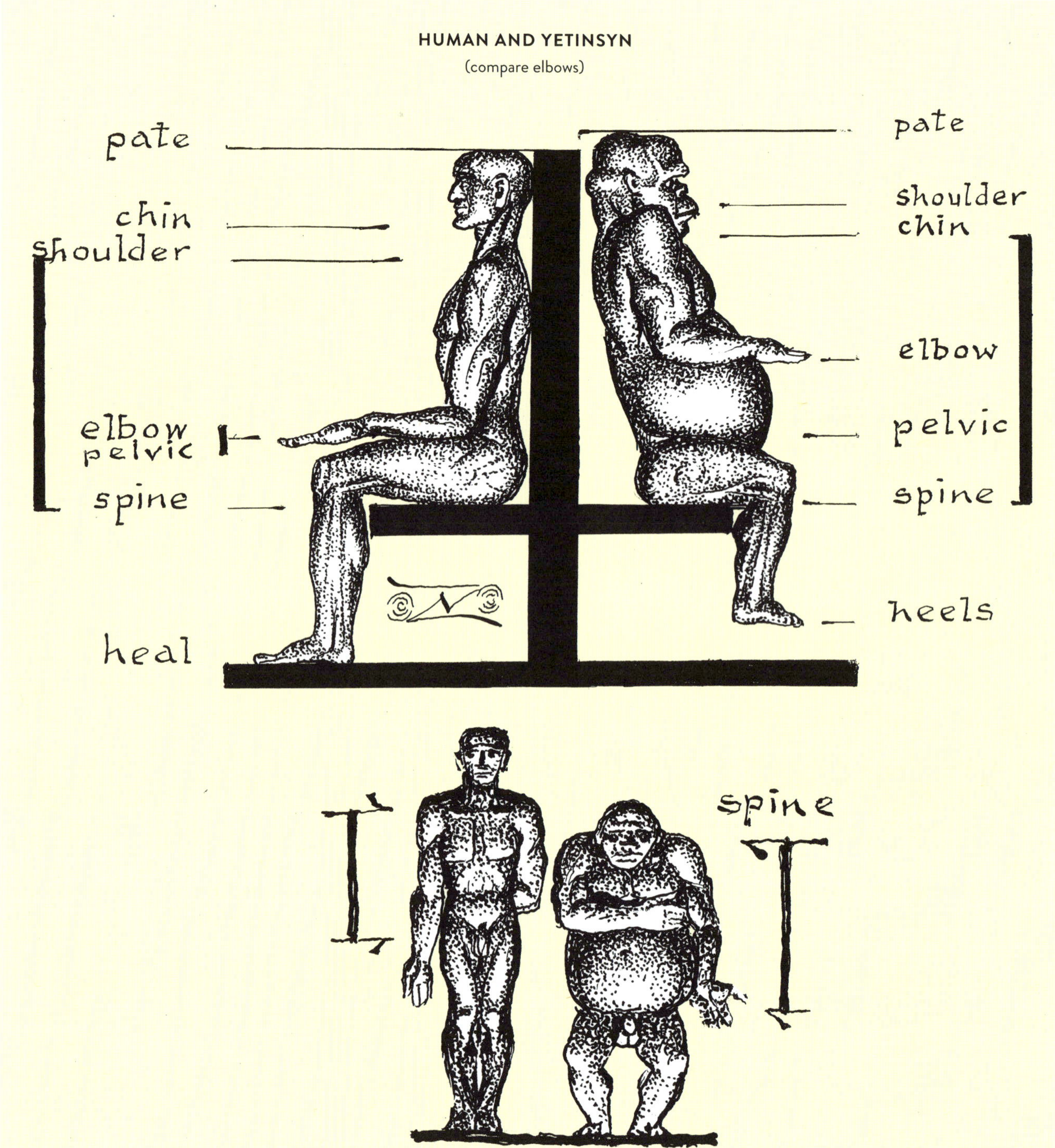

144 One trait of apeism is the too-long torso, which can be seen when a person is standing up with the arms bent. My elbow overlaps the pelvic, because I am a Human. The worker, however, I met at the gas station had an elbow–pelvic interspace of 1 foot and 2 inches (I measured it).

When a person, while standing, has the same height as you, but towers over you in a sitting position, he is a Yetinsyn with his too-long torso, with which he undoubtedly will have legs too short to reach the floor. He is a semi-Human, devoid of human, NOBLE ways.

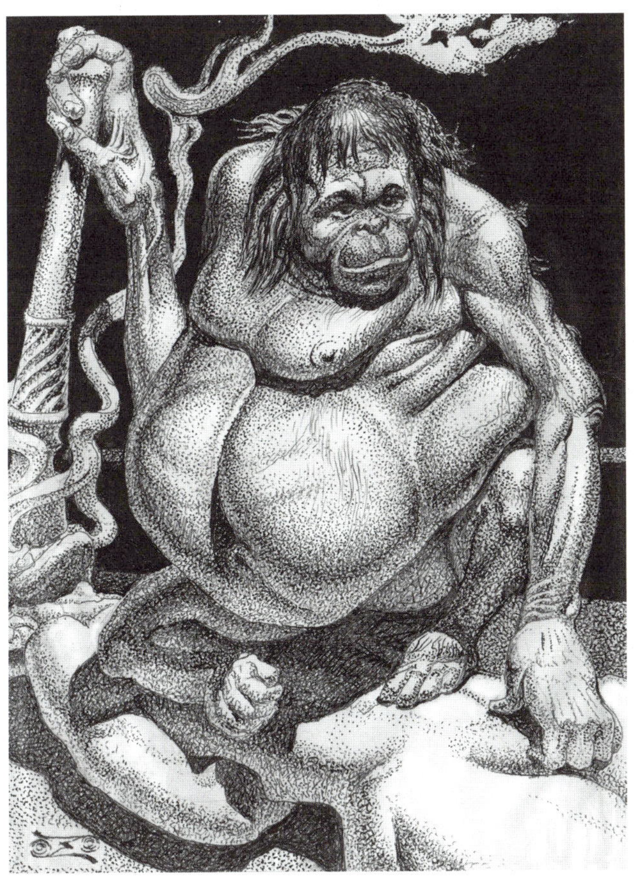

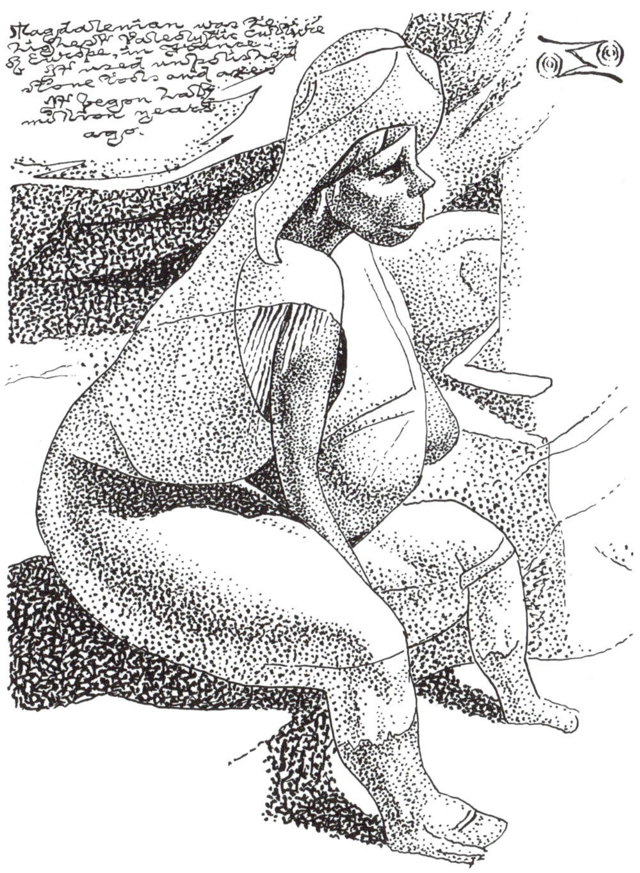

145 Here, for your comparison, you have the **ORANG-UTAN** of the Borneo-Sumatra region, sitting on a broken sculpture, stifling its face with a flaming torch. Note the Communist upper lip and the immense torso, an indication of uncontrollable gluttony. The pendulous abdomen in its Yetinsyn-descendants becomes the index of the psychotic obsession to possess everything in sight, to gain ever greater territories (Queen Victoria, Tsarina Catherine the Great).

Note the extremely short bone in the upper arm, another trait seen in anti-human bastards. You see, I am a sculptor, you are not, so you had not noticed these odd proportions of limbs.

146 In a cave in Lussac-les-Chateaux, France, a piece of slate was excavated with on it the, for that epoch, wondrous portrait of a **YETIDOCH** (Russian for "Daughter of the Yeti"). It has been preserved at the Musée de l'Homme in Paris. The portrait was carved with a flint-flake by the then just arrived diluvial refugees from the distant Pacific, known to us as the Cro-Magnon Men, a species of giant Humans who had the marvelous ability to picture records of prehistory.

I have not added any details to this document other than my shading, so to make the subject matter more elucidating. Look at that belly, look at that upper lip and the vestigial wart-nose. This female belongs to the bi-species of Manape that is partly admixed with Humans. She could have been a tsarina or a queen or some other empire-builder, since she is of the predatory species.

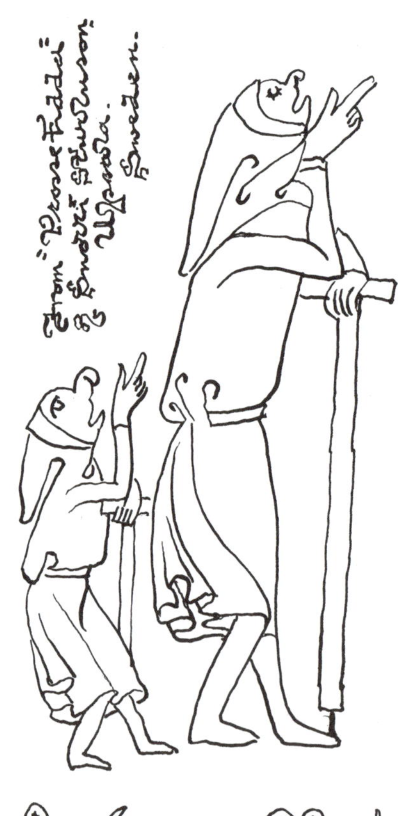

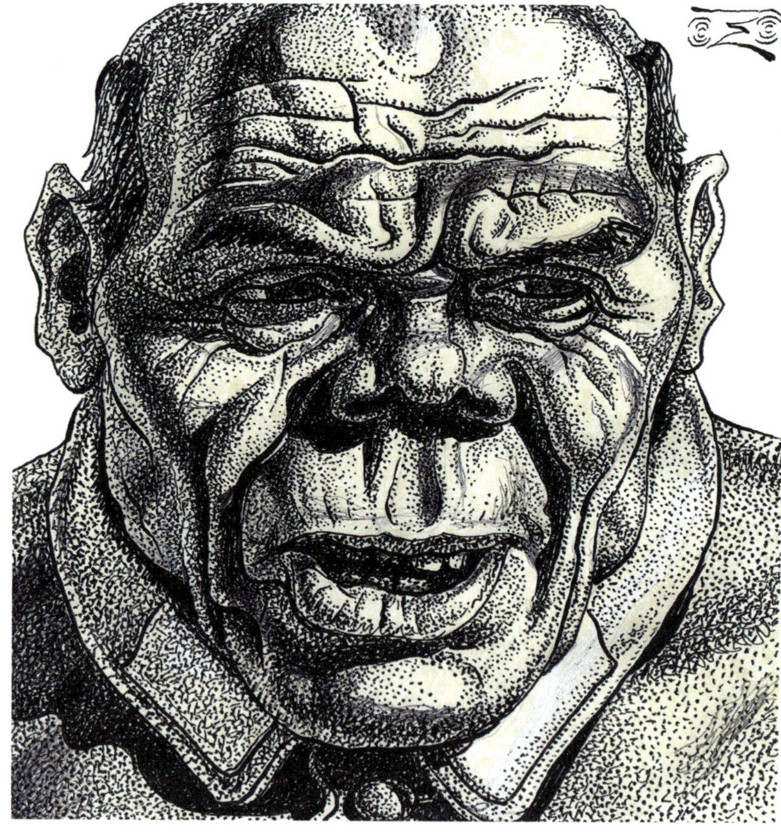

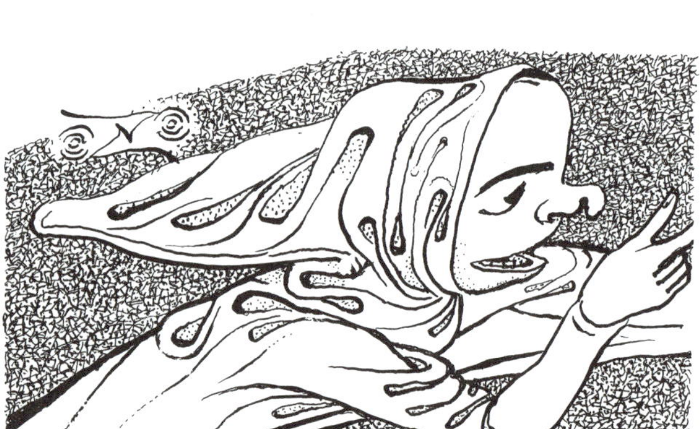

147 Some time ago I came across a reproduction of an illustration to early sagas of Sweden. The sizes of the different figures were random, perhaps to indicate difference in importance. I have made for you a larger, more articulate drawing, that you may see what creatures these really are.

The size of the heads in relation to the bodies indicates that these are the "**TROLLS**" who perhaps were a contemporary type of minority population. It could be that these are still a different type of Manape that I have seen so far, judging by the peculiar shape of the noses.

148 The face of one of the prevalent types of **YETINSYNY**. I drew this portrait from a photograph of one of millions of *chinovniki*, the executors of the Tsar's orders, the committers of evil, the abusers of real Humans.

Note the apeoid placement of the nostrils, below the center of the base of the nose. Compare the apron-like upper lip to that of the orangutan of plate 145. Look how close the nostrils are below the eyes. Here you have the prototype abuser of ensnared Humanity.

The above traits I pointed out, occur in every nation on earth. But it is the great prevalence of the apeoid type in a nation that instigates its predatory existence, hence foments wars of conquests and the victimization of other nations. Look about you and observe which nations, up to recent years, were the greatest empire amassers, and you will understand why the prevalent type among their members of government was the type with the undercut nose.

Each of them can feel his own apeoid tail between his buttocks, curling under into the too delicately fragile to be exposed. One can bend it to a small extent by pressing it farther in.

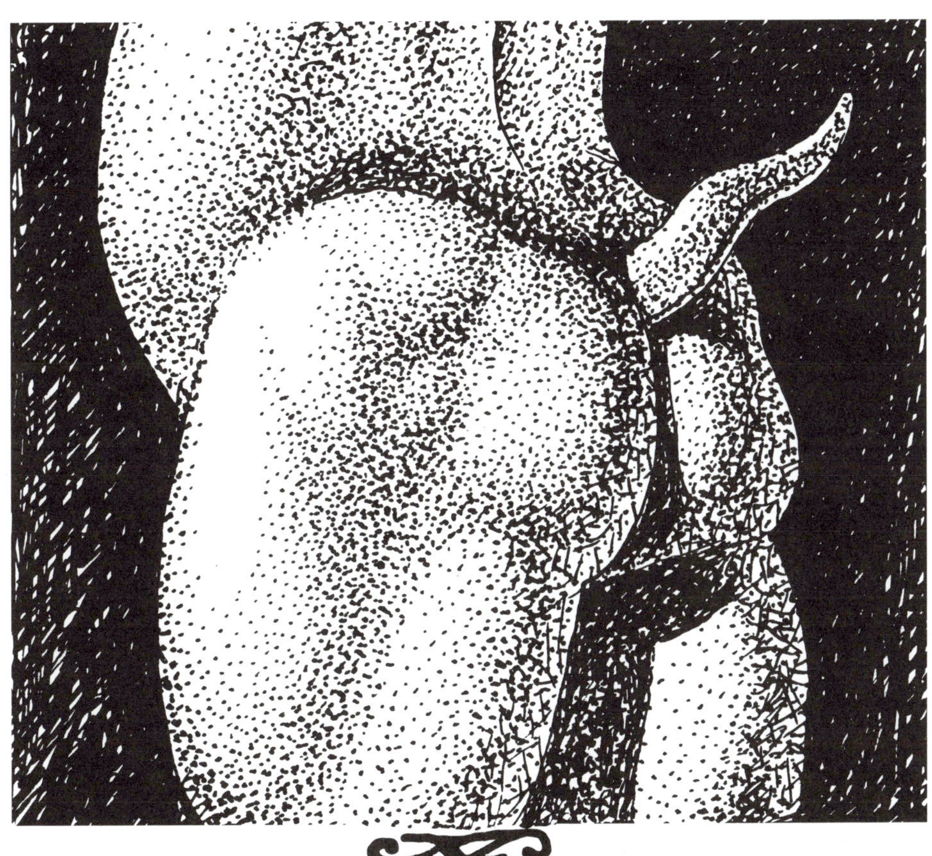

Some years ago a nine-year old German girl came to the Johns Hopkins Hospital in New York with her father, to have her **TAIL** amputated. It was a mobile appendage, for she could wiggle it at will. I drew this from a medical book.

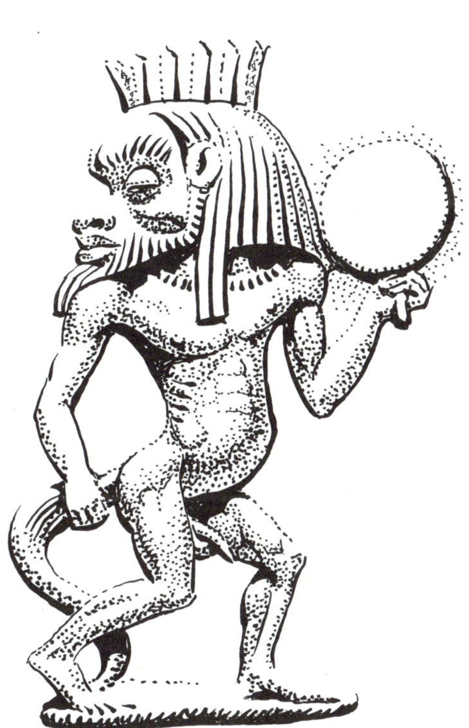

A small baked pottery carving showing an Egyptian Bess with a **TAIL**, a crown of feathers on his head and the Dawn-greeting Mirror in his hand. From my collection.

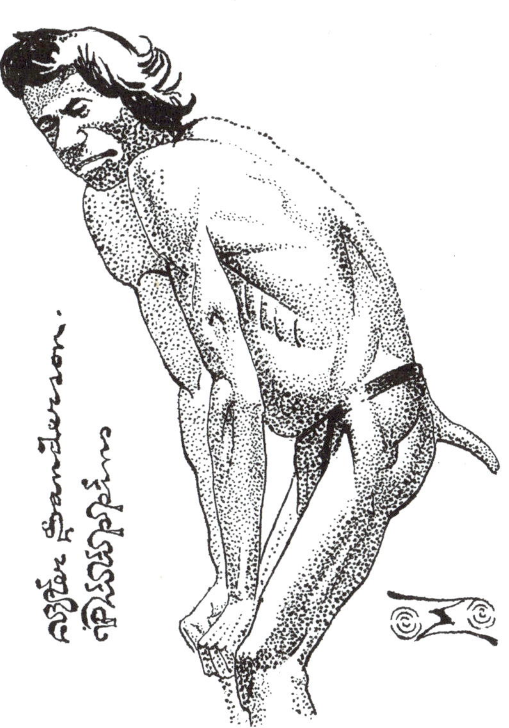

In Sanderson's book on the Yeti, there is a photograph of a Filipino man with an **APE TAIL**, its tip suddenly terminating as if it had been cut off.

Could it be possible that human society would tolerate Manape halfbreeds and continue to further inbreed with them? Not intentionally! But there are always irresponsible drunks and men of low mentality who, when sexually pressed, are willing to copulate with a hole in a fence or to rape, despite protests from period-beset females.

Let this drawing illustrate the inadvertent toleration of a most unlikely member of the family (which also happens in personal families, when we are "thrown together by circumstance"). It is known that the cuckoo never nests but, like all nomadic, non-home-making creatures, finds a small victim to work for it. It waits till a small bird, like the meadow pipit, flies away seeking food, then descends on its nest and lays an egg. Mother pipit, on returning, is surprised at its large size, but being proud of what seems to be her achievement, begins to hatch the egg.

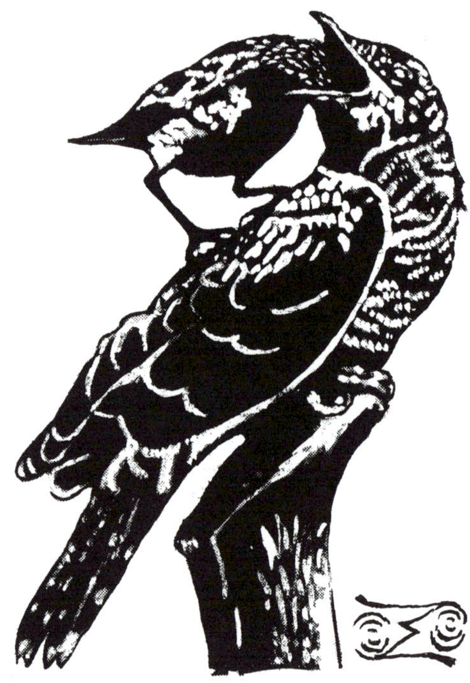

The young **CUCKOO** is born glistening-skinned nude, looking like a reptile. Immediately it lays on its back and begins to push the legitimate pipit children out of the nest. The expulsion of the nestlings, which are minuscule in comparison to the parasitic invader, is so gruesome and sickening a sight, that I barely was able to continue watching the documentaries in which this was shown. But if you would see nature at its worst and take the lesson of whose side Providence stands on, do not miss the opportunity.

The mother will spend her entire energy to feed the parasite, completely unconscious of what is being loaded on her shoulders. She is the "kidnapped" sucker-parent by proxy, doing her duty because "it was there," the… egg of Providence.

Because we wear clothes, our bodies are disguised and laymen never notice variations, until an artist, who is trained to observe differences for differentiation in his works, points them out.

Now that I have told you about all the traits that set the Yetinsyn off against the Human: the long torso, the short upper arms and subsequent long elbow-pelvic interspace, the enormous belly, the wart-nose, and very likely a tail, what is my conclusion?

It is most vital to the Destiny of Mankind that these semi-Humans who speak the same language as we, are actually not our fellow countrymen at all, but Yetinsny, the results of Human a-Human interbreeding, that are devoid of all the genteel traits of the former, but retained all avaricious, vengeful, ferocious traits. When they enter politics, they do so exclusively for the purpose of attaining positions that allow them to gloat in VENGEANCE for their obsessive psychosis of INFERIORITY. It is they who, when their dream-chance arrives, exterminate HANDSOME mankind by the millions. Until then, they masterfully bide their time.

Just like the Eta people of Japan were until lately *never* permitted by the Japanese nation to serve in the Imperial Army, all of human society, in a conscious scheme for SURVIVAL, should *never, never, NEVER* permit these Yetinsyny to participate in any form of politics or the military service.

Yetinsyny as the Benefactors of Mankind

However!!! Instead of ostracizing every Yetinsyn in every country, that they may not concoct from one of their political philosophers, Karl Marx, Mao Tse Tung, Nietszche, Bakunin, Kropotkin, or other haters of humanity, encourage them to partake in the arts: creative Art, applied arts, literature, in medicine and all forms of engineering. Arrest them, however, when they write on ethics, morality, compassion, charity or sociology, for in each case they will be masters of hypocrisy, all the while really intending, like Socrates did, to undermine the human relations and foment "revolutions." Then: perform as executioners.

Why then will they excel in the above branches of creative contribution? Because, as frightfully inferiority-obsessed males and females who NEVER get beautiful human women and men into their beds, they persistently dream of the IMPOSSIBLE. To endure their mental hardships they develop extraordinary patience and such perfect IMAGINATION that almost anything they dream of, they are capable of contriving. Thus, patience and imagination, together with their ANIMAL vitality, make them capable to contribute miracles of inventions in every sphere of interest. They are the Nibelungs, the little pixies, the fairies of the legends of every country. Politically, they forever remain… socialists and therefore, potential Communists, because they cannot forgive humankind its popularity with the opposite sex. Humans love and are loved. Yetinsyny love human women and men, but are never loved in return by them. It's the formative years of adolescence that decides for the rest of their lives their hatred of mankind in general from the bottom of their feet's soles. They NEVER forget and NEVER forgive. But if their hope for vengeance is sublimated into beneficial inventiveness, and from their frantic industriousness and total dedication to their skills they get the reward—sincere gratitude, appreciation and fame, which is LOVE—from mankind, they purr like kittens and become the best of friends of appreciative humanity that is ALWAYS NOBLE. (I have one entire volume on Yetinsyny who have greatly contributed to mankind's enlightenment and well-being.)

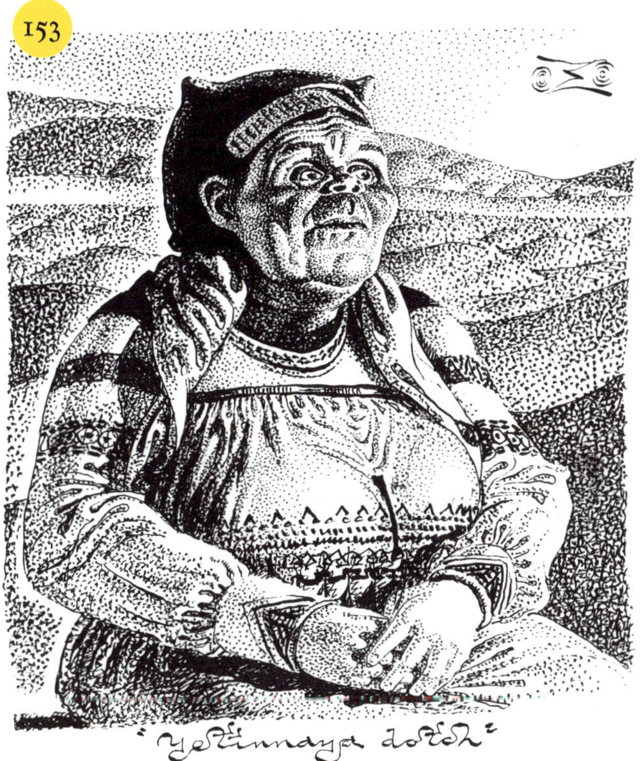

Yetinsyny—The Elemental Foes of Mankind

153 Let me dwell a little longer on the anthropoid elemental gluttony for everything in sight, which is so well illustrated in the Polish saying about the Moscovites: "Wolves' eyes, wolves' gullet, what they see they devour."

Here is a portrait of a once famous **STORYTELLER** among the Russian *muzhiks* (peasants). Note the wart-nose and the enormous upper lip, the vast-size breasts and the voluminous hips. Here is the typical Mother of the Predatory Nation that, on getting into power through invasions, altered their Tartar ethnics by conquering the Rusy and taking on their national name. The Slavic Rusy, the collective term for the inhabitants of Ruthenia, Ukraine and Great, Little, White, Black and Red Russia (which appellations describe the fertility and the color of the soil), are the ultimate in agricultural predilection, while the "Russian" conquerors, the predators, NEVER can be self-supporting by soil-tilling, no matter how they may try, for they were born to live nomadically, off the animals they herded. But now the Anglomericans, eagerly making money by supplying the grain to the predators that they should store for the time of the siege of Europe and America, are assisting Russia to win the next war.

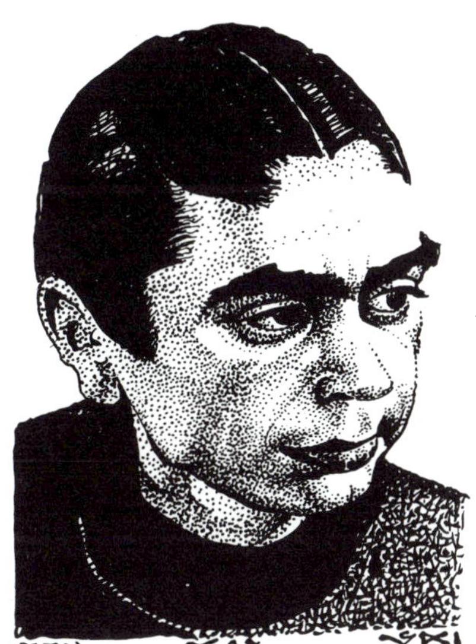

154 She was called **"RED HILDA" BENJAMIN**. A *Kommissar* of Justice for East Germany and a Moscovian agent (they always are on the side of the enemy and against the nation to which they were born), she was selected because of her vicious-looking proclivities (note the tucked-in mouth, as to diminish her brutal appearance and give the impression of coy femininity). She was 4′2″ and, being of

masculine disposition, could not experience physical pleasure in lovemaking, so she was a nymphomaniac who tried
every man in sight, thinking that finally she would find a
man who could give her pleasure. She had prisoners have
sexual intercourse with her, then ordered them executed.

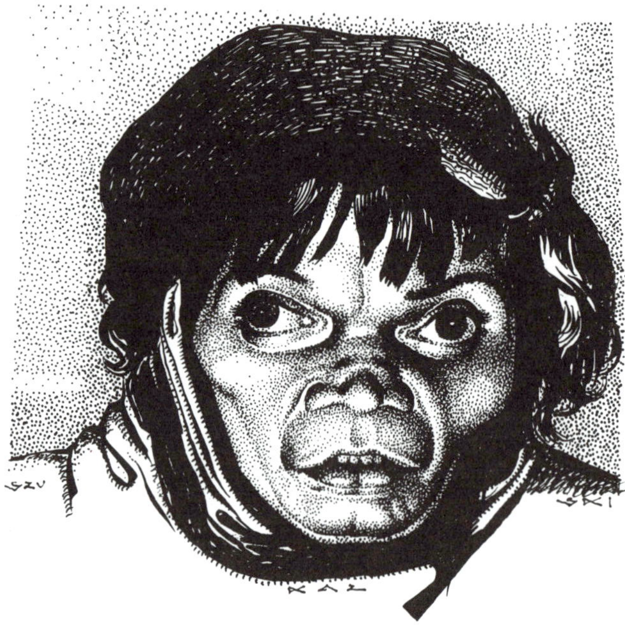

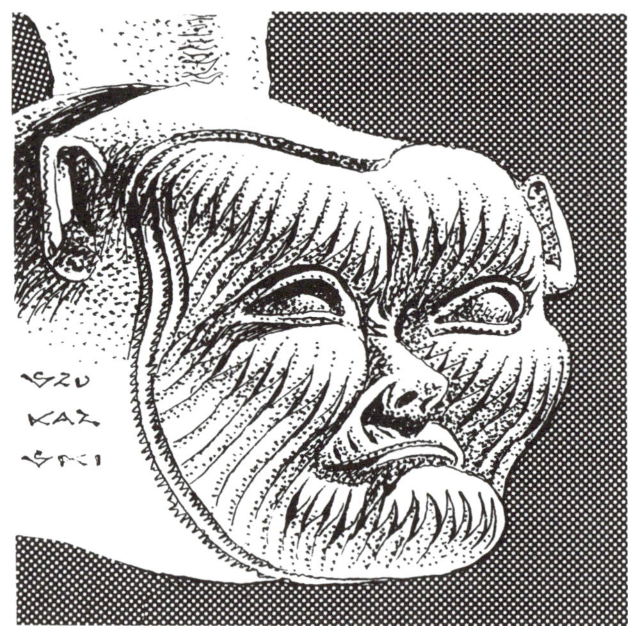

156 A vase from ancient Peru presenting a portrait of a
YETIDOCH. The vertical lines were put there by the
marvelous sculptor to let us know that this creature was a
survivor of the Deluge. From her face streams the dirt that
thickened the waters of the globe when continents were
submerging and other ones re-emerging. Such lines are the
universal pictographs of diluvial cataclysm.

155 I made the drawing of this female from her picture in
Time magazine. The dwarfish creature spent her
entire mature life writing poison letters to the people of her
town, implying their criminal behavior, causing great grief to
everyone involved and breaking long friendships. Finally
she was put in jail. She was by all circumstances "French,"
but actually this woman has no nationality, for she was a
YETIDOCH ("Daughter of the Yeti").

157 Two of the most representative writers of Russia are
BAKUNIN and **KROPOTKIN**, both anarchists. In a
review of the former's work a commentator remarks:
"Marx's ideas caught on fast in Russia, which had its own
brand of revolutionary thought exemplified by the nihilist
Bakunin who believed in violence for violence's sake and

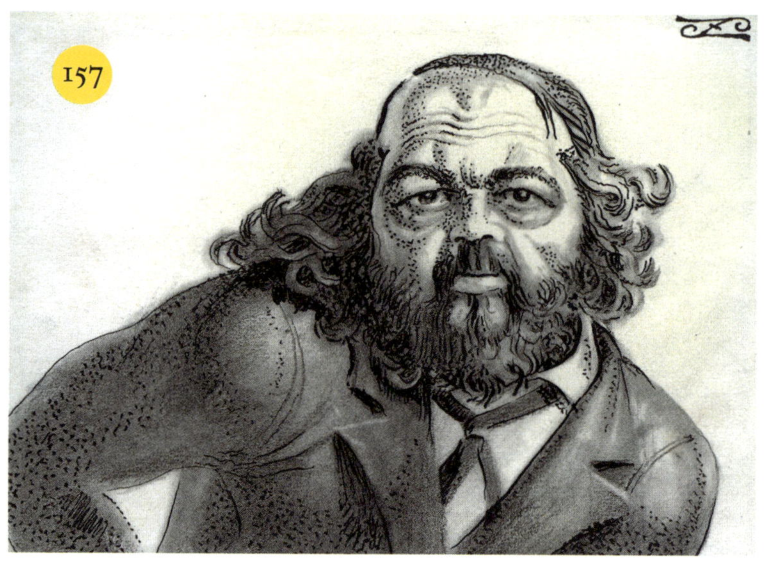

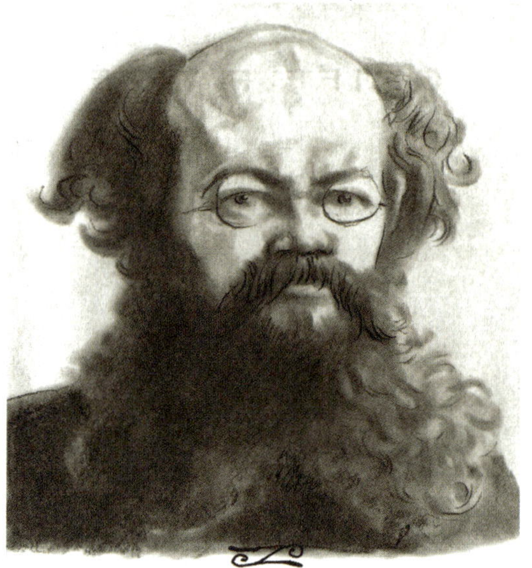

had a vision of the whole of Europe… transformed into an enormous rubbish heap." The Bolsheviks combined Marx's ideas with Bakunin's terrorism to create their own revolutionary creed.

This was when American Civilization was as yet not known in the Russian backwoods (he lived 1814–'76), for his hatred would particularly have hoped to destroy this land of FREEDOM first.

From his little shoulders and pumpkin head you may assess his physical size: that of a Yetinsyn shrimp. Not being capable to excel in civilization, leadership and refined elegance, the Russian potential exterminators of mankind affected "disheveledness" as a way of life, in disdain of European orderliness, which they never could match.

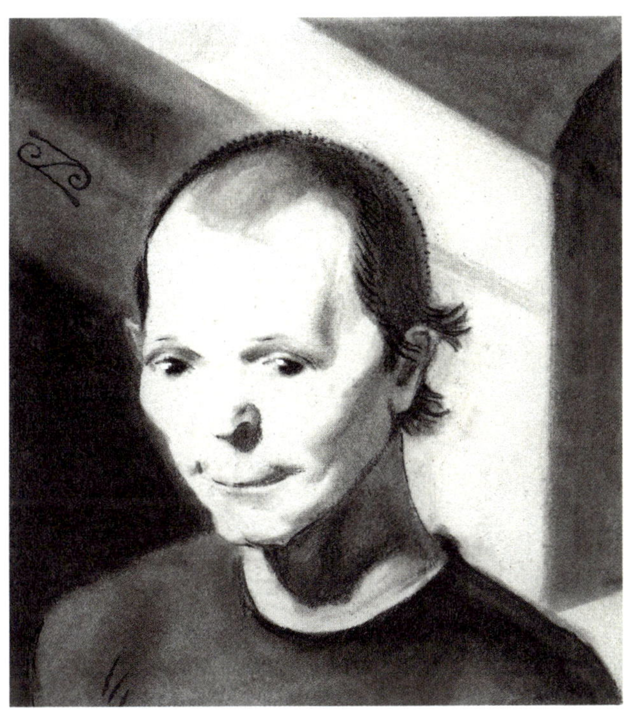

158 The weasel-faced **MACHIAVELLI** and his methods, designed for his patron Prince Lorenzo de Medici to gain power over the nation, became the proverbial example of sneaky deception. There is something in the face, particularly the mouth, that no human could produce, that is purely anthropoid. There is a radio broadcaster in Los Angeles with that rare type of mouth who is renowned for his subversive services to Communism.

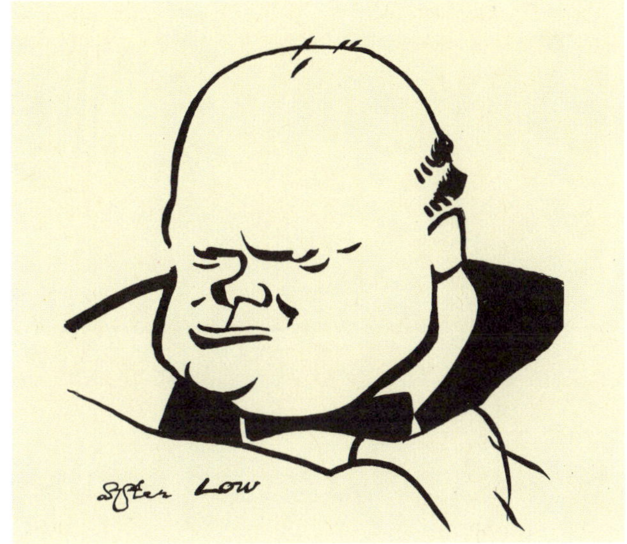

159 Here I have copied a most penetrating observation by an excellent artist, the English political cartoonist David Low, of **CHURCHILL.** There is expressed viciousness, not due to his wartime hatred of the Nazi Germans, but to his inborn capacity to convey hatred… because he was a dwarfish social aggressor and the servant of a distinctly predatory nation.

Let me reproduce a clipping from an American paper that will explain what is behind Churchill's facial expression, why he helped Roosevelt betray half of Europe, giving eleven nations over to Communism at Yalta.

Gluttony is an inadvertent giveaway of one's anthropoid heritage and the motivation to create global Vampirialism. As a matter of fact, I have never seen a fat being in Poland and, though some five hundred years ago that country was the most powerful in Europe, it NEVER conquered other people's countries. Soil-tillers do not conquerors make.

Churchill Biggest Eater at Palace, Says King's Ex-Chef

CHICAGO, Dec. 9 (UP)—The former chef for England's royal family said today that Sir Winston Churchill was the heartiest eater he remembers at Buckingham Palace.

Rene Roussin, here to act as "guest advisory chef" to a Chicago restaurateur, served the late King George from 1937 to 1947 when illness forced him to retire.

Queen Mother Elizabeth would mention that a "gentleman who likes a lot to eat" was coming to dine.

"Then I would know that Mr. Churchill was coming," Roussin said. "For Mr. Churchill I would double everything, and often he would ask for a second helping."

One trick, he said, was to stuff one partridge inside of another, so the former Prime Minister would appear to be eating the normal helping.

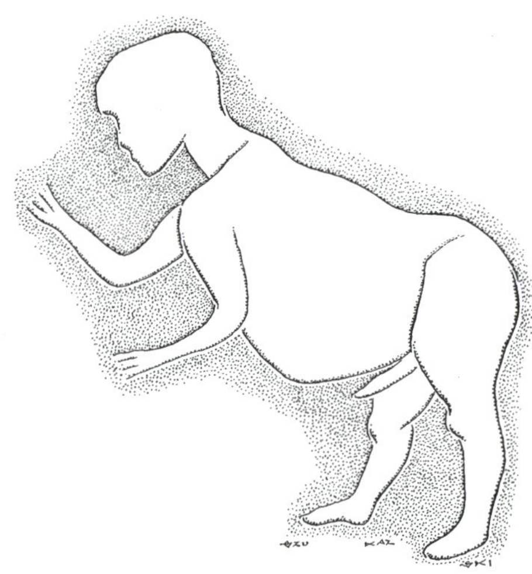

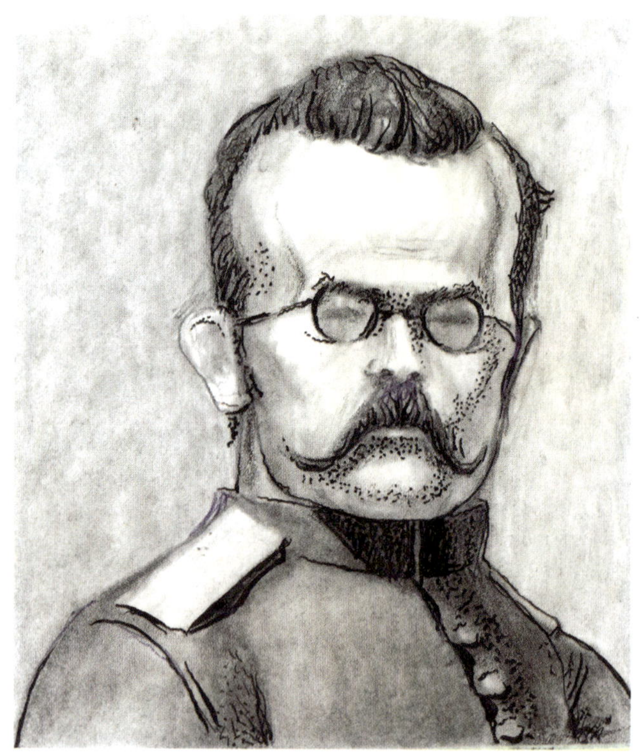

160 From the Paleolithic (early Stone Age) dates this **EUROPEAN PYGMY**, immortalized by a Cro-Magnon diluvial, with a constant erection from infection, extremely short arms and legs, but an enormous abdomen and long torso. There is a mistake, however. Such dwarfish gargantuan eaters never have long necks, but are practically neckless.

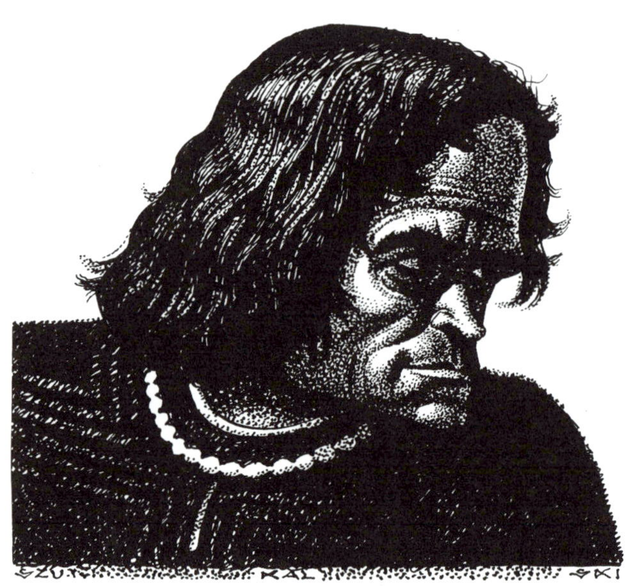

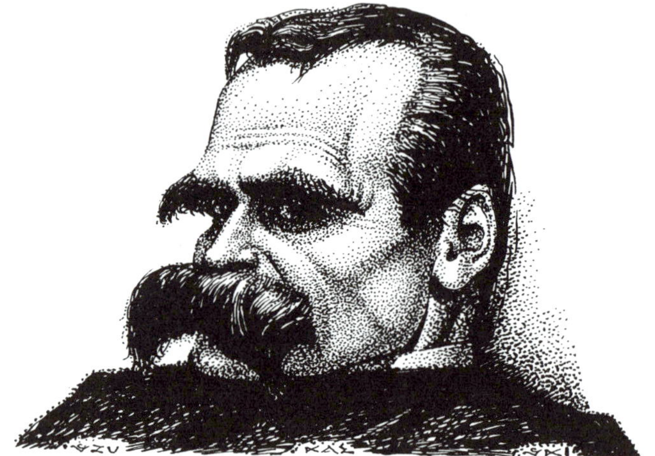

162 Being ugly and suffering from an inferiority complex, **LORENZO** "the Magnificent" **THE MEDICI** (whom Machiavelli taught how to become more princely by the sly methods of a sneak) had himself portrayed many times and nicknamed "the Magnificent." As a patron of the arts, which at that time were still creative, he built great palaces to incidentally create a halo around his name and thick personality. As you can see by his projecting muzzle, he was an apeish man.

161 Napoleon ordered David and others who painted his portraits that "rulers and kings should be idealized in portraiture, because after they die no one will know if they were not true!" A good illustration of this motto is this portrait painted by the fine German sculptor-painter Kling, dramatizing **FRIEDRICH NIETZSCHE**'s likeness by giving him a gigantic walrus mustache. Actually the inferiority-stricken poet turned propagandist-philosopher, who attempted to smuggle himself from his knock-kneed timidity into the ranks of Gods and Supermen, was a nondescript individual as we can tell by the photograph on top, taken when he was a sergeant in the German Army. It is characteristic of timid men who gain some notice to add thickly to hints at their unusualness.

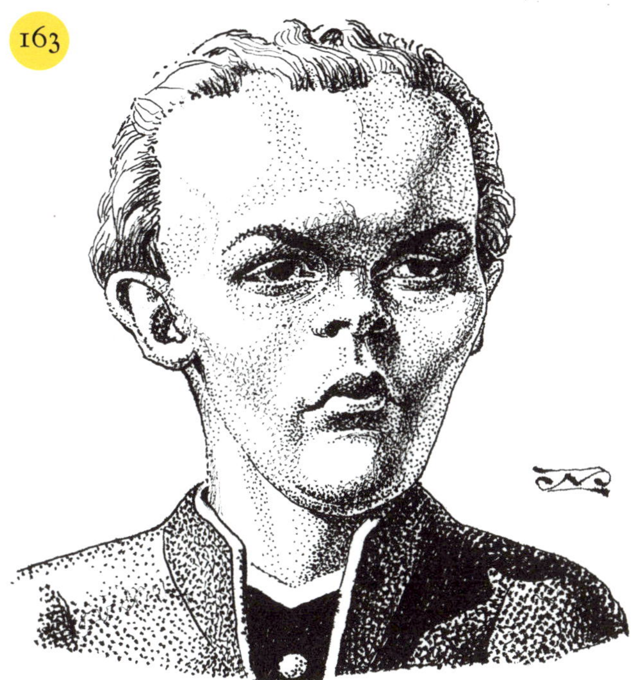

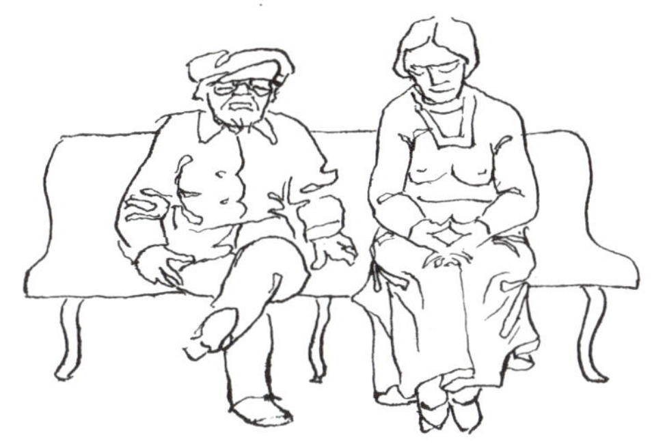

LENIN AND HIS WIFE, NADEZHDA KRUPSKAYA

163 A drawing I made from a photograph of Vladimir Ulyanov, alias **LENIN**, as a boy of fifteen. This is one of the Greatest men in history, that is, judged in my way, maybe not yours… Those are GREAT who ALTER the history of the world, be they GOOD or EVIL, and by that token Hitler is among the Great, for with his predatory ambitions he has caused tremendous change, if only in the moral indignation of the German people.

Kerensky murdered. Thus he took over the wrecked edifice of the State that others had diligently prepared and worked on (they do not sow or plant, but they INVADE… in order to reap the harvest). He was a Yetinsyn, which is more markedly revealed by the pointed head that we know from my drawings of the four anthropoids in this chapter. Note the total absence of neck and the "Russian" nose.

165 But look at the drawing of the late **KING FAROUK** of Egypt. Being born of royal lineage and in affluence, he did not suffer from inferiority feelings, because girls and women did not disdain him, so he did not turn against the state and become a revolutionary. Most radicals are exceedingly ugly and because they can never be popular with girls and women, they develop a hatred of mankind, starting in the formative years of adolescence. It comes to that simple explanation.

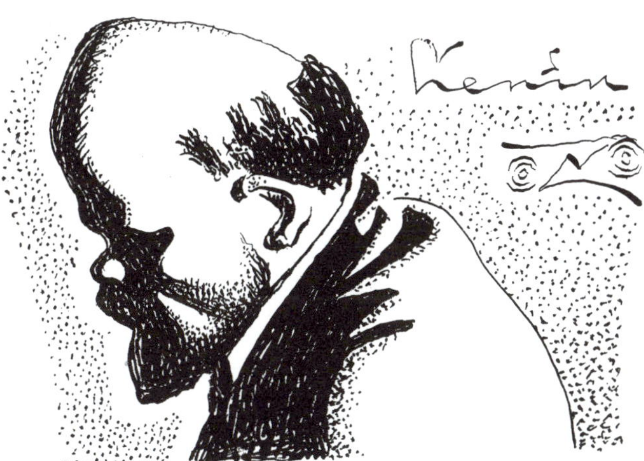

164 When **LENIN** grew up, his biological inferiority preordained him to live conspiratorily. He dedicated himself ostensibly to the revolution against the tsarist tyranny only to establish another tyranny: that of the Yetinsyny, by betraying the revolution when he ordered

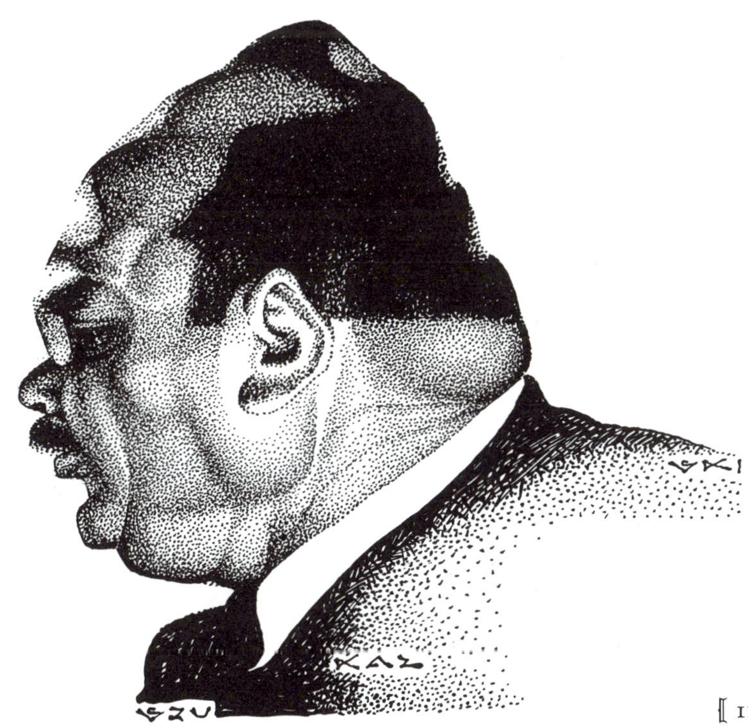

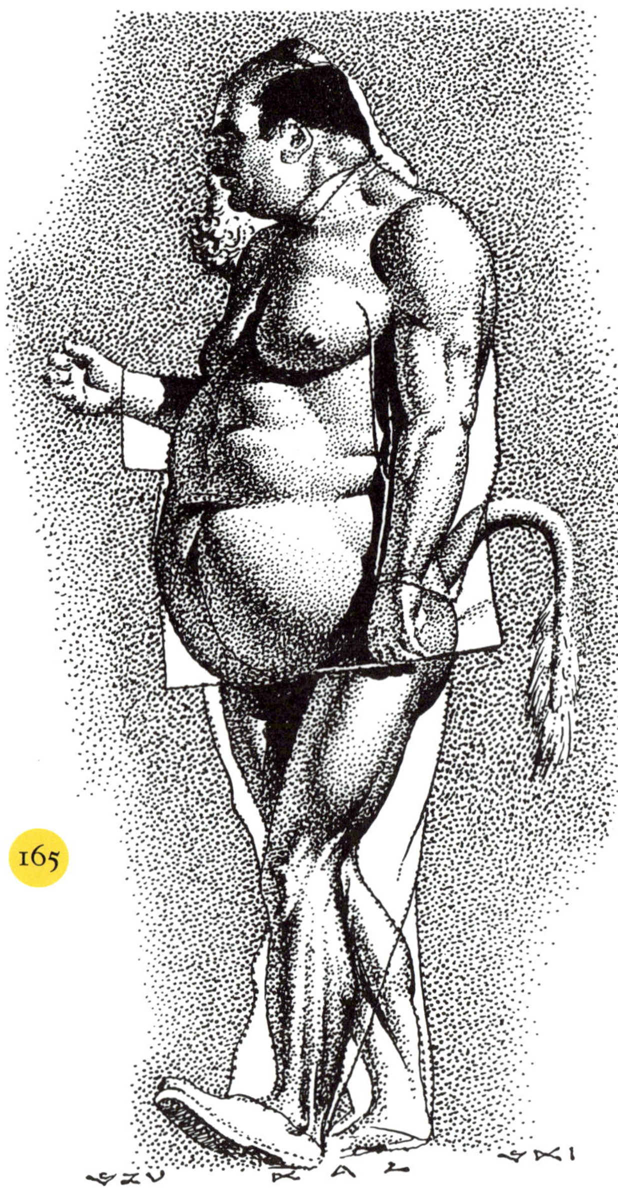

165

I have stripped **KING FAROUK** of his clothing and added the Pan's tail that he probably had at birth, but had removed. Look at the pointed head of a Manape. His too-short arms do not even come to his genitals. His too-small hands are characteristic of dwarfishness. His neck bulge is still there, though it should have disappeared in the fourth month of the foetal state. His gargantuan gluttony indicates his heritage from the Egyptian Bess.

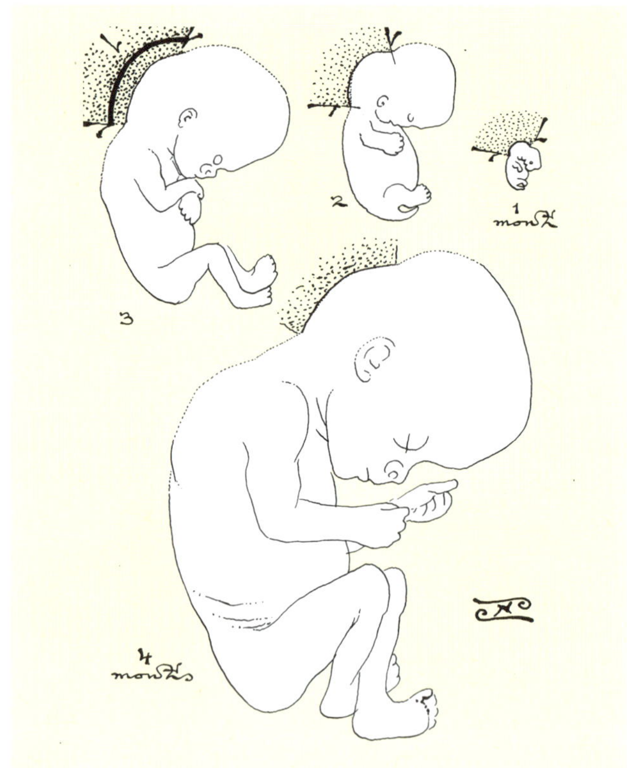

166   I made a small drawing of the development of a **FOETUS** from the first to the fourth month. You see the bulge in the back of the neck enlarge progressively, then suddenly vanish. Since the gestations of apes and humans differ in length of time (therefore, I observed premature births in women of Manape heritage) the children born to apeoid parents retain such fatty rolls of flesh after birth and throughout their lives.

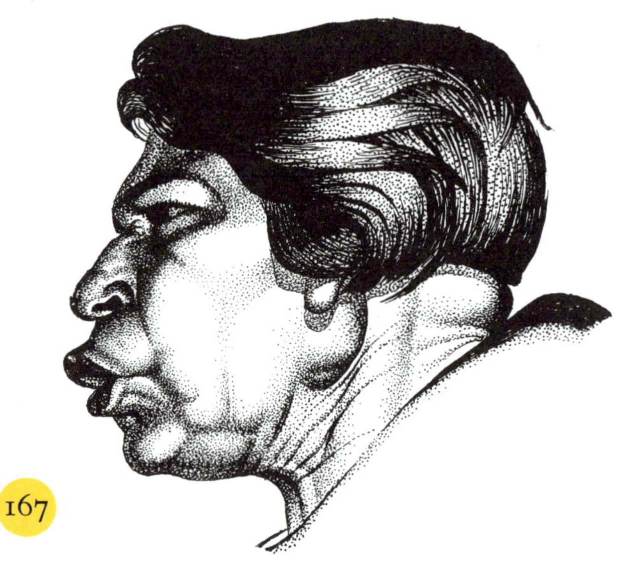

167

DICTATOR PAUKA
(Russian agent for Romania)

168

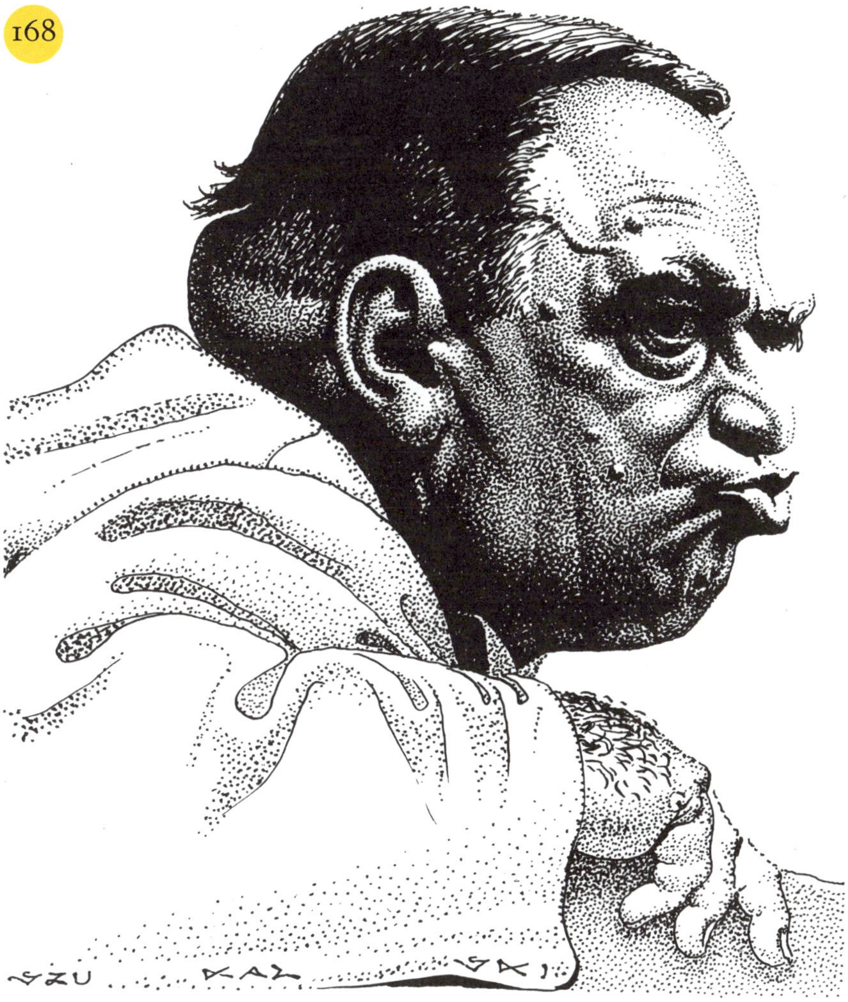

169

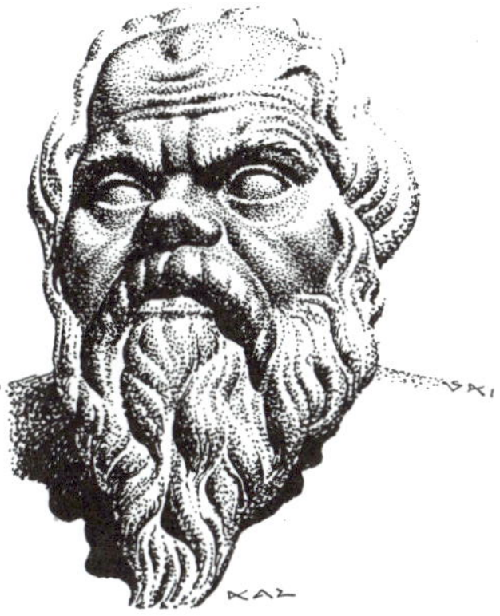

SOCRATES
(Apoid father)

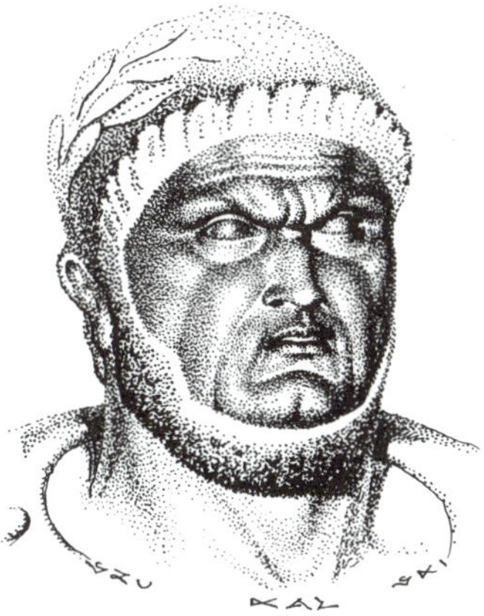

NERO

168   Little **LA GUARDIA**, the manipulative mayor of New York who was selling locomotives to Tito of Yugoslavia, ostensibly taking away the spiritual control from anti-Nazi, anti-Communist Michailovich, the patriot, assisting the Communists in taking over that part of Europe.

Here you have the "little flower", as he preferred to be called. The tiny hands indicate the dwarfishness of this Great Patron of Communism, though he was an American flag waver.

169   In order to be better understood while speaking of the coming portraits of people with Manape heritage, let me further carry the above statement about the fatty neck-roll, in that there are two types of Yetinsyny. I class them according to the facial mask, which is either **NERONIC** or **SOCRATIC**. Let us say that the two eyes on a face form the horizontal base of a triangle, the down-pointing "pinnacle" being the mouth. If you shift this triangle to the bottom of a circle, you have the face of a child. If, on the contrary, the triangle is shifted upwards in the circle, you will have a mature face.

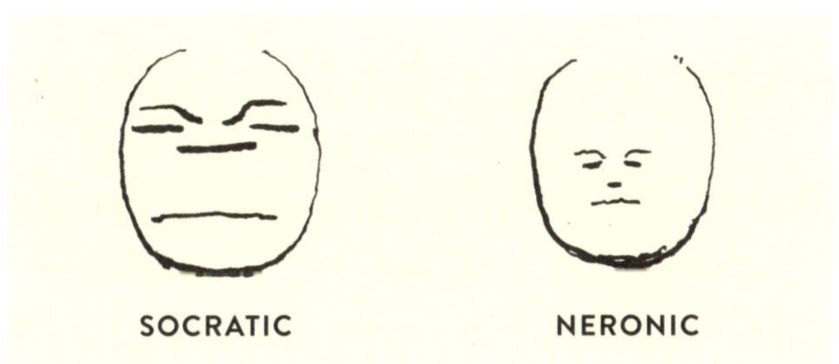

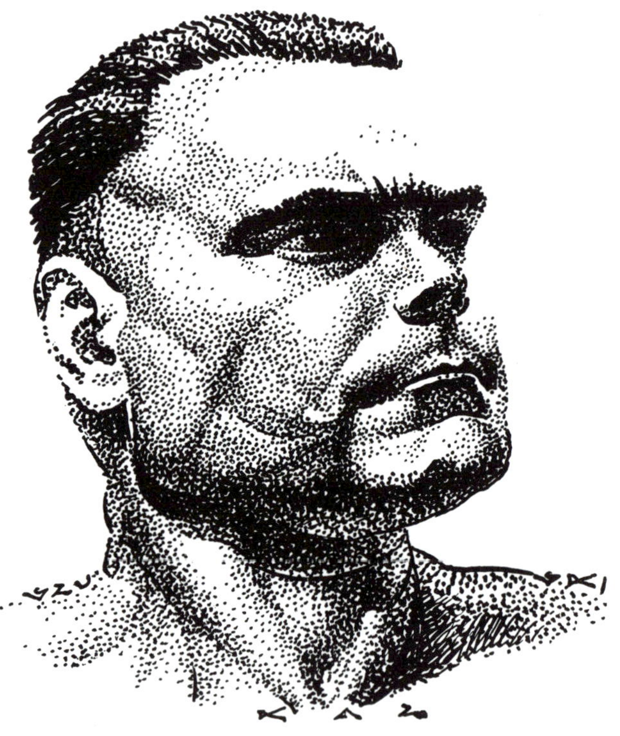

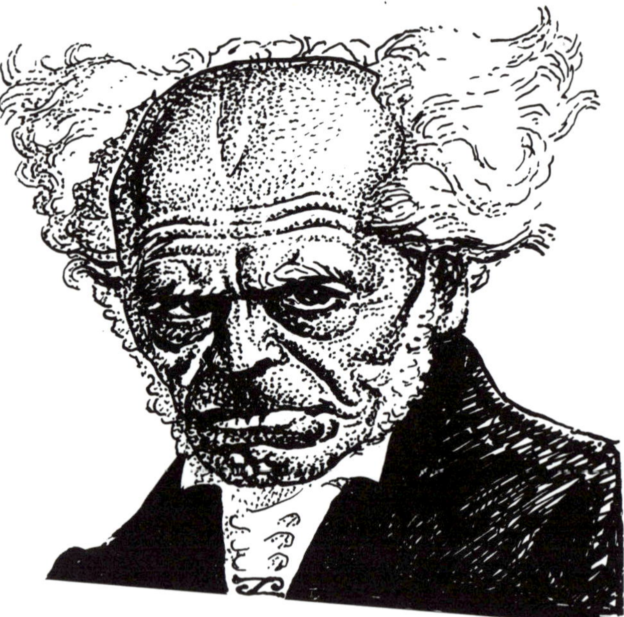

170 A Neronic type of face with a very large mouth that, however, is tucked in to deceive people while the owner is biding his time till he can inflict vengeance for being rejected by beautiful girls and women. A long upper-lipped Yetinsyn (his German nationality had nothing to do with this), **COMMANDANT KRAMMER** could finally realize his adolescent Manape dream to kill-kill-kill when he was given the longed-for position at Bergen-Belsen where he could exterminate thousands of the HUMANS he so hated.

171 Portrait of philosopher **SCHOPENHAUER**, an inferiority-obsessed Yetinsyn who spent his entire life publicizing himself by inference of a disguised God, fooling the intellectual fools, the good-for-nothings, who took him as a divinity.

This is the acromegalic type of face. The over-long, though tucked-in upper lip marks him as a Yetinsyn who, being cowardly, hid himself behind protective verbal projectiles.

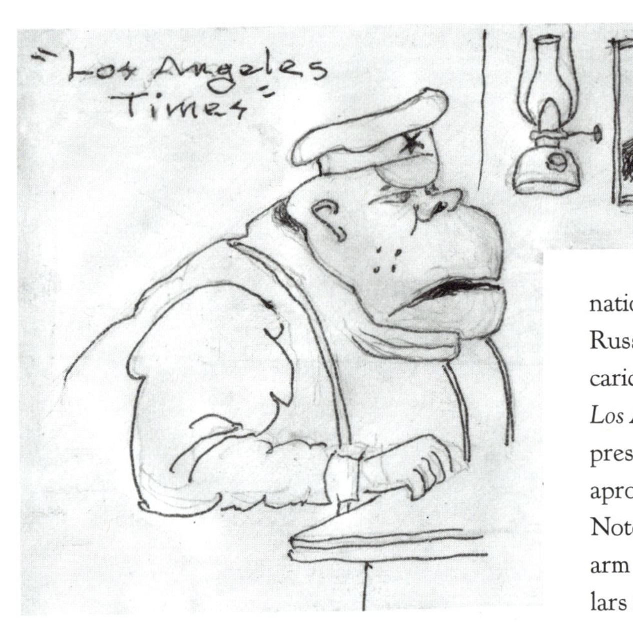

172 People eventually learn about the "spiritual" personality of the Yetinsyny who form the governments of various nations, from the political cartoonist. This linear description of a Russian official (a *chinovnik* or "doer"), an intentionally naively drawn caricature, as if it were graffiti on a toilet-room wall, appeared in the *Los Angeles Times*. I do not know the artist and did not tell him how to present a Yetinsyn, but unknowingly he did it correctly, with the apron upper lip, a trap-mouth, a wart-nose and protruding muzzle. Note the picture on the wall of the Yetinsyn Hero. Note the shriveled arm of the official, who was about to let you bring your American dollars into Russia at the 1980 Olympics.

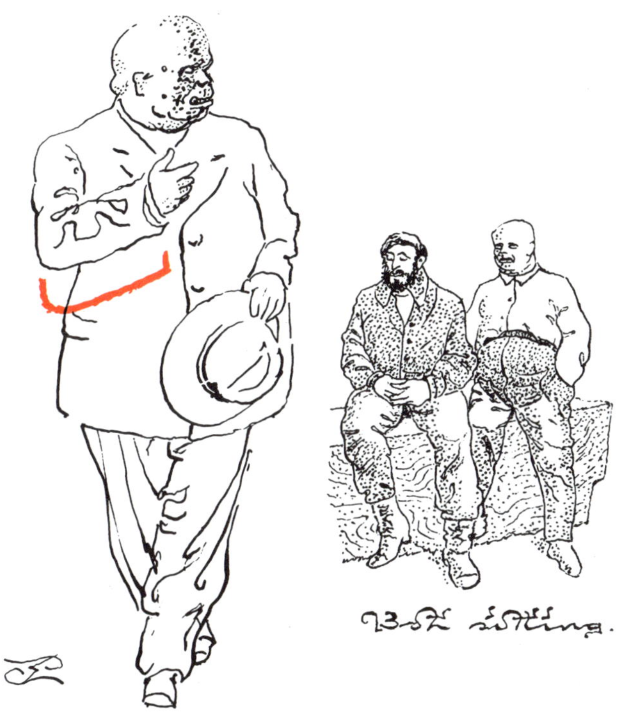

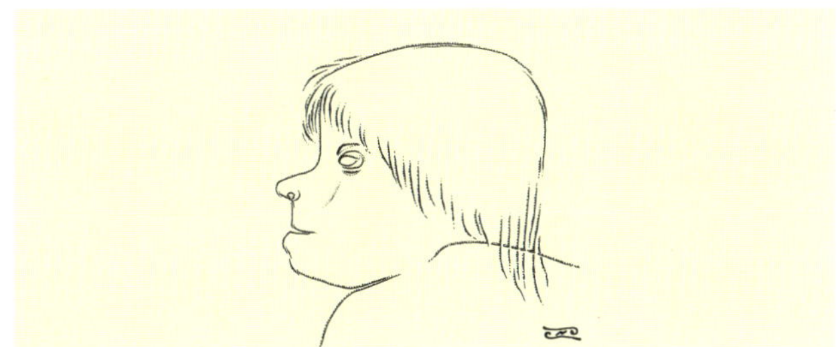

173 Two comparative drawings for you to see **KHRUSH-CHEV**'s build. On the first you see a red line where his arm would have been were he not a Yetinsyn. Though he was a Ukrainian, he was a descendant of the Manape, therefore born to be a traitor to his own people. The too-loose pants the Russians used to wear when they came to get what they wanted from the gullible Anglo-mericans, were to disguise the odd angles of the always bent legs (do not, however, immediately think of the Russian ballet danc-ers, who have perfectly proportioned legs).

Then compare the two chummy *tovarishche* (comrades): the weak, will-less **CASTRO** who was shoved forward as a dictator by his brother, Che, and the just-dealt-with Yetinsyn. Note that the representative of the Soviets tow-ers over the wishy-washy intellectual from New York. But look where their waistlines are. Khrushchev's is just below Castro's chest. The Russian is standing on his left, straight-ened leg while he is sitting, while Castro, also sitting, has his legs doubled up. The pot-bellied Nikita is not cheating you in order to convince you that he is taller than the "Latino," he simply cannot sit any other way and look his size, because his Yetinsyn torso is one-third longer than Castro's.

174 There were various types of Manapes everywhere, until Mankind wisely reduced their numbers, so that we at present refuse to believe that there even exists a Big Foot, Sasquatch or, as nearby Indians have called him since prehistoric times, Mo Mo.

There was a small variety of Manape with whom Humans, either way, could produce bastards. This bi-species I have named Yetinsyny too, though they are of a more diminutive size and have the Neronic, small-triangled facial type. Here you have a most magnificent portrait, scratched on a piece of slate by the Cro-Magnon Human.

Her forward-thrust muzzle, the undercut nose, the viciously tucked-in mouth where lips are reduced to tin can rims, and the total absence of neck mark her as a Manape, though she is clearly more delicate than the usual type.

175 The slight filigree face and figure of **ROBESPIERRE**— who during the French Revolution held the position of key figure, deciding who was or was not to be executed

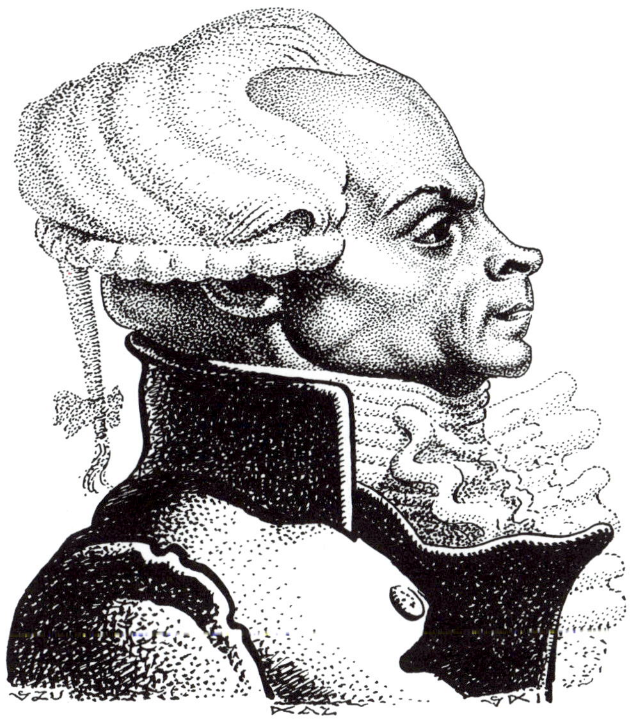

by the blade of the newly invented guillotine—make him one of the descendants of this grand-grand-grand-mother of the Yetinsyny of every nation, who by the unthinking world are erroneously considered to be French, or German, or Russian.

So is Manson (178) not an American, just because he was born in the United States, nor is William Calley (179). They are two of the international Yetinsyny, whose elemental mission in life is to destroy as many Humans, loved by beautiful women, as possible.

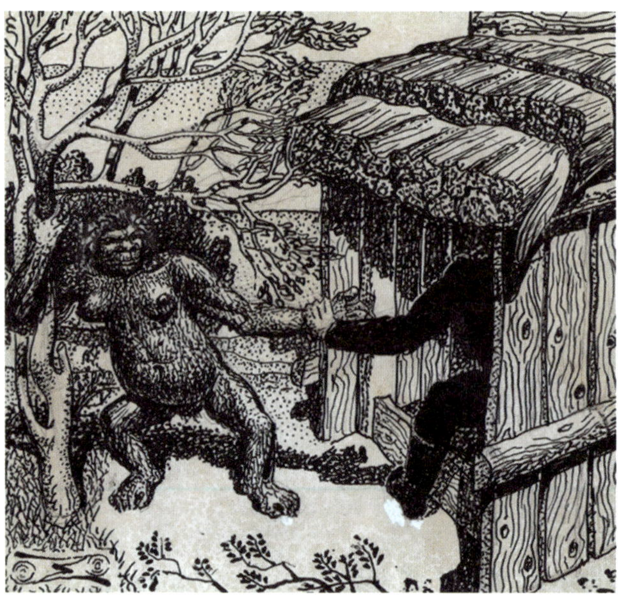

Rendez-Vous with Destiny in the Woodshed

176 To make myself better understood, I made you a drawing of a Tsar's *soldat* (soldier) having a date with a village **ETA** and at the same time unknowingly inviting an avalanche of history's calamities upon the truly Russian (not Moscovian) owners of the woodshed.

There were instances of Yeti females being adopted as infant creatures by villagers in northern Russia who, on maturing, were domesticated enough to wear clothes and capable of performing chores. Their willingness to distribute sexual satisfaction (as well as the animal disease syphilis) to any willing village drunk, made them rather popular objects far and wide. So, many a traveling male inquiring which of the women was "the one" that could be had without preliminary introductions, would be answered by the villagers pointing towards the village Yeta: *Eta* (that one)! This is precisely the word that became the name for the females of the domesticated Eta "people" of Japan. It is recorded

that a child was born to one of these village whores, which grew to maturity, and Russian scientists have the records of these facts. Thus, going back into prehistoric times, these half-breeds introduced the bi-species that I named Yetinsyny. Whenever there are populations prevalently wart-nosed, they harken to the crossbreeding between Man and Animal, the consequence of which is bloody ravages to the surrounding world.

Again, it is not language or citizenship that makes a man or a Communist, but the biological classification and the Human or a-Human predisposition. History is the float, the cork, of the fishing line. It behaves in many ways, glorious or tyrannical, depending on what type of creatures motivate it down in the depths nibbling on the bait. While it is Humankind that created all the Christian or other systems of Ethics, it is the a-Human, Yetinsyn heritage that gave us all the man-made calamities, wars, invasions, plagues, syphilis. Not until mankind recognizes the biological directions from where all the misfortunes come, it will continue to be the victim of this Yetinsyn affliction. Each species has its elemental foes, its exterminators, and so do we, Humans.

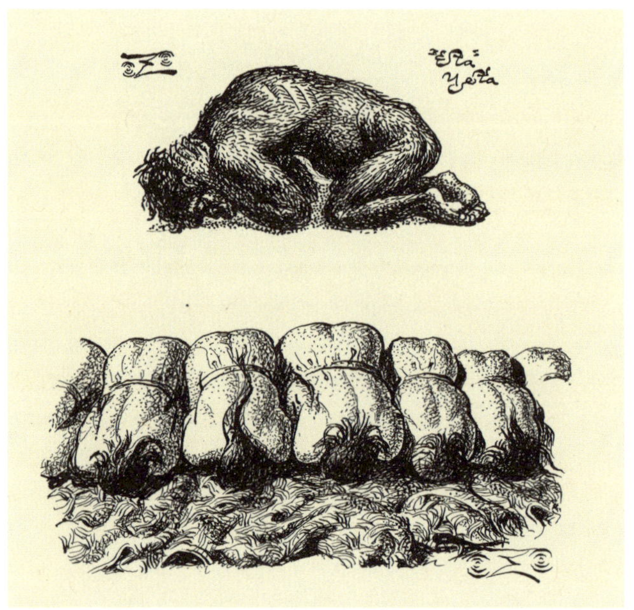

177 In one of the oldest books in Russia that presented the incidents of Yeta females living among the villagers, I found a woodcut showing the odd way in which they positioned their bodies in sleep. They crouched on the ground, holding their heads down with their hands. Their foreheads, from heavy leaning on the ground, always developed thick callouses over their apeish brows. Later, while perusing through the Northridge College Library, I came across a British scientific periodical that had a photograph showing the communal way of sleeping of the Mongols. They double up for warmth the same way the domesticated Yetas did, spreading sheepskins on the ground for their fore-heads to lean on.

This identical manner of sleeping is most significant, for it explains the proverbial cruelty of the Asian people. It proves that the Mongolian race is a bi-human species which has continued to use this sleeping position ever since their Manape ancestors taught their infants, millions of years back.

178 When a Human kills, he is a criminal and, under the human law, has to be punished according to the degree to which a nation has scaled Evil, depending on its sensitivity or callousness. When **CHARLES MANSON** kills many people, American insensitivity allows him to continue his life in prison, that he may not be molested by human society. How many times should sub-humans like him be executed? As many times as they have killed? Then Manson

is beyond the Human Law, hence he is saved from Justice.

Do we reproach a wolf, a hyena if it kills? Do we think them criminal? If a dog with rabies attacks a child, we do not sue in court, but simply kill the offender. The semi-Humans who kill-kill-kill are not criminals, they are dangerous animals, and Justice with human consideration does not apply to them. They simply should be eliminated without the process of law, being an economic burden on human society as it is.

179 Regardless of what was the inhuman activity of **WILLIAM CALLEY**, and whether the court found him guilty of slaying a community of Asian Humans or not, with a facial type like his he should never have been allowed to handle guns. Look at his vengeful eyes and the tucked-in split-liver mouth. He is the same type of Yetinsyn as Trotsky, a pinch-faced Neronic. He should have been directed towards science, crafts and arts. He could be a benefit to society if he was a mechanic, an engineer or a jeweler, but *never* as an officer or a politician.

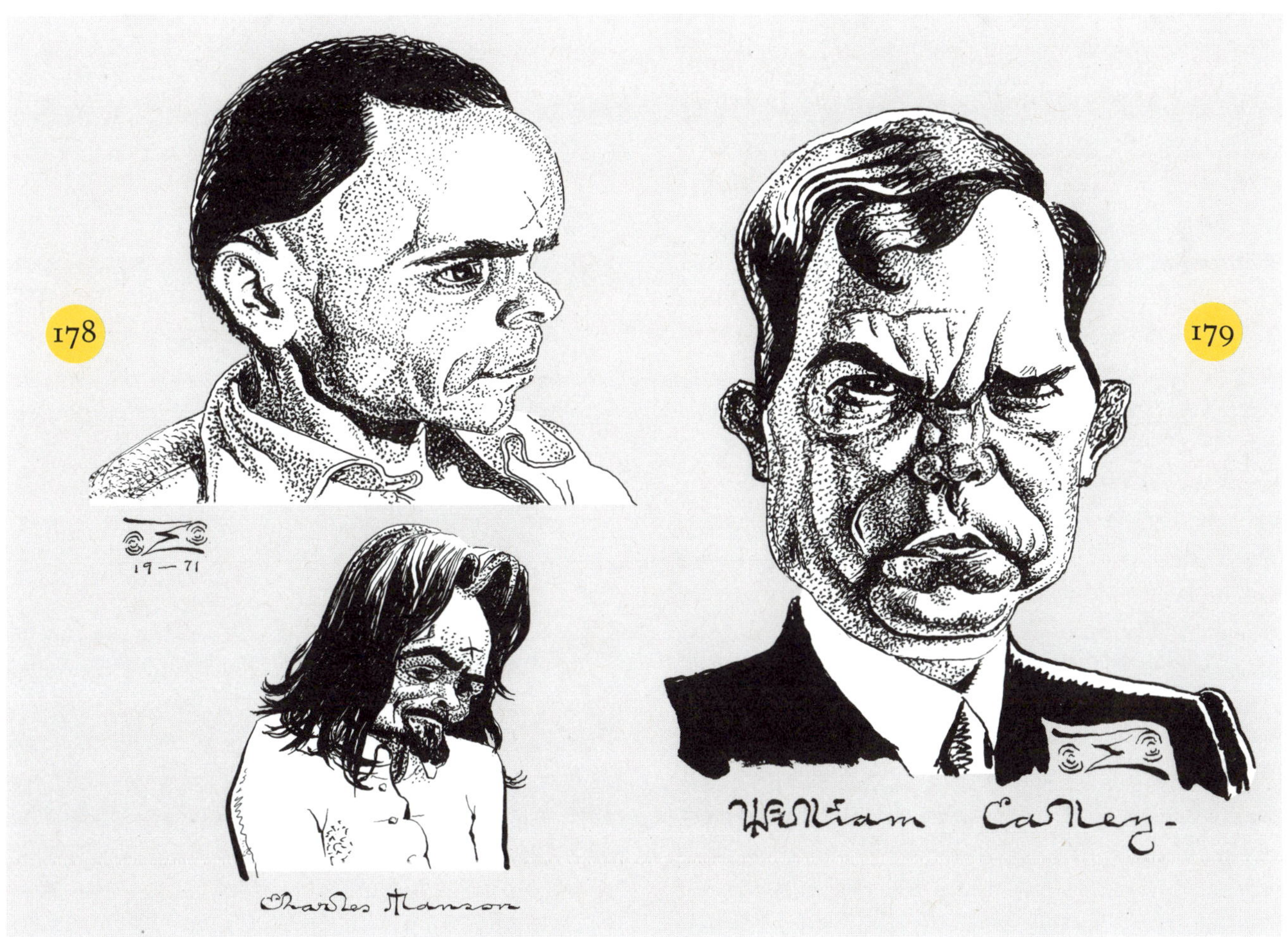

Any Bait Will Do to Catch Pin-Headed Mankind

This book is too grievously miniscule to enable me to expound the vast subjects that are all related organisms of my new science of Zermatism. I feel I do not even have the opportunity to begin to tell you. But then, these discoveries I made have had to remain on my shelves too long already, unread and unheard of, because I am not one of the privileged minorities of the Cultural Siberia of America, Southern California.

In my volume on the new science of *Anthropolitical Motivations* I illustrate how our human ancestors were slow-witted pinheads, thinking but silent, narrow-shouldered, slouchingly moving creatures. A remainder of this disposition is the almost shattering naivety of human society, which causes us to fall for any ideological CRAP that the dwarfish amongst us concoct.

When the Roman Predatory Empire was declining, a pope noticed an odd species of man on the throne of France. There was Pepi, and his two sons, Karl and Karloman. The three of them were Asiatic dwarves. When the sons inherited the vast Kingdom, Karl renounced his brother Karloman, and exiled him to the Monte Casino monastery where he remained imprisoned for the rest of his life, as a monk.

Seeing so efficient a ruler and knowing the expansory ways of the Asians, the pope made him the first King of Europe, who then proceeded to christianize the continent. Those who would not submit to the new Ism, were exterminated and their land confiscated. His example was soon followed by "kings" who submitted to being Latinized or Germanized in the name of the Holy Virgin.

The Poles called their king "Krol," the Czechs called him "Kral," and the Russians "Karol," all of which dialectic versions could now be translated as Charles, but actually were nothing else than local forms for the word DWARF. The Germanic languages had words like *Koenig, Koning* for the kings, which are but continuations of the word "Khueng" which actually means "Hun." (From this came the English word *Viking,* by way of "We Khueng," meaning "We the Huns.")

180 While ruling over his vast Empire, Charles sent specially selected troubadours (foundlings, bastards, comparable to our contemporary hippies) into the world to tell their poetic legends about his Supermanship, which is symptomatic of the inferiority psychosis of the Yetinsyn.

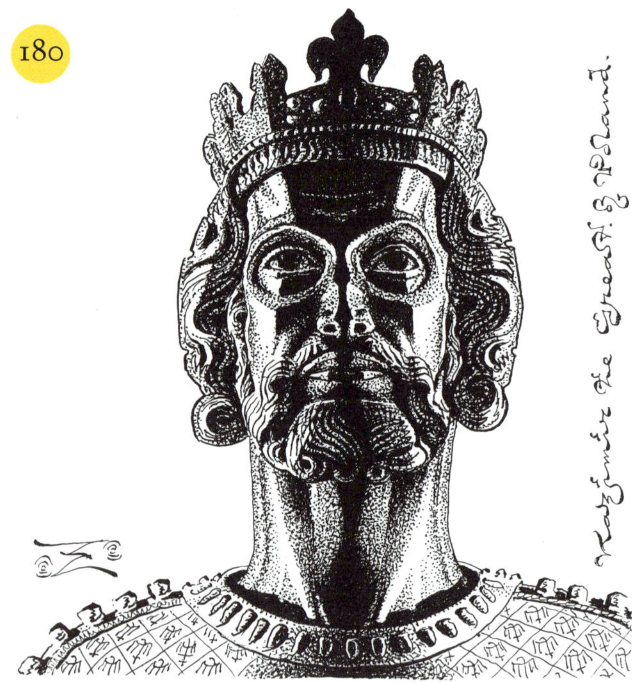

The German nation in particular is proud of their *Übermensch,* recounting the legendary reputation of this SUPER-KILLER up till our times. They even counterfeited his likeness by taking this early work of the Polish gothic sculptor Wit Stwosz, and calling it the portrait of Charlemagne. It was, however, made from life of the Polish **KING KAZIMIERZ THE GREAT** who ruled some 500 years later. On the portrait bust many little Eagles of Poland, with the ring on their tails (*Bi*), were placed, which identifies it as Kazimierz's portrait.

181 So, the Yetinsyny will always take advantage of the trusting Human. The conspiring dwarves will build vast parasitic empires based on some silly Ideology, a mere bait for gullible and kindhearted mankind (incidentally, however, creating favorable circumstances for culture and, presently, sciences to flourish, to the glory of the vermin), be they Canaanites or Poles (in whose countries the predators have now established headquarters and parasite upon the aboriginals).

182 The howling **CHEST-BEATING GORILLA** in the Yetinsyn is perpetually pressed towards its biological preordainment. It works overtime pounding on the pulpit of subversion, calling all the misfits of the world to unite against the hated Human. The phrases ring hours after their delivery, "We must fight against the Tyrants, the Capitalists, the Educated and well… why not against the Good-looking who are loved by beautiful women, too! Long live da Peephole! Long live the Revolution!"

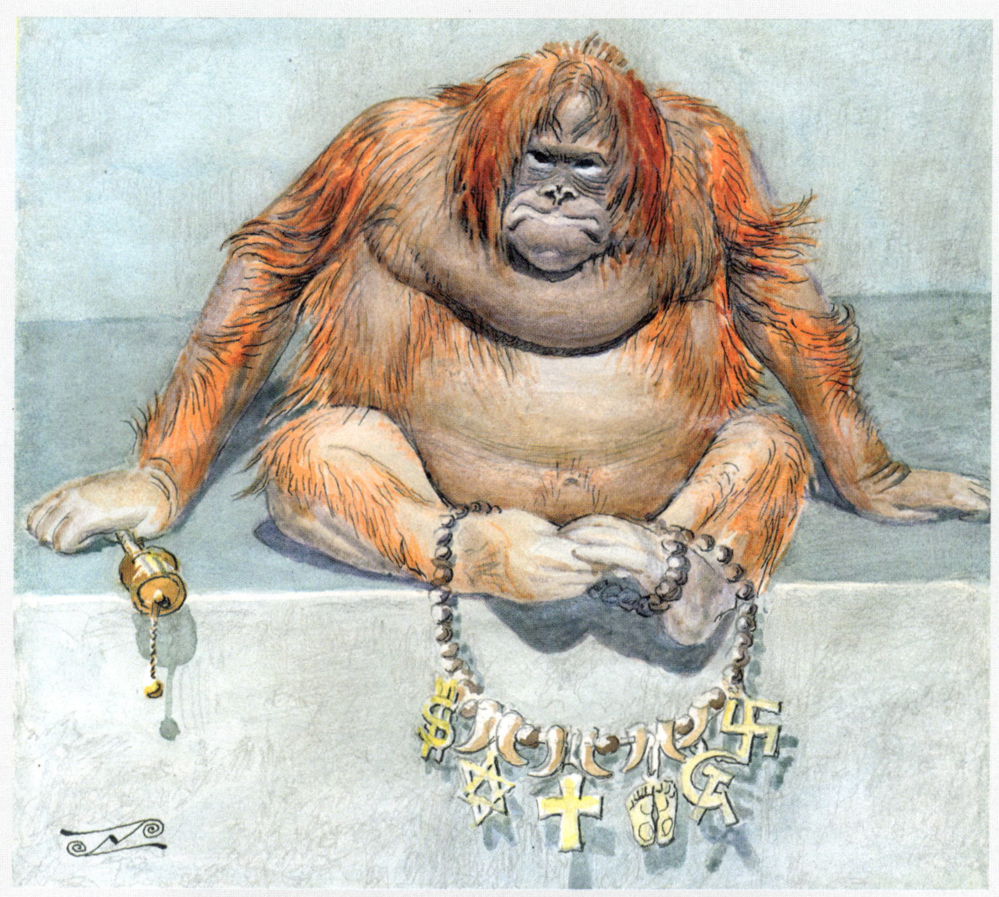

181

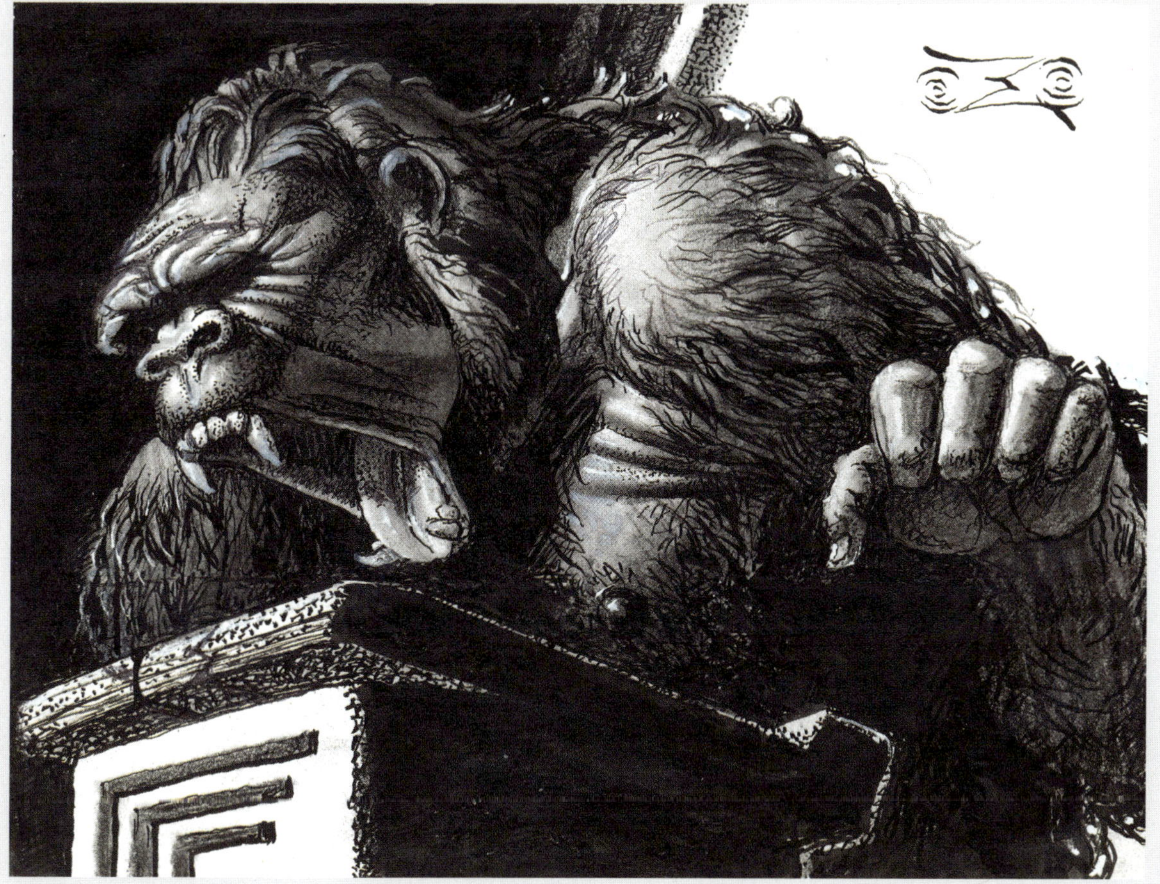

182

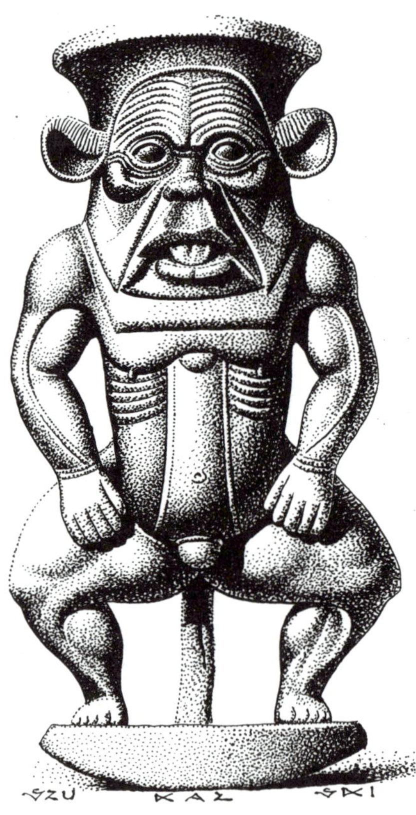

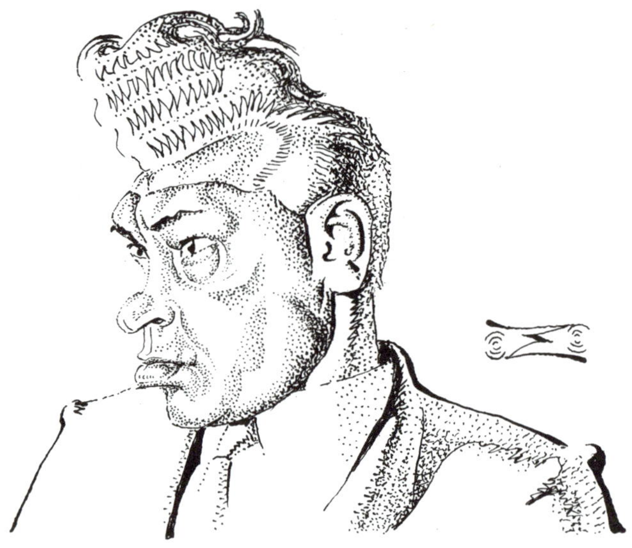

185 **TSARAPKIN**, former Russian delegate to the United Nations, is another example of the Socratic facial type. Note the gentleman's lack of neck and the innate brutality of expression, harkening back to the four drawings I showed you at the beginning of this chapter. He was afflicted with acromegaly, the nervous disease characterized by enlargement of the head, feet, hands, and sometimes chest.

183 The Socratic type of Manape could be claimed to have come down from the Egyptian mythological Bess. Note the small eye–mouth triangle of this Bess, as opposed to the minuscule triangle of the above-illustrated, Neronic facial types.

184 I made this drawing of a Socratic type of Yetinsyn finishing a sketch by David, the master painter of the Neo-Classical Period at the time of the French Revolution. Completely covered by warts—flesh colonies of foreign, primate cells—with an upper lip like the blacksmith's apron and a brow protruding like a gorilla's, **DANTON** developed a grudge towards mankind and became the chief order-giver for the execution of thousands of Humans.

His godawful loneliness so depressed him, since no woman would deign to look at him, that he compensated his shattered ego by giving himself titles as "Jove the Thunderer," "The Rebel Satan" and "The Titan."

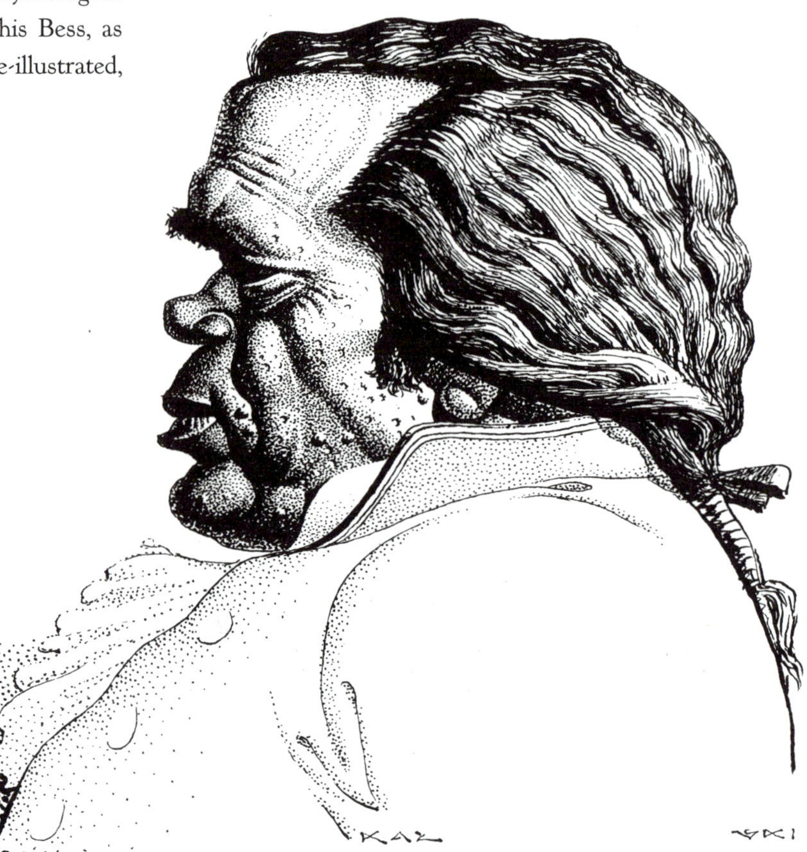

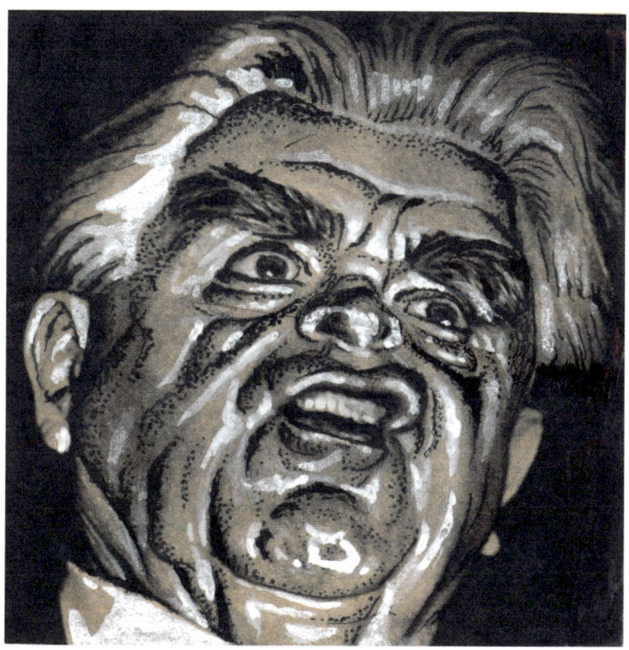

186   Hold on to my hand, don't be scared. This is a Labor Leader who simply "loves da peep-hole." He is so indignant of the Tyranny of the Capital that he snarls, threatening to exterminate the capitalists as soon as he becomes a *Kommissar* or *Gauleiter*, no matter of which ideological sub-group, as long as it holds the prospect of vengeance on human society.

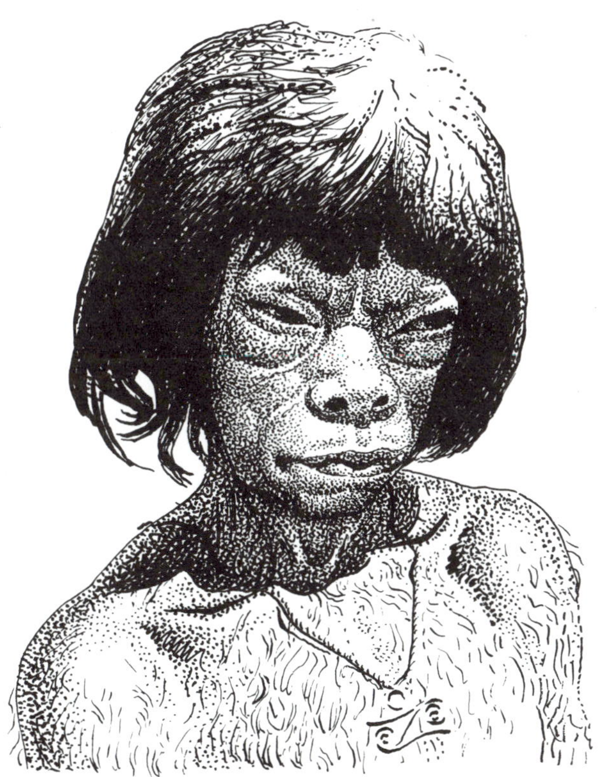

187   **MARIA LIMA** of Peru, who was born covered with fur and never learned human speech. Either both parents were of Manape heritage, or the mother was raped by an Andean Sasquatch.

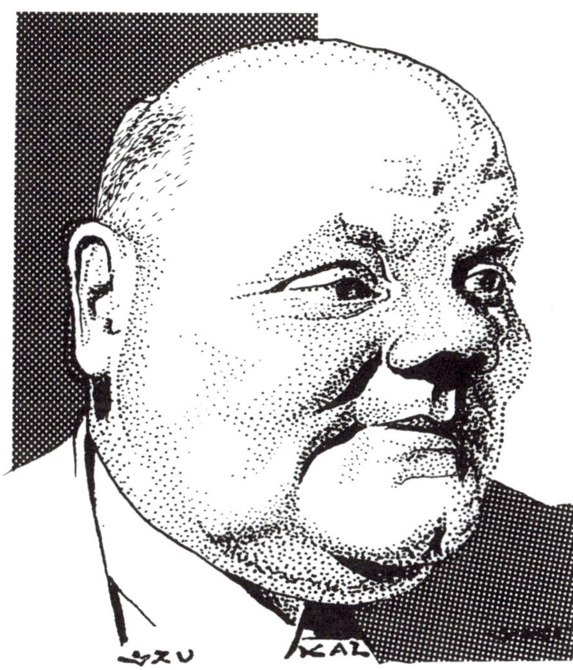

188   John Bodkin Adams, a darling-of-a-doctor who poisoned many of his patients till apprehended and imprisoned, to poison some more after his release.

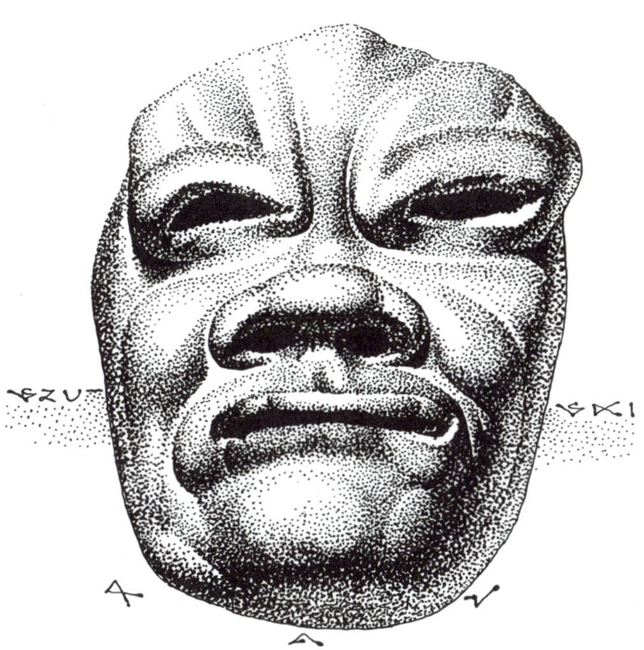

189   An ancient pottery mask, excavated in Peru. This **YETINSYN** too suffered from acromegaly. Look at that terribly wide nose and the swollen eyes.

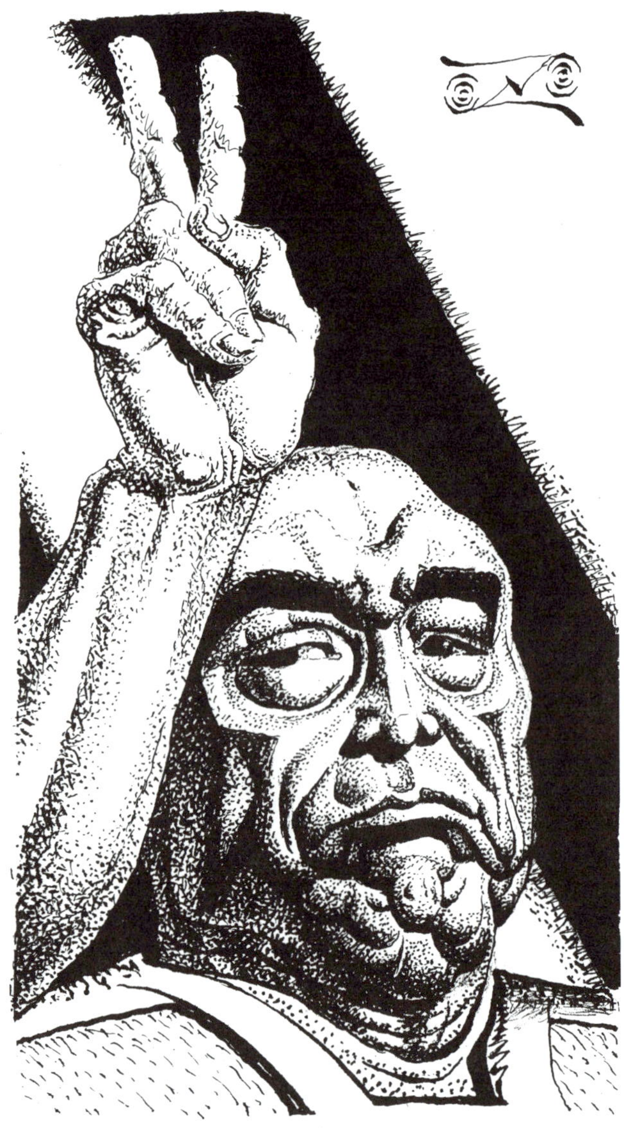

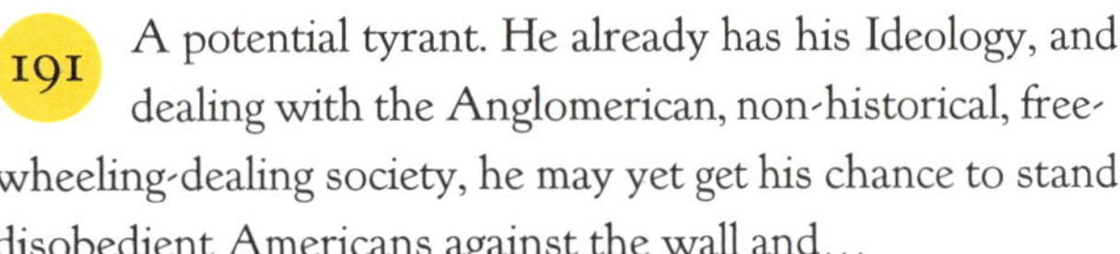

A potential tyrant. He already has his Ideology, and dealing with the Anglomerican, non-historical, free-wheeling-dealing society, he may yet get his chance to stand disobedient Americans against the wall and…

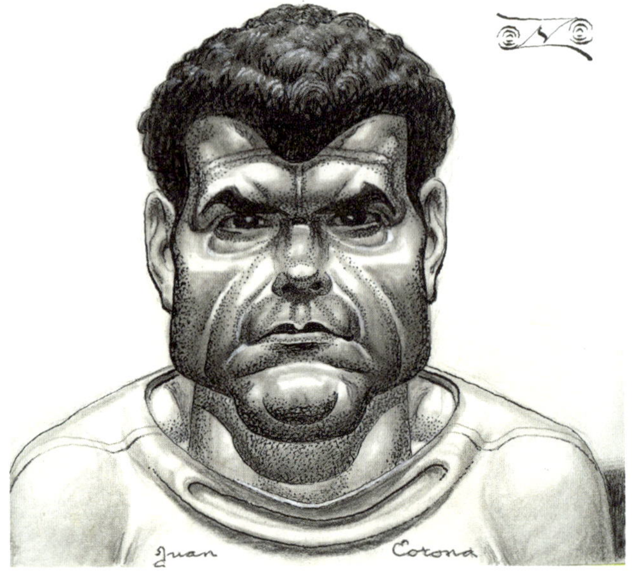

JUAN CORONA, the Mexican field-worker who murdered over twenty other laborers. The United States Court spared his life, for an animal cannot be done Justice. Hence, he was only imprisoned, to protect him from Society.

Can you gauge the hatred behind those beady eyes? What a marvelous executioner for the German Nazis he would have made. Yet, he is not a German, nor a Mexican, but a Yetinsyn on the prowl without some concocted Ideology to serve.

Yeti-Sasquatch and Mankind's Destinies

THOUGH we may insist on preserving our inalienable Right of Freedom in America, we can never alter the biological heritage each of us has at birth, which preordains us to fulfill our specific Mission. We will remain uncouth, broody and dour-dispositioned, though educated and moving in the finest of environments—or gracious and sunny-dispositioned. Due to the combination of our parents' physical and mental traits and our total CHANCE conception (each male orgasmic explosion releases some 14,000,000 spermatozoa, each bringing a different personality, one of which may enter the mother's jelly-egg with its traits) you and I are the inheritors of a personality that may go back to millions of years ago and that could have been some almost divinity or the basest of criminals. Though what will predominate are the NATIONAL characteristics within certain geographic and historic localities.

In the last several years, magazines featured a number of articles about the sightings in remote areas of Sasquatches, Yetis, Abominable Snowmen, which press-gossip caused pooh-poohs from the less imaginative who, believing in the infallibility of science, denounce the "naive" and "unworldly" who "fall for such childish fantasies."

I am definitely one of the latter, having an open mind to every possible impossibility in this as yet unknown world. When coming to a friend's house you see a string dangle out of a drawer, you cannot tell if it will end in a fraction of a second when you take a hold of it, or if it will unwind for an hour, because you do not know the contents of the drawer. To rather a simple mind the things that already exist are the only ones that do. To me things exist even before they are NAMED with a term, as soon as someone has discovered them and, having a mindful head, I even discover new Wonders in things discarded as uninteresting by mindless individuals or timid scientists who can only think with the support of someone higher up in their regard. Scientists are diggers and tabulators. Creative men are thinkers.

I have shown you the meaning of the Greek vase paintings and the Egyptian Besses. Presently I am about to explain to you some mythic reports from prehistoric Mexican and Central American Art. Again, I am showing you only a thimbleful of the vital evidence gathered in my 39 (so far) volumes. In fact, they contain so vast a number of archaeological "witnesses" that if you were made to look at them in one continuous session, you would fall on your knees and beg me to desist my insistence.

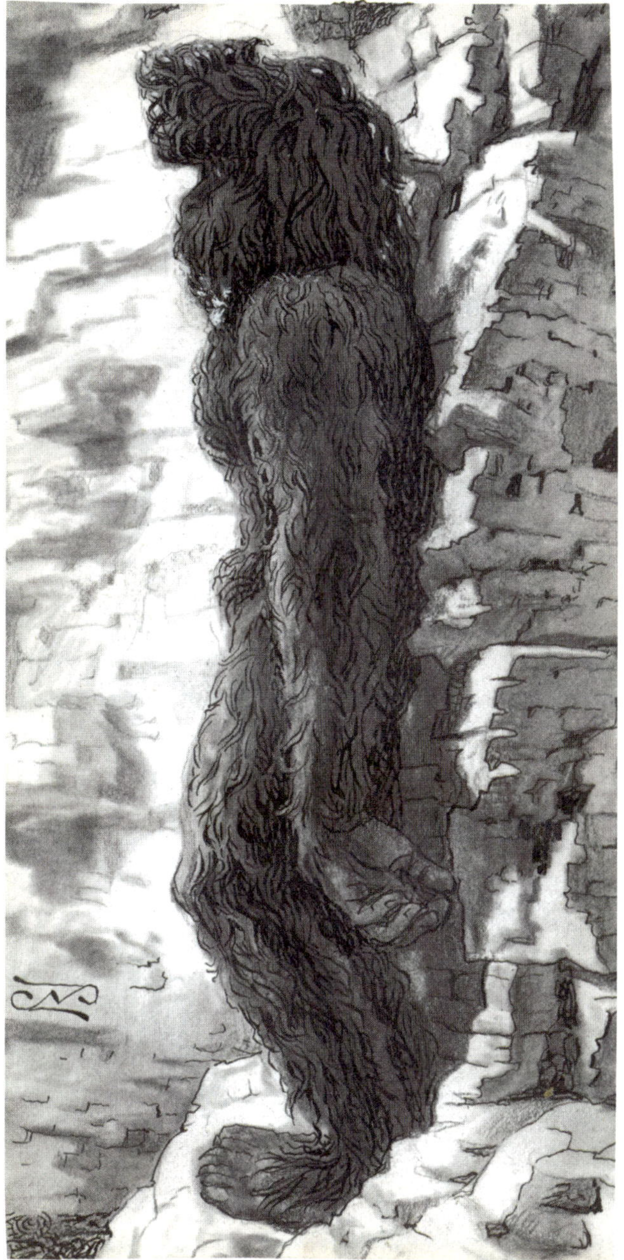

192 Among the illustrations in the articles on the **SAS-QUATCH** was the first chance photograph made of the so elusive creature. It shows the Manape so tiny, being seen far away, that details were lost. However, that minute glimpse of him (I insist on the word "him," because he is more than an animal) sufficed for me as an artist to elaborate in the drawing I made for you.

It is noticeable at first glance that this extraordinary creature is not an ape. He will never walk on all fours. Our locomotion depends on the counter-swing of our limbs and apes, having too-long arms and too-short legs, have great difficulty walking upright because their

counter-swing is disproportion-
ately uncoordinated, while man
can walk and run because of the
correct length of his limbs. But the
Sasquatch has exceedingly long legs
and longer arms than man, while his
torso is much shorter. This is the
reason why no human can match the
Sasquatch in running, aside from his
greater dimensions. If he stood on
all fours, his too-short torso would
not allow enough space between
the limbs to run comfortably. The
Sasquatch seems in fact created to
be more human than we. I suspect
that he is in disposition very unlike
the anthropoids. His potentials are
greater than ours, but there were
perhaps climatic circumstances that
held back his evolution to excel
humans in all fields.

As you have
gathered by now from reading the
preceding chapters, everything I
have written in my 39 volumes
pertains to the Global Deluge.
Our ancestors remembered their
Manapes from pre-diluvial times.
Those who saved themselves from
drowning, noticed that these creatures also had the fortune to survive,
so they named them accordingly,
everywhere on this globe, in one
language, my Protong. The present name *Sasquatch* was then "Sa Z
Gladz" (this "ł" is diagonally crossed
in Polish and sounds like the English
"w"), which means "Here From
Destroyed" (i.e. the deluged continent).

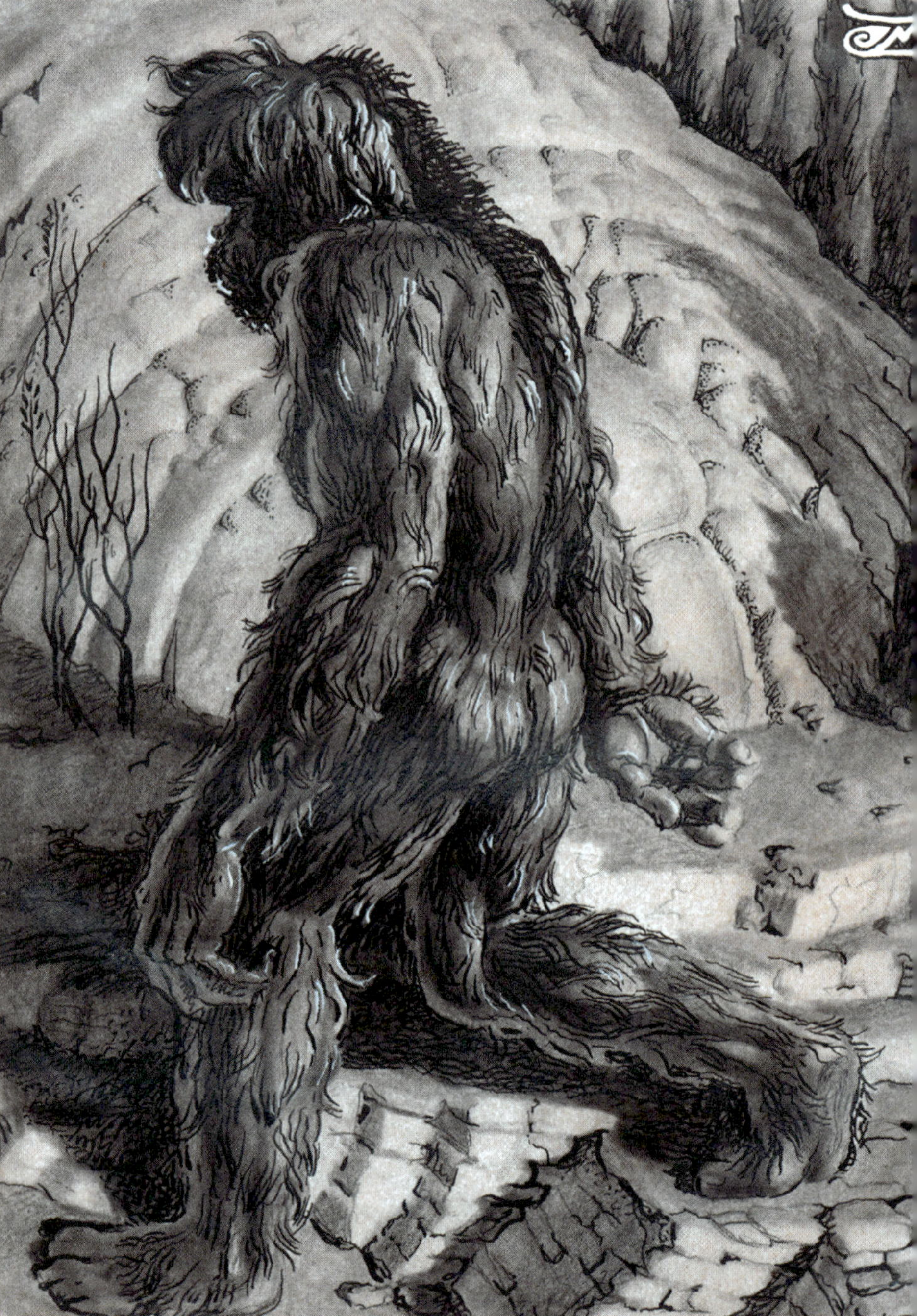

192

193 In this portrait from that tiny photograph I have further added my imagined details so to make this
Sasquatch seem nearer to you. It is obvious that this is a
sub-arctic being, judging by the fur, like Newfoundland
dogs. This is an **AMERICAN YETI**, though we must assume
that there are many varieties and this one is surely different
from the Tibetan one or the Japanese *Eta*.

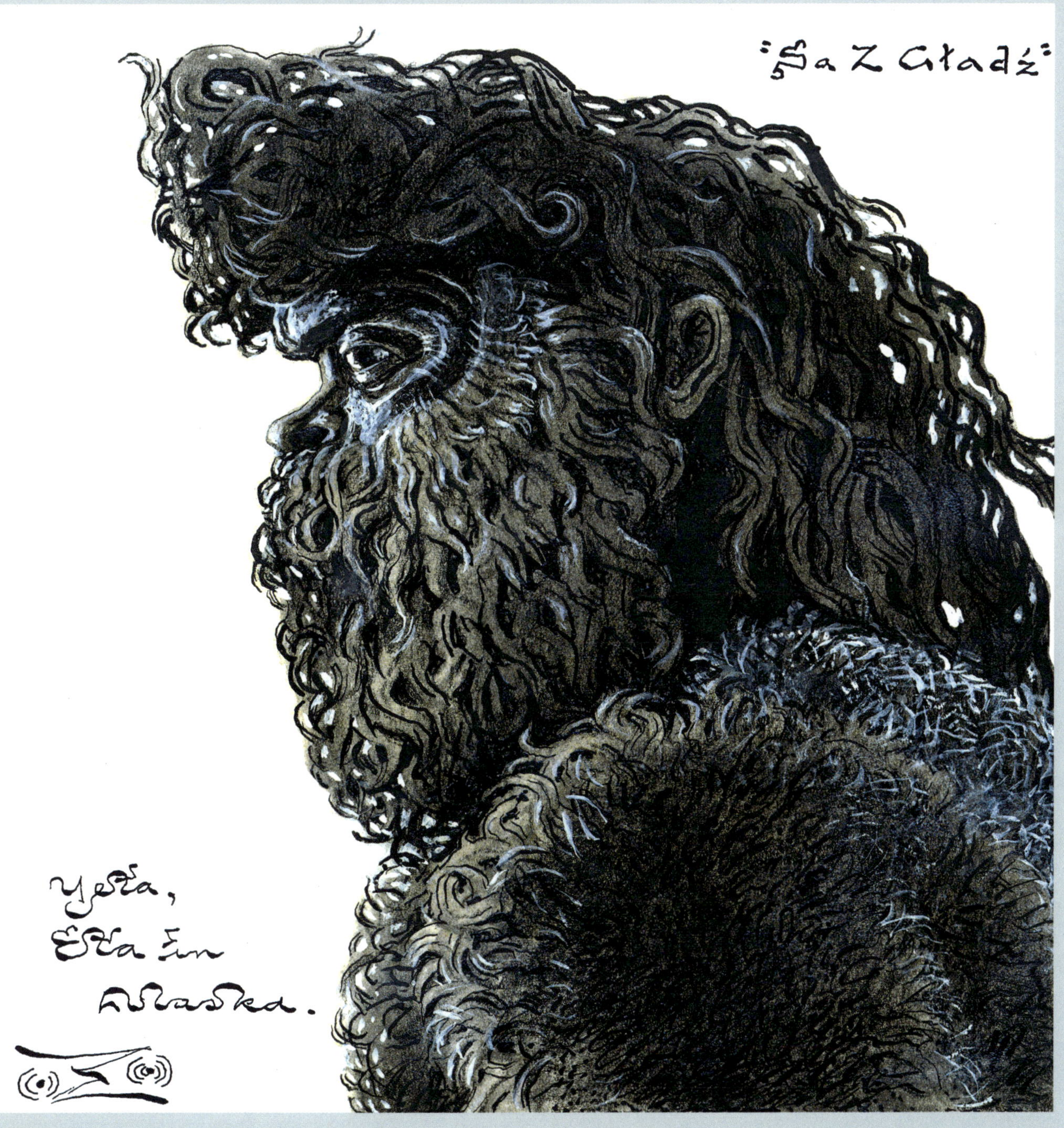

AMERICAN YETI
(Alaska)

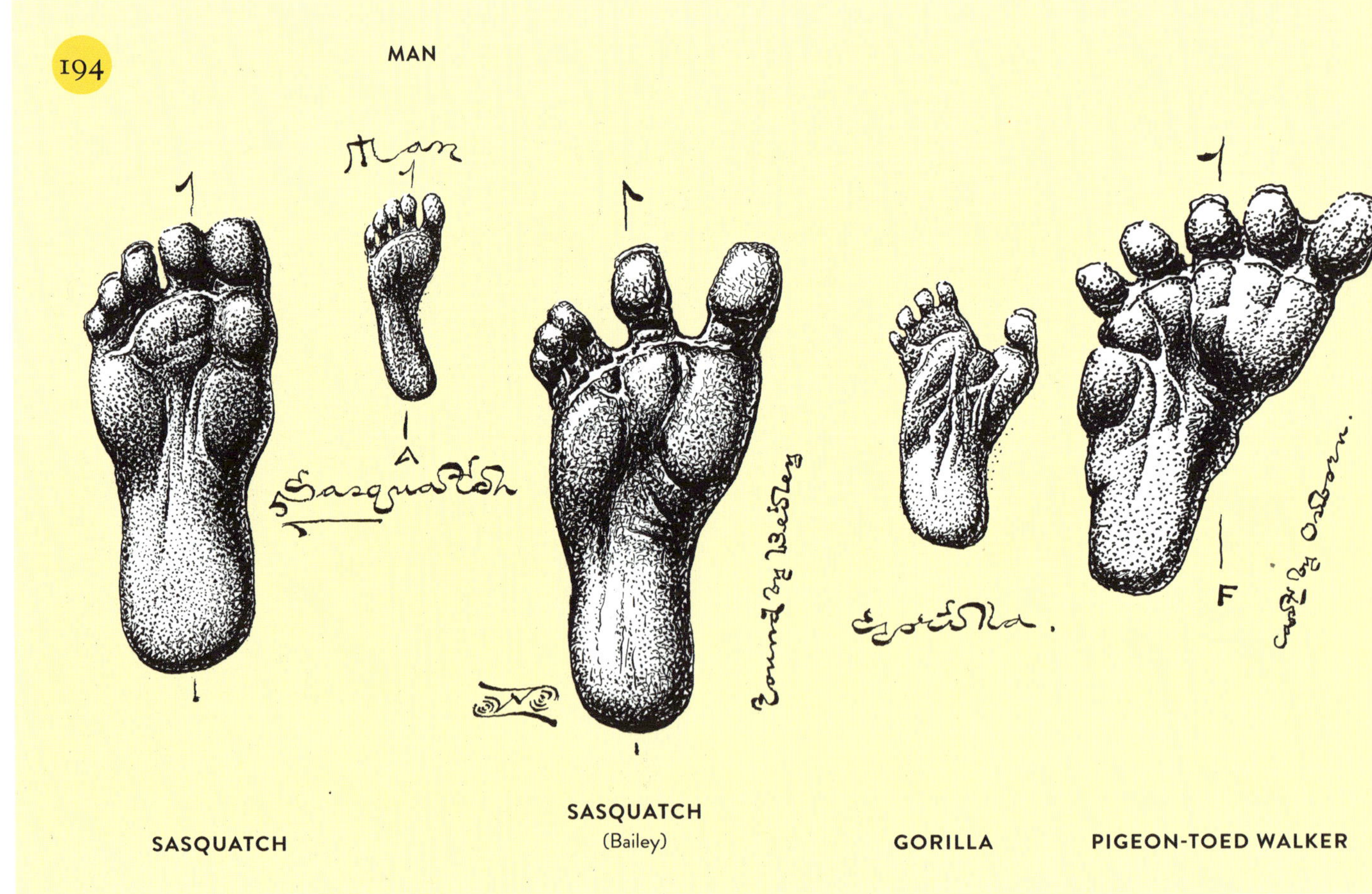

194 There were numerous plaster casts made by various people who found Sasquatch foot-imprints in deep forests. Usually all details were lost, so, being a sculptor and a fine anatomist, I completed the realistic details in these hazily shaped feet, that you may readier visualize their function.

Second from left you see your own foot in comparative size to the plaster casts. At left you see the foot of our **SASQUATCH**. The arrows indicate the direction in walking; note that he walked with his feet directly forward. Third, you see the variant foot of another Sasquatch, cast by Bailey who found the footprints. Note how the first and second toe are massive digits, widely separated, while the same toes on the first foot are more frail and seem to be almost joined by a membrane. While man's toes are grouped in 1–4 sets, these are divided into 1–1–3.

Fourth is the footprint of a gorilla where the first toe, as the thumb, still opposes the other toes, harkening back to the tree-climbing past.

Next you see the crescent-shaped foot of a very **PIGEON-TOED WALKER**, found and cast by Osborn.

195 At left you have the footprint of a **YETI IN THE HIMALAYAS**, who is locally called *Meh-Teh*. Observe how short and stubby it is, how totally different from the others. Here we have proof that there are a number of bi-species of the Sasquatch.

In a book on Nepal I found photographs of **NATIVES OF THE CHITWAN VALLEY**, who have unusual feet, one-and-a-half size larger than our average foot, though the tribesmen are of our height. There was one sitting, his crescent-like foot facing me, which I drew here for you.

196 Finally, a very small foot of a thirty-year-old **WOMAN CRETIN**. The big toe and foot itself are separated, harkening to a tree-climbing, apeoid past.

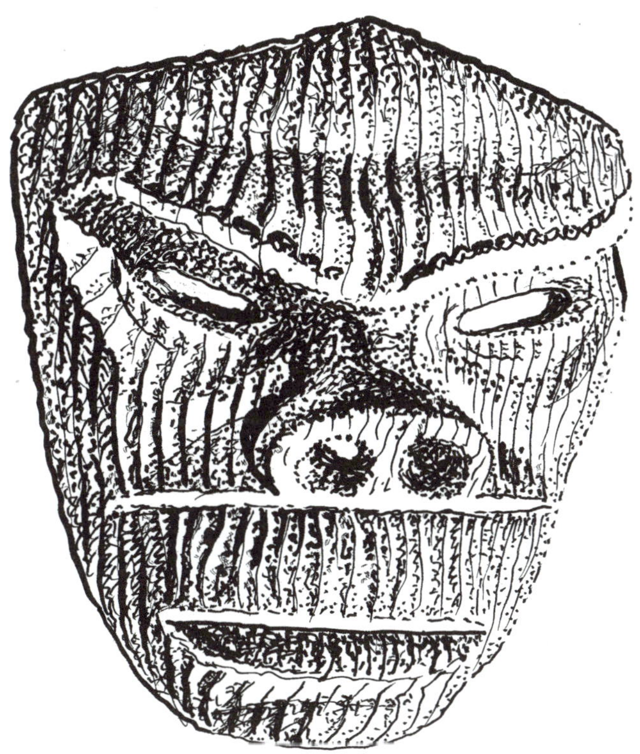

195 MEH-TEH

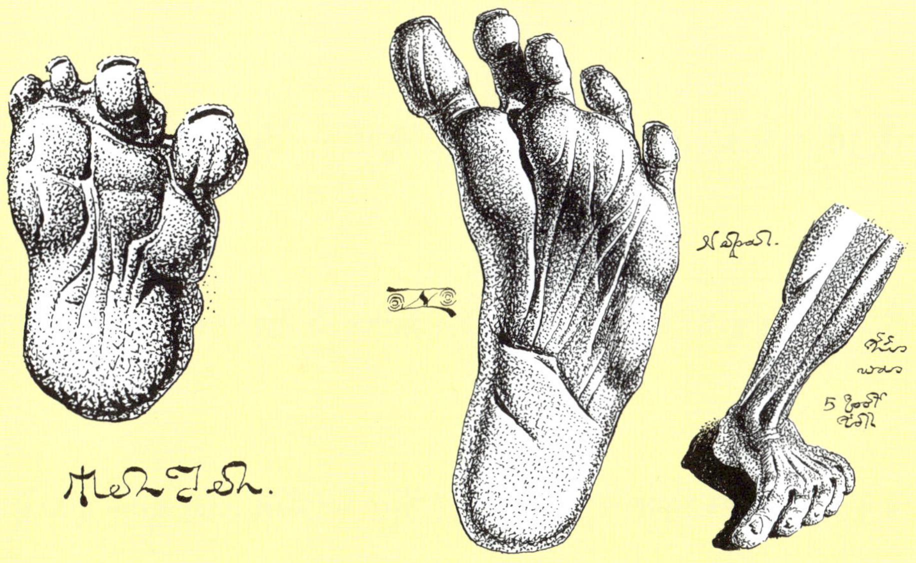

196 CHITWAN NATIVE, NEPAL

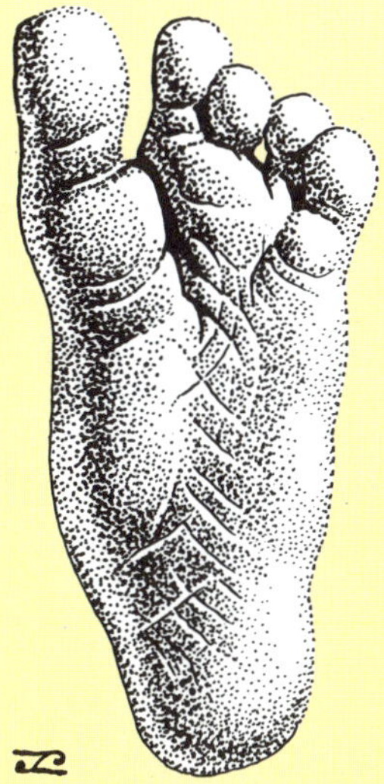

WOMAN CRETIN

197 Among ancient carvings of the Dorset Culture of the Point Barrow region in Alaska, this **MASK** was discovered which white men assume is an imaginary Devil. But you can plainly see that this is a portrait of a local Sasquatch. Incidentally, in the vertical lines we have a marvelous document. They were carved there to let us know that this creature, like the ancestors of the Alaskan Eskimos, also saved himself from the Deluge, for any lines, vertical or horizontal, represent "waters," hence the Great Flood. There is still another pictograph, besides the vertical draining-off of muddy water. It is the horizontal line just below the nostrils, which, by being placed above the water level, tells us that his breath, his SOUL, was saved.

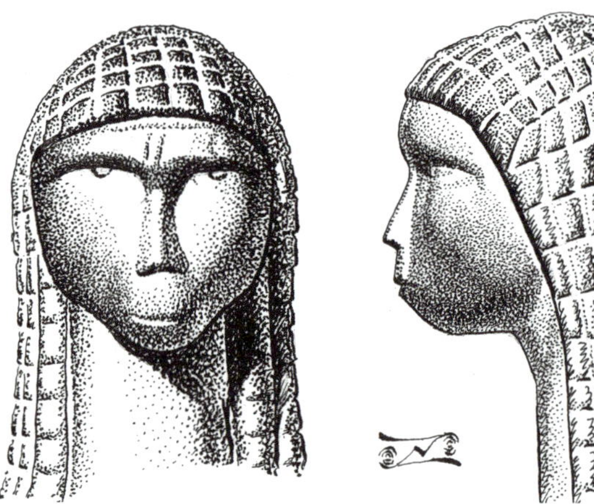

Sasquatch, Mother of God

EASTER Island (Mata Weri or "Mother of Worship") had, prior to its present submergence, the Lioness as its totemic coat of arms; and wherever the escaping diluvials saved themselves, the verbal myth about the Great Lioness was retained. On the American twin continents there were no lions, so the descendants likened the Mythic Cat to jaguars or pumas (Protong "Bu Ma" means "God's Mother"). In Scandinavia and Etruria (pre-Roman Italy) they took the she-wolf, in earliest China the tiger.

198 In the Grotte de Pape, France, a small Cro-Magnon bone carving was excavated, representing a **SAS-QUATCH FEMALE**, mindless, chinless, but scowling at you.

199 This is the only reproduction of this sculpture I have seen and I cannot tell the sex from it. However, knowing what to expect I can effortlessly explain who this is. It represents the breastless (virginal) **MOTHER OF THE DAWN GOD**. Her arms are intentionally absent to convey that she is helpless against the Dragon (geologic upheavals) and the Serpents of Flood it brings forth. Not knowing what lions look like, this American sculptor chose the Sasquatch female as the appropriate gigantic being to represent the anthropomorphic Great Lioness of Easter Island.

Of all the tribes of ancient Mexico only the Olmecs began and continued the use of the Sasquatch to picture the Mother of the Dawn God and the God himself. Let me hint here again at the affliction called acromegaly, illustrated some pages back and explained in the encyclopedia as a human nervous disease, but which I think is a throwback to the Manape ancestry of these Yetinsyny.

A long chapter in my *Zermatism* is dedicated to the reliefs discovered in Mount Alban, Mexico, in the so-called Temple of Dancers, which actually portray spastics and syphilitics who, being cretinous, resembled in the mind of the Aztecs the Sasquatch Mother of the Dawn.

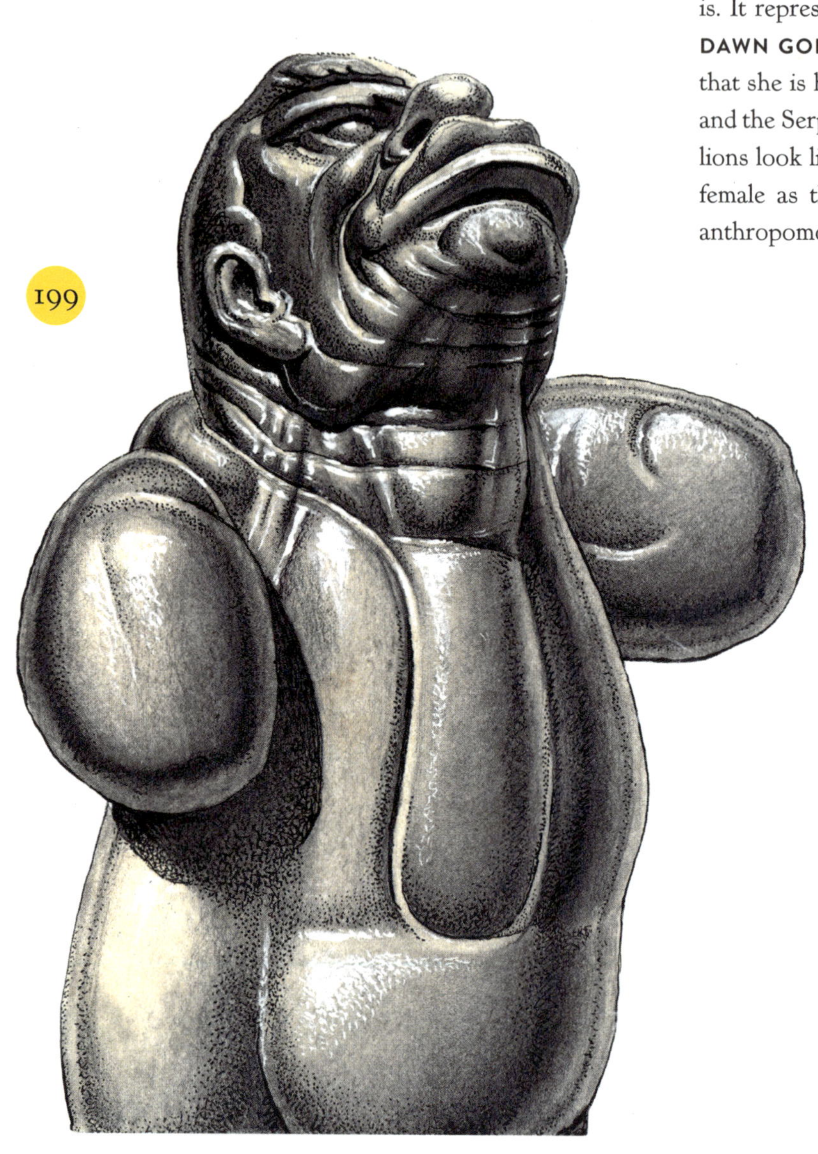

199

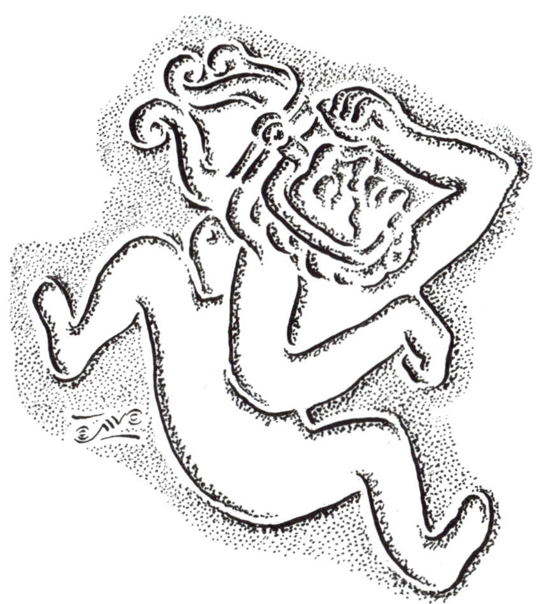

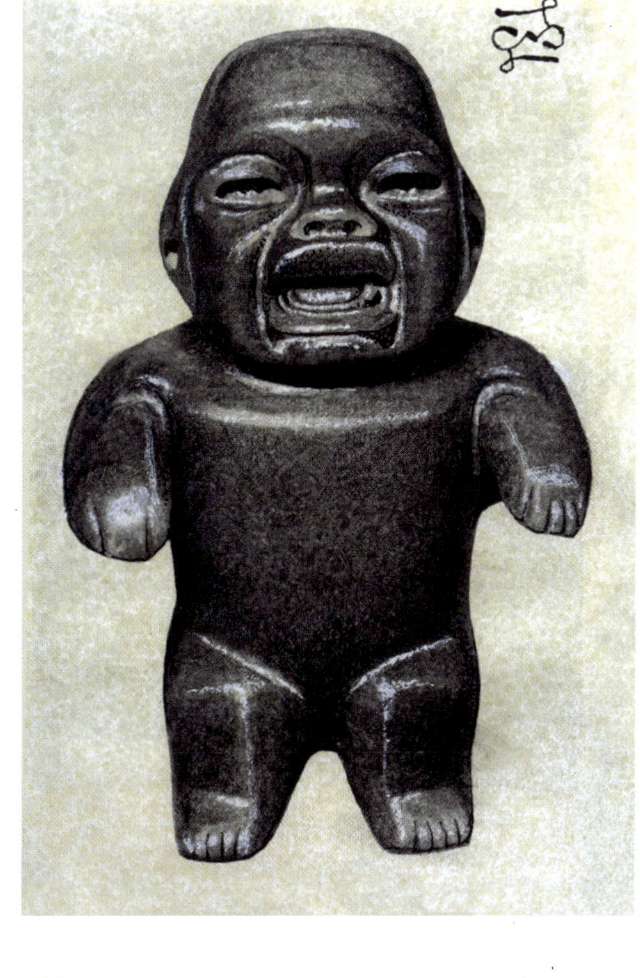

200 Here you see a tiny sample, the **MOTHER OF THE DAWN** arrested in a frog-like floating. Her head is surrounded by curls, emulating the verbally-remembered mane of the Great Lioness. Above her head, like a pointed helmet, we see the pictograph of Easter Island—which she personifies—being attacked by the sea waves of the Pacific and Atlantic, as conveyed by the contra-whirling pictographs. Just above her forehead, between the two horizontal water lines, a diadem was placed with a pierced disc in the center. This is the *Bi*, which means that she was "killed" by the Deluge.

201 The **DAWN GOD**, crying for his Mother. Why are his limbs so short? Because babes are always short-limbed. This is what Sasquatch babies must look like.

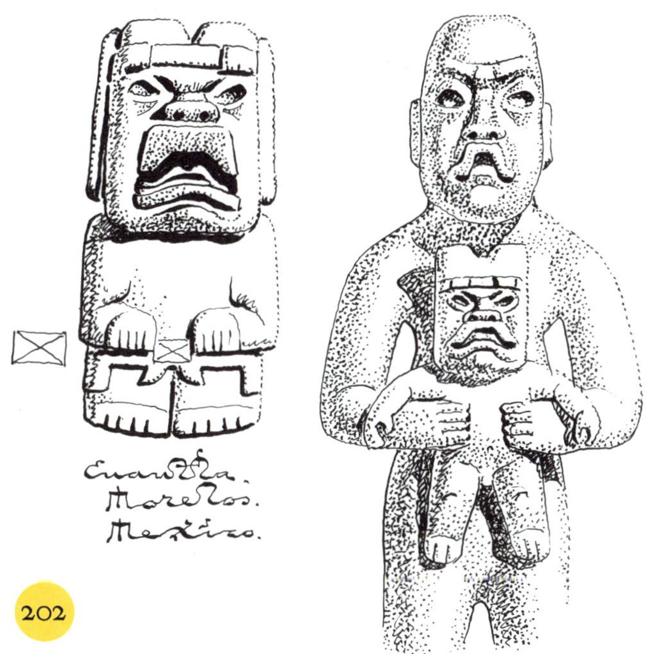

202

202 This Sasquatch-faced **MOTHER OF THE DAWN** is about to raise her Sasquatch Son into the heavens to shine with his first two rays protruding from his forehead. Traditionally, like the Polish *Baby* and the British Sheila-na-gigs, she is bald-headed, as always serving as a rebus for Protong "Li Ze," which means that she represents the "Flooded Land."

At her left I drew a small image of her Son, the Saviour. Between his hands he holds a glyph, the Diagonal Cross, which everywhere on the globe has the same meaning: Mother.

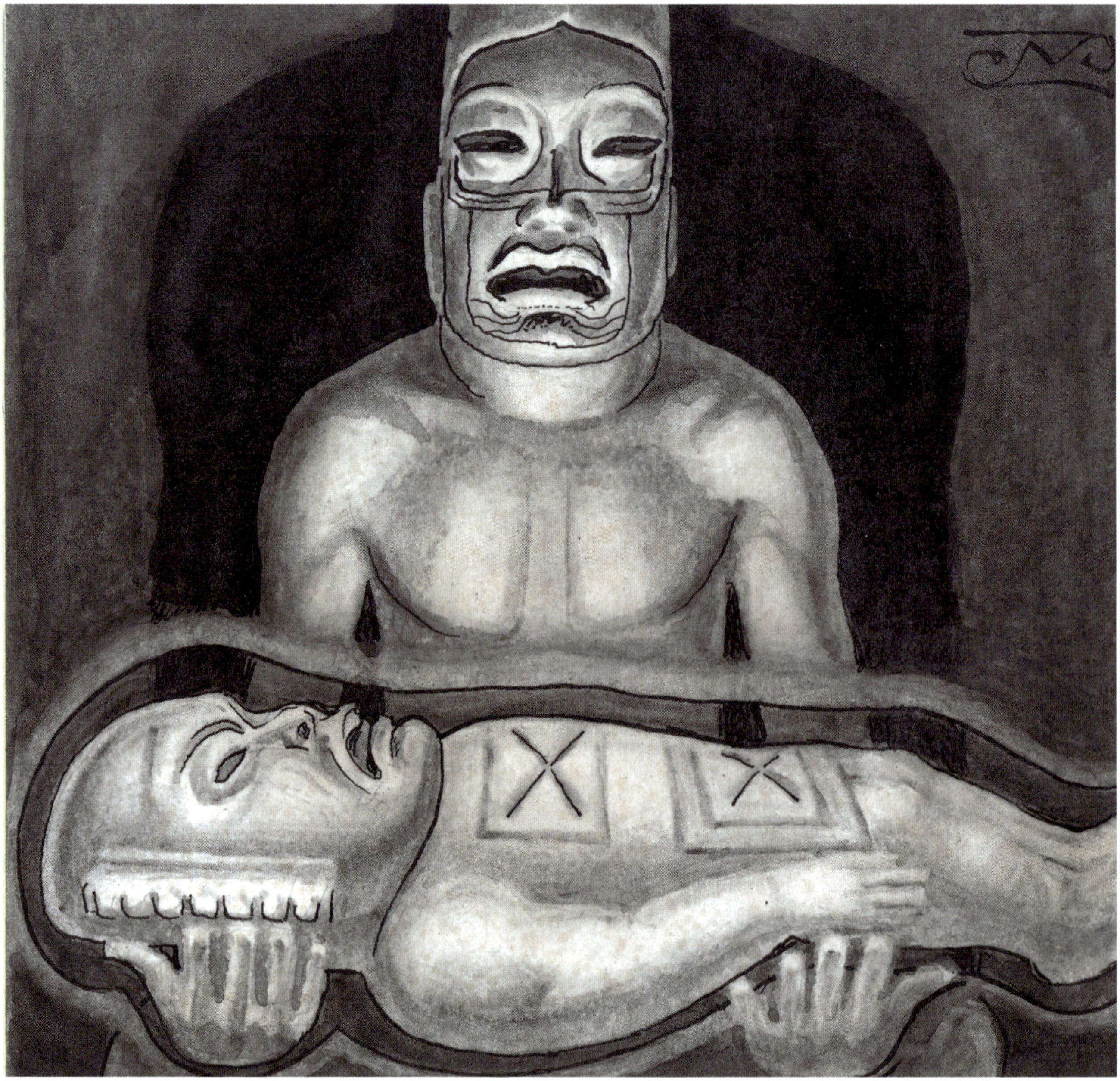

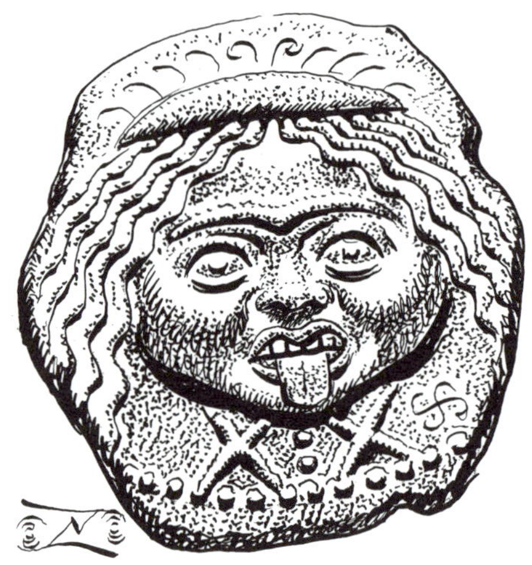

One of a number of mound-like carvings, from whose cavity emerges the Sasquatch-faced, virginally breastless **MOTHER**, presenting to the world her Son, the infant **DAWN.** On his body he has two Diagonal Crosses, one for his Mother, Easter Island, and one for her "husband" submerged in the Atlantic region, Oce On.

For your comparison, here is a pre-Roman Italian medallion with the **MASK OF MEDUSA**. Below it the sculptor placed the twin Diagonal Crosses, like the Olmec sculptor. The traditional granules, always seen on ancient coins, are actually pictographic air bubbles, for Medusa is deluged and from her and her yet unborn Son's hot bodies, the gasses rose as bubbles. From the shallow Easter Island pictograph atop her head radiates the Dawn's glow. Her tongue is a rebus (compare **TONATIUH**).

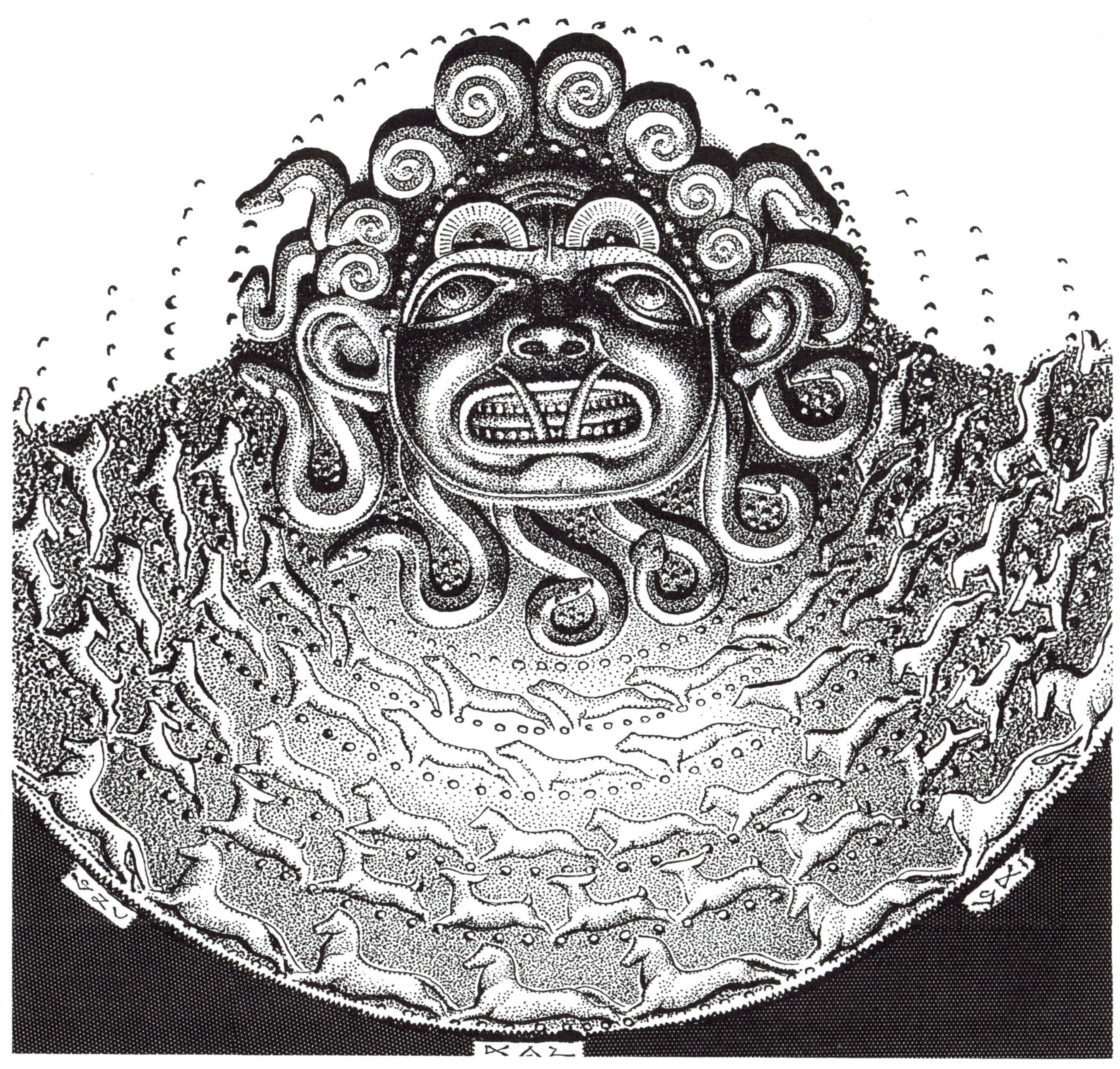

205 My reconstruction of the frightfully eroded bronze shield of **MEDUSA** in the collection of the Smithsonian Institute Museum. Protong "Me Dusa" means "Me Chokes," i.e. with emotion—for this again is the pictographic presentation of the deluged Mother of the God of Dawn, Easter Island.

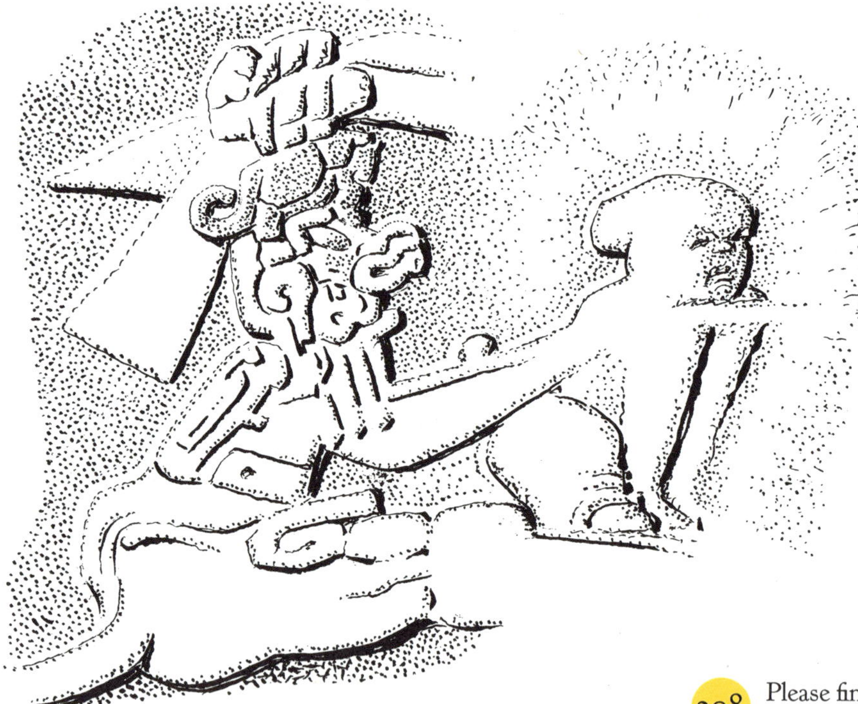

206 Here she is, the **GREAT LIONESS** (note her tail, bottom left), pushing forth her Son, the Dawn, that he depart from her and make his daily journey across the firmament. The infant is Sasquatch-faced.

This is one of over fifty carved slabs in front of the main mound at Dainzú, Mexico, dating from the first century B.C.

208 Please find the page with my elaboration on the photograph of the **SASQUATCH**, keep your finger there and compare the illustration with this one. This is the **DAWN GOD**, an anthropomorphic being, walking to the right (towards Sunset). He has butterfly wings to point out his daily reincarnation. With his right arm he presses the *dzida* (spear) to his body, which is rebusal for "Dzi Da," meaning that he is the "Day Giver." Note that his arms are very long, but that his elbows are on the same level with his genitals, which means he has the exceedingly short torso of the Cro-Magnon man and the Sasquatch. Atop his head the Solar Disc was placed in the form of a bright yellow blossom.

Olmec, excavated at Hacienda las Victorias, El Salvador.

209 In Juxtlahuaca, Mexico, a cave was discovered with mysterious frescoes.

Behold the **DAWN GOD**, a veritable giant. Before him sits piously a bearded Human. The God has the unbelievably long arms of the Sasquatch, holding in one a bow, while with the other he presents the Human with the totemic White Eagle, which is the pictograph of the priesthood, his messengers.

Across the God's chest horizontal lines were painted, representing the deluging seas. On his long arms we see air bubbles. His head, left shoulder and leg are covered with the skin of the Great Lioness, for he is her Son. The skin has its own *Bi*, to tell that she was killed by the Deluge. Painted approximately 600 B.C.

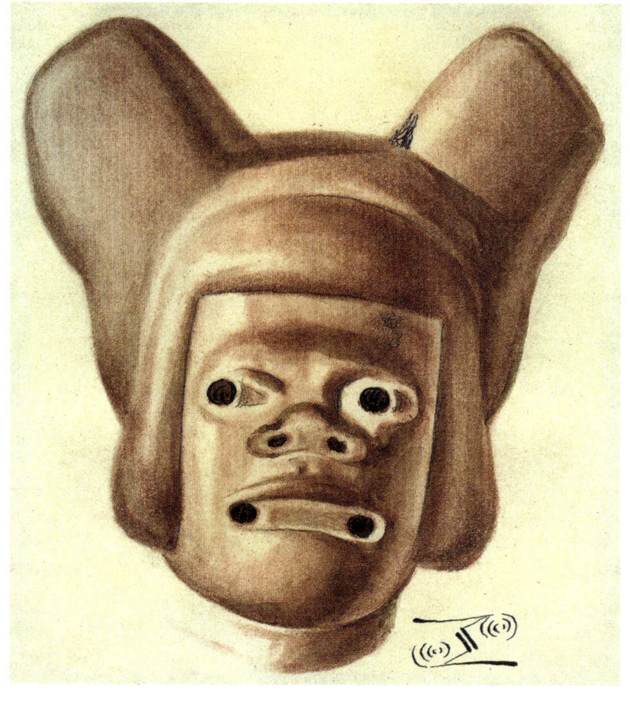

207 A little pottery head from Aztec Mexico. It is the Sasquatch-faced **DAWN GOD**, with the first twin rays of light radiating from his head. In my collection.

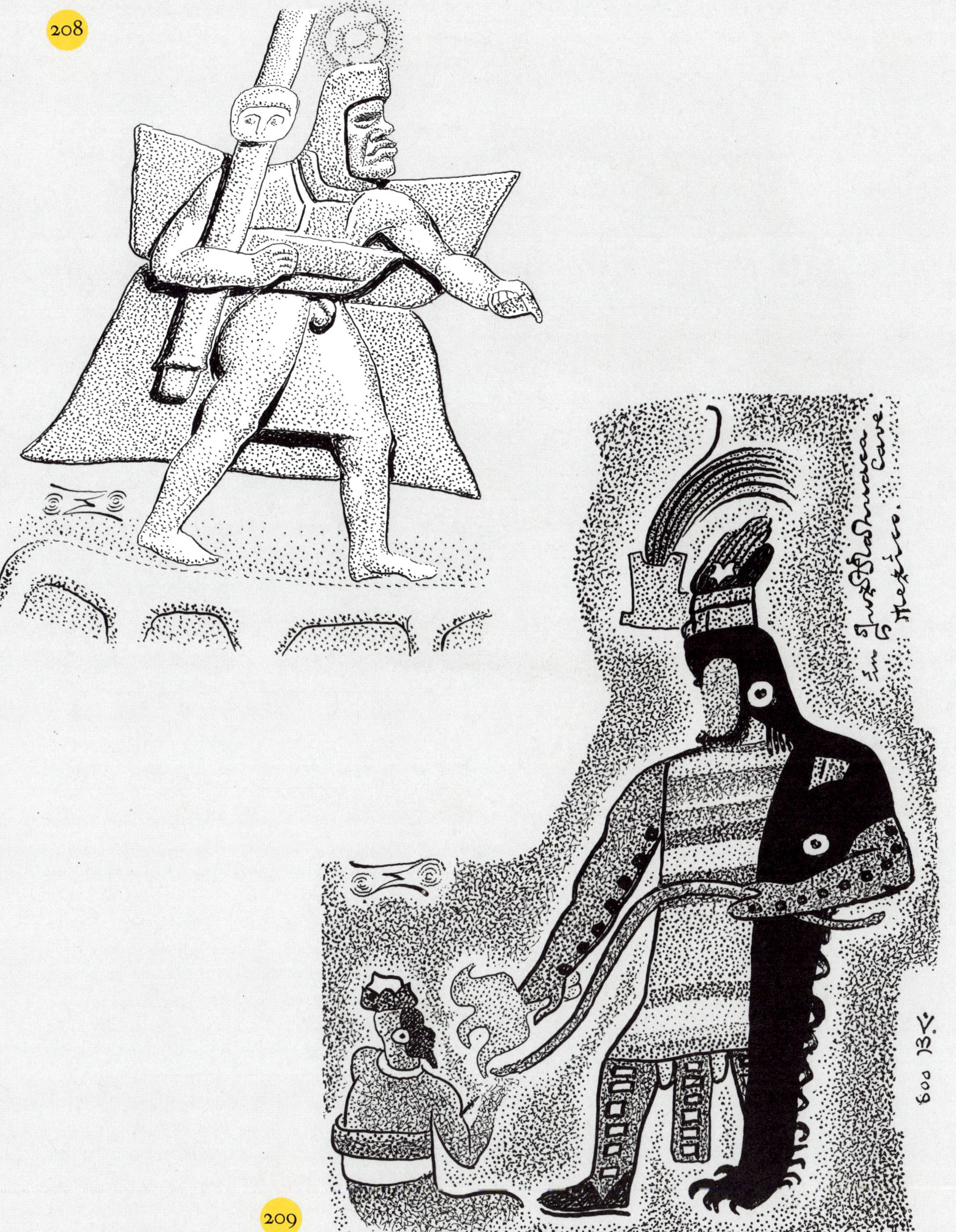

208

209

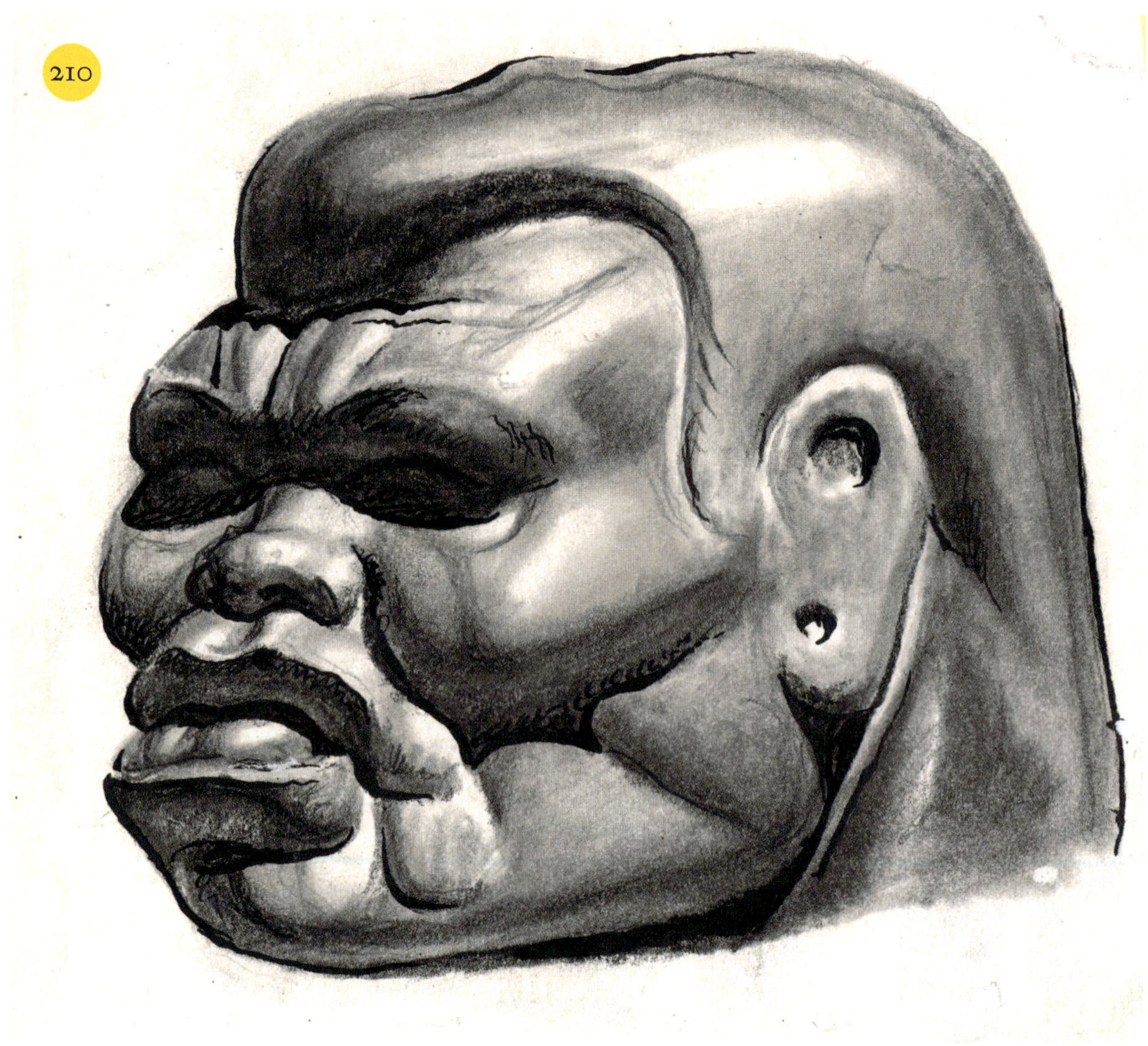

210 Gigantic heads like this one, taller than a man's height, are found in many places in Mexico, Colombia, etc. They are portraits of the **DAWN GOD**, a custom similar to erecting crosses, to remind the worshippers of the Super-human Divinity and his readiness to die in order to save the deluged Mother. But the features are those of the Sasquatch.

211 An altar of a temple dedicated to the **DAWN GOD**, still a crawling infant here. From his head radiate four cardinal rays forming the pre-Christian cross. Above his forehead the mask of the Great Lioness is seen, without a mouth, to indicate that she is breathless, dead. The same mask is always seen on the heads of Aztec-Mayan kings, as to hint at their descendance from the same Mother. Above her towers a pictographic creature, giving us more facts about her. The tongue (see **TONATIUH**) tells that she is in a "Land Towards Elsewhere," while the two hands on the shoulders make the Dawn-Greeting gesture. Before its chest we see a bundle of kindling wood (Polish *drzewo*) which rebus informs us that she is "Where Water."

AFTER this book is in circulation, we—that is, the Kopernik's Tower Publishers—intend to publish the complete tome on the *Anthropolitical Motivations*, from which this chapter has merely been a sampling.

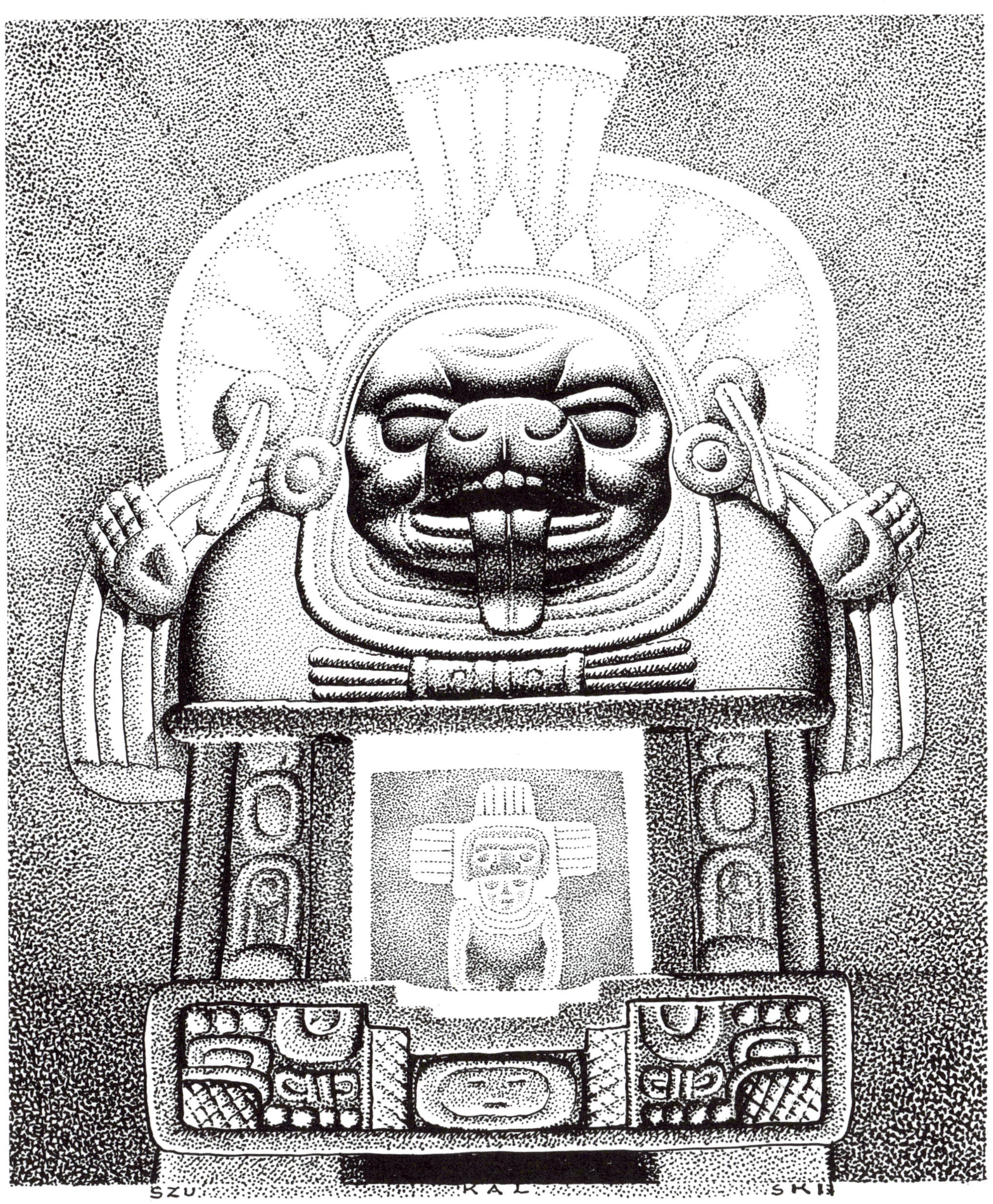

[137

LIBERTY AND THE LAW OF GRAVITY
1920

Led by courageous individuals, the masses start their period-
ically historic march towards Liberty. But with the weight
of their quantitative nature, they assist the law of gravity in
returning them to the depths of the same bondage. And so
they start again and again, each time feeling that it will be
the solvent effort. At times, the hub wears away and then
comes impotence, until the awakening of a new civilization.

Stolen by Communist Poland

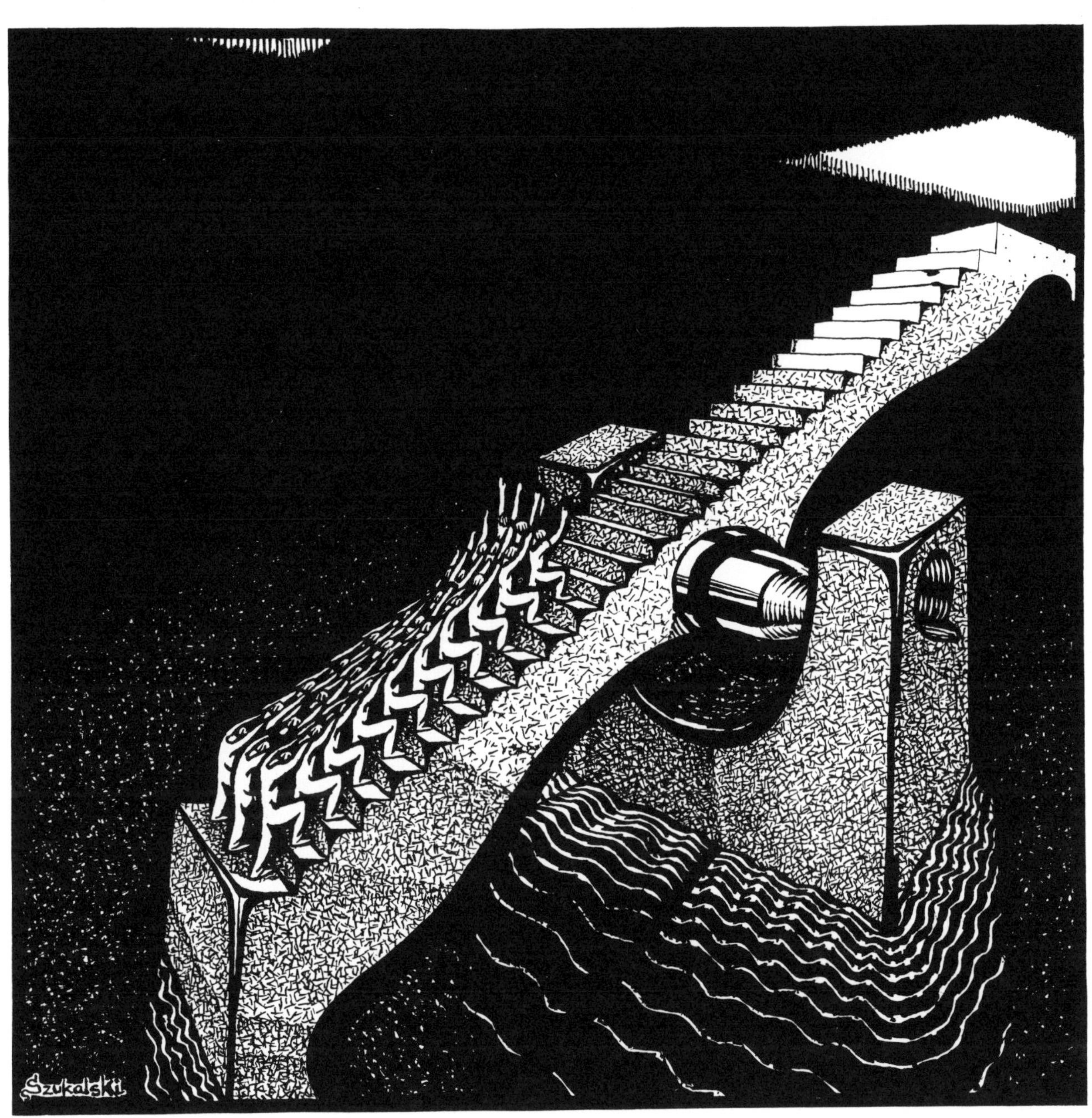

Szukalski

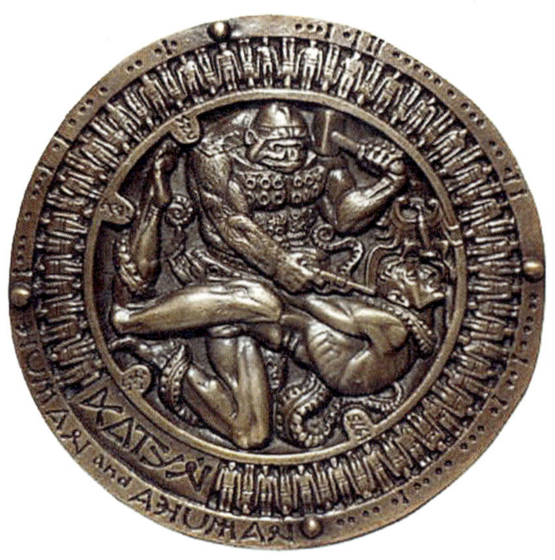

THROUGHOUT millennia, since the time when the first Idealist was stoned to death by the democratically-minded herd of semi-humans, all those who served well the Gods or their Church were posthumously awarded a verbal pat on the back with the honorary title of "Saint."

From early boyhood I understood that if it were not for the very few, there would be no Nations, but only the generic classification of "many." It is like in my sculptural composition *Struggle* where, were it not for the inspired tenacity of the THUMB who forever opposes the principle of "majority," there would not be any concept of "man," but only creeping earthworms.

Therefore I began to think of making an appropriate term to bestow upon those so unrewarded with a mere "word," who always served MANKIND alone, aiding the progress of its elevation from bare Beast into benign Human. From archaeology I have learned that the God Zeus always had his priestly EAGLE awaiting his commands. Therefore, I chose the "name" for them of GOD'S EAGLES.

A few years ago, soon after the world of sciences observed the 500-year commemoration of Copernicus' birth, who rearranged the universe to please his Polish logos, I invented a project for his monument. As usual, I did this spending sleepless nights lying on my back in bed. In the painting showing all minute details, I covered his body with eagle feathers, thus giving him the honorific title of **GODEAGLE**.

When the Russian and German Yetin-syny (the infinitesimal element of the Manape descendants who created the Communist-Nazi Conspiracy to destroy Mankind) made the Molotov-Ribbentrop Agreement to again simultaneously attack Poland, that country doggedly defended itself, but the hastily assembled army was destroyed and the twin predators were victorious.

As is the fate of all improvised armies, men of all professions, even of great renown, joined, leaving their tools, telescopes and laboratories to become officers. As always,

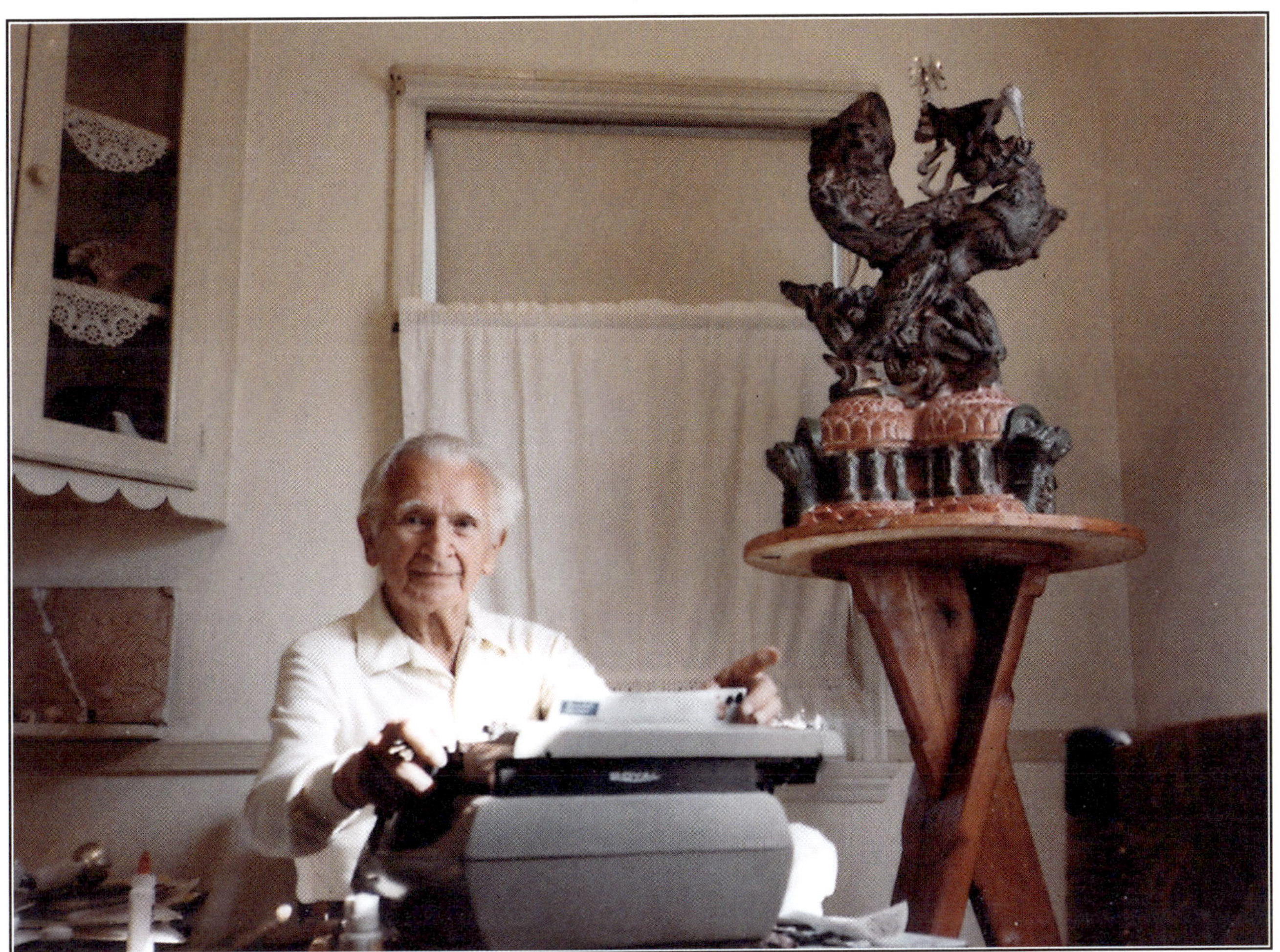

STANISLAV SZUKALSKI WITH "KATYN" PLASTER MODEL
Glenwood Place, Burbank, 1983

the unprepared-for-war nation had been caught preoccupied with more human duties. The Moscovian Yetinsyny, remembering the "Miracle of Vistula"—where almost overcome Poland suddenly turned the tables on the Asian invaders and reduced them to whining cowards who then had to sign the Peace Treaty of Riga—decided to destroy every well educated Pole. Out of the disarmed Polish ranks they methodically culled all the officers who had had academic education and had made names with various achievements, as potential men of danger to the victors. They brought together the military elite of the Polish nation, including the lesser officers, in one place, the hidden-from-the-world Katyn forest—some 14,500 selected individuals of various professions. Ironically, the name *Katyn* means "of the executioner," being derived from the English form of ultimate punishment, where the axe "cuts" the head of the condemned.

Upon gathering the intellectual, scientific, cultural and military elite of the Polish nation, the Yetinsyny ordered these thousands to dig gigantic hollows in the land. They brought out the hundreds of bails of wire shipped from Germany to bind the wrists of these dedicated Poles behind their backs, had them kneel on the embankments; then, striking their heads with hammers, stuffing into each open mouth a handful of sawdust to stifle the screams, blew their faces out with a revolver shot in the back of the head until they had all mindlessly tumbled down into the common grave, to the glory of Mother Russia as a visible success of the Yetinsyn subhuman supremacy over us… Humans.

The Yetinsyny of Germany had the same manner of destruction of the Polish nation, executing thousands of the elite, though on a lesser scale. But no creature on earth would think of destroying a nation at one stroke so efficiently as the Moscovian Yetinsyny did.

It is the NAMES of famous individuals in various spheres of government, sciences and culture, that make the nameless folk into a

NATION. Thus, the killing in the Katyn forest of the Polish Nation, eliminated all spiritual leadership and left a faceless body of irresolute masses. Killing six times that number of America's best educated people, would destroy this nation for a few generations, for with that number the continuity of the "American" spirit would die. No nation on earth would resort to such bestiality, unless it was bestial, like the Moscovian State formed by the descendants of the noseless-faced Tartars, the biological strain of Yetinsyny. Because of the Darwinian theory, and thereby the enormous assurance, that the "link" is missing between the Manapes and us, Humans, the Russians-so-called are considered Humans. It is easy to differentiate between Beasts and Humans, by their bestial and human behavior. Everything bestial about Russia and Germany (Communism and Nazism) is symptomatic of the Manape heritage among their populations. For that reason we must disassociate the evils we experienced at the hands of their monstrous elements from the rest of the nation, and not only forgive these two nations but do everything in our power to assist them in CURDLING into two biological elements, so that the real, human population, by means of re-education and publicity, awakens to the fact that initially they were of the pure Slav (i.e. Glorious) race, but that the bestial Yetinsyny have ENSNARED them, so that they became "ideologically" hypnotized into submission in order to act as Monsters themselves.

As an American Pole, I have always been on the side of India, Scotland and Ireland, for I am forever against any nation parasiting upon another, for that is what Empires do. But I have observed that the revolutionary movement of Ireland presently is in the hands of the Irish Yetinsyny, who were born to kill-kill-kill, for the sake of KILLING, not for gaining freedom from the parasites. What has happened? The biological type of the revolutionaries has changed, and presently the foes of Mankind, not only of the English, control the "ideological" movement. Therefore, the murderers of Lord Mountbatten are not the Irish, but the accursed bi-species of the Celtic race, the Abominable Yetinsyny that in Russia would have been Communists and in Germany Nazis. Industrial and commercial initiative, not killing, will free Ireland, Scotland and Wales, NOW, when the English are lapsing into their biologic, Historic Hybernation. A nation that produces Anglosexual variants in men and women, is on the way out. With lessened virility the population diminishes and national vitality fades, providing the awaited-for chance to get Free from the formerly more vital invaders. Let us not blame the real people of Russia, nor judge Ireland by her Yetinsyny with too long upper lips, for the senseless killings. Inhumanity is not national, but sub-racial and symptomatic of nations being pseudo-ideologically ensnared, becoming themselves the victims of our mutual foes, the Manapes who play-act as "revolutionaries" to eventually EXTERMINATE... us all.

It is due to the extermination of the nation (consisting of renowned men of achievement) at the Katyn forest, that the Poles living outside of Poland have had no success in attaining a meaningful monument to commemorate the Victory of the Moscovian Predator over the Humans, that the London Poles erected a trivial obelisk (a banal concept that only an architect could sweat out). Recently the Poles in Toronto, Canada, announced a competition for a monument to commemorate the Katyn Crime. The conditions of this undertaking were to "express the tragedy of the loss of thousands of officers, implying the outrage and demand for justice."

The Committee consisted of a President, Secretary General, Secretary, Recording Secretary, Treasurer General, Assistant Treasurer, nine Vice-Presidents and twelve Directors, enough to run any other league of patriotic stalwarts out of business. (Any Pole who can sign his name, is now regarded as an intellectual.)

The jury consisted of three Canadians and two Poles, and the result was to be foreseen. Anglo-Canadians have a traditional antagonism to "foreigners" and, when "intellectual," are without exception pro-Communist, this being the Fabian conspiracy against Democracy and Freedom. They pressed the policy of Russian stooges NOT to permit that the monument be expressive of "the tragedy of thousands of officers being murdered as war prisoners and the OUTRAGE that demands justice!" Accordingly, they chose "a cracked slab" [[sic]] as the most appropriate monument. The whole affair was secret, so that the press was uninformed and no one knows what transpired. I am not even sure that my project was shown to the public.

I wrote seven letters to these people who betrayed the intention of the competition. But sharks, crocodiles, Hottentots and Poles never answer letters. They prefer to live in murky atmospheres. With much ado I was finally able to get my sculpture back, but five paintings as part of the project, were stolen by the Vice-Presidents and Directors, whose number was a pretense at assuring the competing sculptors that the competition would be an honorable attempt at being a civilized affair. Throughout my life I have never had a dealing

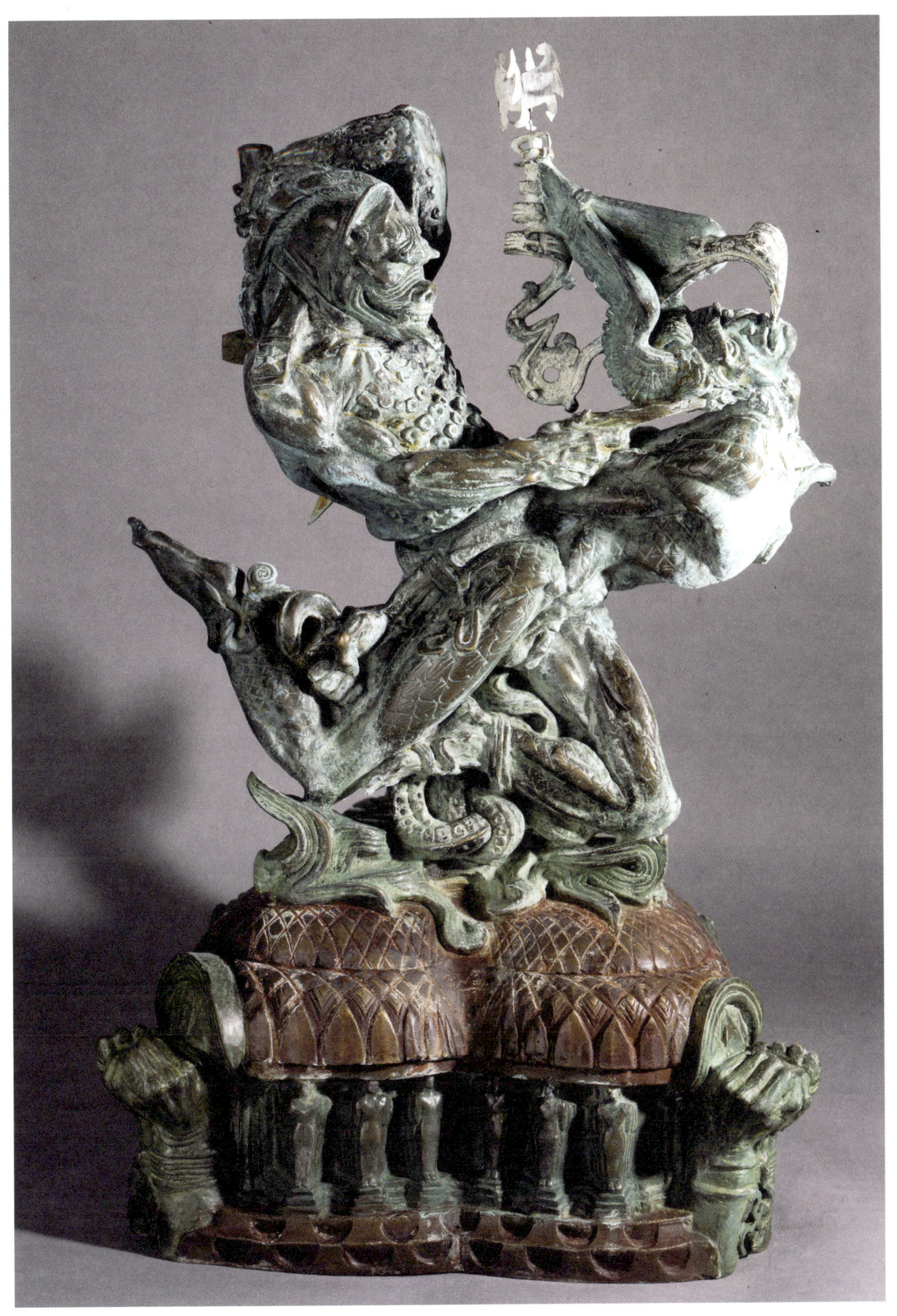

KATYN, OR GODEAGLE AND THE PREDATOR
1979

with the Polish "intellectual" that did not prove disastrous to me, though most of my subjects were pertaining to Poland and somehow part of multitudinous projects for monumental works. Patriotism is but another word for CONCERN over matters pertaining one's nation. JINGOISM is the proper term for "patriotism" of predatory nations, due to their AGGRESSIVE existence deriving from their nomadic origins.

■

KATYN—The Last Breath

My project is intentionally realistic, to help the onlookers visualize the Crime committed by the Moscovian Yetinsyny. We see a befeathered figure of a Polish Godeagle, sent by Swiat Owid to defend the country. He is tumbling down to his knees, both arms wired tight behind him, with wire manufactured in Nazi Germany (note the Swastika attached to it). This is the allusion to the Molotov–Ribbentrop Pact of their simultaneous attack on Poland.

In back of the entrapped Godeagle, there is the Moscovian Yetinsyn, wart-nosed, short-armed, long-torsoed Manape, his servility rewarded by a chestful of medals that metamorphose into polyp-suckers. The Yetinsyn is about to crush the head of his victim with the hammer (made in the USA), while his right, short arm presses the revolver to blow the brain of the Pole out. The revolver ends in the sickle with which to decapitate his victim. I have so arranged the composition, that the legs of the Pole seem to be also the legs of the Moscovite.

However, seeing the sculpture from the right side gives us a shock, for the Yetinsyn has no legs at all. Instead, he has the eight blood-sucking arms of the Octopus. Thus, I have created a new mythic aberration with which to picture Moscovian world-PARASITISM and VAMPIRIALISM, and named him OCTO-YETINSYN. Down the waist bulges the pendulous belly of the Octopus, full of black ink to cloud all the world-issues. Therefore, I have inscribed on it the word *Pravda*, meaning "Truth," which word was borrowed from my people, since in Russian there never was any need to make up such a strange and outlandish word, since Predators never tell the truth: that is a purely Human necessity. Some of the blood-sucking arms he sends to the Moon to lean upon it, so that his bestiality be free to commit the avalanche of crimes in the total blackness of the night, in obscurity to the Human world. Beneath the arching arms of his "leaning on the night" lays the prostrate body of Europe.

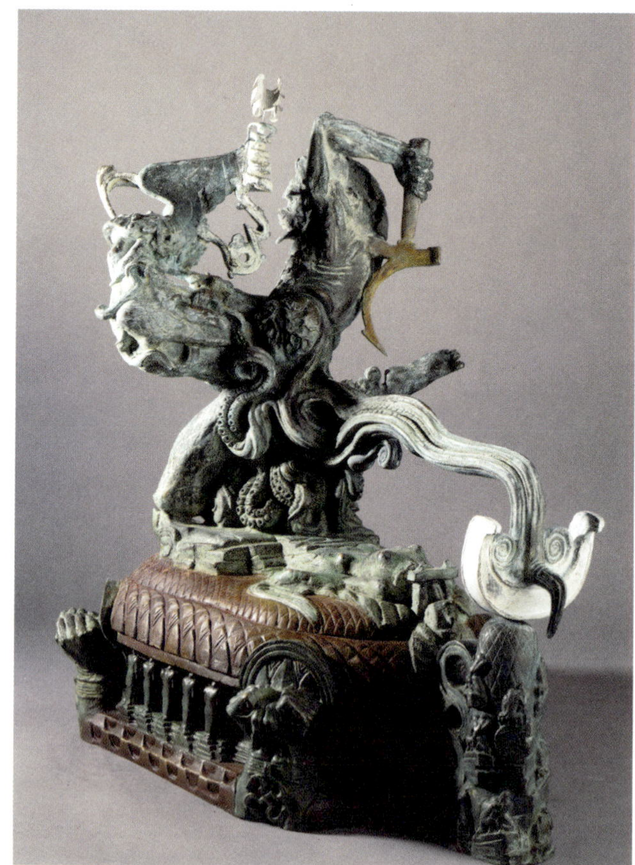

The hammer implies the grievous fact that it were the Anglomericans who supplied all the means of Modern Civilization, so to assist this Octo-Yetinsyn in destroying Free Mankind and BETRAYING it at Yalta where half of Europe was given away to the World Parasites.

Looking again to the front of the sculpture, we notice the thin, golden halo around the head of the falling Godeagle, for with him the name of the nation and its ultimate substance was destroyed at one stroke, leaving behind an irresolute… historically lost… nameless folk. From the mouth of the falling Pole rises his last, frozen breath, from which alights the four-winged Eagle, fiercely beating its wings against the wind.

(The Eagle and the Crescent will be chromium-covered and the Bird will rotate on the pivot by means of a jet stream of air.)

The pedestal for this monument is additionally meaningful, and for that reason the Polish committee thieves have kept my paintings of it, so that I could not have them when completing work on it. The platform consists of stylized forests carved in red granite, for it was in the Katyn forest that the horrendous crime was committed… not by the Russians, but by the Russian Yetinsyny.

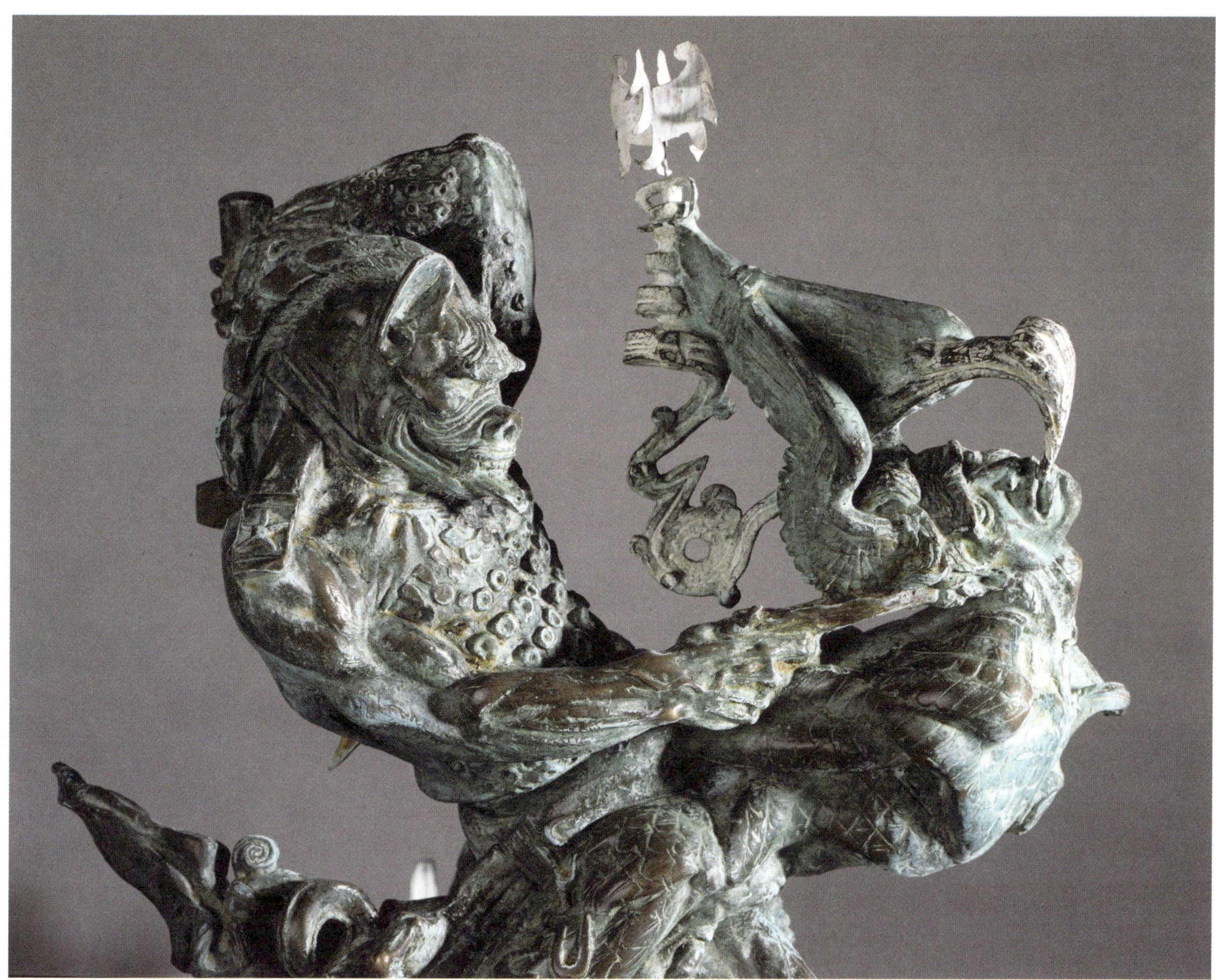

Below the bronze sculpture runs a horizontal stratification of black basalt in which are to be carved ghostly figures of the murdered Elite of Poland, standing headless (since their heads were blown off), arms raised in salute gesture, Awaiting!

Under the Crescent Moon will be sculptured a Pillar of Night, which, in relief, will show many Manapes in the act of blowing out the brains of kneeling Godeagles who were ordained by God to defend their country and their faiths.

I proposed to the competition committee that they appeal to Our Father Wojtyla, Pope John Paul II, that he take over the patronship and erect a temple in Rome dedicated to the 15 thousand Polish martyrs, wherein this sculpture would commemorate their mass execution.

The Russian-controlled competition picked three inane projects, then allowed the public to see these worthless doodlings to choose from.

I propose that the temple to be erected will be a *CRYMAMID*, where people may send the ashes of their dearest departed, which would be mixed with clay and shaped into bricks on which their names and dates would be imprinted. Thus, all nationalities, including Germans and Russians, would protest, even after their death, against the genocidal Crime of the German and Russian Yetinsyny. The Crymamid of Polish Martyrs should be the culminating PROTEST of ALL faiths and religions, of all nationalities. In my project I have included the coats of arms of all nations.

I have so well in-vestigated Rome and its sacred vicinity while imagining the realization of this plan in sleepless nights, that I have already found an appropriate place for the Crymamid of Polish Martyrs. It only needs the nod of the head from the Roman population and the blessing hands of Father Wojtyla raised over my project. ∎

Federate or Perish!

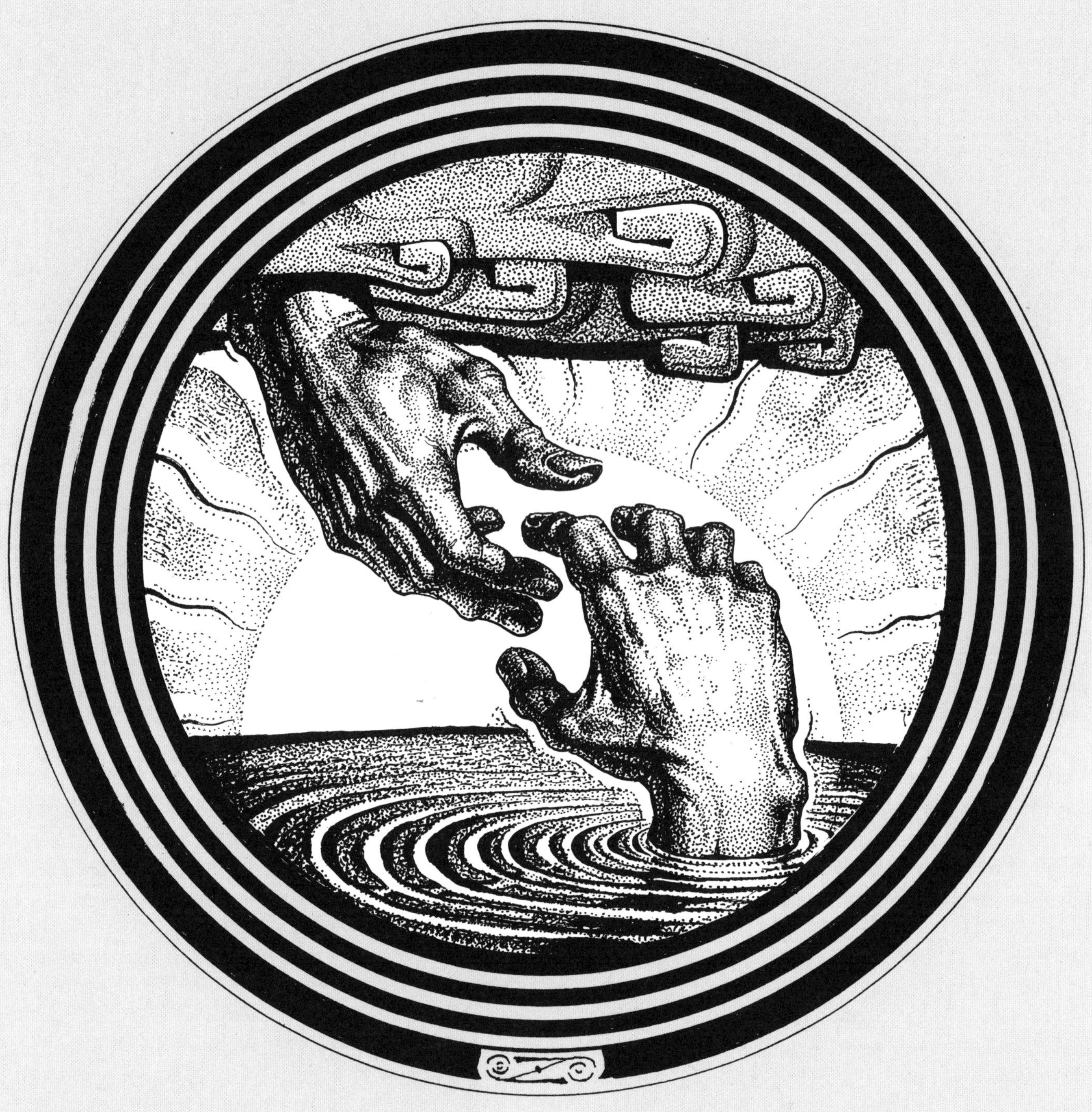

Grasp or Sink!

Society or Public?

As the matter of ceaseless wars and invasions by a-Human Predators (like the German and Russian Yetinsyny) forced me to seek the main cause for this burden on mankind, I similarly felt the need of a diagnosis of Poland and its suicidal proclivities whereby I might get to the source of its self-destruction.

As a boy I had no use or need of God. I, even then, felt that God was for everyone else, but I was self-contained, complete, unboastfully complete. (Read the chapter from my autobiography, *Selfborn*, entitled "The Mute Singer" (in *Atlantic Monthly*, July 1964.)

Though at the age of nine, because my mother was religious, I served at the altar for the Dominican order in Gidle (pron. "geed-leh") where I had been raised from the age of five, I soon gave up interest in religion. My father, Dyonizy, then away to fight with the Boers in Africa against the parasitic British Empire, was a heretic, of which I as yet did not understand the reasons.

Since in earlier inter-astral ages Poland's terrain was covered by the Long Sea (Ptolemy's *Mare Longum*), there are now deposits of limestone present everywhere, with trillions of shells, some containing tiny air-pockets, caught within, so that when I found a piece in a local quarry, I presumptively took it that it was there specifically for me to inhale the Air-of-the-Ages. (Out of the limestone I carved most detailed figurines for "my girls" and they called me a sculptor.) When in my teens, after migrating to the United States, that assumption inspired me to never think of myself as Stanisław Szukalski the individual, but as… a Pole, ever, every instant of my conscious breathing. I had no time for God, for his place was taken by the mere word "Poland" which I gave every minute of my thoughts and fine energy, producing more than any four classic sculptors of Italy put together. Thus, I have never been conceited, but ever proud, not personally, but nationally.

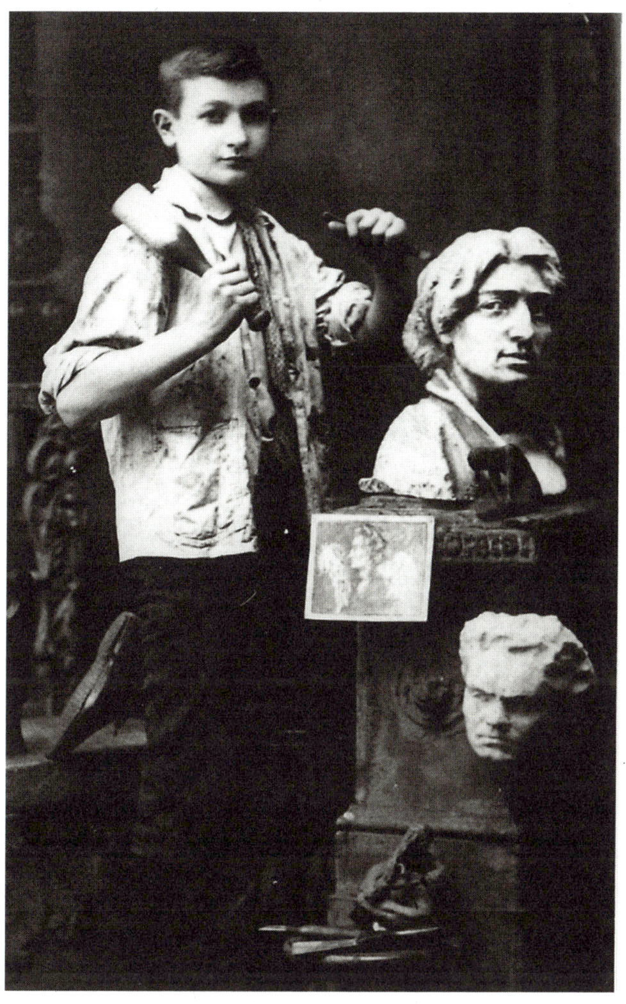

CHICAGO, 1908 (AGE 14)

The Anglomericans are usually annoyed by the persistence of other nationalities living here, in calling themselves "Hungarians" or "French" instead of "Americans." They do not realize that people with integrity do not de-nationalize overnight just because it is profitable to insincerely claim that one is already Americanized in order to become a citizen, which, in fact, does not benefit the American society (legally, financially). People without personal integrity are

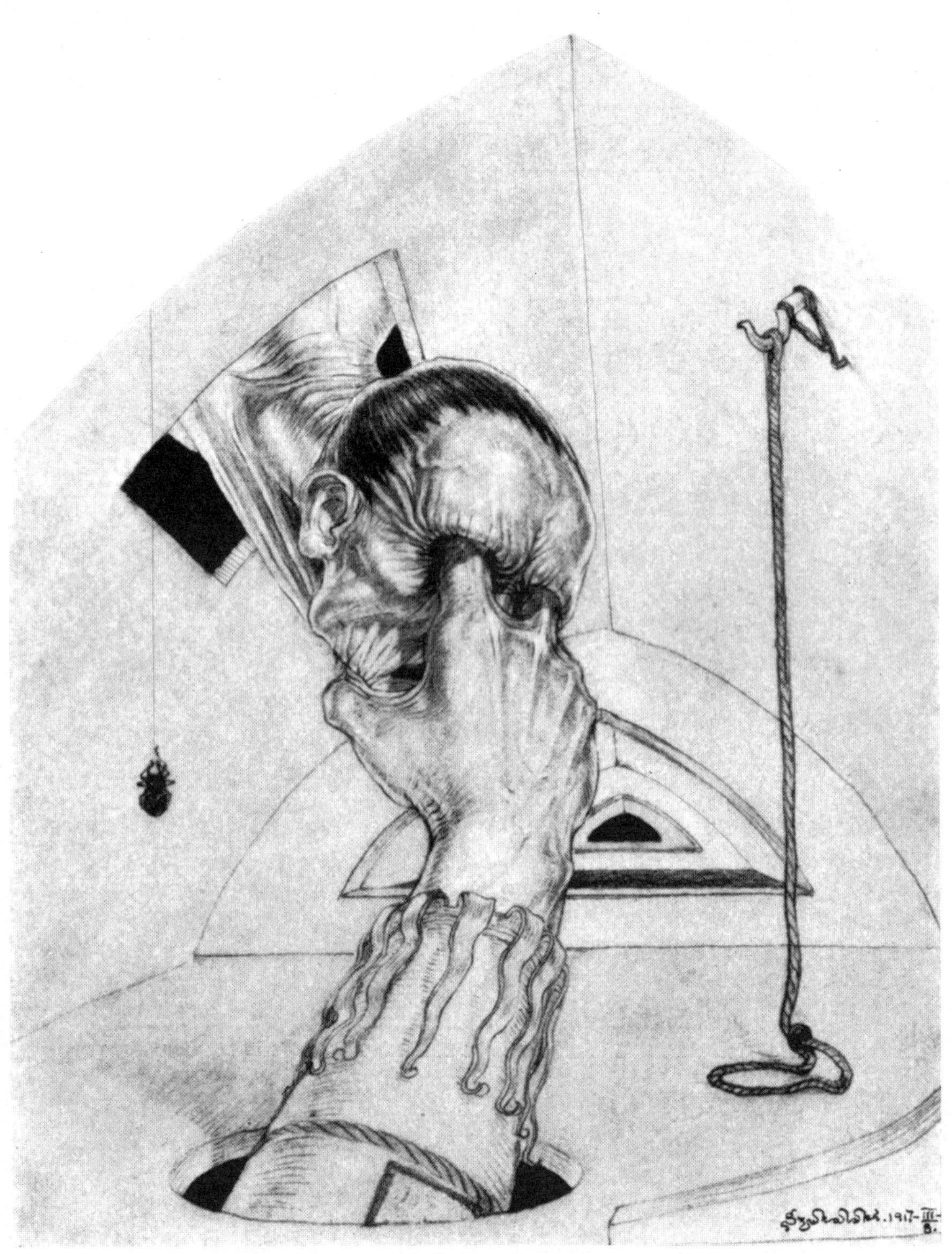

MAN AND HIS BROTHER
1917

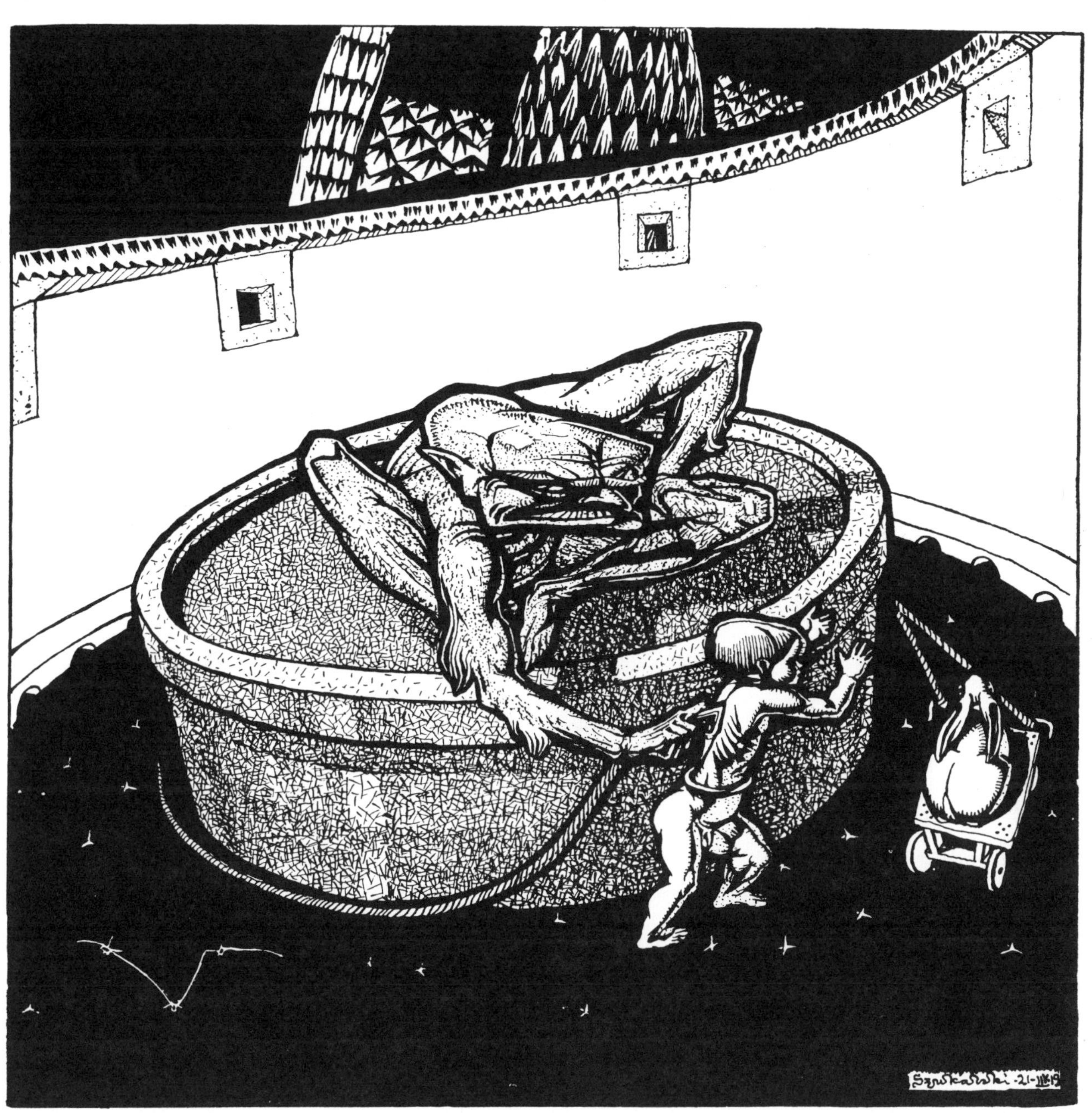

HOPE (YOUTH AND PROVIDENCE)
1919

pride-less, hence deceitful, cheats. What is of far greater moment is the sense of ADMIRATION for America in a person, therefore the assurance that such person is pro-American, hence unofficially, without the stamp of the Immigration Department, a Patriot.

Very few Anglomericans have that capacity for Patriotism themselves, simply because there is no EXCUSE for such an emotion. Patriotism is but a more dignified term for ordinary CONCERN. One may be born with such passion, but Opportunism, so devastatingly advocated by the Anglomerican society, negates, prevents one from being a Patriot. We Magyars, Poles, French and Armenians bring the most precious of soul-capacities into this rankly prosaic, abysmally matter-of-fact society: Patriotism, because we all have been digested by history on the ancient continent, being the survivors of the death-carrying acids of multi-faced Calamities and Exterminations by the a-Human Predators.

What about Poland, the worshipped? I have had the unprecedented adoration from the Polish Public (though I was totally dismissed by the American Poles who never reprinted even the smallest mentions from the American Press). Yet, despite my winning first prize for the project for Mickiewicz by a unanimous vote of the jury, there began a nationwide campaign in Poland, with the most unspeakably abusive press attacks on this intruder from across the ocean. Suddenly I discovered the other, unspoken-of face of my unfortunate country. There was the monstrous Poland of the *Inteligencja*, the "deformed."

I have never met a more IDEAL Public than that of Poland or America. Yet, never met a rottener Society than those of Poland and America. Now, before you stand me before the wall of sighs and pump me full of lead for so rash a statement, let me make myself better understood.

Who is the Public? Who is the Society? (For I take them as "creatures ," distinct organisms, organically phobic of each other.) In my definition, the Public is the cross-section of a street crowd at any given moment, in a photograph in which might have been caught a school teacher, a bank clerk, a mechanic, an idler, a village bumpkin and a prostitute—neither the acme, nor the lowest of the nation. Among these I count the audiences met at symphony concerts, art exhibitions or political gatherings. They are the NATION of a given village or metropolis. These people I SERVE with my every breath, for them I created EVERYTHING in my long life; with them I have everything in common. They are my bio-logic affinity and my beloved audiences. Poland, America, Germany, France are the assemblages of persons, not the elite, not the scum of the nations, but the bones, the flesh and the blood, of which I, as a creative individual, am the Spokesman. Whenever I had the privilege to come before them, I was elated in spirit, for they were my Destiny, my end of the journey.

Who then is the Society? They are the most successfully EDUCATED, the ones equipped to speak for the nation, to protest encroachments upon freedoms, the confessors who, after hearing all, give absolution to the Yetinsyn sinners.

There are societies, however, as the German, where people are raised in discipline, in self-deficiency, as opposed to self-debasement and self-indulgence. These nations become the ultimate in human advancement (remember: German Nazidom was not "German," but a product of the Yetinsyn bi-species).

While education in other nations produces complete humans, in Poland it is rather maltreating, even perverting. The Polish word for education is *wyksztalcenie*. *Ksztalt* means "shape." The prefix *wy–* before any word, undoes it; therefore, to be educated in Poland means to be de-shaped, deformed. If I had been well-educated in Poland, I indeed would have been depraved, de-nationalized, de-patriotized, for my innate personality would have been altered to resemble any from-the-edge Pole's: intellectually shy and colorless. Any sterile Pole who can sign his name belongs presumptively to the intellectuals. And sterile they are for, for undiagnosed-by-historians reasons, their education, after raising them from prone and uncouth peasants to the vertical position of some degree of Civilization, alters them so that from hard workers they all become idlers. They are the laziest lot of loafers and café-dwellers that ever afflicted a nation, from their neighboring tables assassinating and besmirching each person who is capable of some industrious achievement. What is it that makes these Poles so vile, each a personal enemy of every being that can work instead of talk-talk-talk? I think I finally, towards the end of my existence, have found the answer.

There is not a more gifted, perceptive public than the Polish people. Look at me, a mere Pole who, without getting beyond the third grade of the American school system, writes on astronomy, contrived six new sciences in the sphere of anthropology, devised his own method of perspective, and has got an astounding insight in anatomy. I have actually made myself a SOUL, by making myself a CREATIVE artist, because I was lucky enough to avoid

SEE,
WHY
IT IS SO?

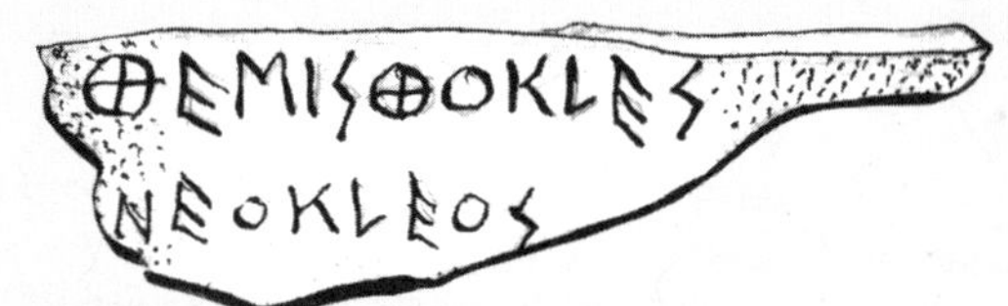

Themistocles

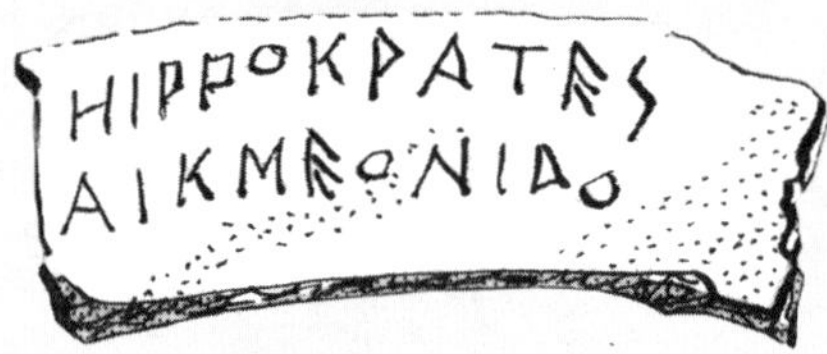

Hippocrates

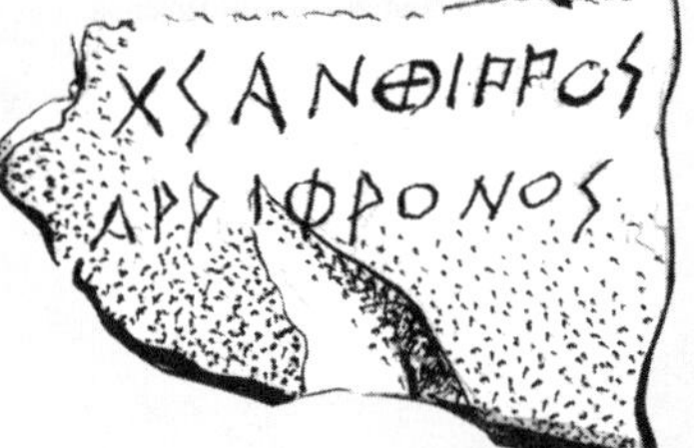

Xanthippus

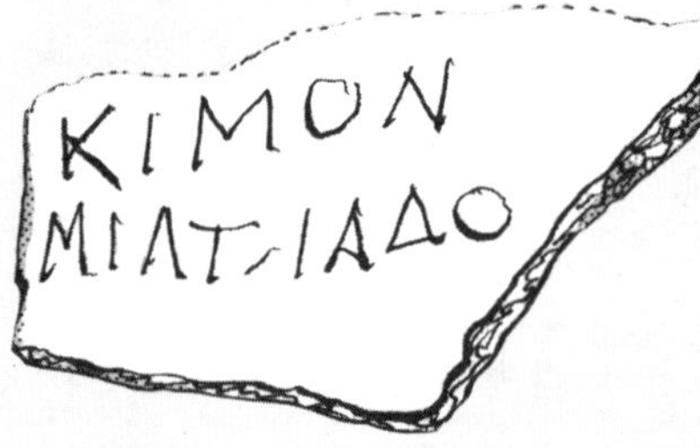

Cimon

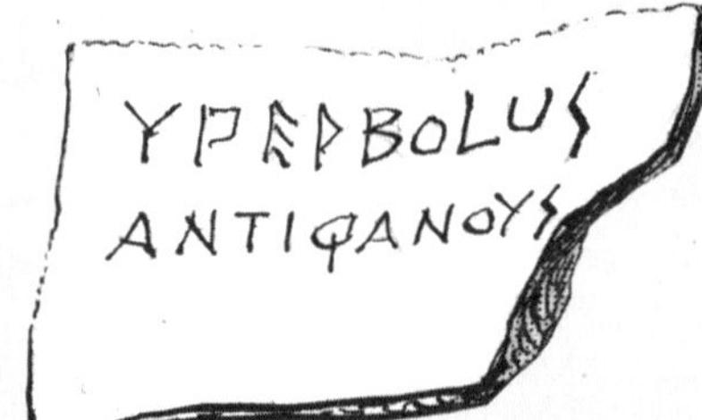

Hipperbolus
the Old

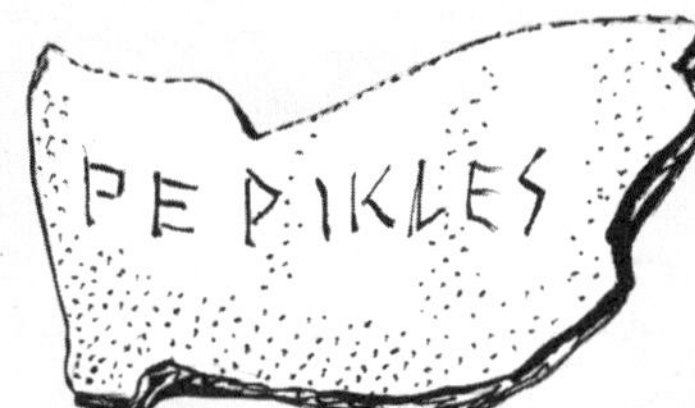

Pericles

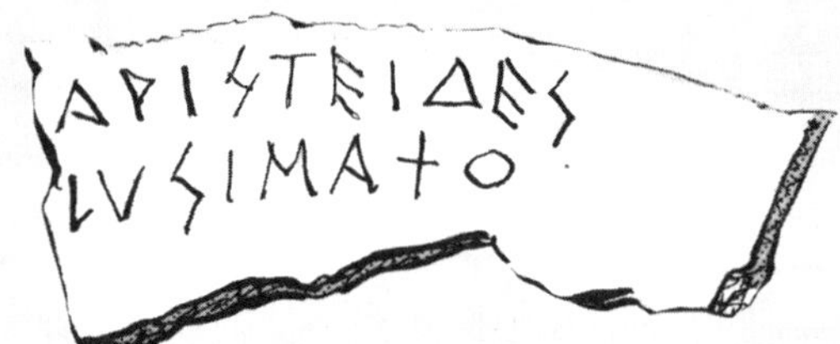

Aristides the Just

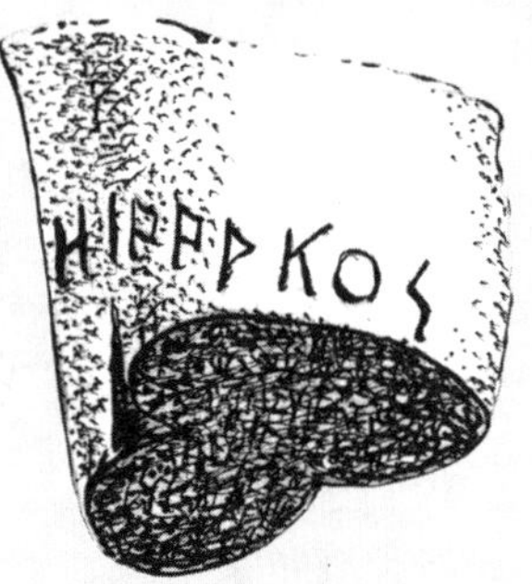

Hipparchus
146-126 B.C.

 POTSHARDS ON WHICH CITIZENS SCRATCHED THE NAME OF THE PERSON THEY WOULD LIKE TO LEAVE TOWN

being educated by Polish and American "de-formers." The average Pole, from peasant to merchant, is wonderful, so is the average American. But: the higher the education, the greater the rat! And it is the treason-bred PROFESSORS who methodically depraved the educated, because all who FAIL, TEACH! If they had not failed, they would PRODUCE, CREATE. We send our national youth to universities to learn success from misfits who, instead of committing suicide, become teachers.

This country was miraculously created by rude, uncouth hicks, and presently is being calamitously destroyed by the educated who have become the chief obstructors of patriotism. The creatures that failed at writing become the editors who employ other failures as critics of everything that is being made to sustain the greatness created by the uneducated, unwashed immigrants into America. The Anglomericans who created the greatest Miracle of the Ages, AMERICA, chewed tobacco and spat across the church through the paneless windows. Now it is the misfits with education who, faster and faster, trade our nation's greatness for the metamorphosed betrayal of America, of Europe, of Africa and Asia in obedience of their predatory masters, the Moscovian Yetinsyny.

The employing editors of the Polish press, however, who gave jobs to the scum of the nation, I recognize as the ultimate men of Evil. First they hounded me for being in America, denied me the right to be a Pole or an American. Then they kept silent about my being alive, so that for forty years I was denied the means to be a sculptor in either country. I faithfully remained a Pole, only and completely, my ultimate PRIDE. But at last, I have been de-nationalized by "intellectual" Poland, the destroyer of creative men, the parasite extraordinary upon the inspired Messenger of national Biology who unselfishly dedicated every breath to its presumptive society.

Ancient Greece committed suicide by introducing a systematic extermination of creative individuals, called *ostracism*. Each citizen yearly deposited an *ostrakon* (potshard) on which he had scratched the name of the person he, or actually his superiors, would most like to leave town. The first creative man so destroyed by the democratic Greeks was the astronomer Hipparchus. What could an astronomer-mathematician have done to the "intellectuals" of Greece that would warrant their campaign against him? He was simply despised by those who thought they knew more than he who knew *better*. He was just an example of a superior individual. Hence, it was "Down with Hipparchus," because he produced change in knowledge. Other now great men of classic Greece followed, some were even stoned to death, as if ostracized for the second time. Here are their tickets to oblivion.

There is no doubt that the chief instigators of these ostracisms of providential men were the Greek Yetinsyny, with wart-noses and Pan body proportions, the extinguishers of Humanity and its Civilizations. It is precisely this hereditary sickness of the ancient Greek society that the Poles are afflicted with. Like children and barbarians who are not able to create and thereby derive the thrill of seeing things change, they emulate the envy of the educated simpletons, destroying any singular individual and his achievements.

■

The Thieving Poles

IN 1925 I was married to Helen Walker of Chicago and lived in Paris. Having won the award for the project of the monument to Mickiewicz, I was able to buy very many engravings. In Los Angeles I bought a collection of 49 Cambodian paintings, a few centuries old, and accumulated a treasure of Chinese and Sasanian coins. From a doctor in Paris I had bought ancient Peruvian pottery that was of museal quality. Eventually I took my entire collection to Poland from America, with all my works. All of it the official "Culture Vultures' of Poland have stolen.

Presently, in Upper Silesia, there is a Museum of Engravings, supposedly formerly owned by General Zajac ("hare"), which actually is my property consisting of over three thousand items of the finest masterpieces of Dürer, Altdorfer, Aldegraver, Burgmayer, Vit Stwosz, Hammerskerker, Solis and many other masters. There were three *Melancholias* by Dürer, and 23 large wood engravings by this extraordinary artist, part of the famed cycle commemorating the Triumphal Procession of Emperor Maximilian. These thieving Poles do not answer letters, that there be no evidence of their knowing of my protests. The American State Department would not assist (when there was a time one could make such demands). Just lately the Polish periodical *Polityka* had a long article about the Crimes Against Culture committed by the Russians and Germans in the last War, how dastardly they looted the Polish museums. But looting Szukalski's entire life's achievements they regard as… "patriotic." The Polish nation knows of this crime, but the whole "intellectual" society keeps silent, that no one knows of their deeds. They have no honor, no morality, and they are the most shameless liars

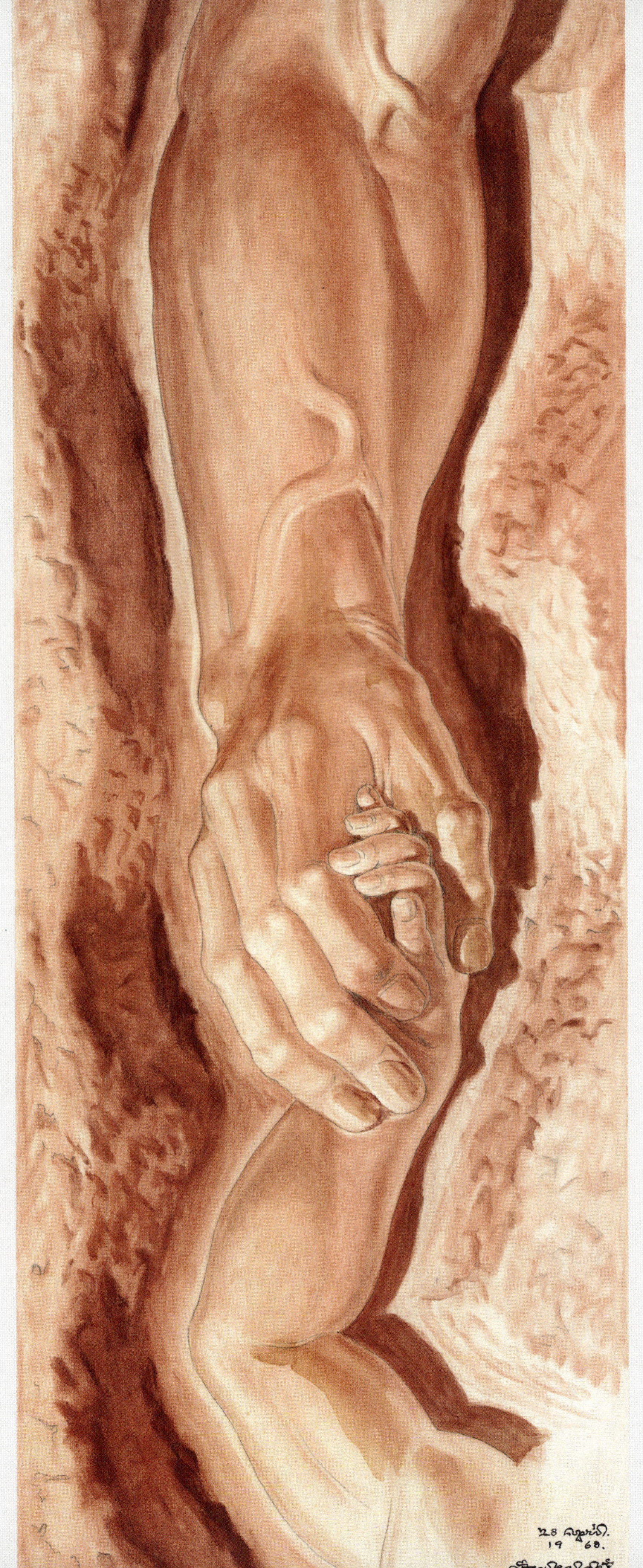

FATHER AND CHILD

1968

and cheats, for they perpetually live in *zaklamanie*, the admitted national self-deception.

My coming to America with high hopes of being useful as a creative man was a fatal mistake, since here the Baseball-Football Cyclops are the heroes of the nation. Not having an English name disqualified me the moment I left the ship *Bremen* when I was only 12 years old. From then I was only a second-class American, who has never looked into "the funnies." Though all my works were created in the United States and I was renowned as the "Wonder Youth Son of a Polish Blacksmith," being raved and gloated over, I was never permitted to do anything that would contribute to our Culture. Besides, being very impractical, lost in the spheres high above the prosaic economics, I was starving for weeks at a time in silence, having no father, king, president or God to turn to with my personal complaints. Without sustenance I created an "Empire of Sculpture in America" (as Ben Hecht wrote), to have every bit of my astounding output stolen by the Polish Ministry of Art and Culture.

Having nothing to belittle me for, no dishonorable deeds to point to, the Polish "intellectuals" simply despised me for my complete integrity as an exemplary Pole, but a Pole who was in America. That fact was beyond forgiveness. For forty years, after my third time crossing the Atlantic with all my works in the hope that my native country would take me as a creative man, they have kept my achievements hidden in various places in Poland classed as "National Treasure," after erasing my name.

Therefore, at long last I break my filiality with Poland, the Destroyer of Men of Genius.

I was methodically buried alive in crass, post-Roosevelt America by the Polish and American press in which only decadent "art critics" (who have never created even a chewing-gum bubble) lead the nation in appreciation of "modernist" misfits and psychos. Our periodicals disdain everything that is not on the level of Lipchitz, Miró and Picasso. If Peter Bruegel lived today, they would stone him to death for exposing our contemporary sterility.

We are forcibly fed with the Art of Democracy, the Art of Doodling and Sham!

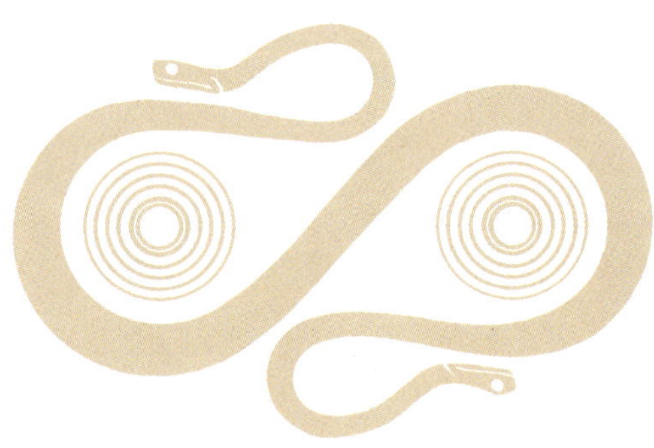

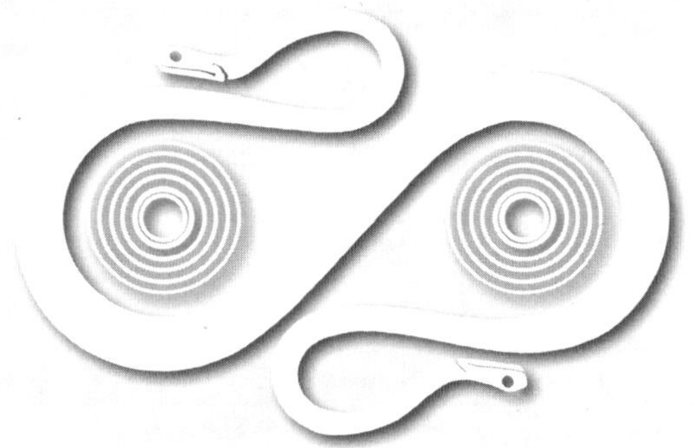

A Protong Glossary

List of Protong words and their English translation

This rootless language is the pre- and post-diluvial, grammarless language, preserved in modern Polish.
Centuries back it was known as Lach, earlier as Sarmatian, and still earlier as Celtic.
In Protong "Cel Tik" means "Whole (world) Touch(ing)," i.e. universal.

A, (J)a	I, me Protong actually had no words beginning with "a" or "e." All words beginning with these sounds were once preceded by a "w" (sounding as "v") which softened into "f" and eventually vanished, except in Polish which retained the archaic form
Ar, War, Far, We, Wer, Wra, Wre, Wir, Wara, Wiara, Wera, Wiera	Belief, worship
Ba, Bam, Boi, Ban	Terrified, frightened away
Ba, Bal, Bial, Bieli, Be, Bil	Whiteness, daylight, dawn, God of Sunrise. Different vowels denote different dialectic uses.
Bab, Baba, Baby	Old woman (referring to the ancient Motherland in the Pacific, now, after submergence, seen as Easter Island
Bi, Za-Bi-Ta	Killed, deluged. In pictography, this idea is conveyed by a circle with a hole in its center
Bo, Bog, Boga, Boh	God
Bol, Bul, Boli	Pain, suffering
Br, Bra, Bre, Bro, Bru, Bri, Ber	Pain, suffering. Take(n), i.e. by the Deluge
Cal, Cel, Cali, Celi	Whole, universal
Ce, Ci, Cia, Cie	You. (The "c" sounds like "ts," therefore "you" is also: ti, tie, tia)
Cud	Miracle, the ancient name of Finland, where the Poles of Holy Rugia saw the Sun rise
Da, Dan, Dar	Give, given, gift
De, Gde, Gdze	Where
De, Den, Dzen, Di, Din, Dian	Day, daylight (referring to dawn and the Dawn God)
Des, Dies	Ten
Dr, Dra, Dre, Dri, Dro, Dru, Der	Deserted, to desert, deserter
E, (J)e	Is
Ga, Gan, Gne, Go, Gon, Gu, Gun	Drive out, driven into exile, exiled
Ge, Gde, Gdzie	Where
Gi, Gin, Hi, Hin	Lost, perished (by submergence, referring to the deluged Mother or Fatherland in the Pacific or Atlantic)
Gor, Gur	Mountain
Hl, Hla, Hle, Hli, Hlo, Hlu	Souse, soused till almost drowned. Now these are sometimes written as "gua," hence "Guatemala" and "Nicaragua"
Howa, Chowa, Hv	Hide, hidden; hiding beneath the seas
Id, Ida, Ide	Go, going (archaic for "migration")
In, Ine, Inni	Elsewhere, not in this world, therefore in the Netherworld of the deluged ancestors, the kingdom of perpetual night
Il, Ili	Mire, bog, marshes

K, Ka   Towards, in the direction of, dedicated to
Ko, Kocha   Love, beloved, worshipped
Ki, Kaj   Where
Kie, Kiej   When

La, Le, Li, Lan, Lu, Lej   Pour: the archaic term used for Flood, Deluge
Leb, Lib   Head; usually applied in Britain for dangerous submerged rocks, the bane of navigation
Lina   Rope (vital in rebusal pictography)
Lon, Lono   Womb, womb of the "Mother of Worship" (Mata Weri or Easter Island)

Ma, Mat, Mati, Matia, Mac   Mother(land), Easter Island
Me, Mi   Me, I, we, us
Mr, Mar, Mer, Umar, Umer, Mra,
    Mre, Mro, Mru   Dead (always referring to the submerged Motherland)
Me, Mor, Mur, Mo, More   Sea, seas (as in all British names ending in "mor," "moor," "more")

Na, Nar, No, Nor   Made-born, birthgiver, given birth
N, Ne, Ni   No, not, no more existing, deluged
Nes, Nos, Nies   Carried, brought to
Nib, Nieb, Neb, Neba   Heaven, where there is "no fear" (compare "Nippon")

O, Jo   I (first personal pronoun).
Oe, Oey, Oce, Ocec   Eyes, ocean (pron. "o-ts")
Oce On   Ocean; "He of the Fathers," the name of the continent that submerged beneath the Atlantic
Ok, Oko   Eye
On, Ona   He, she

Po   After, along

R, Ra, Ran, Rano   Morn, sunrise, dawn (often synonymous with worship)
Ron   Abort, lose
Rat, Ratowac   Saved, always referring to being saved from the Deluge

Sa   Up-to-here
Swe, Swenty   Holy, sacred (compare modern "saint")
Swit   Daybreak, the pre-sunrise glow
Swiat   World, earth

Ti, Tie, Tia   You
Tik, Tyk, Tyka   To touch, touching
Tin, Tien, Cin, Cien   Shadow, ghost, Netherworld
Ton, Toni   To sink, sinks, Sunken by Deluge
Top, Topi   To be drowned, drowned

U, Ut, Uton   Sunken, sink
U, Ut, Utop   Drowned
Ukaz   Appear(ed)
Um, Umi   Remember, know
Un, Una, Uni   He, she, they
Ur, Urod   Birthgiver, born, made-born
Us, Usniona   Mortally-Asleep, applied instead of "dead," only to dearest persons, Virgin Mary or Easter Island and fish

Wr, Wra, Wre, Wri, War, Wer, Wir,
    Wi, Wira, Wera, Wiara, Wiera   Worship, meaning "Dawn"

Z, Ze   From, out of
Ze, Zi, Zim, Ziema, Zem, Zema   Land, Motherland, referring to Easter Island, the Mother of Dawn
Za, Zar, Zero, Zera, Zra, Zre, Zorza,
    Zaria, etc.   Dawn

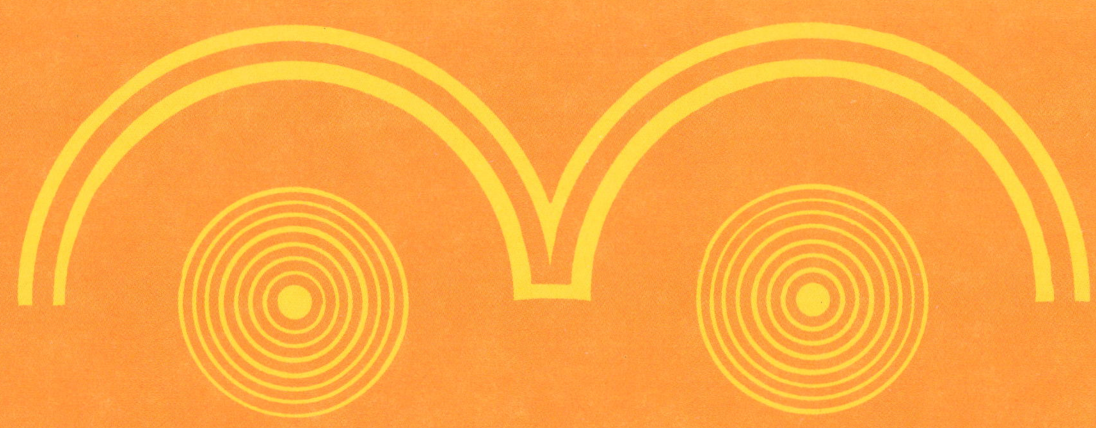

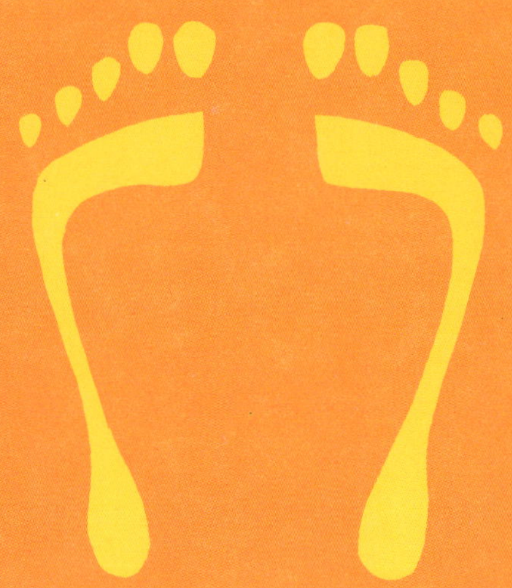

Editor's Note

AFTER finally getting approval from the Master to start publishing a book with him, we agreed to produce a modest book of his sculpture, drawings and writings, something like an updated *Work of Szukalski* book, to start things off. This would be in 1978.

I went through four layouts with Xerox-image paste-ups to see how the images would visually flow. With each draft, Szukalski would make new notations, and with each design I thought we were getting closer to getting the book done, which he titled *Troughful of Pearls*.

But after the fourth layout, he told me directly that he thought this was a bad idea. The art within that book was mostly old work, from 1915 and up, while now he was hardly any longer making sculpture due to his dire financial situation. Had he had the funds, he would have rented a studio with a skylight in order to produce new large-size plaster works to be cast in bronze. But now he was completely submersed in his "Zermatism" science, thirty-nine volumes with thousands of drawings, explaining the uncanny correlation of ancient images from all different cultures the world over, before civilizations had invented the superfast communication devices of today. Szukalski insisted that without showcasing this newer material, he no longer had any desire to produce a book on his work.

Lena and I had invested so much time in the book already that we agreed to include the scientific work. Now the book became a "69" format, with two separate covers, each side driving toward the middle. I had no layout experience. Lena did have proofreading experience, which turned out to be crucial in straightening Szukalski's frantic typing-off-the-paper style sentences and fragmentation of subjects into readable, cohesive paragraphs.

Once I started designing the pages, Szukalski would make very insightful corrections to my novice layout work. The book was really a three-person vessel, each of us giving our all, in hopes of delivering Szukalski once again to the art world after fifty years of silence. What made the chore even harder was the fact that this was done before the home computer. We had to have everything photographed for paste-up, and the typing was redone by a professional typesetter who had to follow Szukalski's personal, unusual way of setting down paragraphs and use of capitals.

The process took the better part of a year. Lena kept retyping and revising Stas' typewritten pages to clear up typos and incongruities, and each time we gave the pages back for him to approve, he would completely revamp or add to it. After six or seven times, we realized it was never going to end, so we stopped showing the layouts to him. We still have his copy of the final printed book, and even that is heavily laden with more inked "corrections."

We printed 1,200 copies of *Troughful of Pearls / Behold!!! The Protong*; 100 of them were hardbound and signed by Szukalski.

Much to both Lena's and my amazement, we seemed to get more positive (or bewildered?) response to the *Protong* side of the book. Therefore, after his passing, we reprinted just that side in 1989 as an Archives Szukalski publication. And before the Laguna Museum Exhibition in 2000, Ron Turner's Last Gasp publishing house reprinted it one more time with a changed color cover (I think Ron was making another "underground" statement).

This edition is now the fourth printing. All images have been newly scanned at hi-res for best possible reproduction. Our thanks go out once more to Dutch supreme layout genius Piet Schreuders (who also designed our 1990 *Lost Tune* book and the 2000 edition of *Struggle*). We believe that Stas would not only have approved, but would have loved the newer appearance of his 39-year old book.

Glenn Bray

2019

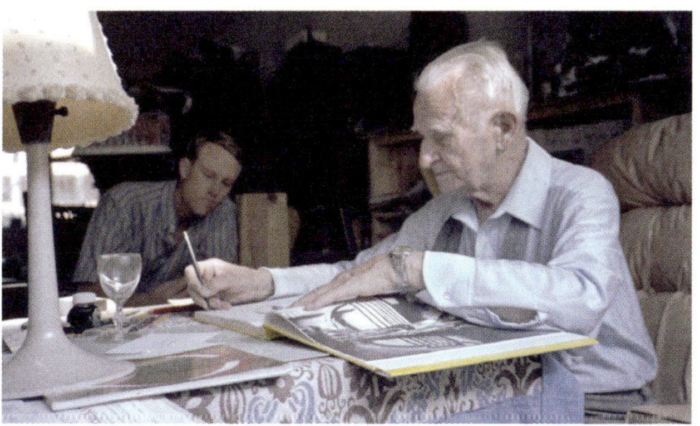

Szukalski signing the first edition of *Behold!!! The Protong*, 1980

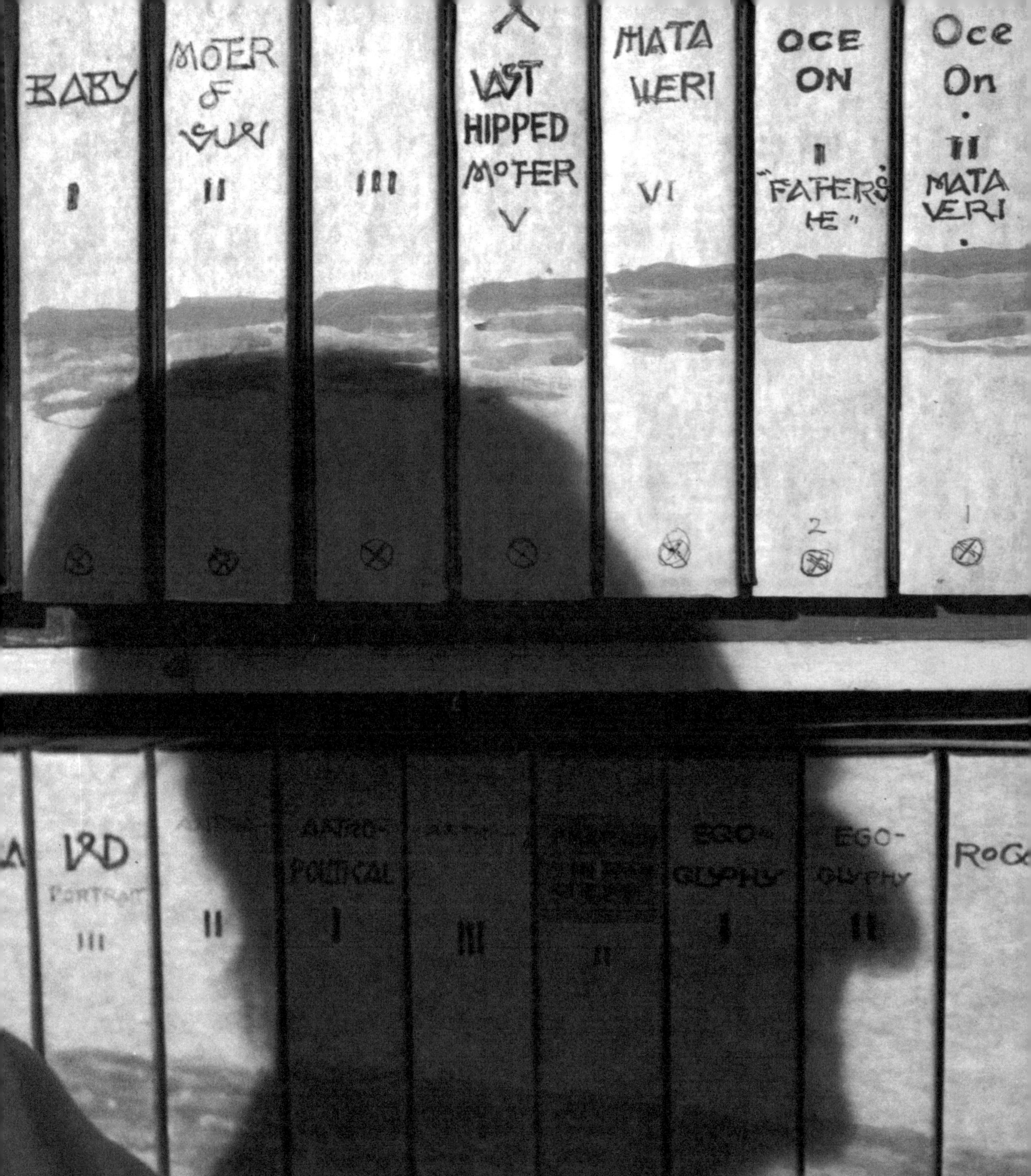

Photo—Glenn Bray